The Three Faces of Discipline for Early Childhood

Empowering Teachers and Students

Charles H. Wolfgang
Florida State University

Mary E. Wolfgang
School for Young Children, Inc.
Tallahassee, Florida

Allyn and Bacon

Boston London Toronto Sydney Tokyo Singapore

A Division of Paramount Publishing
160 Gould Street
Needham Heights, Massachusetts 02194

Library of Congress Cataloging-in-Publication Data

Wolfgang, Charles H.
The three faces of discipline for early childhood : empowering teachers and students / Charles H. Wolfgang, Mary E. Wolfgang.
p. cm.
Includes bibliographical references and index.
ISBN 0-205-15649-5
1. School discipline--United States. 2. Behavior modification--United States. 3. Classroom management--United States. 4. Early childhood education--United States. I. Wolfgang, Mary E.
II. Title.
LB3012.2.W65 1994
371.5--dc20 94-981
CIP

Printed in the United States of America
10 9 8 7 6 5 4 3 2 1 98 97 96 95 94

Contents

Preface

Disciplining is an active teaching and learning process of helping young children become cooperative people who can acquire the ability to become self-disciplined. When children first come to early childhood classrooms, they are the products of many months and even years of past experiences of having been disciplined. Some children have been well nurtured, and life has granted them the best; they are charming and require little guidance, and typical misbehaviors are dealt with using the lightest request. Other children are more demanding and challenging, requiring strong limit setting. We are also faced with very difficult children who bite, hit, and attack classmates and teachers, as well as passive children who are nonresponsive. These diverse types of children require very different responses and behaviors from teachers. If these varied children may be viewed as if they are on a continuum with regard to the demands and difficulty that they present to the teacher, so too should our discipline-related actions be seen on a behavior continuum.

There are many discipline models and systems available for the teacher to deal with misbehaving children. All are good models, most of them based to varying degrees on psychological theory. Each has a fairly narrow and differing view of the motivation of children and misbehavior, and each prescribes various techniques for dealing with it. Some models rely on very light requests of the child, whereas others make clear demands to stop misbehavior. Still others use strong controlling actions to extinguish the misbehavior. These models may be categorized as reflecting three schools of thought, which may be called Relationship-Listening, Confronting-Contracting, and Rules and Consequences. These approaches progress along a continuum from minimum to maximum power exerted by the teacher. If we view the continuum of so-called difficult children in our classroom side by side with the continuum of discipline models with regard to the power these techniques give us as teachers, we may see that some models might be quite effective with some children but totally ineffective with others. No one model can work successfully for all children at all times, nor will the same model always succeed for the same child as he experiences and exhibits different kinds of misbehavior. The approach taken in this text will be characterized as a Three Faces of Discipline construct—the Relationship-Listening Face, the Confronting-Contracting Face, and the Rules and Consequences Face—taking the view that all models have strengths and techniques that can improve the skill of the teacher and that the most effective approach relies on a continuum of behaviors by the teacher.

The Three Faces of Discipline for Early Childhood will present in a practical manner three broad philosophies, orientations, and techniques for dealing with misbehavior and the difficult child. The teacher of young children will be skilled in a host of techniques and methods that will permit this professional to make judgments as to what intervention or method is appropriate for which child at any given time in her development. The Three Faces of Discipline philosophy holds that even when strong and demanding techniques are needed to handle daily incidents with a difficult child, repeated success with that child will enable the teacher to *deescalate the power used until the child can be self-disciplined.*

Many readers of this text will be familiar with Wolfgang and Glickman's (1980) *Solving Discipline Problems: Strategies for Classroom Teachers* (2nd ed.) (Allyn and Bacon) and Wolfgang's (1977) *Helping Aggressive and Passive Preschoolers through Play* (Merrill). This book builds on the best of these older texts, but updates the content and reshapes the knowledge so that it will have more relevance for the young child ages 2 to 7 years. It also adds classroom management and the value of play and play intervention for the problem child.

The Three Faces of Discipline for Early Childhood is written for the early childhood teacher, child-care provider, prekindergarten teacher, and kindergarten or first-grade teacher who teaches and works with children ages 2 to 7 years in a classroom setting. Classroom procedures are most likely organized to use one of the following curriculum models: direct instruction, thematic teaching, or play-activity. Some of the discipline models and techniques will be more helpful because of certain teaching philosophies; for example, the Rules and Consequences techniques may be logically related to direct instruction. Others may not be as helpful and some readers might even professionally reject and feel uncomfortable in using some of these discipline techniques. The Three Faces of Discipline position described in this book does not make a value judgment as to which discipline model is "best." It does not conform to one model; instead, it presents all of the most commonly used models in such a manner that the reader will be skilled and knowledgeable in making his or her own decision in building classroom discipline strategies.

A style note: In order to avoid the awkward writing construction of *his or her* and *he or she* to refer to the teacher, we will simply use one gender at a time. Because teaching is a field shared by women and men alike, we will use both genders at various times throughout this text, although we recognize that early education is predominantly staffed by women. Similarly, we describe discipline incidents involving a child of one particular gender, without wishing to suggest that such incidents could not just as well involve children of the other gender. The use of only one gender at a time should not be taken as an indication that the concepts being presented or the problems encountered would be more often associated with or relevant for one gender than the other.

ACKNOWLEDGMENTS

A special thanks to all our colleagues and the many teachers who read this manuscript and gave us their insights and suggestions. Dr. Jamileh Mikati, the Director of School for Young Children, Inc., has put many of the suggestions found in this book into practice. The staff at School for Young Children—Rosemary Stromberg, Mary Simonds, Maurica Peacock, and Cathy Harrell—made many valuable suggestions. Also, a special thanks to Dr. Jeryl R. Matlock, Director of the Educational Research Center for Child Development at Florida State University, and to the fine teachers at that center: Sherry Taylor, Ashley Dobert, Diane Gomez, and Deborah Madden. Further thanks to Gwen Wolfgang, school nurse at Hempfield Area High School in Westmoreland County, Greenberg, Pennsylvania, for her work on the medication chart. We also gratefully acknowledge Sharon Kane (State University of New York at Oswego) and Susan Trostle (University of Rhode Island) for their expertise in reviewing the manuscript. And, finally, our thanks to Jon Peck for his wise advice and excellent editing.

SECTION I

The Three Faces of Discipline

Section I contains four chapters that deal with how to handle day-in, day-out misbehavior of young children. Chapter 1 offers an overview of the Teacher Behavior Continuum (TBC), a systematic teaching process a teacher might use to intervene on a daily basis with the kind of minor misbehavior normally seen in most young children. With an understanding of the general teacher behavior categories on the continuum, one will begin to understand that these behaviors will be reflective of three distinct philosophies of how to facilitate, stop, and shape children's behavior. These are the Relationship-Listening, Confronting-Contracting, and Rules and Consequences techniques, also referred to as the three faces of discipline. Subsequent chapters will expand on the TBC to include many more techniques under each of the categories along the continuum. Chapter 2 provides a detailed explanation of Relationship-Listening techniques, and Chapter 3 presents Confronting-Contracting techniques. Finally, Chapter 4 describes Rules and Consequences techniques. With an understanding of the many techniques found under these three distinct philosophies, we as professionals may now understand the tools or techniques related to a power continuum that are available to us in dealing with misbehaving children. This knowledge will permit the teacher to choose which techniques and how much power are needed for intervening in daily incidents with a particular child over a period of many months.

Each of the faces of discipline—Relationship-Listening, Confronting-Contracting, and Rules and Consequences—requires a clear awareness of ourselves and our actions as we deal with young children and their incidents of misbehavior. We will need to "step outside ourselves" and look at our own actions when confronting misbehavior, and ask ourselves why we are taking a particular action with a particular child in a particular situation. More importantly, are our actions effective? What is the child really learning from these incidents and our intervention? Where are we going or what will we do next as we attempt to work with this child?

We tend to mother the way we have been mothered and we tend to father the way we have been fathered. We also tend to teach the way we have been taught. We may hear our own parents' or past teachers' words coming out of our mouths as we work with children ("Young man, get your feet off that coffee table right now! I mean now!"). Teachers will spend much time planning how to teach a lesson or concept, but spend no time thinking about what they will do if "little Johnny" spits at them or swears at a peer. During these explosive moments of dynamic actions that require us as teachers to respond, we may draw on a deeply rooted memory of "how it was done to us." This may be fine, and even effective, if we received good to excellent parenting ourselves or had excellent teachers and have a data bank of healthy past experiences to draw on to deal with spitting and swearing. However, *The Three Faces of Discipline* suggests that we can take the natural behaviors that we have within us and gain new knowledge and techniques that may permit us to dramatically increase our skills to help and deal with children during these valuable teachable moments.

In describing the Relationship-Listening techniques, a collection of nonintrusive techniques will be employed to help children become more purposeful. The Confronting-Contracting techniques require that we assume a new "face" (attitude or philosophy) to stop or confront misbehavior and then counsel the child through a contracting process that allows him to find social acceptance. Finally, Rules and Consequences techniques are employed when we need to escalate our methods to clearly state the behavior we want from children and to set about through reward systems to obtain that behavior.

Figure 1 provides a list of various books authored by psychologists and educators from which the many techniques under these three large categories, or "faces," were drawn.

Figure 1 Today's Discipline Models

←——— TEACHER'S POWER ———→ **MINIMUM POWER**		**MAXIMUM POWER**
Relationship-Listening Face	**Confronting-Contracting Face**	**Rules and Consequences Face**
Gordon, *T. E. T.: Teacher Effectiveness Training*[1] Gordon, *Teaching Children Self-Discipline: At Home and at School*[2] Harris, *I'm OK—You're OK: A Practical Guide to Transactional Analysis*[3] Raths, Harmin, & Simon, *Values and Teaching*[4]	Dreikurs & Cassel, *Discipline Without Tears*[5] Albert, *A Teacher's Guide to Cooperative Discipline: How to Manage Your Classroom and Promote Self-Esteem*[6] Glasser, *Control Theory in the Classroom*[7] Glasser, *Schools Without Failure*[8] Glasser, *The Quality School: Managing Students Without Coercion*[9]	Madsen & Madsen, *Teaching/Discipline: A Positive Approach for Educational Development*[10] Alberto & Troutman, *Applied Behavior Analysis for Teachers*[11] Dobson, *Dare to Discipline*[12] Canter & Canter, *Assertive Discipline: Positive Behavior Management for Today's Classroom*[13] Canter & Canter, *Succeeding with Difficult Students*[14] Alberti, *Your Perfect Right: A Guide to Assertive Living*[15] Alberti & Emmons, *Stand Up, Speak Out, Talk Back*[16] Jones, *Positive Classroom Discipline*[17]

Endnotes

1. Gordon, T. (1974). *T. E. T.: Teacher Effectiveness Training.* New York: David McKay.
2. Gordon, T. (1989). *Teaching Children Self-Discipline: At Home and at School.* New York: Times Books.
3. Harris, T. A. (1969). *I'm OK—You're OK: A Practical Guide to Transactional Analysis.* New York: Harper & Row.
4. Raths, L. E., Harmin, M., & Simon, S. B. (1966). *Values and Teaching.* Columbus, OH: Merrill.
5. Dreikurs, R., & Cassel, P. (1972). *Discipline Without Tears.* NewYork: Hawthorn.
6. Albert, L. (1989). *A Teacher's Guide to Cooperative Discipline: How to Manage Your Classroom and Promote Self-Esteem.* Circle Pines, MN: American Guidance Service.
7. Glasser, W. (1985). *Control Theory in the Classroom.* New York: Harper & Row.
8. Glasser, W. (1969). *Schools Without Failure.* New York: Harper & Row.
9. Glasser, W. (1992). *The Quality School: Managing Students Without Coercion* (2nd ed.). New York: Harper Perennial.
10. Madsen, C. H., & Madsen, C. K. (1981). *Teaching/Discipline: A Positive Approach for Educational Development.* Raleigh, NC: Contemporary Publishing.
11. Alberto, P. A., & Troutman, A. C. (1990). *Applied Behavior Analysis for Teachers.* (3rd ed.). New York: Maxwell Macmillan International Publishing Group.
12. Dobson, J. (1970). *Dare to Discipline.* Wheaton, IL: Tyndale House.
13. Canter, L., & Canter, M. (1992). *Assertive Discipline: Positive Behavior Management for Today's Classroom.* Santa Monica, CA: Lee Canter & Associates.
14. Canter, L., & Canter, M. (1993). *Succeeding with Difficult Students.* Santa Monica, CA: Lee Canter Associates.
15. Alberti, R. E. (1982). *Your Perfect Right: A Guide to Assertive Living.* San Luis Obispo, CA: Impact Publishers.
16. Alberti, R. E., & Emmons, M. L. (1975). *Stand Up, Speak Out, Talk Back.* New York: Pocket Books.
17. Jones, F. H. (1987). *Positive Classroom Discipline.* New York: McGraw-Hill.

1

Child Misbehavior

How Should the Teacher Respond?

Jimmy stands before the paint easel. Using a large, thick paintbrush, he dips the end into the paint pot. Soon the brush reappears, dripping with a large glob of paint. As a peer walks by, Jimmy turns and sticks out the brush as if it is a sword and attempts to "stab" his schoolmate. The peer screams and runs off, much to the delight of Jimmy.

How shall we intervene with Jimmy after this kind of incident? Our goal is to alert a child such as Jimmy that we are aware of his actions and to use a minimum amount of teacher power, granting the child time to self-correct. If we are unsuccessful, we will escalate to more powerful teacher behaviors until we get Jimmy to halt his actions. Let's watch the skilled teacher as she intervenes with Jimmy "El Zorro."

The teacher observes Jimmy's actions and physically moves toward the boy, positioning herself behind the easel and in direct eye contact with him. She tries to catch his eye and signal him (modality cueing) of her presence. In his excitement, and near emotional "flooding" with the use of a paintbrush as a power tool to scare his peers, Jimmy fails to see the teacher's cues or signals.

Teacher: *(Nondirective statements) "Jimmy, paints can be scary and sometimes hard to control. That is fun and exciting for you but other children are frightened by the paintbrush." (Jimmy is still excited as he repeatedly dips his brush into the paint and looks for another "victim.")*

Teacher: *(Questions) "Where does the paint go?" (The teacher waits a few seconds for a reaction from Jimmy.) "Do you need my help to control the brush and paint?" (Jimmy still appears to be "flooded" with excitement.)*

Teacher: *(Directive statement) (The teacher states his name, makes eye contact, and places her hand lightly on Jimmy's shoulder.) "Jimmy, keep the paint on the paper." (The teacher tells the child what to do,* not *what not to do! Still no compliance by Jimmy, who turns around to the classroom looking for another child to scare.)*

Teacher: *(Directive statement and preparatory command) "Jimmy, what you are doing shows me that you have forgotten the rules on how to use the paints, and if that is done again, you will need to leave the painting area and find something else to do." (A peer passes by and Jimmy stabs out with the paintbrush.)*

Teacher: *(Physical intervention) (The teacher moves in firmly in a controlled but nonaggressive manner to Jimmy, takes his arm, and physically takes the brush from him and returns it to the paint pot. She physically turns him about to face the classroom, and points to the various play centers in the classroom.) "Choose another area to play or you may rest in the beanbag chair." (Jimmy skips over to the puzzle shelf and selects his favorite puzzle.)*

For purposes of this example, the incident ends successfully with Jimmy skipping off to a new play area. However, the experienced teacher realizes that after a physical intervention, Jimmy is more likely to strike, kick, bite, or use similar forms of aggression toward the teacher. Later, methods and constructs for dealing with raw aggression will be provided, but first it is important to understand the preceding incident in order to explain the construct of the Teacher Behavior Continuum (TBC) [1,2,3] and the concept of "escalation from minimum to maximum use of power" (see Figure 1–1).

When a child acts in an inappropriate manner in the classroom, the teacher should ask herself, "What should be done to stop this behavior?" The natural tendency, especially for a beginning teacher, is to move to the child, tell the child what not to do ("Don't do that, Jimmy, stop scaring others!"), and then, if compliance is not obtained, take the paintbrush (as in the preceding physical intervention example) away from the child. Telling the child what *not* to do is generally ineffective on a number of accounts.

Erikson,[4] a child development expert, characterizes the span from ages 3 to 7 as the period of *initiative versus guilt*. The child this age appears to be emotionally pulled between two extremes. He wants to *initiate* his own creative ideas (the "sword" paintbrush), while at the same time he may feel *guilt* for his actions because his "creative ideas" are forbidden by adults. The feeling of guilt is a surface emotion ready to effervesce during the 3 to 7 age period in the child's development. "Don't do it!" brings quick and strong guilt feelings from the child (at this particular age) and is highly likely to "flood" the child with emotion. This flooding clouds his logical thinking on how to respond to the teacher's demand. Thus, "don't do" statements may cause a child to flood with guilt and respond in an aggressive manner back at the teacher.

Viewing this in the "Don't stab others with the paintbrush" incident, it is important to keep in mind the way in which young children hear and absorb

FIGURE 1–1 Teacher Behavior Continuum

MINIMUM POWER	MAXIMUM POWER
Step 1: Modality Cueing Step 2: Nondirective Statements Step 3: Questions Step 4: Directive Statements (preparatory command) Step 5: Physical Intervention/Modeling (reinforcement)	

verbal communications. If we as teachers read children a story or tell them a two-line statement, and then ask them what happened in the story or what they remember about the two lines, they generally will remember and repeat only the last few words and statements. Because of their irreversibility[5] of thinking, they do not begin at the beginning of the story and then progress step by step through the story sequence. When required to recall something, it is the last actions that children remember. After reading *Peter Rabbit* to young children, we may ask, "What happened in the story?" The young child's typical response is, "Peter was sent to bed"—which is the very last action of the story. When children hear, "Don't stab others with the paintbrush," what they often hear and remember is "Stab others with the paintbrush." Unknowingly, we might actually be suggesting that the children perform the very actions we do not want.

Words also trigger *motor-meaning responses* in young children. If we are reading a story that says, "The tiger growled and showed his ghastly teeth," a look at the young audience will show most of the children "growling" and showing their teeth. Words suggest, to young children, a motor-meaning response, which they seem impulsively unable to control. Therefore, if we state to a child a sentence that ends with an action or motor meaning, even when the sentence begins with the word *Don't,* we are likely to get the young child to perform the motor meaning of the last words. Therefore, we should tell the child what *to do,* not what *not to do.* In this way, we are presenting a reality solution to the child as to what actions we want, and are suggesting the motor meaning of our desired actions ("Keep the paint on the paper").

The final difficulty with the "don't do so and so" approach is that if this is a child motivated by power, he will most likely take us on in a power struggle. As a toddler, the child begins to test out his autonomy[6] by attempting to get around the limitations set by his parents and other adults. If this limit setting by adults has been erratic and inconsistent, the child might have come to the conclusion that *Don't* really is a word that triggers a game of "let's see if the adult really means what she said" or "can I beat the adult and do as I wish?" The "don't" statement as a directive statement on the Teacher Behavior Continuum places us with our backs against the wall, requiring an immediate confrontation or physical intervention with the child who challenges our power. The goal in using and understanding the TBC is to grant the child maximum power to change his own behavior, but when the attempt is unsuccessful in gaining compliance, the goal then becomes to gradually escalate the power until we get results.

THE SEVERITY CLAUSE AND "DON'T" STATEMENTS

For every rule there is an exception. If we see a child about to perform some action that is life threatening, is likely to produce injury, or will destroy expensive property, the *severity clause* applies. In such a case, of course, we state firmly or even shout a "No, Stop!" statement to attempt to get the child to immediately desist. If we have followed the rule and have regularly told the child what to do, not what not to do, our emergency "No, Stop!" statements are more likely to be immediately obeyed. But if the child has an hourly diet of "don't do this, don't do that" and is told repetitively, "No, don't do so and so" a thousand times a day, he is desensitized to the prohibition of "No, Stop!" statements, and is now less likely to immediately obey an emergency command. Save "No Stop!" statements until they are really needed.

CONFLICT OVER POSSESSIONS

Let's look at another example of the use of the TBC, as the teacher uses the techniques to mediate two children's conflict over a possession.

> *The class has just gone out to the playground. Kate has found a shovel in the sandbox and is just about to fill a bucket. Mark, seated nearby, has a bucket but no shovel. His solution is to reach out and take Kate's shovel.*

How should we handle such incidents, which are seen again and again in the early childhood classroom? We have what will be described later as a *teachable moment*, but what exactly do we want to teach? The answer is that young children must learn to resolve conflict through language and not through aggression (see Figure 1–2). Our goal is to have Kate retrieve the shovel by using language and not by being passive, physically aggressive, or verbally aggressive, and for Mark to realize that others have rights and that he needs to respond to language used by peers.

Step 1: Modality Cueing

We begin by bringing the two children together, either at a private corner of the sandbox or by simply holding each child's hand and bringing them together face to face, called *knee-to-knee conferencing*. We employ modality cueing by simply looking at the children, moving our eyes from face to face in a nonjudgmental manner (i.e., we are not frowning). We give the children a period of time, by saying nothing and simply looking, to see if they can resolve the situation without any more intrusion on our part.

Step 2: Nondirective Statements

Our target is Kate, because she has the immediate problem and may be considered the victim—her shovel was taken. Kate can respond in a number of nonproductive ways: by being passive (just leaving or surrendering her toy), by being physically aggressive (striking out at Mark), or by being verbally aggressive (calling Mark a name, swearing, or crying). However, we want social conflict to be resolved through impulse control and expressive language (Figure 1–2). Therefore, if Kate does not assert herself, we move up and escalate our power on the

FIGURE 1–2 The Passive-Aggressive Construct

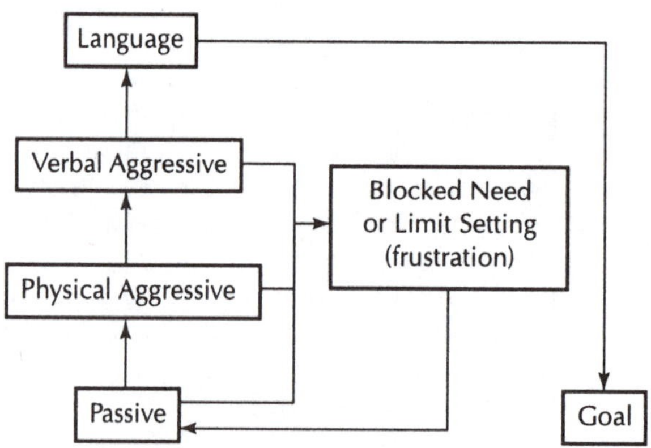

TBC to incorporate nondirective statements: "Kate, I can see by your face that you are unhappy; you have lost your shovel." We have verbally encoded both Kate's feelings and the problem needing to be solved, without being directive.

Step 3: Questions

If there is no reaction from Kate, we escalate to the question strategy: "Kate, what could you say to Mark so he would know what you want?" The teacher now retreats to a posture of simply looking on, to give Kate some time to think and respond. If she *does* speak up, the target child for our efforts now becomes Mark (see below), but if she *does not* speak up, we would escalate to directive statements aimed at Kate.

Steps 4 and 5: Directive Statements and Modeling

The teacher may state, "Tell Mark (directive statements), 'No, that is my shovel, I was using it. I want it back!'" (modeling). The teacher again retreats to a posture of simply looking on, to give Kate some time to think and respond. As before, if Kate *does* speak up, the target child becomes Mark, but if she *does not,* we continue with our modeling. At this point, if Kate does not respond, we might say, "You are having a difficult time using words with Mark. Would you like me to tell him for you this time?" If she indicates yes, we repeat the language model directly to Mark: "Mark, Kate wants me to tell you that she was using the shovel and wants you to give it back to her" (modeling). The teacher does this for a child like Kate, who cannot or will not speak up, only once. From that time on, the teacher will continue using the TBC techniques; however, after verbal modeling, the teacher will simply leave, telling the child that she must use language to get what she needs. Some children have learned that by acting passive with expressions of sadness, they can get others to serve them. We do not want to fall into such a passive-aggressive trap.

Some teachers may feel this is unfair and that Mark is getting away with something. But there will be many other occasions to deal with Mark, and right now Kate needs a lesson in asserting herself. If we relieve Kate of all the stress in the situation, getting what she wants *for* her, she will have no need to learn to act for herself. We permit Kate to own her problem.[7] If our overdeveloped sense of teacher "fairness" pushes us to play judge and jury, to return all objects to the rightful owner, we will be continuously exhausted because all the children in the class will be pulling at our skirt or pants to have us settle countless conflicts daily! Rather, when clashes over possessions occur, we should continue to intervene using the TBC techniques, until one day Kate will assert herself and gain real power to use language to deal with a conflict. There can be no more valuable lesson—and, developmentally, a 3-year-old should be ready to begin learning this skill.

TEACHER BEHAVIOR CONTINUUM (TBC)

If, during the sandbox incident, Kate does respond or simply says, "No, stop, that is mine," Mark then becomes the target child for attention through the TBC.

Step 1: Modality Cueing

Mark must learn to respond to the language used by a peer, and we help teach him this by using the TBC. First, we simply look on (modality cueing) as Kate and

Mark stand face to face, giving Mark time to think and act. (We have encoded his feelings and the situation or problem.)

Step 2: Nondirective Statements

If a sufficient period of time brings no action on Mark's part, we move to nondirective statements, such as, "Mark, it is hard to give up toys that you want so much to keep."

Step 3: Questions

After encoding his probable feelings, if there are still no results from Mark, we move to questions: "Mark, do you need my help to return the shovel?" If he indicates yes, we gently take the shovel from his hand and return it to Kate. If he says nothing, we give him some wait time and then move to directive statements and modeling.

Steps 4 and 5: Directive Statements and Modeling

Having received no response from Mark, we move on: "Mark, Kate said to give it back, that she was using the shovel." The teacher again retreats to simply looking on, to give Mark some time to think and respond.

(Optional) Step 6: Physical Intervention

Finally, after some wait time, we escalate to physical intervention by taking the shovel and returning it to Kate. If Mark then has a temper tantrum or attempts to strike us, we would use the techniques of mirroring and diversion (described in a later chapter that deals with raw aggression). Notice that in this resolution there is no attempt to discuss guilt or improper behavior. Our ultimate goal is to teach the children to use expressive language to resolve social conflicts, and to do it with no or minimal guilt.

The incidents of the "paintbrush Zorro" and the sandbox conflict over a possession are two examples of those myriad small misbehaviors—which may be called *teachable moments*— that a classroom teacher working with young children faces daily. The incidents are dealt with in a matter of minutes, and the teacher escalates up the TBC power continuum as she intervenes. With some children, especially physically and verbally aggressive children, these teachable moments may arise five or six times in an hour and occur daily. Therefore, we may spend many weeks and months handling such incidents with one particular child. This demands that we be skilled as teachers, knowing how much power to apply and how quickly to progress up and down the Teacher Behavior Continuum. In the Jimmy "El Zorro" incident, we were required to progress up to the most controlling teacher techniques of physical intervention. By the end of perhaps three more weeks of similar intervention, we may only have to escalate to directive statements, still later progressing only to the question level, then back to nondirective statements. Finally, we would only need to signal Jimmy by looking on (modality cueing). Ultimately, Jimmy will become highly socially adaptive and rarely will our intrusion as a teacher be required.

This escalation to more powerful techniques on the TBC will also reflect a very real attitudinal change on the part of the intervening teacher. This attitude change may be characterized as the *Three Faces of Discipline:* Relationship-Listening, Confronting-Contracting, and Rules and Consequences.

The *Relationship-Listening* face involves the use of minimum power. This reflects a view that the child has the capability to change his own behavior and that if the child is acting out in aggressive behavior, it is because of inner emotional turmoil or flooded behavior. Our goal would be to signal or make the child aware of his actions and get him to talk out his emotional concern. This talking it out by the child would lead him to become more purposeful in his behavior, and the acting-out behavior would stop. The "face" of the Relationship-Listening teacher would rely only on such minimal intervention techniques as modality cueing and nondirective statements found on the TBC (see Figure 1–3).

The teacher's face when escalating to a *Confronting-Contracting* method of intervention is one of, "I am the adult. I know misbehavior when I see it and I will confront the child to stop this behavior. I will grant the child the power to decide how he or she will change, and encourage and contract with the child to live up to a mutual agreement for behavioral change." The Confronting-Contracting position primarily involves the use of questioning techniques found on the TBC (see Figure 1–3).

The last and most powerful intervention technique of the TBC is a teacher attitude of *Rules and Consequences.* The teacher's Rules and Consequences "face" is one that communicates an attitude of, "This is the rule and behavior that I want and I will set out assertively to get this action. I will teach and reward new positive behaviors acquired by the child." Drawing from the TBC, the Rules and Consequences teacher's "face" will use the powerful techniques of directive statements and physical intervention and modeling, demonstrating to the child the behaviors that the teacher desires (see Figure 1–3).

The Teacher Behavior Continuum and the escalation and change between these attitudes, or faces of discipline, may also be used in the following two ways to help young children's behavior move to a more mature level:

- First, for the child who is simply having a rare misbehavior (possibly an uncontrollable moment), we would within a few minutes escalate across the TBC. This was demonstrated in the example of Jimmy "El Zorro."
- Second, for the aggressive or passive child whose "life-stance" position is one of a day-in, day-out series of classroom disruptions, we may stay with a single face of discipline—with its accompanying techniques—for many weeks. We would gradually change our face of discipline to increase power if these tech-

FIGURE 1–3 The Three Faces of Discipline

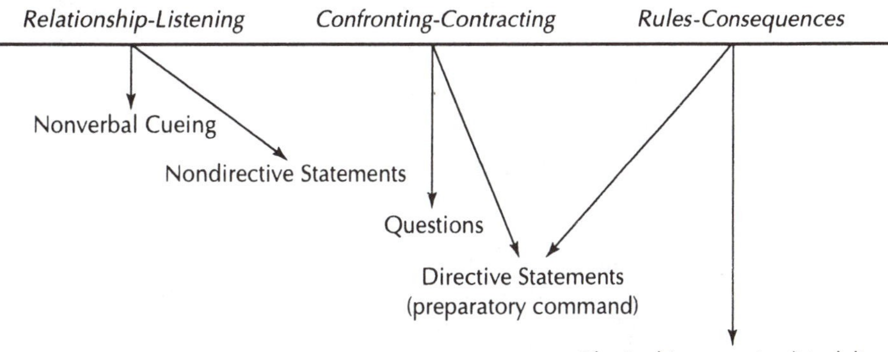

niques are unsuccessful, or to decrease our power to less intrusive techniques if the child's behavior begins to change and becomes more purposeful and guided.

THE THREE FACES OF DISCIPLINE: A CONCEPT, NOT A RECIPE

The concept of the Three Faces of Discipline, with the use of the TBC power continuum and its accompanying teacher behaviors, is not for the purpose of giving the teacher a recipe for responding to misbehavior. One example of a recipe is suggested in *Assertive Dicipline,*[8] which calls for the teacher to place a child's name on the board as a warning of misbehavior, followed by a check mark for each new act of misbehavior; after three checks, the child suffers some form of punishment. This approach takes the skill out of the teacher's hand by assuming that this recipe will be effective with all children. The TBC and the concept of the Three Faces of Discipline simply provide an orderly arrangement of teacher techniques that may be used as they relate to degrees of power. This concept permits the teacher to use skills to decide how much power is needed for which child under what type of circumstances.

For example, with one misbehaving child, the teacher may choose to state, "Carol, stop that, this may not go on!" (Confronting-Contracting techniques). Carol, without any undue stress, realizes what she must do to comply, and the discipline incident is over. With another child who is getting out of hand, the teacher simply needs to make eye contact (Relationship-Listening techniques) for the child to gain an awareness of what he is doing wrong and how to stop doing it. Still other children require the teacher to assertively state the rules and demand immediate compliance (Rules and Consequences techniques), and the child does stop. The teacher, based on past experiences with these children and an intimate knowledge of them, has made a decision on how much power and which techniques would be most effective with each individual child. The Three Faces of Discipline concept would go one step further in that for those children requiring the strong Rules and Consequences (and to a lesser extent Confronting-Contracting) intervention, the teacher over many weeks would gradually teach or lead the children to respond with techniques of less and less power, until they could effectively control themselves.

Subsequent chapters contain a more detailed explanation of the teacher behaviors found on the Teacher Behavior Continuum, with many new subbehavioral techniques defined and presented under each of these larger behavioral categories. One may recall that in the Jimmy "El Zorro" teachable moment example, the teacher first used the behavioral category of directive statement ("Jimmy, keep the paint on the paper") and then progressed to a subdirective statement under this category called a *preparatory command* ("If that is done again, you will need to leave"). Other behaviors on the TBC will also contain subbehaviors and techniques under these broader categories.

TEACHER PERSONALITY TYPE

There are many teachers who do not escalate or deescalate their power along a continuum, but wear one "face," generally repeating or doing two to five discipline actions consistently with most children. These teachers tend to have a set philosophy or orientation.

Each teacher has a deep memory of the child within. This memory is an accumulation of how parents, teachers, and other significant adults conducted discipline when this teacher was a child. Therefore, people parent the way they have been parented and teach the way they have been taught. When we as teachers set limits with children, we are projecting the amount of autonomy we feel comfortable giving to children for controlling their own behavior, or how much we are in need of control as the teacher "in charge." Therefore, for some teachers, the Rules and Consequences techniques may be too strong a form of teacher control, or the Relationship-Listening too "touchy-feely" in nature, or the process of bringing discipline issues for group discussions in Relationship-Listening too phony. Many teachers, then, based on their own personalities, naturally and unthinkingly use methods and techniques that tend to cluster under one of these three schools of thought (or faces) or eclectically piece together a collection of unrelated techniques. The question arises: Which one of these three faces philosophically fits your personality best? The Beliefs about Discipline Inventory will permit the teacher to answer a series of value questions that will help assess which philosophical "face" comes naturally to the teacher—based on the child within.

Stop now and complete the inventory, so that after you are more knowledgeable about the methods under each of these three positions, you will be able to determine whether your values have changed.

SUMMARY

As a teacher intervenes with a young child who is behaving inappropriately, the teacher must use some degree of power through which she takes control of the situation or grants the student the autonomy and time to change his unwanted behavior. This use of power by the teacher may be viewed on a Teacher Behavior Continuum, ranging from minimum to maximum use of power, with the teacher moving from one "face" to another as she deals with the student's actions.

While wearing the Relationship-Listening face, the teacher relies primarily on the behaviors of visual looking and nondirective statements. The teacher using the Confronting-Contracting face often uses questions. Finally, the teacher wearing the Rules and Consequences face uses the techniques of directive statements, modeling, and physical intervention.

The Teacher Behavior Continuum does not provide a rigid set of steps for carrying out a discipline program, but rather gives the teacher the tools to deal with each discipline situation and each misbehaving child, individually. A Beliefs about Discipline Inventory helps the teacher identify the face and philosophy with which she feels most comfortable and, in conjunction with the TBC, will provide a construct for use in subsequent chapters.

Beliefs about Discipline Inventory

It is valuable to determine where your personality and the techniques you tend to use today would fall under the three philosophical positions, or "faces." The following 12 questions will give you those insights about yourself. In each numbered question, you are asked to choose between two competing value statements. With some questions, you will definitely like one statement and dislike the other, making it easy for you to choose. With others, you will like or dislike both options; this likely will be frustrating to you, but you must choose the option that most closely resembles your view.

Forced Choices

Instructions: Select the statement you value more and circle the corresponding letter, *a* or *b*. You must choose between the two statements in each item.

1. a. Because young children's thinking is limited, rules need to be established by mature adults for them.
   b. Each child's emotional needs must be taken into consideration rather than some preestablished rule.
2. a. During most group time (snack time, circle time, etc.), the teacher needs to give each child his or her own desk, table space, or floor space and to teach each child to routinely take that space after transitions.
   b. Groups of young children can, through class meetings, decide what rules they need to govern themselves.
3. a. During preplanning, children should be given choices as to what interest center they wish to choose that morning and then, once chosen, they must keep to that decision for most of that period.
   b. What children must learn and what tasks to be performed must be determined by the teacher, and a specific sequence of instruction to accomplish these goals must be followed.
4. The books in the classroom library are being misused, soiled, and, at times, destroyed; I will most likely:
   a. Hold a class meeting, show the damaged books to the class, and ask the children how we may solve this problem, including what action should be taken toward a child who misuses books.
   b. Physically remove or limit the number of books available, and observe closely to see who was misusing the books, then tell that child how such action was affecting other students and how I felt about such loss of books.
5. Two children of equal power and abilities are in a rather loud verbal conflict over a toy or classroom materials; I would:
   a. Approach the children, tell them of the classroom rule, and demand that they desist in their actions, promising a sanction if they fail to comply.
   b. Avoid interfering in something that the students need to resolve themselves.
6. a. A child strongly requests not to come to circle time today. This will be permitted because the teacher feels that this child has some emotional concerns related to the group experience.
   b. One child is being refused entrance into group activities. The teacher will raise this as an issue in a class meeting and request a discussion for reasons and solutions by the child and the group.
7. The noise level in the classroom is at such a high level that it is bothering me; I will:

a. Flick the classroom lights to get the students' attention, request the students to be quiet, and later praise those who are talking quietly.
b. Select the two or three children who are making most of the noise, take them aside, and ask them to reflect (think) about their behavior and how it might affect others, and get an agreement from them to work quietly.

---

8. During the first few days of class, I would:
   a. Permit the children to try out or experiment in getting along as a new group and make no predetermined teacher rules until the children feel they are needed.
   b. Immediately announce the class rules and the sanctions that will apply if the rules are broken.

---

9. a. A child is frustrated by a classmate and responds by swearing. I do not reprimand the child but encourage him to talk out what is bothering him.
   b. I bring two children who are swearing together in a "knee-to-knee" confronting relationship and attempt to get them to work out this conflict while I ask questions and keep the focus on the negotiation.

---

10. A child disrupts circle time while I am trying to read a story; I will:
   a. Ignore the disruption if possible and/or remove the child from circle time as a consequence of his misbehavior.
   b. Express my feeling of discomfort to the child about being disrupted from my task.

---

11. a. Each child must realize that there are some school rules that need to be obeyed, and if a child breaks the rules, he or she will be punished in an equitable and fair manner.
   b. Rules are never "writen in stone" and can be renegotiated by the class, and sanctions will vary with each child.

---

12. A child refuses to put away her work or play materials after using them; I will:
   a. Express to the child how not putting away materials will affect future activities in this space and how frustrating this will be to everyone, and then I will leave the materials where they are for the remainder of the day.
   b. Confront the child to reflect on her behavior, think about how her noncompliance affects others, and tell her that if she cannot follow the rules, she will lose the use of the materials in the future.

Scoring Key and Interpretation: Circle your responses on the tables below.

Table 1		*Table 2*		*Table 3*	
4a	1b	2b	4a	2a	1a
6a	5b	3a	6b	3b	5a
9a	8a	7b	9b	7a	8b
12a	10b	11b	12b	11a	10a

Total number of responses in Table 1 _____
Total number of responses in Table 2 _____
Total number of responses in Table 3 _____

The table in which your total number of responses was the highest is the one where your values are clustered under that school of thought, or "face." Table 1 is Relationship-Listening, Table 2 is Confronting-Contracting, and Table 3 is Rules and Consequences. The table with the next highest score would be your second choice and the table with the least number may be the "face" you value least. If your responses are equally distributed across all tables, you may be an eclectic teacher who picks and chooses from all philosophies. In Chapter 5, we will return to this inventory—after you have read Chapters 2 through 4, which will present all of the techniques under the three "faces."

Test Yourself

Test your understanding of the concepts related to the TBC by writing your answers in the column on the left. You will find the answers at the end of this chapter, following the Endnotes.

A. _____ questioning B. _____ cueing C. _____ physical intervention D. _____ directive statements E. _____ nondirective statements	1.–5. Place a number from 1 (minimum) to 5 (maximum) before the teacher behavior on the left, as if you are escalating up the TBC using more and more power.
	Select one answer for each of the following questions, choosing from the answers on the left.
A. _____ teachable moment B. _____ motor meaning C. _____ physical intervention	6. The new music teacher attempts to get cooperation from a group of 4-year-olds and states,"Now, I want you all to sit up and sing like birds!" The children respond, "Chirp, Chirp."
A. _____ life-stance position B. _____ uncontrollable moment C. _____ wait time	7. Sarah is a child who spends all day with a drooped head and an expressionless face; she rarely talks or plays with other children.
A. _____ escalated in power B. _____ deescalated in power C. _____ stays the same in power use	8. Mike is standing on the outside picnic table. Teacher: "Mike, climb slowly down from there and have your feet here on the ground." (Mike refuses to move.) Teacher: "Mike, you're saying by your behavior that you do not know the rules, and I will take you down from there."
A. _____ escalated in power B. _____ deescalated in power C. _____ stays the same in power use	9. Teacher (during snack): "Throwing snack trash away permits us to use the table for play." Teacher: "William, what is the rule after you are done with snack?"
A. _____ escalated in power B. _____ deescalated in power C. _____ stays the same in power use	10. Teacher: "If the ball is thrown against the school wall, that behavior says that you do not know the rules, and I will need to take the ball away." Teacher: "Who could you get to join you for ball play?"

Glossary

Confronting-Contracting The Confronting-Contracting face attempts to maintain an adult relationship with a misbehaving child, by requesting the child to "stop and change." The solution for how the child will change will still be in the child's hands. (These methods are based on Glasser's Reality Therapy[9] and Adlerian theory as defined by Rudolf Dreikurs.[10])

Directive Statements This is the fourth behavior on the TBC and is a powerful direct statement whereby the teacher tells the child what to do, not what not to do ("Keep the paint on the paper!").

"Don't" Statements It is ineffective to tell children what not to do; rather, the teacher is encouraged to tell the misbehaving child what to do. "No, Stop!" statements are used if the incident is serious and if harm may occur.

Escalation/Deescalation of Power The gradual movement across the TBC through the use of stronger or more demanding teacher behaviors as an escalation of power; or a retreat back through this continuum with lesser intrusive behaviors as a deescalation.

"Faces" (teacher attitude) This is a metaphor for the idea that a teacher may act toward a misbehaving child in a number of conscious predetermined manners, and that the teacher's attitude and methods can change (take on a new "face") to match circumstances.

Irreversibility of Thinking For young children (ages 3 to 7), thinking is preconceptual; they are not naturally reflective in their thinking. After experiencing a number of sequential events, they remember and retell only the last incident. Their thinking is irreversible.

"Knee-to-Knee" Conferencing The teacher deliberately brings together, by physically intervening, two or more children, seated in an isolated area "knee-to-knee," and sets the stage for conferencing and discussion between these children. The teacher and child may also do a "knee-to-knee" conference.

Life-Stance Position When a child (or adult) becomes so overwhelmed by a world of frustration and accompanying inner emotional turmoil, he may defensively take a passive or aggressive stance, 24 hours a day, toward life experiences.

Modality Cueing The first (minimum power) behavior on the TBC, which the teacher uses to signal the child—through a modality of looking, a touch, or a sound—to become aware of his own actions.

Modeling Placed on the maximum end of the TBC, this is a teacher technique of demonstrating the positive behavior desired by the teacher, either through a verbal explanation or a physical demonstration.

Motor Meaning If a toddler sees a set of stairs, he feels compelled to climb them; if he sees a light switch, he will attempt to switch it. These actions occur because the young child has limited impulse control to stop himself from doing these motor actions. Just as objects can set off a child's impulsive motor meaning response, so too can words.

Nondirective Statements The second behavior on the TBC, which the teacher uses words to describe to the child the feelings, problem, or situation the child is facing regarding some episode (e.g., difficulty with another person or objects and materials).

Passive-Aggressive Construct (See a fuller definition of this construct in Chapter 9.)

Physical Intervention This strongest and most intrusive action is placed at the end of the TBC, whereby the teacher physically takes the child by the hand or body and stops an action that is occurring.

Preparatory Command This is a subbehavior under the larger category of directive statements. Once the teacher has told the child what to do and the teacher sees that she is not getting compliance, the teacher verbally gives a preparatory command—a promise to follow up with a strong physical intervention action if the child does not quickly comply ("If that happens again, it tells me that you don't know the rule for using that item and I will have to take it from you").

Questions The third teacher behavior on the TBC, in which the child is called on to intellectually reflect on the situation and to think of new ideas to solve the situation ("What could you say to Mark, who has your shovel?"); alternatively, questioning could be the teacher's offer to provide help ("Do you need my help to give up the shovel?").

Relationship-Listening The least intrusive of the three discipline faces, this position views children as inherently good; thus, if they are misbehaving, it is because they are suffering some blockage of an inner emotional need. The teacher's role is to establish a nonjudgmental relationship and encourage the child to "talk out" the problem while the teacher listens. This talking helps empower the child to solve her own problems and needs. (These methods are based on Rogerian[11] theory.)

Rules and Consequences This is the most powerful or controlling of the three faces, with philosophy and methodology that clearly state rules for behavior and assertively take actions through reward to get the positive behavior wanted by the teacher. (These methods are based on theories of assertiveness training[12] and behavior modification.[13])

Severity Clause If the child's actions endanger himself or others or destroy significant property, a teacher would be justified in escalating up the continuum to the most intrusive or demanding teacher behaviors of physical intervention.

Teachable Moment An occasion in which the teacher, facing a slightly frustrated child with a blocked need, may intervene to get her to change her behavior.

Teacher Behavior Continuum (TBC) A systematic teaching process that a teacher might use daily to intervene with the kinds of misbehavior normally seen in most young children in classroom settings. The TBC contains a group of five general teacher behaviors (modality cueing, nondirective statements, questions, directive statements, and physical intervention/modeling) placed on a continuum, suggesting that the behaviors move from minimum teacher intrusion or power to maximum teacher control.

Three Faces of Discipline A concept of discipline that takes the position that teachers may consciously be aware of actions toward children and that the attitude and action (or "face") teachers use may change to reflect the faces of Relationship-Listening, Confronting-Contracting, or Rules and Consequences.

Wait Time Once an overture to the child (such as the behaviors on the TBC) is made, the teacher waits for a reasonable amount of time so as to permit the child to intellectually consider her actions and comply with her wishes.

Uncontrollable Moment A short-lived emotional flare-up of anger, or similar emotions, that most normal children and adults have as they experience life's frustrations.

Related Readings

Wolfgang, C. H. (1977). *Helping Aggressive and Passive Preschoolers through Play.* Columbus, OH: Merrill.

Wolfgang, C. H., & Glickman, C. D. (1980). *Solving Discipline Problems: Strategies for Classroom Teachers.* Boston: Allyn and Bacon.

Wolfgang, C. H., Mackender, B., & Wolfgang, M. E. (1981). *Growing & Learning through Play.* Poali, PA: Judy/Instructo.

Wolfgang, C. H., & Wolfgang, M. E. (1992). *School for Young Children: Developmentally Appropriate Practices.* Boston: Allyn and Bacon.

Endnotes

1. Wolfgang, C. H. (1977). *Helping Aggressive and Passive Preschoolers through Play.* Columbus, OH: Merrill.
2. Wolfgang, C. H., Mackender, B., & Wolfgang, M. E. (1981). *Growing & Learning through Play.* Poali, PA: Judy/Instructo.
3. Wolfgang, C. H., and Wolfgang, M. E. (1992). *School for Young Children: Developmentally Appropriate Practices.* Boston: Allyn and Bacon.
4. Erikson, E. H. (1950). *Childhood and Society.* New York: Norton.
5. Piaget, J. (1971). *The Construction of Reality in the Child.* New York: Ballantine. See also: Piaget, J. (1971). *The Language and Thought of the Child.* New York: World Publishing.
6. Erikson, E. (1950). *Childhood and Society.* New York: Norton.
7. For a detailed explanation of the concept of problem ownership, see: Gordon, T. (1974). *T. E. T.: Teacher Effectiveness Training* (pp. 126–129). New York: David McKay. See also: Dinkmeyer, D. G., McKay, D., & Dinkmeyer, J. S. (1989). *Parenting Young Children* (pp. 90–98). Circle Pines, MN: American Guidance Service. In our opinion, the concept of problem ownership is helpful, but we do not feel that problems for

young children with limited conceptual ability can be left to them to solve. We feel that the ultimate goal is to have children solve their own problems, but if they cannot, to escalate up the TBC to provide them with gradually more help.

8. Canter, L., & Canter, M. (1976). *Assertive Discipline: A Take-Charge Approach for Today's Educator.* Seal Beach, CA: Lee Canter and Associates.
9. Glasser, W. (1969). *Schools Without Failure.* New York: Harper & Row.
10. Dreikurs, R., & Cassel, P. (1972) *Discipline Without Tears.* New York: Hawthorn.
11. Rogers, C. (1969). *Freedom to Learn.* Columbus, OH: Merrill.
12. Canter, L., & Canter, M. (1976). *Assertive Discipline: A Take-Charge Approach for Today's Educator.* Seal Beach, CA.: Lee Canter and Associates.
13. Alberto, P. A., & Troutman, A. C. (1982). *Applied Behavior Analysis for Teachers.* New York: Merrill.

Answers to Test Yourself

A3, B1, C5, D4, E2, 6B, 7A, 8C, 9A, 10A

2

The Relationship-Listening Face

In Chapter 1, examples of Jimmy "El Zorro" and the sandbox conflict over the shovel demonstrated how the teacher can easily escalate along the Teacher Behavior Continuum (TBC). In each case, the teacher first used modality cueing, then progressed to nondirective statements, questions, directive statements, modeling, and physical intervention. This is a short version of the TBC that may be used for minor incidents of misbehavior that offer so-called teachable moments. For the more difficult child who requires a much longer intervention, a host of related techniques may be found under each of the TBC behavioral categories. What follows is a fuller explanation of each of the techniques on the TBC and additional new techniques that a teacher may use under each category while wearing the Relationship-Listening "face" (see Figure 2–1).

TEACHER BEHAVIOR CONTINUUM (TBC)

Modality Cueing

Young children become self-absorbed in exploring exciting materials and interacting with each other as peers. As a result of this self-absorption, they lose an awareness of the consequences of their actions. In using the first, least-powerful techniques on the TBC, the teacher tried to signal Jimmy to desist his paintbrush sword play, but with limited or no guilt imposed (see Chapter 1). This can be done, with a Relationship-Listening attitude, through the use of *low-profile correction.*[1] The teacher moved to Jimmy and attempted to signal (modality cue) him of her awareness of his actions through the modalities of sight, sound, or tactile senses. The teacher does this by moving to the child and making eye contact, or moving to the child and making a sound to catch his attention, or moving to the child and laying her hand lightly on his shoulder to get his attention. The teacher may cue for the child's attention by any or all of these modalities: eye contact, sound (making an acknowledgment sound such as clearing her throat), and touching his shoulder. This minimum signal might be all that is needed to make the child aware of his behavior and to get him to stop his inappropriate actions.

FIGURE 2–1 TBC: Relationship-Listening Face

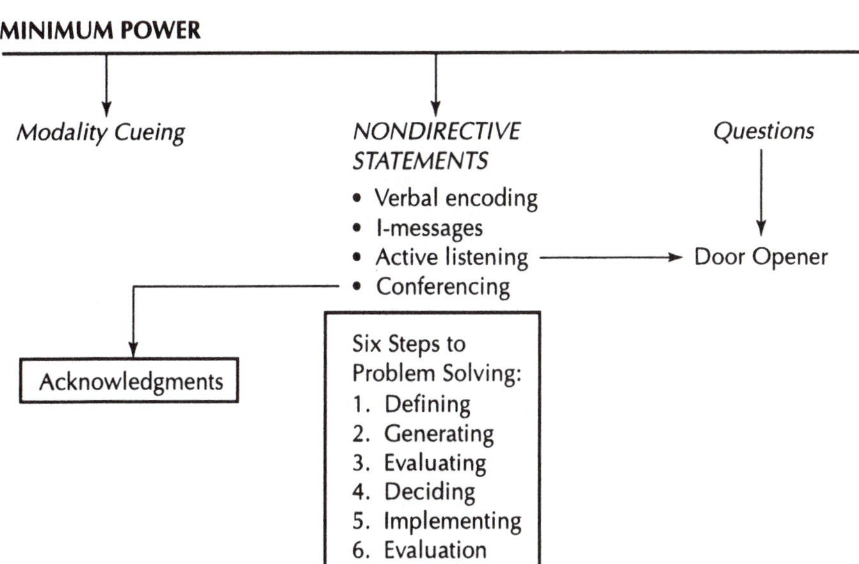

Gear Shifting through Modalities Some children have weak or even depressed modalities. That is, one or more of the senses—vision, touch, or hearing—has been desensitized so as to be an ineffective modality for taking in information from the outside world. For instance, if Jimmy "El Zorro" has a weak visual modality, the teacher's attempts to cue visually with him might be unsuccessful. This would now require the teacher to shift gears to another modality, such as tactile (placing a hand on his shoulder) or auditory (making some modality acknowledgment sounds or even saying his name softly), or a combination of the various modalities.

The point is that when a teacher wishes to signal or cue a child to desist by using only one modality, simply looking at him (visual), saying his name (sound), or placing a hand on his shoulder (touch) may not work. Shifting to other modality forms might be required and be more effective. Of course, the teacher becomes even more skilled and effective if she has analyzed in advance the stronger and weaker modalities of each child in her classroom.

Nondirective Statements

If the use of modality cueing (the first step on the Teacher Behavior Continuum) and its subbehaviors of visual, auditory, tactile, and gear shifting are unsuccessful, the teacher now escalates her power by moving up the TBC to nondirective statements. In using nondirective statements, we as teachers use our words, with verbal encoding, to describe the *situation* and/or the *feelings* of the child as we see them.

Verbal Encoding *Verbal encoding* is a very "soft," or minimal power, technique. It has the sole purpose of bringing to the child a conscious awareness of his action, his and others' feelings, and his effect on others. In the Jimmy "El Zorro" example, we see:

Teacher: (nondirective statements/verbal encoding) "Jimmy, paints can be scary and sometimes hard to control. That is fun and exciting for you but other children are frightened by the paintbrush."

The I-Message (Behavior-Effect-Feeling) An *I-message* is another teacher subbehavior under the general category of nondirective statements on the Teacher Behavior Continuum. When a child (such as Jimmy with his paintbrush "sword") is acting in such a manner that it disrupts the class or has a similar tangible effect on you as the teacher, the I-message is the most nonguilt-inducing method of directly expressing to the child how his actions are affecting you and his peers. Here is an example of an I-message:

Teacher: "When friends are stabbed with a wet paintbrush (behavior), it soils their clothing and scares other children (effect). I need to keep people safe and clean, and it frightens me (feeling) when people are jabbed."

The I-message is a way to inform the child of the problem that *you* the teacher are facing. The I-message is not saying, "You did something wrong" (the word *you* is not permitted in an I-message) and it is not saying, "Here is how I want you to change." It is saying, "Child, *I* the teacher want to let you in on how my world is being affected by your behavior." This nonjudgmental statement still gives the child the power to cognitively reflect on his actions and come up with his own solutions on how he will change; thus, there is no coercion by the teacher.

Generally, after an I-message is delivered by the teacher, the child might respond in one of three ways. First, he might simply stop the misbehavior (Jimmy stops the sword play and returns to painting a picture on the paper at the easel),

EXAMPLES OF POOR AND GOOD I-MESSAGES

Poor Example: "I want you to get your feet off that table now!"

This is a you-message implying guilt. It contains a poor definition of the improper behavior, no example of the effect, and a lack of expression of the teacher's feelings.

Good Example: "When feet are put on the table (behavior), germs come off our shoes and get on the table. We must rewash the table before we eat (effect), and I get angry (feelings) having to do more work."

Poor Example: "When the school flowers are picked (behavior), I don't like it!"

The message starts effectively with a good statement of behavior, but no effect is given, and "I don't like it" is a value judgment rather than an expression of the teacher's feelings.

Good Example: "When the school flowers are picked (behavior), they will soon die and we will have no beautiful flowers to see grow and smell (effect), and that makes me sad (feelings)."

EXAMPLES OF GOOD I-MESSAGES

"When Legos are left on the floor (behavior), people might slip on them and fall (effect), and I worry (feelings) that someone will get hurt."

"When tables are not cleaned after snack time (behavior), spilt milk and other 'gooey stuff' will damage the puzzles when we put them on the table (effect), and I am afraid (feelings) we will soon have no puzzles to enjoy."

"When I am told to 'shut up' when I am speaking at circle time (behavior), I am not able to explain the rules to everyone (effect), and I am fearful (feelings) that someone will get hurt using this new toy."

"When children stand on the table (behavior), I am afraid (feelings) that they will fall and get hurt (effect)."

"When people scream indoors (behavior), it hurts my ears (effect) and I get angry (feelings)."

"When people write or scribble in our good children's books (behavior), it destroys them (effect), and I am afraid (feelings) we soon will have no books to share or read."

"When sand (or toys or other materials) is thrown (behavior), it gets into people's eyes and hurts them (effect), and I am the teacher who must keep people safe and that scares (feelings) me."

thereby ending the teachable moment. Second, the child might continue to defy the teacher, prompting an escalation of power along the Teacher Behavior Continuum to the questioning stage. Finally, the child might respond back to the teacher with some form of language. This language is typically of two types: defensive language (verbal aggression, denial, or attempting to distract the teacher to a side issue) or real verbal communication (how the child may wish to solve a specific dilemma he is facing). The following is an example of defensive language:

> ***Teacher:*** "When friends are stabbed with a wet paintbrush (behavior), it soils their clothing and scares other children (effect). I need to keep people safe and clean, and it frightens me (feelings) when people are jabbed."
>
> ***Jimmy "El Zorro":*** "I didn't do anything! (denial) (The teacher simply looks on.) You're a butt-head! (verbal aggression) Carol was playing 'sword' and you didn't say anything to her!" (sidetracking)

In viewing Jimmy's defensive verbal response, we must simply see these statements as an immature child's attempt to find some defensive way of handling this situation. We must not view "I didn't do anything" (denial) as lying. We simply ignore these denials. This may be a natural tendency for a child to

FEELING WORDS FOR TEACHER AND CHILDREN

At times, when using I-messages with young children, our encoding of our feelings seems repetitive, such as overusing "that scares me." At the same time, we are helping children learn to put words and labels to their own feelings. The following list of feeling words[2] might help to broaden the teacher's feeling vocabulary:

Negative Feelings		Positive Feelings	
angry	sad	appreciate	great
confused	scared	better	happy
disappointed	sorry	enjoy	like
frightened	unfair	excited	love
hate	unhappy	glad	pleased
hurt	want to give up	good	proud
left out	worried		
mad			

deny reality as he is faced with it. In addition, some children emotionally "flood" and are quite frightened; they actually may not remember what they did, even though it occurred just seconds before.

We also must not be frightened, angered, or offended by "you're a butt-head" (or sexual or swear words) because if we accept the passive-aggressive construct (Figure 1–2) as explained in Chapter 1, that verbal aggression is a better or more productive response than a physical aggressive response to us. The teacher might respond with, "When those words are said to me, I hear anger, but I don't know why you're angry, and I feel sad that I am not able to help you (I-message). What words could you use to help me understand what you want?" (door opener; discussed below) (see Figure 2–2).

It is important not to be drawn into a power play by the child's attempt to make us feel guilty ("Carol was playing 'sword' and you didn't say anything to her!") and respond to this assertion by trying to deny the child's criticism or explain our behavior to him. It has been said that the best defense at times is a good offense, so the teacher should just see this as an attempt (and a fairly sophisticated one) to sidetrack her down a blind alley and take the focus off the child and his actions. We may simply ignore sidetracking statements or use some of the following techniques to respond to denial, verbal aggression, or guilt statements used by children to distract us.

Note: The statement, "I don't like that when so-and-so is done!" is not an I-message. It is an expression of the teacher's value judgment.

Active Listening/Door Openers/Acknowledgments Children can become emotionally "flooded" as a result of teachers' actions that are intended to demonstrate to them that their behavior is not appropriate and will need to change. When this happens, their verbal response to us might be verbal aggression (see Figure 1–2).

FIGURE 2–2 I-Messages

CHILD'S ACTION	TEACHER I-MESSAGE
Joe starts to talk during circle time to Perry while the teacher is reading a story. They talk loudly enough that they start to disturb everyone listening to the story.	"When children talk during circle time (behavior), I have a hard time reading so everyone can hear (effect), and that makes me feel frustrated (feelings)."
After getting up from her nap, Jordan leaves her blanket and stuffed animal on the floor and starts toward the snack table.	"When children leave blankets and animals on the floor (behavior), I am fearful (feelings) that others will fall over them and get hurt (effect)."
Ann finishes eating and she departs with her lunch box, leaving her trash behind.	"I get frustrated (feelings) when I have to clean up the snack table (effect) when trash is left behind (behavior)."
When the door is opened to go out to the playground, Caitlin runs through the door and down the stairs.	"When children run down the stairs (behavior), I am fearful (feelings) that people will fall and get injured (effect), and my job is to keep people safe."
Sara is trying to tie her shoe when she stops, begins to cry, and comes to talk to the teacher through the crying.	"When children cry and talk to me at the same time (behavior), I can't understand what is being said (effect), and I am disappointed (feelings) that I can't help."
The teacher is talking to a parent when Carlos interrupts and starts talking.	"It makes me sad (feelings) when I cannot understand two people who are talking to me at the same time (behavior), and I become confused (effect)."
Margaret deliberately splashes Julie while washing her hands.	"When water is splashed (behavior), people's clothes get wet and the floor gets wet and dangerously slippery (effect), and that frightens me (feelings) because I need to keep people safe."
Tom and Beth are fighting over a book by pulling it back and forth.	"When books are pulled (behavior), I am fearful (feelings) that they will get damaged and destroyed and we will not have them any more (effect)."

Calling the teacher "butt-head" or shouting out "I hate you!" should simply be viewed as the child's first attempt at using language; the child is trying to communicate with us by taking a step up from physical aggression. We should not be offended or frightened by this immature behavior, but instead should accept the verbal aggression as an attempt at verbal communication. If we avoid reprimanding the child, and even encourage him to verbalize or speak more, we will see that the hostility feelings will soon leave the child's language and more reasoning and verbal problem solving will begin.

The philosophical orientation of these Relationship-Listening techniques views the child as an inherently good and rational being. If the child's behavior is destructive, the Relationship-Listening explanation would be that the child is having some form of inner turmoil, which we call flooding, and this inner tension results in "acting-out" behavior. Thus, the child, under Relationship-Listening, should never be viewed simply as being naughty. The teacher's helping role is to establish a nonjudgmental and supportive relationship with the child and to encourage the child to communicate these feelings in words by using the teacher as a "sounding board."

Communication is a very difficult process among adults; it is even more difficult for young children with their limited intellectual and verbal ability. The following is an attempt to understand how communication would be explained by Thomas Gordon,[3] one of the leaders among the Relationship-Listening school of discipline. Gordon has suggested that adults and children constantly maintain one of two internal states: equilibrium or disequilibrium. A child who is full and not hungry, and who is playing happily, is at equilibrium. An hour or two later, the child begins to tire and gets inner messages that she is now beginning to get hungry, indicating a growing disequilibrium. When this hunger is very strong, the child attempts to communicate this inner need to her mother. The first and surface communication, when listened to by the mother, is not always what the child really means.

Child: "Mom, when is dad going to get home from work?"

Mother: "Ann, you know that dad always gets home at six o'clock."

The child has failed to communicate her real need and the mother has failed to hear what was *really* being said—thus, poor communication. What the child really meant to say was, "Mom, I am very hungry and I don't think I can wait until dad gets home to eat."

When a child has an inner need, she must express it externally, and so she tries verbally encoding that need to express her wants. Now, let's replay the discussion, this time with the mother using active listening:

Child: "Mom, when is dad going to get home from work?"

Mother: "At six o'clock, but you would like dad to get home sooner?" (active listening)

Child: "Ah, he'll be late again!"

Mother: "You are worried that he might not be on time today." (active listening)

Child: "I don't think I can wait for dad if he's going to be late."

Mother: (Looks at child, nods, and smiles) (acknowledgments)

Child: "I'm starving!"

Mother: "You are very hungry, and you'd like to eat now and not wait for daddy because he might be late?" (active listening)

Child: "Yeah. Uh-h-h..."

Mother: "You would like to tell me more?" (door openers)

Child: "Yeah, while waiting for the bus, it rained and I forgot to bring my lunch into the shelter. It got wet and was ruined, and all I had to eat for lunch was a banana."

Mother: "Oh, that does make a difference. The rule is that we wait for dad so we can all eat dinner together, but because you missed out on lunch today why don't you have a glass of milk and two oatmeal cookies to tide you over."

Active listening is a technique for improving communication between child and teacher whereby the child is encouraged to "talk out" repetitively, and the adult's role is to attempt to mirror back to the child the emotional feelings we think we are hearing from the child. If we take first or surface communication statements from the child as fact, especially when the child is flooded, we may not hear what the child is really attempting to communicate. The adult's nonverbal behavior of nodding our head (called acknowledgments) and asking questions such as, "You would like to tell me more?" are called door openers. They simply serve to encourage the child to continue to talk and attempt to communicate.

Let's take another teacher-child example:

Teacher: (nondirective statements) "Jimmy, paints can be scary and sometimes hard to control. That is fun and exciting for you but other children are frightened by the paintbrush."

Jimmy: "I don't like him!" (meaning the peer, Walter, who just passed by and was the target of Jimmy's latest attempt to stab with the paintbrush)

Teacher: "You're angry with Walter?" (active listening)

Jimmy: "He is mean!"

Teacher: "Walter has been mean to you?"

Jimmy: "Yes. I am his best friend, and he let Robert sit beside him at snack!"

Teacher: "You're angry because you were not able to sit by your friend." (active listening)

Jimmy: "Yes, could I sit beside Walter?"

The teacher's efforts to determine the cause of Jimmy's sword play have exposed a deeper problem that Jimmy is facing, and now the teacher can begin dealing with it from a new perspective (see Figure 2–3).

FIGURE 2–3 Communication

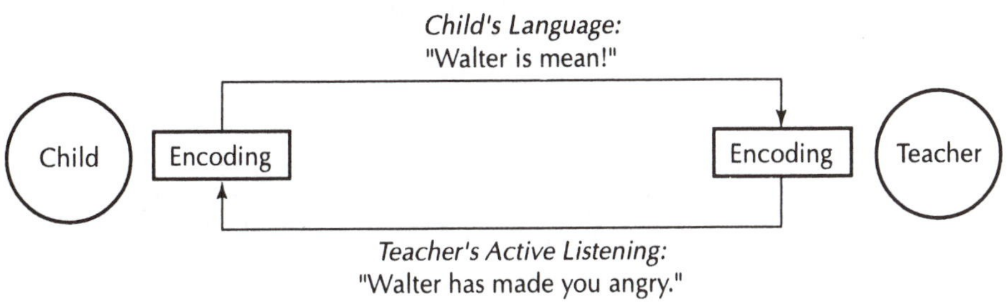

THREE SPHERES OF RELATIONSHIP

Adults who are put in charge in institutions (hospitals, prisons, schools, etc.) or businesses (airline counter attendant, store check-out personnel, etc.) and who are under day-in and day-out stress may start to show *institutional behavior*. They might begin dealing with the public in a mechanical manner, using curt speech, exhibiting flat expressionless behavior, and showing an unthinking administration of the rules. They may exhibit little consideration of the needs of the individuals with whom they are dealing and communicate no warmth. If we are not very careful, this same attitude can begin to be seen in the behavior of teachers in the early childhood classroom, especially if the classroom is imbalanced with too many children, not enough teacher help in supervision, and a general lack of equipment and classroom materials.

The airline counter attendant is burned out because she has to manage too large a number of passengers (in a classroom it would be children). A snow storm has grounded five flights and she must deal with literally hundreds of angry passengers—the situation is obviously out of balance. Teachers working in an imbalanced classroom (too many children, not enough toys or materials) may begin to become burned out and take on institutional behavior. Young children ages 3 to 7 may spend 8 to 10 hours in day care and early childhood centers, and they must have significant emotional investment by caregivers and teachers. To go days, weeks, or months being cared for by adults who are "depressive" and "burned out" can have a real and lasting destructive effect upon young children. Even a busy parent caring for a very small number of her own children, after a few busy weeks, suddenly stops and asks herself, "When is the last time I just stopped and totally listened to my child?" She feels guilty when she realizes that it has been many weeks or that she cannot remember how long it has been. We cannot permit this to occur in early childhood classrooms, and thus we use the *three spheres of relationship* construct to determine how we use our time with children.

There are three basic spheres in a teacher's relationships with students—Sphere 1: one to one, Sphere 2: one to group, and Sphere 3: one to all (Figure 2–4). Viewed in reverse order, we see that the *one-to-all sphere* is a lecture format when the children must sit passively, refrain from communicating, and listen to the teacher speak. This format can sometimes lend itself to children feeling no affec-

FIGURE 2–4 Spheres of Relationship

One to One	A teacher interacts with one child (knee to knee).	The child receives near total emotional attention by the teacher and may dominate conversation.
One to Group	A teacher interacts with a small group of 6 to 8 children.	The child feels more emotional connectedness with the teacher and peers, but needs to share conversation with peers.
One to All	A teacher speaks or teaches to the total group of children.	The child feels little emotional contact—a spatial distance—with the teacher, and must generally inhibit the desire to talk, but simply listen.

tion coming from the teacher and feeling depersonalized because there is just one teacher to all children. In the early childhood classroom this might occur at circle time or story time if such occasions are handled in an authoritarian manner.

The *one-to-group sphere* occurs when the teacher is seated together with a group of six to eight children and there is conversation among all members of the group. An example of this would be when the teacher is seated at the snack table. There is much more warmth felt among this smaller group, but they do have to share the teacher's warmth and attention with their table mates—one teacher to a group of up to eight children.

The *one-to-one sphere* is the time when the teacher and child are totally alone with one another. The child can receive total warmth and attention from the teacher and is free to dominate the conversation. Relationship-Listening techniques such as active listening, door openers, and acknowledgments can be very helpful in communicating with the young child during this one-to-one sphere of relationship and, to a lesser extent, with a group of children in the one-to-group sphere.

As described in more detail in Chapter 6, which deals with key time periods throughout the child's school day, we cannot leave it to chance and hope that every child will get sufficient personal time with a teacher, because the quiet and less assertive children will fall through the cracks. In staff meetings and during teacher planning time, we must use this three-sphere construct in planning the children's day to assure that every child will have a relationship with the teacher in each of the three spheres. We can have a rich collection of toys and materials and a well-designed classroom but still have teachers who are spending 100 percent of their time dealing with children in the third sphere of one to all. These types of teachers are "life guarding," directing traffic and activities and dealing with the children in a custodial manner. In such a case, they are expressing cold institutional behavior. We can test to see if this is occurring by asking, "What are the teachers doing at snack or eating time, and what are they doing when children settle down for a nap?" If the teacher is playing waitress, then no adult is seated with the children. At the beginning of rest time, does the staff quickly depart for coffee? These are two critical times when young children emotionally need us. At snack time, we can be seated with groups of children and have one-to-group dealings. At rest time, when a child is having difficulty falling asleep, we can have one-to-one dealings as we rub the child's back or talk softly, giving the child a feeling of warmth and intimacy.

MEETINGS, DISCUSSIONS, AND COMMUNICATION

Because young children are small in stature and have limited language ability compared to adults, we as adults may underestimate their need to communicate; thus, again we may often see institutional teacher behavior toward the child. Let's examine how meetings, discussions, and communication in adults occur and then set some principles and techniques for facilitating communication with young children.

Imagine yourself seated in a doctor's waiting room (or any waiting room). It is a long, boring wait and you find yourself face to face with a stranger also suffering the same boredom—you are spatially confined together. One adult feels a need to reach out and establish a human relationship with others in the room, and she may do that by finding some topic to talk about. She may ask questions such as, "Where do you work? Are you married? Do you have any children? How old are they?"

Your response to these questions, which can be personal and even intrusive into your privacy, is basic to establishing a relationship. If you do not want a relationship with the waiting room stranger, you might respond flatly and coldly, "Why do you need to know this?" Well, the person does not really need to know this information but is simply opening up lines of communication, by requesting *free information*.[4] Communication occurs when two or more people are willing to transact in a ping-pong manner, each offering small bits of personal *free information* (information about oneself, opinions, feelings, etc.) that tells the other who one really is. You might respond, "Well, I am married and have identical twin daughters who are age five." "Oh, oh—double trouble! My neighbor has a set of twins. Oh, are they a handful. How are yours?" This verbal transaction may go on indefinitely.

If a transaction, through a sharing of free information, is able to continue for many days over a long period of time, such communication will enable a deep friendship to develop between two people. This is also true for young children, both peer to peer and teacher to child. Therefore, through the use of the Three Spheres of Relationship, we as teachers deliberately set up meetings to teach and encourage discussion and communication among peers and staff (see Figure 2–5).

Class Meetings

The teacher may hold weekly class meetings (either Sphere 1: one to one; Sphere 2: one to group; or Sphere 3: one to all) that bring the children together in a circle for one of three specific purposes: free information, topical, or problem solving (see Figure 2–6).

Free-Information Meetings Children simply transact verbally by providing the teacher with *free information* on a topic that interests them. If a child is motivated simply to give information, the teacher uses *active listening, acknowledgments,* and *door openers*. If the child questions the teacher, she responds naturally with *free information.*

FIGURE 2–5 TBC: Relationship-Listening Face

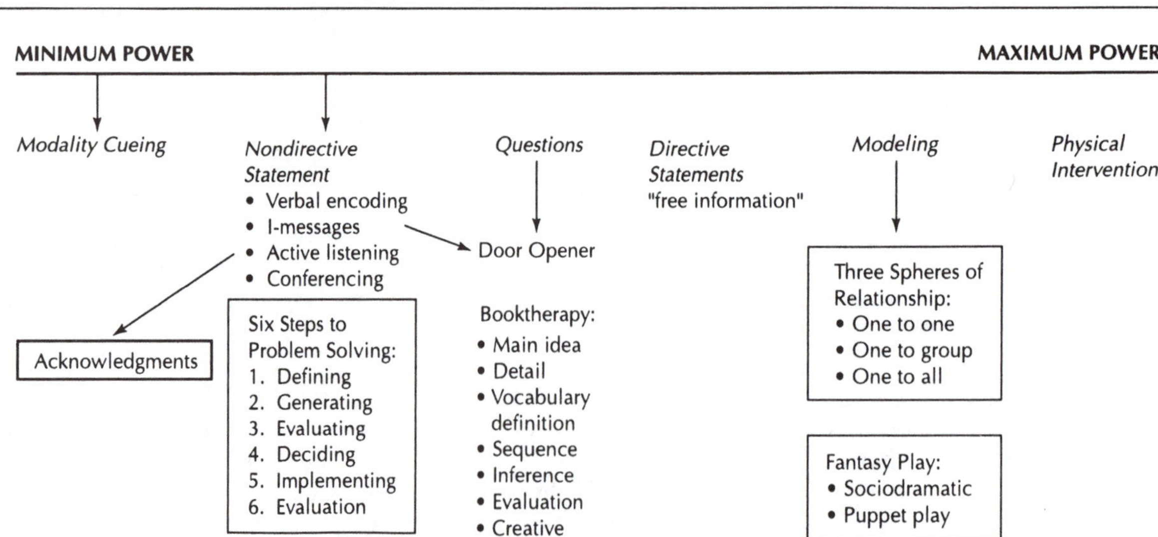

Topical Class Meetings Generally, children are brought to the circle to discuss a topic that is of high interest to them (e.g., a recent children's video they have seen) or of great emotional concern (e.g., the arrival of a new baby brother). If the child has a strong motivation to give information and simply talk about things of great emotional concern, the teacher uses active listening, acknowledgments, and door openers. If the child questions the teacher, she gives free information by carrying on discussions with the child or perhaps reading a children's book on the child's topic or emotional concern, and permits the child to discuss the book afterwards. (See the list of bibliotherapy books categorized by topics located at the end of this chapter.)

Problem-Solving Meetings The teacher holds a meeting to discuss a topic that involves some incident of social conflict repeatedly occurring within the classroom. For example, the teacher might begin such a meeting with, "Friends, let's talk about what you may do when someone takes your toy." The children are then led through the Six Steps to Problem Solving. This is a structure for helping children think out problems and come up with creative solutions.

Briefly, the six steps are:

1. Define the problem.
2. Generate solutions.
3. Evaluate the solutions.
4. Decide which solution is best.
5. Implement the solution.
6. Evaluate the solution.

SIX STEPS TO PROBLEM SOLVING

To help children learn to think through a problem logically, the teacher might model a six-step process that may be used in all three spheres of relationship. The example that follows is in the one-to-one sphere of teacher to child, but the same steps may be followed in a one-to-group or one-to-all relationship, possibly as a part of a class meeting. Each of the six steps will be used.

Teacher: "You have a problem and that problem is, 'How may you sit beside Walter at lunch?' (Step 1: Defining the Problem) Let's think together of ways that you might solve this problem. What are your ideas?" (Step 2: Generating Possible Solutions)

Jimmy: "I could get to the table first."

Teacher: "That may work, but let's think of a lot of other ways, too."

Jimmy: "I could ask Walter to sit by me. But Robert always gets there first. I could sit at the little table [has only two seats] and ask Walter to sit with me. But Robert would come and push me out of my seat. I could push him back or tell the teacher on him!"

Teacher: "Robert wants to eat with Walter, too." (active listening)

Jimmy: "Yes, could he eat at the little table? We could have three chairs and be best friends."

FIGURE 2–6 Class Meetings

RELATIONSHIP SPHERE	TYPES OF CLASS MEETINGS
	Free Information
Sphere 1: One to One Seating Arrangement: The child and teacher are in a knee-to-knee spatial relationship.	The child simply verbally transacts by providing the teacher with free information on a topic that interests the child. If the child is motivated to simply give information, the teacher uses active listening, acknowledgments, and door openers. If the child questions the teacher, she responds naturally with free information.
Sphere 2: One to Group Seating Arrangement: The children and teacher are in a shoulder-to-shoulder spatial relationship, preferably at a round table or on a rug on the floor in a circle where everyone can clearly see the face of all other members.	The teacher brings together a group of children (no more than eight) and permits conversation to develop naturally or does a door opener to get conversation going. The children simply transact through talking by providing the teacher and peers with free information on topics that they wish to discuss. The teacher's techniques are active listening, acknowledgments, and, especially, door openers with those children wanting to speak but seeming not able to initiate. If the child questions the teacher, she gives free information.
Sphere 3: One to All Seating Arrangement: The children and teacher are in a shoulder-to-shoulder spatial relationship in a circle on a rug or on chairs where everyone can clearly see the face of all other members.There will likely be too many children for a circle, so the children could be arranged in three or more semicircles facing the teacher, who is seated in an elevated position (on a chair).	The teacher uses the same general guidelines as above (one to group) for the discussion, but in Sphere 3: one to all. The free-information meeting must be short in duration and move quickly, requiring the teacher to be more directive so that one member does not dominate with an overly lengthy egocentric monologue that does not interest the other members of the group.

FIGURE 2–6 (Continued)

TYPES OF CLASS MEETINGS	
Topical	**Problem Solving**
Generally, a child brings to the teacher a topic that is of high interest (e.g., a recent children's video he has seen) or of great emotional concern (an arrival of a new baby brother). If the child has a strong motivation to give information and simply talk about things of great emotional concern, the teacher uses active listening, acknowledgments, and door openers. If the child questions the teacher, she gives free information by carrying on the discussion with the child or perhaps reading a children's book on the child's topic or emotional concern, and permits the child to discuss the book afterwards. (See the list of bibliotherapy books categorized by topics under headings of general emotional concerns of children this age at the end of this chapter.) If the book is free of emotional content, the teacher uses the questioning taxonomy.	The teacher brings to the child a topic that involves some concrete incident of social conflict repetitvely recurring with this child. "William, let's talk about what you may do when someone takes your toy." The teacher then leads the child through the Six Steps to Problem Solving.
The teacher brings a topic to the group or a topic may spontaneously arise from the group that is of high interest to them (e.g., a recent children's video that they have seen) or of great emotional concern (e.g., an arrival of a new baby brother). If the child has a strong motivation to give information, the teacher uses active listening, acknowledgments, and door openers. If the child questions the teacher, she gives free information by carrying on the discussion with the child or by reading a children's book on the child's topic or emotional concern, and permits the child to discuss the book afterwards. (See the list of bibliotherapy books listed under topical headings of general emotional concerns of children this age.) If the topic is not emotionally laden, the teacher will avoid yes-no questions and use the questioning taxonomy.	The teacher brings to the group a topic that involves some concrete incident of social conflict repetitively recurring with these children. "Friends, let's talk about what you may do when someone takes your toy." The teacher then leads the group through the Six Steps to Problem Solving. The teacher also symbolically models various positive solutions with the use of puppets (puppet modeling).
The teacher uses the same general guidelines as above (one to group) for the discussion, but in Sphere 3: one to all. The free-information meeting must be short in duration and move quickly, requiring the teacher to be more directive so that one member does not dominate with an over lengthy egocentric monologue that does not interest the other members of the group.	The teacher brings to the group a topic that involves some incident of social conflict repetitively recurring with these children. "Friends, let's talk about what you may do when someone takes your toy." The teacher then leads the group through the Six Steps to Problem Solving. The teacher also symbolically models various positive solutions with the use of puppets (puppet modeling).

Teacher: "Which one of your ideas is best?" (Step 3: Evaluating the Solutions)

Jimmy: "Having three chairs."

Teacher: "Is that what you will do tomorrow?" (Step 4: Deciding Which Solution Is Best)

Jimmy: "Yes."

The next day, the teacher watches as Jimmy adds a third chair to the small table and invites both Walter and Robert to eat with him. (Step 5: Implementing the Solution) After lunch, the teacher talks to Jimmy.

Teacher: "Was your solution to your problem a good one?" (Step 6: Evaluating the Solution)

Jimmy: "Yes, it was *great*, and I figured it out all by myself!"

The teacher has used the Six Steps to Problem Solving to help Jimmy through a process of on-the-spot conferencing. First, we saw Jimmy performing an aggressive act toward Walter. Then, through active listening, we discovered that Jimmy had an inner disequilibrium, or a "blocked" need—he wanted his best friend to sit beside him at lunch. The teacher did not solve Jimmy's problem for him but was willing to take the time to listen and encourage Jimmy to communicate (speak out) about this problem until a solution was obtained. The communication was guided by a rather simple sequence of procedures: (1) helping to define the problem, (2) trying to stimulate creativity toward generating solutions but without evaluating them, (3) conducting an evaluation of the solutions, and then (4) deciding on a solution. We also saw the teacher observing Jimmy (5) implementing the solution, and finally asking him to (6) evaluate the effectiveness of the solution (see Figure 2–5). *Note:* Since the six steps take much time, the teacher normally will use this problem-solving process with a single child only on a special occasion, but will more likely use these techniques in large group meetings with a group of children or the entire class. This process may be effective in all three spheres.

Who Owns the Problem?

Notice that with Jimmy, who wanted to be seated by a friend, the teacher did not solve the problem for him. Jimmy owned this problem and the teacher facilitated his thinking by defining the problem and then acting. We as teachers are solidly motivated to nurture and help children. Some of us may act as "super-teachers," seeing our role as the person who solves all problems in the classroom. If we do that, we rob the children of the authentic experience of clashing with others and objects. Such experience allows children to acquire skills in solving their own problems and become autonomous. In order to classify the problems that we see involving the children in the classroom, we must determine whether the child owns the problem or the teacher owns the problem. These questions will help:

1. Do the actions or problems of the child take away the teacher's or classmates' rights? (The child has had three servings of the special snack for today while others have only had one, and by her actions she is moving to take a fourth helping. This requires the teacher to intervene.)
2. Is the safety of the materials, the classmates, the teacher, or the child involved? (A child eats the paints. This requires teacher intervention.)

3. Is the child too young and incapable of owning or solving this problem? (The child is trying to get the lid off the nail storage can in the carpentry corner, which takes more strength than the 3-year-old has. This requires teacher intervention.)

If the answer to any of these questions is yes, the teacher owns the problem and must respond. The responding techniques will be I-messages, active listening, door openers, acknowledgments, and possibly the Six Steps to Problem Solving. But the concept of problem ownership says clearly to the teacher to stop and to inhibit "rescuer" tendencies. (For instance, if Maria complains to the teacher, "Michael took my tricycle!" the teacher will respond with a door opener, "What are you going to do to get your tricycle back?")

In reality, 80 to 90 percent of all problems faced by children in the classroom belong to them. The guidelines for problem ownership suggest that we as teachers must not, out of our need to help or fear that chaos will occur, rob them of the experience of solving their own problems by moving too quickly and unthinkingly.

BOOKTHERAPY[5]

The reading of books to children as a form of bibliotherapy (or booktherapy) has benefits for helping them find answers to many day-in, day-out emotional pressures they face. "Reading provides insight into [a child's] own problems, and offers clues to how to best solve them. In their everyday lives, many children lack people they admire enough to want to identify with and use as a pattern for their own development. In reading, they find sources of identification which fit their needs and provide motivation in the molding of their personalities."[6] Literature provides children with a chance to interact with characters who face similar circumstances, to identify with the feelings and experiences of others, to acquire clues for remedying problems, and to "serve as mirrors for children, reflecting their appearance, their relationships, their feelings and thoughts in their immediate environment."[7]

These books might be read to children within all three spheres of relationship. They might serve as a topic for a topical class meeting or for a child known to be facing a unique emotional concern at this point in life. After reading such books to young children, the teacher may follow up with a series of questioning techniques to enable the children to intellectually "talk out" their ideas and feelings and critically think about these issues. Some of these questioning techniques might be the following:

1. *Main idea questions.* The children are asked to identify the central theme of the story. "Why did Scott get so upset in the story?" These questions help children become more aware of the details of the story and their relationship to each other.

2. *Detail questions.* The teacher asks for bits of information the materials convey. "What kind of cake was Cindy baking for Asa? When did Asa see the cake?" Since very little depth of comprehension is necessary for these questions, they should not form the bulk of the questioning.

3. *Vocabulary definition questions.* The teacher assesses the children's understanding of words with which they may be unfamiliar. "Children, what do you

think the wren said to Peter Rabbit when he was stuck in the gooseberry bush and *implored* Peter to get loose?"

4. *Sequence questions.* The teacher checks the children's understanding of the order of events. "Were Matt and Christopher alone after their mother and father left the house?" is not a sequence question since there is no order of events which may have taken place. "What did Matt and Christopher do after their mother and father left the house? Then what happened?" is an example of a sequence question.
5. *Inference questions.* The teacher asks questions that require the children to infer elements from the story that were not directly stated in the story. "Would mother have liked The Cat in the Hat being in the house while she was gone? Why do you think that?" Children can answer these questions within their particular level of comprehension.
6. *Evaluation questions.* The teacher asks the children to make judgments about the reading materials that require the children to have sufficient background experiences related to the situation involved. "Was Angel doing the right thing when she decided to play with her daddy's VCR? Why or why not?"
7. *Creative questions.* The teacher asks the children to go beyond the facts in the reading to create new ideas. "What are some ways Delbert could have helped Rosalind in the block room when she was building her house, instead of kicking the blocks down?"

The key skill in using booktherapy for young children is to determine their emotional needs and match this with our knowledge of similar content found in children's books appropriate to their age. (See the list at the end of this chapter.) After many of these engaging stories are read to the children, we ask them to talk out their ideas through the questioning techniques just listed. We would also encourage discussion after asking these questions by using active listening, door openers, and acknowledgments.

SOCIODRAMATIC PLAY AND PUPPET PLAY

Having the children discuss emotional concerns after being motivated and focused by children's literature is only one form of language that the children have for understanding. The second hidden language is the make-believe language of play. Therefore, the teacher might wish to support this language by adding new props and puppets to the sociodramatic play and puppet area. Many children will follow up on the understanding they have gained by hearing and discussing books, and will enact this same content in make-believe play with puppets in the sociodramatic play corner.

SUMMARY

The "face," or attitude, of Relationship-Listening takes the position that when children act out in a negative manner, there must be some form of need being blocked, causing an inner emotional disequilibrium. The emotional tension, or flooding, is ineffectively expressed by the child's negative behavior. In using the Relationship-Listening techniques, we view the child as a capable person with the inner strength and ability to solve his or her own problems; through solving such problems, with our nonjudgmental help, the child becomes more empowered as an adaptive maturing person. Let the child find the solution for his or her own problems; if adults provide the solution, they will make the child dependent and weaken his or her future problem-solving ability.

When we see misbehavior, the Relationship-Listening techniques would direct us to first do a low-profile correction as a form of modality cueing. Awareness of our presence helps the young child maintain self-control; we therefore cue with that child, gaining the child's awareness through some modality (vision, sound, or touch). These first attempts at modality cueing might be ineffective if we are trying to cue a child with a weak or depressed modality, and thus we are required to cue again by gear shifting to a different modality to attempt to signal the child once more. If the child is flooded, the cueing may not raise his conscious awareness and we would be required to move to nondirective statements.

Carrying out the teacher techniques under nondirective statements, as a form of verbal encoding, we may be required to deliver an I-message (behavior–effect–feeling) to consciously make the child aware of his actions. We do not take verbal aggression and similar denial statements expressed by the child at face value, but we do value the expression itself and encourage it to continue through door openers or acknowledgments. In order to know whether we are hearing the child's true communication to us, we mirror back our summary and judgment of what the child is saying and feeling by using an active listening response. Through repetitive "talking it out" by the child and our parallel active listening, we begin to hear the child gradually change from expressions of strong emotion to more effective thinking about his or her situation and problem. With this renewed rational thinking on the child's part, the teacher may choose to do on-the-spot conferencing by taking the child through the Six Steps to Problem Solving process.

If these techniques are effective, the end result will be a child who is free to express inner thoughts and feelings, knowing the teacher will respond in a nonjudgmental manner. In this way, a binding relationship is formed between child and teacher. It is through this relationship and the ability to express needs that the child now becomes free to solve his or her own problems and gain greater maturity.

Test Yourself

Take the following test to see how well you understand the Relationship-Listening techniques. Check one answer. Answers may be found at the end of this chapter, following the Endnotes.

A. ___ gear shifting B. ___ modality cueing C. ___ door opener	1. Tommy is off task; the teacher approaches and places her hand lightly on his shoulder.
A. ___ low-profile correction B. ___ active listening C. ___ I-message	2. "When blocks are knocked down, the sound hurts my ears and I become nervous and irritable."
A. ___ low-profile correction B. ___ active listening C. ___ I-message	3. "I see by your face that you are angry and would like to have your shovel back."
A. ___ door opener B. ___ gear shifting C. ___ acknowledgments	4. "Gee, Bill, that must have made you very angry. Would you like to tell me more?"
A. ___ generating solutions B. ___ implementing C. ___ evaluating solutions D. ___ deciding on solutions E. ___ evaluating effectiveness F. ___ defining problem	5. On the left are the Six Steps to Problem Solving. Number them 1 to 6 in the order that a teacher would progress through the steps.
	Read these statements and determine if they meet the full criteria to be called I-messages.
A. ___ Yes B. ___ No	6. "You are making too much noise. I don't like it, and you are disturbing the whole group."
A. ___ Yes B. ___ No	7. "When chairs are carried high above children's heads, I am afraid that they may fall and hurt someone."
A. ___ Yes B. ___ No	8. "When someone says those swear words at me, I am not able to determine why that person is angry, and I feel frustrated not being able to help."
A. ___ Yes B. ___ No	9. "When books are scribbled on, I know it will destroy them."
A. ___ True B. ___ False	10. When problem solving with young children, teachers must give them good solutions because they are still too young to make decisions themselves.
A. ___ True B. ___ False	11. Strong verbal aggression is unacceptable for young children to express, and they must be corrected for hostile language directed toward a teacher.
A. ___ True B. ___ False	12. Active listening is a useful tool for helping children who are "flooded."
A. ___ True B. ___ False	13. When generating possible solutions under the Six Steps to Problem Solving, the teacher should immediately point out through an I-message that the suggested solution is not acceptable.
A. ___ True B. ___ False	14. When used sparingly, time out can be a helpful discipline procedure when wearing the Relationship-Listening face.

A. ___ "You" B. ___ the punishment C. ___ feeling D. ___ defining the problem E. ___ two choices F. ___ behavior G. ___ rule H. ___ effect	15. Check each of the elements or parts that should be found in an I-message.

Glossary

Acknowledgments A modality behavior, such as making eye contact or nodding one's head, to indicate that when the child is talking, the teacher is listening and understanding.

Active Listening The process of "mirroring" back to a child his emotional feelings and the problem being expressed, to the extent the teacher can understand it.

Conferencing A meeting—either planned or spontaneous—held between the child and the teacher to work out either the child's or teacher's problem and how either might change behavior accordingly.

Door Openers When a child is having difficulty expressing something that is troubling him, the teacher uses a question as a "door opener" to invite the child to talk about his concerns.

Gear Shifting through Modalities When the teacher signals a child that his behavior is off task or not appropriate through the use of one modality (such as looking or eye contact) and it fails to gain the child's attention, the teacher shifts gears, or changes, to another modality (such as touch).

I-message A teacher technique of expressing to a child that a behavior is having a negative effect on the teacher. This statement must contain three elements: the child's *behavior,* its *effect* on the teacher, and the teacher's *feelings* as a result of the behavior.

Low-Profile Correction A nonintrusive process of signaling a child that he is off task, without disrupting the ongoing activities of classmates and with minimum or no guilt imposed on the child.

Modality Cueing The first (minimum power) behavior on the Teacher Behavior Continuum through which the teacher—using the modalities of sight, touch, or sound—signals the child to become aware of his actions.

Six Steps to Problem Solving A structure for carrying out a problem-solving conference between the teacher and student or group of students, such as a class meeting. The steps are:

1. **Define the problem.** Before any discussion may occur in a conference, a clear statement of the problem must be given by the teacher or child.
2. **Generate solutions.** Encourage all parties—teacher and children—to come up with a creative list of solutions, no matter how unrealistic the solutions may be, without evaluating the merits of the suggestions.
3. **Evaluate the solutions.** All solutions are openly evaluated to determine if they are "good" or "bad."
4. **Decide on a solution.** All parties—teacher and child or children as a group—must decide on a solution that is acceptable to everyone.
5. **Implement the solution.** All parties must decide what their role is in carrying out the solution and commit themselves to the actions required. Everyone must agree on when a later evaluation of the effectiveness of the solution will occur.
6. **Evaluate the effectiveness of the solution.** A later follow-up meeting will occur to see if the solution was effective and what other actions might now be needed.

Verbal Encoding Labeling the child's emotions and feelings, both positive and negative, through the use of the teacher's words.

Related Readings

Books on Relationship-Listening Techniques

For Teachers

Axline, V. M. (1965). *Dibs: In Search of Self.* Boston: Houghton Mifflin.

Axline, V. M. (1971). *Play Therapy.* New York: Ballantine Books.

Gordon, T. (1974). *T.E.T.: Teacher Effectiveness Training.* New York: David McKay.

Moustakas, C. (1972). *The Authentic Teacher.* Cambridge, MA: Howard A. Doyle Publishing.

Wolfgang, C. H., & Glickman, C. D. (1980). The supportive model: Gordon's Teacher Effectiveness Training. In C. H. Wolfgang & C. D. Glickman (Eds.), *Solving Discipline Problems: Strategies for Classroom Teachers.* Boston: Allyn and Bacon.

For Parents

Brazelton, T. B. (1984). *To Listen to a Child: Understanding the Normal Problems of Growing Up.* Reading, MA: Addison-Wesley.

Ginott, H. G. (1965). *Between Parent and Child.* New York: Macmillan.

Ginott, H. G. (1969). *Between Parent and Teenager.* New York: Macmillan.

Gordon, T. (1970). *P. E. T.: Parent Effectiveness Training.* New York: Peter H. Wyden.

Greenspan, S., & Greenspan, N. T. (1985). *First Feelings.* New York: Viking Penguin.

Muriel, J., & Jongeward, D. (1971). *Born to Win: Transactional Analysis with Gestalt Experiments.* Reading, MA: Addison-Wesley.

Literature with Special Meaning for Preschool Children[8]

Accomplishment

Krauss, R. (1945). *The Carrot Seed.* Illustrated by Crockett Johnson. New York: Harper & Row. *Story of planting a seed and watching it grow. Ages 5–7.*

Anger

Armitage, R., & Armitage, D. (1980). *The Bossing of Josie.* London: Andre Deutsch. *Josie feels that she is being bossed by her family and so tries to boss her baby brother. Pretending to be a witch, she casts a spell on him, which she believes caused him to disappear. She is relieved when he is found. Ages 4–6.*

Berman, L. (1983). *The Goodbye Painting.* Illustrated by M. Hannon. New York: Human Sciences Press. *Nick's babysitter moves away, and he feels anger and loss. Ages 4–6.*

Bottner, B. (1980). *Mean Maxine.* New York: Random House. *Ralph pretends to be a dragon so that he can tell off Maxine and do wicked things to her, but they end up playing together. Ages 4–6.*

Chorao, K. (1982). *Kate's Quilt.* New York: E. P. Dutton. *Kate throws a tantrum when her mother makes her a quilt instead of a doll. Ages 4–6.*

Fujikawa, G. (1983) *That's Not Fair!* New York: Grosset and Dunlap. *Competition among four friends ruins their play, and they realize that it is more fun to play together than alone. Ages 4–6.*

Goodsell, J. (1986) *Toby's Toe.* Illustrated by G. Fiammenghi. New York: William Morrow. *A boy gets angry and takes it out on his sister, causing an effect on many different people all day long. Ages 3–8.*

Hautzig, D. (1986) *Why Are You So Mean to Me?* Illustrated by T. Cooke. New York: Random House. *A little boy feels hurt and angry when others tease him about not being good in sports. Ages 2–7.*

Hurwitz, J. (1983) *Rip-Roaring Russell.* Illustrated by L. A. Hoban. New York: William Morrow. *A little boy feels anger and jealousy over a new baby girl in his family. Ages 4–8.*

Marron, C. (1983) *No Trouble for Grandpa.* Illustrated by C. Burstein. Milwaukee: Raintree Publishers. *A young boy is angry for having to share his baby sister with his grandfather, but the boy changes his attitude when he rescues his sister from a stranger. Ages 4–8.*

Preston, E. M. (1969). *The Temper Tantrum Book.* Illustrated by R. Bennett. New York: Viking Press. *A variety of young animals tell why they get angry. Ages 3–6.*

Sharmat, M. J. (1985). *Attila the Angry.* Illustrated by L. A. Hoban. New York: Holiday House. *Attila is a squirrel with a temper problem, and his friend Angelica Squirrel gives him techniques to calm down. Ages 4–6.*

Simon, N. (1974). *I Was So Mad!* Illustrated by D. Leder. Chicago: Albert Whitman. *A variety of children explain what makes them angry, leaving the impression that it is all right to feel that way. Ages 4–up.*

Arguing

Winthrop, E. (1983) *Katharine's Doll.* Illustrated by M. Hafner. New York: E. P. Dutton. *A doll interrupts the friendship of two girls, until they realize that the doll cannot replace their friendship. Ages 4–8.*

Attention Seeking

Cohen, M. (1985). *Liar, Liar, Pants on Fire!* Illustrated by L. A. Hoban. New York: Greenwillow Books. *Alex has a habit of lying in order to win the approval of his new school mates. Only after he stops lying does he win new friends. Ages 4–7.*

Hoban, L. A. (1985). *Arthur's Loose Tooth.* New York: Harper & Row. *When Arthur falls and cuts his lip, he yells for the babysitter, thinking that he had swallowed his loose tooth. Later, he devises a plan to have his sister unknowingly pull his tooth for him. Ages 4–6.*

Krensky, S. (1983). *The Lion Upstairs.* Illustrated by L. Grant. New York: Atheneum. *Sam's imaginary lion begins to cause trouble when Sam cannot do his homework or other chores, and blames the lion for this and for taking things out of the kitchen. This gets his family's attention and they devise a creative solution. Ages 4–6.*

Lampert, E. (1986). *A Little Touch of Monster.* Illustrated by V. Chess. Boston: Atlantic Monthly Press. *Parker wants to be noticed, so he behaves like a monster to get the attention of his parents, until he gets what he wants. Ages 4–7.*

Bedtime Fears and Monsters

Brown, M. W. (1942). *Goodnight Moon.* Illustrated by C. Hurd. New York: Harper & Row. *A bunny says goodnight to everything in his room before going to sleep. Ages 2–4.*

Fenner, C. (1963). *Tigers in the Cellar.* New York: Harcourt, Brace & World. *A little girl believes there are tigers in the cellar. She has a dream in which the tigers are friendly and the fear goes away. Ages 4–7.*

Hoban, R. (1960). *Bedtime for Frances.* Illustrated by G. Williams. New York: Harper & Row. *Frances is a little bear who has a difficult time going to sleep. With help from her parents, she finally goes to sleep. Ages 3–6.*

Kauffman, L. (1965). *What's That Noise?* Illustrated by A. Eitzen. New York: Lothrop, Lee & Shepard. *A boy can't sleep because of a noise in the night. He and his father try to find out what it is. Finally, the boy goes to bed with his father and finds that the noise is his father snoring. Ages 4–8.*

Viorst, J. (1973). *My Mama Says There Aren't Any Zombies, Ghosts, Vampires, Creatures, Demons, Monsters, Fiends, Goblins, or Things.* Illustrated by K. Chorao. New York: Atheneum. *A little boy reaffirms his trust in his mother's opinion that monsters don't really exist. Ages 4–7.*

Blame

Cummings, P. (1985). *Jimmy Lee Did It.* New York: Lothrop, Lee & Shepard. *A little boy finds a perfect person to hang the blame on when things go wrong. Ages 4–6.*

Change

Davis, G. (1985). *Katy's First Haircut.* Illustrated by L. M. Shute. Boston: Houghton Mifflin. *A girl cuts her long hair and then wonders if she made the right decision. Ages 5–7.*

Freedman, S. (1986). *Devin's New Bed.* Illustrated by R. Oz. Chicago: Albert Whitman & Co. *A child moves from the family crib to his first bed. Ages 2–6.*

Singer, M. (1985). *Archer Armadillo's Secret Room.* Illustrated by B. L. Weiner. New York: Macmillan. *The story of an armadillo's move to a new home, and his grandfather's help in getting him to accept the move. Ages 3–6.*

Girard, L. (1986). *Jeremy's First Haircut.* Illustrated by M. J. Begin. Chicago: Albert Whitman & Co. *A little boy with shaggy hair worries about his first haircut. Ages 3–5.*

Child Abuse

Anderson, D., & Finne, M. (1986). *Jason's Story: Going to a Foster Home.* Illustrated by J. Swofford. Minneapolis, MN: Dillon Press. *This is a story of a young boy's placement into foster homes until his mother is capable of taking care of him. Ages 3–7.*

Stanek, M. N. (1983). *Don't Hurt Me, Mama.* Illustrated by H. Cogancherry. Chicago: Albert Whitman & Co. *A single, out-of-work mother with a drinking problem abuses her daughter, until the school nurse intervenes and helps both of them. Ages 4–8.*

Death

Brown, M. W. (1938). *The Dead Bird.* Illustrated by R. Charlip. New York: Young Scott Books. *Children find a dead bird and bury it. Ages 3–up.*

Viorst J. (1971). *The Tenth Good Thing About Barney.* Illustrated by E. Bleguad. New York: Atheneum. *A cat dies. Ages 5–8.*

Eating

Hoban, R. (1964). *Bread and Jam for Frances.* Illustrated by L. Hoban. New York: Harper & Row. *Frances wants only bread and jam for every meal. Her parents give it to her until she is sick of it. Ages 3–6.*

Fear

Sharmat, M. W. (1983). *Frizzy the Fearful.* Illustrated by J. Wallner. New York: Holiday House. *Frizzy the tiger is afraid of everything and takes small steps to overcome his fears. Ages 3–7.*

Fear of the Unknown

Carlson, N. (1985). *Louanne Pig and the Witch Lady.* Minneapolis, MN: Carolrhoda. *Louanne Pig and her friends believe that a witch lady lives in a house on a hill. Ages 4–7.*

Carrick, C. (1984). *Dark and Full of Secrets.* Illustrated by D. Carrick. New York: Clarion Books. *A boy is afraid to swim in a pond that appears dark and murky until he explores the bottom of it. Ages 5–8.*

Collins, J. (1983). *Josh's Scary Dad.* Illustrated by D. Paterson. Nashville, TN: Abingdon Press. *Josh's father is big, with a bald head and a beard, and all of Josh's friends are afraid of him. Ages 3–5.*

Feelings

Barrett, J. (1975). *I Hate to Take a Bath.* Illustrated by C. B. Slackman. Englewood Cliffs, NJ: Four Winds Press. *Children give reasons why they hate to take a bath, then what they like to do in a bath if they have to take one. Ages 3–8.*

Buckley, H. E. (1971). *Michael Is Brave.* Illustrated by E. McCully. New York: Lothrop, Lee & Shepard. *Michael is afraid to climb the ladder of the slide. His teacher asks him to help a girl who is frightened at the top. As he helps her, he overcomes his own fear. Ages 4–8.*

Dunn, P., & Dunn, T. (1971). *Feelings.* Words by J. Dunn. Minneapolis, MN: Creative Educational Society. *A variety of feelings are described and photographed. Ages 4–8.*

Iwasaki, C. (1968). *Staying Home Alone on a Rainy Day.* New York: McGraw-Hill. *Allison is staying home by herself and is afraid. Ages 5–8.*

Friendship

Cohen, M. (1971). *Best Friends.* Illustrated by L. Hoban. New York: Collier. *A child goes to a nursery school and is worried about having a best friend. Ages 4–6.*

Cohen, M. (1967). *Will I Have a Friend?* Illustrated by L. Hoban. New York: Macmillan. Deals with making friends at school. Ages 3–6.

Lobel, A. (1970). *Frog and Toad Are Friends.* New York: Harper & Row. *Stories about the friendship of Frog and Toad. An easy-to-read book. Ages 5–8.*

Minarek, E. H. (1960). *Little Bear's Friend.* Illustrated by M. Sendak. New York: Harper & Row. *Little Bear makes friends with Emily. Ages 5–8.*

Udry, J. M. (1961). *Let's Be Enemies.* Illustrated by M. Sendak. New York: Harper & Row. *Two friends are angry with each other and become enemies. They resolve their conflict and go skating together. Ages 4–7.*

Grandparents

Buckley, H. E. (1959). *Grandfather and I.* Illustrated by P. Galdone. New York: Lothrop. *A boy and his grandfather enjoy things without being rushed. Ages 3–7.*

Buckley, H. E. (1961). *Grandmother and I.* Illustrated by P. Galdone. New York: Lothrop. *A girl and her grandmother spend time together. Ages 4–8.*

Lenski, L. (1967). *Debbie and Her Grandma.* New York: Walck. *Debbie visits her Grandma by herself. Ages 3–6.*

Minarik, E. H. (1961). *Little Bear's Visit.* Illustrated by M. Sendak. New York: Harper & Row. *Little Bear spends the day with his grandparents and tires himself out. Ages 3–6.*

Hospital Fears

Rey, J., & Rey, H. A. (1966). *Curious George Goes to the Hospital.* Boston: Houghton-Mifflin. *George, the monkey, goes to the hospital and enjoys it. Ages 4–7.*

Rockwell, H. (1973). *My Doctor.* New York: Macmillan. *A woman doctor and all her instruments are described. Ages 3–6.*

Rockwell, H. (1975). *My Dentist.* New York: Macmillan. *A dentist and all his instruments are described. Ages 3–6.*

Shay, A. (1969). *What Happens When You Go to the Hospital.* Chicago: Reilly Lee. *Photo essay of the hospital experience. Ages 3–6.*

Stein, S. B. (1974). *A Hospital Story.* Photography by D. Frank. Chicago: Walker & Co. *A girl goes to the hospital to have her tonsils removed. Ages 4–7.*

Loss and Recovery

Brown, M. W. (1942). *The Runaway Bunny.* Illustrated by C. Hurd. New York: Harper & Row. *A young bunny tells his mother all the places he will run to. She reassures it that if it did, she would be there as well. Ages 2–7.*

Flack, M. (1933). *The Story of Ping.* Illustrated by K. Wiese. New York: Viking. *A duck becomes separated from its family on the Yangtze River and, after a series of adventures, finds them again. Ages 5–up.*

Krauss, R. (1951). *The Bundle Book.* Illustrated by H. Stone. New York: Harper & Row. *A mother tries to guess what kind of bundle is in the bed. The child pops out in the end, and they give each other a hug. Ages 3–5.*

Lionni, L. (1959). *Little Blue and Little Yellow.* New York: Obolensy. *Two friends, Blue and Yellow, mix together to become green while they are playing. They separate and become individuals again. Ages 3–8.*

Potter, B. (1902). *The Tale of Peter Rabbit.* New York: Warne. *Peter ventures into forbidden territory and is quite glad to return home. Ages 2–7.*

Tariashima, T. (1966). *Umbrella.* New York: Viking. *A 3-year-old girl become aware of growing up as she goes to preschool in her new boots and umbrella. Ages 3–6.*

Love

Jewell, N. (1972). *Snuggle Bunny.* Illustrated by M. Chalmers. New York: Harper & Row. *A bunny wants to snuggle. It finally finds an old man and they snuggle all winter. Ages 3–5.*

Messiness

O'Brien, A. S. (1985). *Where's My Truck?* New York: Holt, Rinehart and Winston. *A little boy finds his truck only after picking up all of his toys. Ages 2–4.*

New Baby

Berger T. (1974). *A New Baby.* Photography by H. Kluetmeier. Milwaukee, WI: Raintree Editions. *A young boy and his family have a new baby, and he realizes the baby will someday be his friend. Ages 3–6.*

Greenfield, E. (1974). *She Come Bringing Me That Little Baby Girl.* Illustrated by J. Steptoe. Philadelphia: Lippincott. *A black boy is confronted with a baby sister when his mother returns from the hospital. He feels resentment, then begins to like her when he holds her. Ages 3–6.*

Holland, V. (1972). *We Are Having a Baby.* Photographs illustrate the story. New York: Charles Scribner's Sons. *A little girl tells the story of the arrival of her brother, including the funny feeling in her stomach that causes her to lose her appetite for lunch. Ages 3–6.*

Stein, S. B. (1974). *That New Baby.* Photography by D. Frank. Chicago: Walker & Co. *This is a realistic account of the arrival of a new baby into a black family. The two older children show rivalry in a variety of ways. Ages 2–8.*

Parental Absence

Dupasquier, P. (1985). *Dear Daddy.* New York: Bradbury Press. *Sophie's father works on a cargo ship and is away for long periods of time. While he is gone, she writes him about herself and her family. Ages 5–8.*

Parent-Child Relationships

DeRegniers, B. (1963). *The Little Girl and Her Mother.* Illustrated by E. Gilman. New York: Vanguard. *The little girl imitates her mother, then realizes that there are things she can do that Mother is too big for, and that some day she will grow up to be like her mother. Ages 4–6.*

Fassler, J. (1969). *All Alone with Daddy.* Illustrated by D. L. Gregory. New York: Behavioral Publications. *When the mother goes away for a night, the girl tries to take her place, cooking, wearing makeup, and trying to sleep in Daddy's bed. Mother returns and she realizes that some day she will grow up and marry someone like Daddy, but not him. Ages 4–6.*

Lexau, J. (1967). *Everyday, a Dragon.* Illustrated by B. Shecter. New York: Harper & Row. *Father and child play dragon. Ages 5–8.*

Zolotow, C. (1971). *A Father Like That.* Illustrated by B. Shecter. New York: Harper & Row. *The boy lives with his mother and he tells her what his father would be like. His mother replies that the boy can grow up to be a father like that. Ages 4–7.*

Sex Roles

Levy, E. (1974). *Nice Little Girls.* Illustrated by M. Gerstein. New York: Delacorte. *Jackie changes some of the sex-role stereotypes in her classroom. Ages 5–8.*

Zolotow, C. (1972). *William's Doll.* Illustrated by W. P. DuBois. New York: Harper & Row. *William wants a doll. Only his grandmother doesn't laugh at him, and she gets him one. Ages 4–7.*

Sibling Relationships

Conta, M., & Reardon, M. (1974). *Feelings Between Brothers and Sisters.* Photography by J. M. Rosenthal. Milwaukee, WI: Advanced Learning Concepts. *A variety of brother and sister relationships are presented. Ages 4–7.*

Hoban, R. (1969). *Best Friends for Frances.* Illustrated by L. Hoban. New York: Harper & Row. *Frances learns to be friends with her sister. Ages 5–7.*

Hutchins, P. (1971). *Titch.* New York: Macmillan. *Titch is the littlest and always has the smallest things. In the end, he has the little seed, which is most important. Ages 3–5.*

Sibling Rivalry

Alexander, M. (1971). *Nobody Asked Me If I Wanted a Baby Sister.* New York: Dial Press. *A little boy tries to give away his baby sister. She begins to cry and it is discovered that he is the only one who can quiet her. He decides to keep her. Ages 3–6.*

Hoban, R. (1964). *A Baby Sister for Frances.* Illustrated by L. Hoban. New York: Harper & Row. *Frances becomes annoyed with her baby sister and runs away, under the kitchen table. She returns. Ages 3–7.*

Hoban, R. (1968). *A Birthday for Frances.* Illustrated by L. Hoban. New York: Harper & Row. *It is Gloria's birthday, and Frances buys her sister a candy bar that she almost eats herself. Ages 3–7.*

Keats, E. J. (1967). *Peter's Chair.* New York: Harper & Row. *Peter's father paints all his old furniture pink for his baby sister. He runs away with his little blue chair, but finds that he no longer fits in it. He comes home and helps his father paint. Ages 3–5.*

Wells, R. (1973). *Noisy Nora.* New York: Dial Press. *Nora is a noisy little mouse who wants some attention. She finally gets it by running away to the broom closet. Ages 3–7.*

Zolotow, C. (1966). *If It Weren't for You.* Illustrated by B. Shecter. New York: Harper & Row. *The older brother tells all the things he cannot do because of the younger one, but the story ends with him realizing that without the younger brother, he would be alone with the grownups. Ages 5-7.*

Special Toys

Brown, M. (1960). *First Night Away from Home.* Illustrated by D. Marino. New York: Franklin Watts. *A boy stays overnight with a friend but can't go to sleep. His mother brings his favorite stuffed animal. Ages 4–8.*

Freeman, D. (1968). *Corduroy.* New York: Viking. *A bear in a store is purchased by a girl who makes a home for him. Ages 4–8.*

Pincus, H. (1972). *Minna and Pippin.* New York: Farrar, Straus. *Story of a little girl and her doll. Ages 3–7.*

Skorpen, J. M. (1971). *Charles.* New York: Harper & Row. *Story of a boy and his bear. Ages 3–7.*

Total Family Relations

Ehrlich, A. (1972). *Zeek, Silver Moon.* Illustrated by R. A. Parker. New York: Dial. *Experiences from Zeek's first few years are told. Ages 4–8.*

Kraus, R. (1970). *Whose Mouse Are You?* Illustrated by J. Aruego. London: Macmillan. *A young mouse explores his feelings concerning his relationships with each member of his family. Ages 4–7.*

Scott, A. H. (1967). *Sam.* Illustrated by S. Shimin. New York: McGraw-Hill. *Sam is excluded by each member of his family and finally cries in frustration. His family realizes what they have done, and his mother finds a way for him to help her. Ages 3–7.*

Endnotes

1. Kounin, J. (1970). *Discipline and Group Management in Classrooms.* New York: Holt, Rinehart and Winston. An example of high-profile correction would be, "James (in a loud, sharp voice), sit down, and keep quiet!" This statement not only punishes James but makes all other members of the group feel the guilt for his actions; if they are busy trying to follow the teacher's instruction or the story being read, their thinking is disrupted and they will have a very difficult time returning to the story line.
2. Dinkmeyer, D., McKay, G. D., & Dinkmeyer, J. S. (1989). *Parenting Young Children.* Circle Pines, MN: American Guidance Service.
3. Gordon, T. (1974). *T. E. T.: Teacher Effectiveness Training.* New York. David McKay.
4. Alberti, R. E., & Emmons, M. L. (1978). *Your Perfect Right: A Guide to Assertive Behavior.* San Luis Obispo, CA: Impact Publishers.
5. This section was partially written by Callum B. Johnston.
6. Bernstein, J. (1977). *Books to Help Children Cope with Separation and Loss.* New York: Bowker.
7. Rudman, M. K., & Pearce, A. M. (1988). *For Love of Reading: A Parent's Guide to Encouraging Young Readers from Infancy to Age 5.* Mount Vernon, NY: Consumers Union.
8. This section was created by Callum B. Johnston.

Answers to Test Yourself

1B, 2C, 3B, 4A, 5F, A, C, D, B, E, 6B, 7A, 8A, 9B, 10B, 11B, 12A, 13B, 14B, 15C, F, H

3

The Confronting-Contracting Face

We have seen that the Relationship-Listening face uses minimal force by the teacher in an attempt to gently guide the student in the direction of appropriate behavior. When that minimal force does not achieve the desired results, we progress on the Teacher Behavior Continuum to the Confronting-Contracting face.

A NEW FACE

The Confronting-Contracting face is much more demanding of the child and uses greater power by the teacher. The purpose of Confronting-Contracting techniques is to have the child mentally reflect on his past behavior and come up with an idea of how to live within the rules. The teacher does not solve the problem for the child but expects him to come up with an acceptable solution himself. The Confronting-Contracting face includes five steps—Step 1: "Stop!" statements; Step 2: "What" questions directed to the student; Step 3: Contracting; Step 4: Isolation (circumstances may call for this step to be employed *before* Step 3); and Step 5: Notify parents (see Figure 3–1).

Jimmy stands before the paint easel. Using a large, thick paintbrush, he dips the end into the paint pot. Soon the brush reappears, dripping with a large glob of paint. As a peer walks by, Jimmy turns and sticks out the brush as if it is a sword and attempts to "stab" his schoolmate. The peer screams and runs off, much to the delight of Jimmy. A second child unknowingly wanders by and Jimmy positions himself for a second attack.

Teacher: *"Stop! What are you doing, Jimmy?" (Step 1—confronting: "Stop!")*

Jimmy "El Zorro": *"Wha-at?" (Jimmy is now aware that the teacher is present and is aware of his actions.)*

Teacher: *"What are you doing?" (Step 2—confronting: "What" question)*

Jimmy "El Zorro": *"I didn't do anything! (denial) Carol was playing 'sword' and you didn't say anything to her!" (sidetracking)*

FIGURE 3–1 TBC: Confronting-Contracting Face

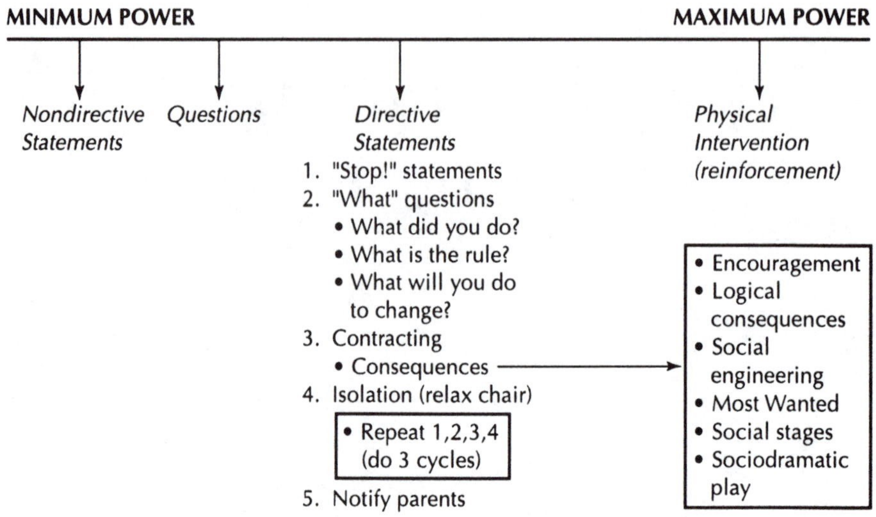

MINIMUM POWER → **MAXIMUM POWER**

Nondirective Statements

Questions

Directive Statements

1. "Stop!" statements
2. "What" questions
   - What did you do?
   - What is the rule?
   - What will you do to change?
3. Contracting
   - Consequences →
4. Isolation (relax chair)
   - Repeat 1,2,3,4 (do 3 cycles)
5. Notify parents

Physical Intervention (reinforcement)

- Encouragement
- Logical consequences
- Social engineering
- Most Wanted
- Social stages
- Sociodramatic play

Teacher: *"What did* you *do, Jimmy?" (Step 2—confronting: "What" question)*

Jimmy "El Zorro": *"You're a butt-head! (verbal aggression; see Chapter 6) Let me alone! No-o-o!" (Jimmy becomes intense, puts the brush back into the paint pot, and runs off to the block corner, attempting to hide.)*

Teacher: *(Goes to Jimmy, takes one of his hands in hers and brings him back to the easel) "Jimmy, we need to talk about this. What did you do?" (Step 2—confronting: "What" question)*

Jimmy "El Zorro": *(Drops to the floor, kicking into the air, and throws a minor temper tantrum.)*

Teacher: *(Picks up Jimmy and gently places him in a large overstuffed chair nearby.) "Jimmy, this is a safe place for you to be. I want you to relax here, and when you are ready to talk I will come back and talk to you about the painting." (Step 4—isolation: "relax chair")*

Jimmy "El Zorro": *(Slouches down into the chair, drops his eyes, pouts with a frowning face for a period of 4 to 6 minutes, and then begins to sit up in the chair watching other children.)*

Teacher: *(approaches) "I need to talk to you about the painting. What did you do?" (Step 2—confronting: "What" question)*

Jimmy "El Zorro": *"I don't know." [or the child might say, "I painted people!"]*

Teacher: *"Well, I saw what you did, and you were using the paintbrush to paint Mark. What is the rule of how paints are to be used?" (Step 2—confronting: "What" question requesting a verbal statement of the rule)*

Jimmy "El Zorro": *(eyes drop) "A-a-h, keep the paint, ah—paper."*

Teacher: *"Yes, when paints are used, our rule is to keep paint on the paper. (Teacher restates the rule so it is very clear.) Now you and I must work this out. (Step 3—contracting) We must have an agreement." (Teacher moves to Jimmy, takes him gently by the hands, and makes eye contact.) "What will* *you do to change? When you use the paints again, how will you use them?" (Step 2—confronting: "What" question, requesting change)*

Jimmy "El Zorro": *"Keep the paint on the paper."*

Teacher: *"Yes. Do we have an agreement on this? Can I depend on you to remember the rule?" (Step 3—contracting: verbal agreement)*

Jimmy "El Zorro": *"Yes." (Jimmy looks up and makes eye contact with teacher.)*

Teacher: *"Good, we now have an agreement. If you agree, I want to shake hands to show a special agreement between us." (Teacher holds out her hand to Jimmy and smiles warmly.) (Step 3—contracting)*

Jimmy "El Zorro": *(Returns the teacher's smile and shakes the teacher's hand.)*

Teacher: *"Good, we now have an agreement! If you can now remember the painting rules, you may paint. But if you forget the paint rules, your behavior will say that you do not know how to use paints and you will not be able to use the easel. (Step 3—consequence) Now, you may feel free to come back to work and play with us when you feel that you are ready." (handling isolation)*

Jimmy "El Zorro": *(Hops up, takes off the paint smock, hangs it on the appropriate hook, moves over to the puzzle shelf, and selects a puzzle.)*

CONFRONTING STEPS

At the beginning of this example, the teacher utilized the confronting techniques of Step 1—"Stop" statements and Step 2—"What" questions. Notice that the teacher did not tell the child what *not* to do but simply stated, "Stop." The "What" questions related only to what the child did, to the rule, and to a challenge for the child to come up with his own ideas of how to change.

Because of young children's irreversibility of thinking after such a confrontation—especially when it is emotionally charged with a minor temper tantrum—the child does not necessarily mentally reflect on his entire sequence of behavior. The child simply knows he is being confronted by the teacher, and most likely his mind is racing through thoughts of "Will the teacher punish me?" or "How can I get out of this situation and away from the teacher?" The "What" question asks the child to be mentally reflective. If the child cannot remember what happened—and some will not or cannot say it—the teacher will tell the child what did occur; however, it is preferable to have the child verbally state his own actions.

The teacher does not stop the confronting process when the child responds by crying or throwing a temper tantrum, because young children have discovered that such strong expressions of emotion can serve as a power technique to get the adult "off their back" and thereby free them of facing up to their behavior. The teacher responds to this emotional "flooding" by taking the child to a "relax chair" or an isolated space (see Figure 3–2) and using Step 4 to isolate the child for the sole purpose of permitting the child to calm down and get relaxed. The teacher reassures the child that this is a safe space and no one will bother him. This is not a punishment because when the child is ready to contract and rationally discuss the incident, he is free to return. The teacher's voice inflection and nonverbal expressions are not ones of guilt but reflect a rather matter-of-fact problem-solving attitude toward the child. The teacher is not sidetracked by the child's claims of unfairness or denial, or by another emotional outburst or crying (sometimes humorously called "water power"). Instead, the teacher remains

FIGURE 3–2 Different Views of Isolation			
MINIMUM POWER			MAXIMUM POWER
Relationship-Listening	**Confronting-Contracting**	**Rules and Consequences**	**Punishment***
Not Permitted	"Relax Chair"	Time Out	Retribution
Isolation of a child while wearing the Relationship-Listening face is not permitted because a near total nonjudgmental position toward the child must be maintained.	The child is placed in a chair or an isolated space not for punishment but to permit him time to calm down so the contracting and rational thinking can occur. The child may rejoin the group when he decides he can handle himself in the social situation.	This is a technique used when the social situation is actually reinforcing the child's misbehavior. The child is placed in an isolated area, possibly a chair, where others can't see him and he can't see others (social stimuli is withdrawn). A teacher establishes minimal time (perhaps using an egg timer with bell preset) for when the child may return.	The child knows the rule and the punishment and is warned that he is breaking the rule and is to desist. When the child does not desist and defies the adult's authority, he is isolated as retribution or punishment for his actions. The teacher sets an arbitrary period of time for the child to return, but this must be long enough for the child to feel some discomfort.

*An explanation of punishment, which might include isolation and corporal punishment, can be seen in the writings of Dobson, J. (1970). *Dare to Discipline.* Wheaton, IL: Tyndale House. However, the *Three Faces of Discipline* model clearly takes the position that punishment in any form is developmentally inappropriate for this age child, and possibly for any age.

focused on the child's behavior in this particular incident, attempting to limit any implication of guilt. The teacher's use of the Confronting-Contracting face toward the child is, "Look, this is not appropriate behavior here. We are faced with a problem, and I want to work with you to understand the problem and your behavior. I want to give you the power to change, I want you to commit yourself to this change through a contract or agreement, and, finally, I want you to understand the logical consequences of failing to live up to this contract."

Repeating Steps 1, 2, 3, and 4

In living within the Confronting-Contracting face, the teacher's interaction with the child after an incident of misbehavior is *confined* to these four steps—Step 1: "Stop!"; Step 2: "What" questions; Step 3: Contracting with statement of logical consequences; and, if needed, Step 4: Isolation. After a contract is established between teacher and child, the child is to return to the classroom with a "clean slate," meaning that we as teachers must maintain an attitude of optimism. We must believe—and show by our actions that we believe—that Jimmy "El Zorro" can and will change his behavior. If we as teachers are angry at Jimmy because of his actions and we communicate this anger nonverbally, Jimmy and his classmates will sense this and he most likely will live up to our *non-belief in his ability to change—the power of expectations.*[1]

It is inevitable that some contracts by a child will be broken. When this does occur, the child will have to experience the logical consequence (to be explained

QUESTIONS OFTEN ASKED REGARDING CONFRONTING-CONTRACTING

What do I do if the child does not come up with a solution?	If the child is not simply being defiant but really cannot think of a change in behavior, make two to three suggestions and ask him to pick one and commit to it. If he agrees to your suggestion, be sure he knows the *"motor rule,"*[2] or the response to which he has committed, by teaching him his choice in a *Directive Lesson of Say-Show-Check* (explained in Chapter 9).
What if the child refuses to make a contract?	Permit the child to continue staying in the "relax chair" until he is ready to negotiate. His refusal indicates he is still angry or flooded.
What if the child's action endangers himself, others, or valuable property?	Endangerment of any type calls into effect the "severity clause," and the teacher immediately moves to physical intervention. The accompanying verbal response could be Step 1: "Stop" followed by Steps 2, 3, and 4, or an assertive command (explained in Chapter 9).

later) of his actions. After the child experiences this logical consequence, the teacher repeats Steps 1, 2, 3, and 4 in a similar manner, as seen in the earlier example. "Stop it! What did you do? What is the rule? What will you do to change?" Again, contracting with consequences will be requested by the teacher, and isolation will be used if needed. The child will again return with a "clean slate," with the teacher being optimistic.

If the child's behavior still does not become more positive, or even regresses to more destructive behaviors, the sequence of Steps 1, 2, 3, and 4 would be repeated at least three times. After three cycles of these Confronting-Contracting steps, we may make the judgment to escalate along the Teacher Behavior Continuum to the Rules and Consequences techniques (to be described in the next chapter). At this time, we do notify the child's parents of our difficulties and the actions we are taking (Step 5: Notify parents). But before we abandon the Confronting-Contracting techniques, we must give some time for the remaining proactive Confronting-Contracting techniques (encouragement, social engineering, etc., which will be discussed next) to take effect.

PROACTIVE CONFRONTING-CONTRACTING TECHNIQUES

The Confronting-Contracting face reflects the attitude that the teacher is the adult and clearly knows what is acceptable and unacceptable behavior. When the teacher sees a young child misbehaving, she will clearly confront that child to get him to desist and make it clear that she will not permit this to continue. The Confronting-Contracting view is that there is *one* central motivation for all children, and that is to attempt to find ways of socially belonging. If this social acceptance is blocked and the child feels unwanted and not included, the child will begin to disrupt the social situation in the classroom with a host of negative behaviors in an attempt to get excessive attention or to control you and others through power techniques. It is almost as if the child is saying, "If I can't get recognition for being the best *good* kid, I will be the best *bad* kid!" Thus, being the most difficult child brings him social acknowledgment and recognition, even though it is negative. This misbehavior, motivated by a sense of not belonging, produces a self-defeating cycle in which the teacher and peers begin to have feelings of dislike for this child because of these offensive misbehaviors. The child now feels even more rejection, and may become revengeful or so hurt that he retreats into a shell of passive helplessness. In short, here is a child who feels unwanted and unaccepted by others, and cannot find social acceptance. Our role as teachers is to take clear actions or be proactive to help the child find acceptance.

> *Megan is standing at the corner of the housekeeping area watching four children playing together. One of these children used to be her constant companion. Megan asks, "Can I play?" The four children respond in unison, "No-o-o! We don't like you. You stink! Stay out!" The leader of the group now whispers to her playmates, "Let's give her poison!" The girls use a small pot, water, and red food die and joyfully mix a secret concoction in the corner of the play kitchen. Meanwhile, Megan has wandered off aimlessly throughout the classroom. The girls put the red liquid into a tea cup and run after her. "Megan, you can play with us. Here is some tea for you to drink at our tea party. You drink it!" Megan smiles and slowly places the cup to her mouth and drinks. All four girls squeal, "That's poison, that's poison, you're dead, you're dead. Ha-ha-ha!" They grab the cup from Megan's hands, laugh with much delight, and run off, leaving Megan behind. Ten minutes later, a commotion occurs at the sand table when Megan throws sand into the eyes of a younger, less powerful child.*

The incident with Megan and the "gang of four" shows clearly that Megan has lost her past friend and companion, and is now being socially isolated. The Confronting-Contracting position would be that Megan's acting out (the aggressive actions of throwing sand) was a result of built-up "revengeful" feelings being directed at an innocent party—a less powerful schoolmate. All misbehavior by children in the classroom—whether attention-getting, power acts, revengeful acts, or passive behavior—is seen by Confronting-Contracting as a failure to find social acceptance. However, teachers rarely get such a clear observation as in the Megan incident to actually verify this position. Instead, teachers typically see a repetitive host of misbehaviors and aggressive actions that, on the surface, do not appear to be related to immediate behavior by other children. ("He bites other children without any provocation.") Children's first feelings of acceptance come out of the home setting with parents and siblings. If they feel they were rejected in early family interaction, they will assume that they will be rejected in a classroom situation and will set out with negative actions *to prove* that others do not like them.

The less skilled teacher might bring the "gang of four" aside and verbally reprimand and lecture them for their actions, applying large doses of guilt for their behavior. Such actions might unknowingly make the four girls even more hostile to Megan, and now they will be revengeful toward her in more subtle ways that the teacher will not see or detect. The target child is Megan, and she needs to acquire social skills that will enable her to find acceptance.

There are a number of techniques that enable the teacher to be proactive in helping children to acquire social skills. Before they are presented, however, it may be helpful to first explore the "outside aggressor" phenomenon.

The Outside Aggressor Phenomenon

A visitor to a early childhood center is asked by a 3-year-old child on the playground, "What's your name, mister?" The man responds, "Mr. Wolfe." The child, hearing woof, *jumps up and runs screaming to the opposite end of the playground, shouting, "Woof, Woof!" Then each member of the child's group picks up a light twig that had fallen during a storm the night before. They "stalk" the visitor, walking up behind him on tip-toe, and then each child forcefully strikes the man in the back with the sticks. They run off, again screaming, "Woof!" Mr. Wolfe has become an example of an outside aggressor.*

Since young children still have two large islands of emotional extremes—when they love they love totally and when the hate they hate totally—and their feelings of rivalry are still very strong, they have a difficult time coming together in groups. One of the more primitive and base levels of social interaction, which first begins during the early years, is coming together in a group and finding an outside person, object, or fantasy object against which to project their strong competitive feelings and aggression. This creates an implicit agreement not to take aggressive action against each other and establishes a temporary feeling of belonging. Megan became the common outside aggressor object to the "gang of four," as Mr. Wolfe did to the 3-year-olds.

Although the outside aggressor phenomenon begins in early childhood,[3] examples can be seen among adults. Perhaps you can recall the interaction at a dinner party when one person must depart early, leaving behind everyone else to talk about him or her in the most negative manner. The "leaver" becomes the dinner group's outside aggressor. By default, members of the group informally agreed to project their aggressive criticism at the departed person, and not to speak ill of each other. The game works if nearly everyone says something derogatory. Thus, for a short period of time, the members of the "dinner gang" have a superior feeling of being above someone else—a feeling of primitive belonging to this "in" group. Throughout history, politicians have used this outside aggressor phenomenon to gain control of groups; perhaps the most glaring and frightening example was the way in which Hitler controlled an entire nation by casting one race as the outside aggressor.

Reaction to the outside aggressor is an expectable, normal behavior among young children. The teacher's role, of course, is to engineer ways through which children can learn to be social in a more healthy manner and to help children like Megan find belonging and acquire social skills.

Social Engineering

After the "poison tea" incident, but before any actions like throwing sand could occur, Megan's teacher, Mrs. Anderson, calls Megan to the "cooking" table, summoning her in a voice loud enough for the "gang of four" to hear. She says, "Megan, we are going to make cookies today, and I am going to let you be the boss of cookie making. You may choose three helpers to work with you!" Three other children step forward, and they all begin to make cookies, following instructions the teacher gives to Megan. The "gang of four" sees what is happening. The excitement of their make-believe play in the housekeeping corner has deflated, and they begin to wander over to the "cooking" table and look on. They loiter about and then gradually plead in a whining voice, "Mrs. Anderson, can we make cookies, too?" The teacher responds, "I don't know. I am not the boss of the cookie making—Megan is! You will have to ask her." The gang approaches Megan and asks, "Can we help make cookies?" Megan hesitates for a few seconds, then smiles and says yes. The teacher hovers nearby, watching all the girls making the cookies. Her presence helps Megan to maintain her power. Later, when the entire class is eating the cookies, the teacher tells the children how Megan shared her activity, and that her work and her working with others have resulted in the entire class eating the delicious cookies. (This topic of *encouragement,* will be described later in this chapter.)

In the use of social engineering, we as teachers take a child who is acting out or misbehaving and view that child as being powerless, lacking the skill to find social belonging. We deliberately "engineer," or set up, activities whereby we empower children such as Megan and help them enjoy the experience of successfully working within a group. We deliberately and genuinely point out to classmates how she has given and contributed to making the classroom a happy and accepting place. Thus, we purposefully engineer positive experiences for misbehaving children. We may, after the cookie making experience, question Megan with Confronting-Contracting "What" questions, such as, "Megan, what did you do at cookie making? What worked for you as you worked with friends? What did not? What will you do next time when you want friends?" Notice that we do *not* tell Megan how well she did, or make any value judgments, or offer a prescription for her in further interactions. Through our questions and counseling of this child who is having difficulty socially, we want her to become reflective after social experiences, to become consciously aware of her own behavior, to evaluate her success, and to come up with ideas of how she may be even more effective the next time.

Disengaging

Odd as it may sound, young children can frighten teachers. Suppose Al bites a classmate, producing an ugly blue toothmark on Gwen's arm. Now suppose Gwen's mother is the most vocal member of the center's governing board on the school's PTO. Under these circumstances, a teacher would feel "under the gun" and of course quite empathic with Gwen's plight. When this happens hourly or even daily, teachers must acknowledge their own feelings. Such feelings may consist of being frightened of Al, and gradually feeling hurt and angry.

Teachers are not robots who are emotionless, who never get angry, and who always have good feelings toward all children. This is an unrealistic image and simply does not happen. Some children are appealing and some are very unappealing; the unappealing children generaly are the ones who cannot find acceptance in their homes and from fellow classmates. As stated earlier, because of feelings of rejection, the nonsocially adjusted misbehaving child in a classroom begins to seek excessive attention and power, becomes revengeful, and, finally, retreats into a passive state of helplessness. If we as teachers acknowledge that we are human beings with a range of feelings, we will allow that the excessive attention-getting child produces feelings of annoyance in us, that we feel at times

FIGURE 3–3 Nonsocially Adaptive Children

Child's Motivation	Behavior Characteristics	Teacher's Feelings	Techniques
Attention getting	Repetitively does actions to make him the center of attention. When requested to desist, he will comply but will start again later.	Annoyed	Channel the child's energies into producing products (painting, clay, etc.) through which he receives attention from others and encouragement from the teacher. Employ social engineering and sociodramatic play.
Power	Repetitively does behavior to make him the center of attention. When requested to desist, he becomes defiant and escalates his negative behavior and challenges the adult.	Beaten	Do not confront but set up logical consequences for negative behavior. Give the child power over the object world (things), never others. Use logical consequences and encouragement. Employ social engineering and sociodramatic play.
Revengeful	Hurts others for no apparent reason.	Hurt	See Chapter 7 for a specific intervention process.
Helplessness	Wishes not to be seen, is passive and lethargic, and rejects social contact.	Inadequate	See Chapter 7 for a specific intervention process.

beaten by the power-needy child, that we feel hurt by the revengeful child, and that we feel inadequate in working with the passive-helpless child (see Figure 3–3).

We must acknowledge to ourselves that we have these feelings toward these children. Our feelings become a problem only when we begin to regress into becoming revengeful and feeling helpless toward these children. Therefore, we now have a second reason to use isolation as described in Step 4 of Confronting-Contracting—that is, to *disengage* ourselves. If we are angry and overcome by our own feelings because of the repetitive demands that the problem child is presenting to us, we may become emotionally flooded in the middle of a teachable moment. We need to confront skillfully, yet we are not able to handle this successfully and professionally because our clear thinking has been flooded by emotions. We then may place the misbehaving child in isolation (the "relax chair") for a period of time or move the child temporarily to another room or into a different play area under the supervision of another teacher. Feeling emotionally flooded, we must spatially move away from this child for many minutes or even an hour until we have disengaged from these strong emotions. Once we are calm and relaxed, we will have the energy to reapproach the difficult child to begin our steps of Confronting-Contracting. We cannot do Confronting-Contracting when we are angry.

Unknowingly, the entire school staff collectively begins to have these same angry, revengeful, and helpless feelings toward this one child. The child with the "If I can't be the best good child, I will be the best bad child" attitude is known in schools by the bus driver, playground supervisor, and cafeteria worker, and in early childhood centers by all the parents of the other children. The child has a reputation that precedes him. By analyzing the staff and the reaction of the problem child's classmates, it is soon easy to see that everyone has made this child the outside aggressor in the classroom, the bus, the playground, the cafeteria, and so on. He gets blamed by *all* children and staff for *all* accidents and negative occurrences. Others, including teachers, do not want him at their snack table or sitting near them at circle time. Most everyone, including adults, has unknowingly begun a process of shunning the problem child. This shunning and being the object of the outside aggressor phenomenon now severely complicates the intervention and dynamics of ever helping this child to change. The difficult child has dug a deep social hole that he will never be able to climb out of by himself.

Aside from disengaging (if necessary) before confronting such a child, how, then, do we handle this collective anger and shunning toward the child?

The Most Wanted

A staff meeting involving all adults who come into daily contact with the difficult child must be called; if you are one teacher by yourself, you may need to sit down during a quite period and in essence have this meeting with yourself. At the start of this meeting, it might be helpful if members of the group of adults are permitted some time to express their honest feelings toward the child. Staff members who are frightened by their own negative feelings toward the difficult child might receive some reassurance if they hear a skilled and respected teacher state, "I am wondering how you are feeling about Al these days. I must confess that at times I find myself getting angry and even frightened by him. At times I don't want him in my group, and at times I am having a hard time liking him." The first step in changing staff's negative behavior toward a difficult child is to voice honest feelings.

The problem child has dug a deep social hole that he cannot climb out of by himself. Because he feels rejected, he sits around day in and day out, his negative actions evoking further rejection from classmates and adults. A child younger than age 7 is still in the formative years of development. The early childhood years are the most robust years for making a positive impact on the child's development that will serve him—or mis-serve him—for the remainder of his life. Love begins with love! The very nature and *the central role* of the early childhood teacher is to make a lasting contribution to such difficult children. Research into the lasting effects of early childhood programs on children from poor economic backgrounds shows that more of these children graduate from high school, more go to college, more are employed, and more have intact marriages, whereas fewer have criminal records, fewer are in prison, and even fewer die before reaching middle adulthood.

These dynamic effects can be traced back to what we do as early childhood teachers. That is the challenge—and the opportunity—before us as we deal with this one particular difficult problem child. If we do not do it, who will? Almost anyone can teach the well-adjusted child who has been well mothered and fathered, but it is the difficult child who enables us to "earn our stripes" as teachers of young children. This is a big responsibility, but we may be the only and the last hope of these children, because once they get older and into the later years of formal schooling, they will rarely find another adult so willing to take the time to help them.

Now, exactly how do we do this? We do this in a staff meeting by using the Confronting-Contracting procedures on ourselves. We ask, "What are we and his classmates really doing to Al?" The answer is that we are, unknowingly, shunning him and making him the outside aggressor. We want most staff members to express in language past incidents in which they have moved away from this problem child. Mrs. Anderson confesses, "I am embarrassed to admit it, but one time when I was seated at the snack table with a group of children, we had one chair remaining at our table. I saw Al approaching, and—again, I'm embarrassed to admit it—but I grabbed another child and had him take this free seat so that Al would not be at my table." This outward admission is most important! (The teacher working alone might want to write this out.) Mrs. Anderson's candor may then encourage other staff members to share similar experiences or feelings.

We then move to, "What will we do to change?" The answer is that for the next two weeks, we will put Al, as our difficult problem child, on the "Most Wanted" list. Unlike a police Most Wanted list, however, this list will single Al out for special *positive* behavior. Recall the behavior of staff and children when a child, possibly visiting from another country or state, has enjoyed special status while spending a day in our classroom. We roll out the "red carpet" for this visitor, who is greeted warmly at the door, shown where to be seated at circle or snack time, told how and where to use the toilet, and so on. Placing the difficult child on our Most Wanted list means treating him as an honored guest throughout the two-week period. When every staff member—even those who do not have him in their group—sees the difficult child passing by, they are to give him special attention. The teacher says hello, makes eye contact, says the child's name, makes some pleasant verbal overture, and physically touches the child. The teacher helps him and invites him to be near her at circle and snack time and on the playground. During *every* time period throughout the day for the two weeks, some adult should be helping the child as if he were new to school procedures and practices—a stranger visiting without friends. At circle time and during any discussion group involving the entire class, the teacher will point out to classmates any and all positive behavior by the difficult child as statements of encouragement (described in detail later).

Almost as if a whistle has been blown, all adults deliberately change their behavior toward the difficult child. If we as teachers do not change, then classmates and the child himself cannot change. We help the problem child climb out of the deep social hole in which he was imprisoned by changing the entire social environment in the school. At first, we will feel phony acting in such a manner, but we must push and commit ourselves to perform such "motor actions." If we are also using the techniques in the Three Faces of Discipline and the direct intervention techniques demonstrated in later chapters, a campaign of welcoming the child day in and day out can have a real impact to change the problem child's behavior and help him gain a feeling of acceptance. In contrast, if we do all the intervention techniques described in these many pages but the school climate—the actions of the adults and classmates—is still shunning the difficult child as an object of outside aggression, it will be unlikely that progress can be made.

At the end of the two-week period of the Most Wanted program, another staff meeting must be held. This will be a follow-up meeting to evaluate the success or lack of success of our welcoming process. The remainder of the staff meeting should follow the Six Steps to Staffing described in Chapter 12, in which we focus on the child's problem behaviors and address what actions can be taken individually by the teacher or staff in dealing with misbehavior. Also, it is given that the welcoming and accepting attitude toward the difficult child should and must continue.

WHY DO STUDENTS OBEY RULES?

How old does a child have to be before understanding the concept of right and wrong? Does the infant who throws up on mother's new blouse know the "wrong" that she has done? Does the toddler who throws his empty bottle and strikes his older sister, causing her injury, know the "wrong" that he has done? The answer in both cases is of course not. Does the 3- to 7-year-old know the "wrong" he has done when he "stabs" Mark with the paintbrush that is dripping with globs of wet paint? Now the answer might be yes or maybe. The difficulty in answering regarding the paintbrush incident is that no one is quite sure how the young child's mind works and how much he can fully appreciate how his action takes away another's right. Thus, a way is needed to view the young child's growing sense of right or wrong. Psychology has provided insights into understanding the stages through which young children move as they develop a full intellectual understanding of right and wrong and begin to obey rules. Answering the question, "Why do children obey rules?" has to be based on the type of intellectual ability of the young child. This question has two possible answers: fear of authority or feelings of social responsibility.

Fear of Authority

When we as adults stop our cars at a red traffic signal, is our reason for stopping that we fear being punished, such as being fined, arrested, or deprived of our opportunity to drive (fear of authority)? Or do we stop because we understand that in a society where we live and work, we are dependent on others and we know that rules are necessary to keep us safe (feelings of social responsibility) so that life's activities might proceed in an orderly, safe, and productive manner?

Fear of authority is the first moral understanding in the very young preschool-age child (ages 2 to 7). Children this age cannot intellectually understand how their actions can deprive others of their rights, and they simply obey parents' rules out of fear of losing their parents' love.[4] In this first childish moral position, what is right or wrong is not related to motive but is tied to mom and dad's punishment or reprimand. As soon as children are out of the sight or supervision of the adult authority figure, they lose the ability to control themselves; when their wants and selfish needs are in conflict with the established rules, selfishness wins out and the rules are broken. It is the adults' discipline action during the early childhood years that will enable children to develop an understanding of how their actions affect others in society. Gradually, with the right educational experiences, children may move to the second moral position of feelings of social responsibility and empathy for others.

Feelings of Social Responsibility

During this developmental period (ages 3 to 8, early childhood and the beginning of the elementary school years), it is the adults' role to build discipline plans and actions on an understanding that these early discipline experiences will help children make the transition from the immature fear of authority position to a more mature social responsibility position. Children at this age are gaining empathy for others, and a developing social conscience enables them to understand that their actions can endanger others and disrupt the social setting in which they live. If the discipline actions of adults are based on fear, power, and authority to simply bend the will of students and coerce them to perform under strict rules and severe punishment, we as adults will retard young children's moral growth and development.

FIGURE 3–4 Moral Development (a Concept of Right and Wrong)

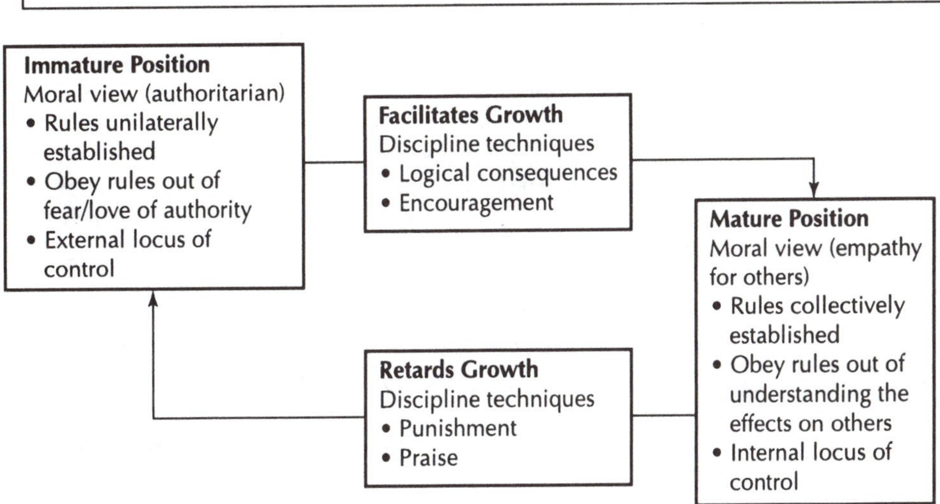

Highly authoritarian early childhood discipline procedures not only mis-serve students but also mis-serve the democratic society in which the students will become adults and assume their responsibility as citizens. A democratic society requires students to develop to the second moral position of feelings of social responsibility. Children must develop the ability to inhibit their self-centeredness of wanting it now, being first, and being childishly indulged. As they grow and mature, they must develop to an understanding of a different moral view. This new view accepts that rules collectively established by citizens serve to give everyone an equal chance, that these rules are for people's safety and society's good, and that they permit an opportunity for everyone to find a chance for their needs to be adequately met.

Why do students obey rules? We as teachers want our students, after their educational experiences in our early childhood centers and schools, to answer this question with the second moral position: feelings of social responsibility (see Figure 3–4).

WHAT ACTIONS SHOULD BE TAKEN WHEN RULES ARE BROKEN?

When rules are broken by children, the teacher needs to act. The actions taken can be morally retarding, such as punishment, or educational, such as logical consequences.[5] To illustrate these options, consider the possible responses to a cafeteria food fight among elementary school students. One set of potential sanctions includes a paddling, two weeks' detention after school, or some similar deprivation. This is punishment; it keeps the student in the first moral position of being *externally* controlled by fear of authority. In contrast, the school authority could instead require the students to clean up the cafeteria floors and tables for a set number of weeks during their after-lunch recess period. This is an example of logical consequences.

Punishment, then, is a legalistic judicial action requiring the educator to take a position that the students are "sinful" or unworthy because of their misbehavior, and therefore must suffer some degree of discomfort as punishment action. *Logical consequence*, in contrast, is educational, taking the position that the students are still immature and are growing, and will make mistakes. The mistake, which appears as misbehavior by the student, is an educationally valuable teachable moment for the school and parents. The actions that adults take toward that "misbehaving" child will serve to enable the student to gain a new perspective on his or her behavior and actions. Logical consequences will allow such students to learn how their actions might have taken away the rights of others and they can become more aware of their social responsibility toward others.

The possible punishment responses to the food fight, such as detention or paddling, require only a passive response from the misbehaving student. He simply has to "grin and bear it" and soon this discomfort will be over. While the student is "suffering" the punishment, he can and will have strong resentment feelings toward the educator and school, and might feel martyred as being treated unfairly. Punishment such as detention or paddling usually has no logical relationship to the child's previous misbehavior.

Logical consequences, as in the example of the food fight, require the student to be active and, by his action, make amends or "give back" to society or others for his negative behavior and actions. This is the case with the directive to clean up the cafeteria for three weeks. Logical consequence, as a sanction, is in direct contrast to punishment in that it is directly and logically related to the misbehaving act of the student. The student, through his misbehavior, trashed the cafeteria; now, as a logical consequence, he must clean up the cafeteria for three weeks. Society, in the form of the school cafeteria, has predictable rules that make it safe and comfortable for people to eat in this space. The misbehaving student has broken the social contract, and now must make amends or take actions to make things right again—in this case, clean up the cafeteria. Through suffering the logical consequences directly related to the misdeed, the student is educated to the cause and effect of his misbehavior.

In many ways, punishment, as a judicial procedure or process, is easy for the student and for the teacher. As mentioned, the student suffering a punishment simply has to "grin and bear it" and it will soon pass. For the educator, punishment requires little or no thought. The student did *X* (misbehaved), and therefore, based on the "rule book" or a discipline recipe system, must suffer *Y* (three hours of detention). This punishment stance by the educator eliminates any real thinking on the educator's part. The result of this punishment is resentment by the student toward the educator and the school. Little or no educational growth or benefit will occur.

But some adults might say, "Yes, but after the harsh punishment of a spanking, the student did not do it again." Normally, this is true only to the limits of this one narrow misdeed, but is not true at a deeper level because new misbehavior will result and might occur unseen by the adult. Punishment rarely educates and stops misbehavior; it simply causes the student to respond passively out of resentment, becoming lethargic and passive at school. This student may take advantage of the first opportunity he gets to drop out of this punishing environment called school. Alternatively, the student may become active by doing other misbehaviors to get even with the educator or school or may become more sneaky or skilled at continuing this same misbehavior. Many motorists who are punished—monetarily fined—for speeding on the interstate highway rarely stop speeding. They simply purchase a radar detector and become more skilled at breaking the law.

How, then, does this relate to discipline for young children? Our goal in early childhood centers and schools is to give up the concept and use of techniques that are defined as punishment and to use, as far as possible, creative and imaginative thinking in the form of logical consequences to the students' misbehavior. Through education, we seek to help the child grow morally as an individual with empathy for others and an understanding that rules are needed in a society of productive people.

The Immature and Mature Moral Positions

To summarize the psychological understandings that enable teachers of young children to gain a perspective on the use of discipline actions toward children who have broken a rule, two opposing models may be used: the immature moral position and the mature moral position.

The *immature moral position* developmentally characterizes young children, reflecting the fact that, because of their nearly total dependence on parents, their first moral position is to view adults as "god-like" or all-powerful. This produces an authoritarian view of what is right or wrong. What is right or wrong is determined by what parents allow or forbid, rather than by an evaluation of the motives of the person and whether he or she intended to do a negative act or even understands how his or her actions affect others. Thus, the young child obeys rules because of an external locus of control related to the love, and the fear of loss of love, from parents and adults (e.g., teachers).

The *mature moral position* normally does not fully develop until near the end of the elementary school years. It is a mature position whereby the older child can understand his or her behavior and actions and how they affect others. The child has developed an empathy for the feelings and rights of others. In this position, the child understands that rules are collectively created and may be changed, and that the unilateral imposition of rules by someone holding more power (authoritarian) does not make these rules fair or right. The higher cognitive understanding of a mature moral position now enables the locus of control to be internal, based on the child's evaluation of concepts of right and wrong and not just because external authorities state it must be so.

As previously stated, our goal is for our discipline actions to facilitate a developmental movement within the young child. By nature, the young child is authoritarian and punishment oriented, and we seek to facilitate a growth toward empathy for others and the mature moral view point. *Punishment,* then, may be defined as an external value judgment by a person in a more powerful position and denotes a failure to please the higher authority; that authority then takes action to retaliate against the less powerful person, causing forms of emotional stress and discomfort by sanctions and actions.

Punishment as an act toward a young child reinforces the immature moral position and retards or prevents development in the direction of empathy and reciprocity toward others. Logical consequence, as an act toward or with a child, is in direct contrast. It educates the child as to his actions and how those actions affect others and himself, and facilitates a growth to a more mature moral position.

Four-year-old William, awakening after nap time, refuses to put his shoes on or have others help him put his shoes on. The school's normal routine is that after children wake up, they use the toilet, wash their hands, and then go outside to the picnic table to get a snack. On this day, the snack is the children's favorite—a juice popsicle. William is motivated by an excessive need for power, exhibited by his refusal to put on his shoes, and he is simply left seated on the floor in the nap room while everyone else goes outside to eat their juice popsicles. Because it is warm outside and the popsicles will quickly melt, the remaining treats are returned to the school freezer. When William finally does appear at the snack table, he sees everyone eating their favorite treat and he is too late to get one. He now demands to have his juice popsicle.

Should the teacher make a return trip to the freezer specifically to get a popsicle for William? The answer is no. William must experience this very important lesson. It is the logical consequence of his refusal to comply with reasonable social routine and rules.

Praise versus Encouragement

Sally has spent nearly an hour drawing, coloring, and pasting an art project. When she is finished, she brings her treasure to the teacher and, putting it in the teacher's face, proclaims, "Mrs. Anderson, see what I did." This is a very important teachable moment and requires a skilled response by the teacher. The teacher may evaluate her response based on an external locus of control (Praise: *"Oh, Sally, I like it. What a beautiful painting!") or an internal locus of control.* (Encouragement: *"Well, you sure did work hard on that this morning; you must be proud of what you have done. I would like to hear you tell about this.")*

Praise is an externally determined value judgment as to how it pleases the speaker (normally someone in a superior position) as to the "goodness" or "badness" of another dependent person's actions. Look at the statement of praise in the preceding paragraph: "Oh, Sally, I like it. What a beautiful painting!" The I-statement signals that the teacher is the one whose judgment is important and Sally has pleased someone in authority upon whom she is dependent. The immature moral position construct is speaking here. The observation that it is a "beautiful" painting is the teacher's value judgment, and from the child's point of view may be totally wrong. Perhaps the painting is of Sally's neighbor's house, which she saw burn to the ground; in this case, the painting expresses a horrible experience and to the child might be an "ugly" painting. These praise statements are widely used by early childhood teachers under a belief that the teachers are being positive and supportive. In reality, based on the moral development position, they are actually teaching a child to be dependent and are retarding the child's own judgments.

Now look at the encouragement statement from the same paragraph: "Well, you sure did work hard on that this morning; you must be proud of what you have done. I would like to hear you tell about this." Encouragement statements place the locus of control not externally on the teacher, but internally within the child—"You sure did so and so; you must be proud." Encouragement does not focus on an evaluation of the end product, but rather on helping the child by recognizing the work effort the child has expended. Encouragement statements should invite the child to evaluate and explain the painting as he or she sees it, not as the teacher sees it ("I would like to hear you tell about this").

The Confronting-Contracting face considers that praise maintains the child in a subservient immature position. Because of the child's high dependence on the teacher, strong praise of the child's efforts ensures that these efforts will be repeated for the sole purpose of getting the teacher's praise, rather than for the learning that the child can acquire for himself in doing the activity. One classroom for 3-year-olds carried out a project in which all the children pressed a foot into clay, dated it, and then had it fired to make it hard. The results were sent home as Christmas presents to parents. For the next three months, each time the 3-year-olds used clay they wanted only to create footprints. The children had received too much praise for this behavior and now it had retarded their expressive use of clay construction.

Praise can also be a two-edged sword and addictive. The child may receive mounds of praise from the teacher for performing a certain act; the next day, the teacher is busy and does not praise the same actions. The child wonders, "Did I do something wrong today?" Other children will want absolutely everything they do to be praised on every occasion, and they will aggressively pursue the teacher, giving her no peace until they get this excessive attention as praise.

HELPING THE MISBEHAVING CHILD ACQUIRE SOCIAL SKILLS

What does it mean to be well disciplined? One answer might be that the person needs to be cooperative, knows how to get along with others, and can work well with others—in short, the individual has well-developed social skills. Terms such as *social skills, cooperative,* and *worker* all need to be understood as developmental concepts if we are going to be able to help young children obtain these skills. We must know how to recognize cooperation, workability, and social skills when we see them.

Social Skills

Does the term *social skills* mean saying "please" and "thank you," waiting your turn at the slide or snack table, and similar customs? Those attributes do represent social skills, but they play a very small part. For the young child, gaining broader social skills comes with the ability to play roles. The young infant does not have social skills, especially as related to cooperation; the young toddler has very limited social skills as related to being cooperative, because he appears cooperative only when it fits his self-centered needs. Near the age of 3, however, the young child takes dramatic steps toward becoming a social being.

For example, 3-year-old Karl ambles down the preschool hallway, wearing a man's hat and a woman's skirt, and carring a baby bottle. His appearance symbolizes the pivotal position in a 3-year-old's life. He is experimenting with a social role that he is not (woman), practices a role that he will become (man), and still clings to a symbol of the role that he must give up (infancy). When a person is socially adaptive, he or she plays roles. First, the individual might play and act out roles involving daily routines of the "driver of a car" or the "customer in a store," or try such occupations as the "plumber who repairs pipes," the "farmer who plows the soil," or similar occupations and life roles—including a teacher, or mother or father.

When people are being social by acting out roles, there are fairly clear rules for appropriate behavior *within these roles.* For example, you take a seat in a restaurant; you are now playing the social role of customer, ready to interact with someone playing the social role of waiter. You are both "scripted" as to how you will act toward each other and the unfolding of events between you: First the waiter will bring a menu, you will then order food, the waiter will bring water and utensils, and so on. If the waiter deviates from this script and tries to look inside your mouth, as a dentist might do, you would of course see this as bizarre and undisciplined, and would probably suggest this particular waiter be restrained because of his unusual and socially unacceptable behavior. Thus, being social is the ability to continually move in and out of roles following fairly defined "scripts"—you are socially adaptive.

It is in the years between ages 3 to 7 that young children are acquiring the ability to be role players, as seen with 3-year-old Karl. In fact, it is critical that by

FIGURE 3–5 Social Stages

Age 2	Age 3	Age 4	Age 5
• Unoccupied • Solitary • Onlooker	• Parallel • Associative		• Cooperative (sociodramatic)

the end of this age period, when they enter formal schooling, children have obtained the ability to play roles. This will permit them to play the role of student in a formal school setting and quickly learn the "script," which, for formal schools, is highly governed by rules. This is truly the adults' goal as we aim to make preschoolers "first-grade ready."

The role-playing with which Karl is beginning to experiment and practice is called *sociodramatic play*. With increased practice and skill as he matures to age 4 and even 4½, Karl will be able to conduct true sociodramatic play by being able to (1) imitate a role, (2) sustain a theme (script) for many minutes, (3) use gestures and objects to represent imaginary objects, (4) interact with others, and (5) use verbal exchange. This sociodramatic play is a complicated learned social skill, one that is not acquired by some children during this age. It is these same children—the nonplayers—who seem unable to "play the game" of later schooling. It is the young child who cannot role-play or do sociodramatic play who lacks the social skills and, more importantly, who cannot find acceptance as a cooperative being with classmates. (Fortunately, this is a fairly small number of children.)

If children cannot find acceptance, we see a return to misguided motivations of the difficult child who needs excessive attention and power, who is revengeful, or who shows a sense of helplessness. In short, the misbehaving young child is the one who lacks the social ability and skills to make solid lasting relationships with others. It is the skill of being able to be a player in sociodramatic play that is central to acquiring these skills. Our central role, in early childhood programs, becomes one of helping the child learn this form of role-play, which will enable him to move out of destructive misbehavior and become a cooperative person able to work with others (see Figure 3–5).

Cooperation

Sociodramatic play is the end goal and skill that teachers wish to see acquired during the latter part of the preschool years, but there are many stages to cooperation before this higher level of sociodramatic play is obtained. These social stages to true cooperative ability are: unoccupied behavior, solitary independent play, onlooker activity, parallel activity, associative play, and finally, cooperative or organized supplementary play. (See Figure 3–5, for the age at which these social stages can normally be expected to develop.)

We may look at these stages to true cooperative ability as developmental railroad tracks across which every child must travel to gain social skills. When evaluating the social skills of a misbehaving child, the teacher may ask, "Where along these six social stages is this child performing?" After observing Jimmy "El Zorro," who has spent large amounts of his time in Stage 2 (solitary independent play), we begin to see him repeatedly near Mark and Walter's activities, watching them do block building or play "Ninja Turtles." His behavior and new interest suggests that he is beginning to move to Stage 3 (onlooker). With this knowledge, the teacher may choose to intervene or facilitate the growth and help him move to

SOCIAL STAGES

Stage #1: Unoccupied Behavior—At this beginning social activity level, the child is not playing and is generally inactive. He may finger his clothing (shoestrings) or body parts (hair), and move physically about with no apparent goal.

Stage #2: Solitary Independent Play—The child uses objects, materials, and toys to carry out play activities without any interaction or regard to other children nearby. He appears to be in a "bubble" of private activity cut off from and unaware of others.

Stage #3: Onlooker Activity—The child stands or seats himself at the edge of other children's play activities, watching their activity intently and possibly talking to them, but making no overt action to enter in their play. He is clearly a social observer and a nonparticipant.

Stage #4: Parallel Activity—The child plays in close proximity or spatially nearby to other playing children and uses similar or the same materials and toys in a similar manner. There is no attempt to interact or to control the other children's activities by his actions. It is apparent that he is socially aware of what his neighbors are doing and he is doing the same.

Stage #5: Associative Play—Two or more children play with each other by borrowing and loaning materials, making attempts to get others to follow their lead, but each child is doing what he wishes to do without complying with the demands of a leader or group definition of the activity. The activity is unorganized with no division of labor and no common theme with a beginning or ending.

Stage #6, Cooperative or Organized Supplementary Play—This play involves two or more children carrying out a task of building some structure, doing a competitive game, or carrying out some form of drama. There are clearly one or two leaders and each member of the group has a clearly defined role. Membership as to who is in or out of this group is clearly defined. The activity is goal oriented, normally with a beginning and an ending.

Source: Adapted from M. B. Parten, "Social Play among Preschool Children," in R. E. Herron & B. Sutton-Smith (Eds.), *Child's Play* (New York: Wiley and Sons, 1971), pp. 83–95.

Stages 4 and 5 (parallel activity or associative play). Consider again Megan's behavior in the "poison tea" and "gang of four" incident. With an understanding of the social stages, the teacher can see that when Megan came to the housekeeping area she was "looking on" and was ready for beginning Stages 4 or 5 (parallel activity or associative play). The teacher, by engineering the cookie-making activity with Megan, was not only giving the child power but was also providing experiences to deliberately lead her to Stage 6 cooperative play, with the accompanying social skills it requires. The teacher may collect this social information more systematically by using the Social Competency Observation System (SCOS), shown in Figure A at the end of this chapter.

Later we will observe Megan and Jimmy "El Zorro" in their attempts at sociodramatic play. As we watch them, we must consider whether they can: (1) imitate a role, (2) sustain a theme (script) for many minutes, (3) use gestures and objects to represent imaginary objects, (4) interact with others, and, finally, (5) use verbal exchange. If the answer to any one of these criteria for sociodramatic play is no, it would become the teacher's objective to attempt to intervene, with the use of the Teacher Behavior Continuum, to help teach these missing elements. Once Jimmy "El Zorro" and Megan find social play among others, the misbehavior will clearly dissipate.

Developmentally progressing up these six social stages is not like climbing stairs, where a person moves in an orderly, predictable fashion up each step one at a time. Many examples of normal and positive regression will be seen in these stages, when children are placed under various pressures and demands. Look at 5-year-old Marcia, who has obtained solid skills in sociodramatic play and the six stages of cooperative play. Marcia's family has moved to a new city and has enrolled this well-functioning child in a new school for young children. The teacher will generally not see high levels of cooperative behavior in this child in the first few days of her enrollment. More likely, Marcia might regress appropriately to unoccupied behavior (Stage 1), appearing listless and inactive. After a few hours or even days, the teacher would expect to see solitary independent play, then onlooker, then parallel activity (Stages 2, 3, and 4). Finally, when Marcia makes friends, the beginning of higher levels of associative play and cooperative play (Stages 5 and 6) will be seen. Although Marcia had the ability to be cooperative all along, because of the strange context (new school), she reverted and had to go back through the stages as she "rehatched" socially.

However, if Marcia did not have the cognitive and emotional strength to handle the change and make these social advancements, the teacher would not see the development through these stages. Marcia would appear as if stuck in one of the lower stages, exhibiting no socially adaptive ability. If she did not "rehatch," Marcia would probably become a discipline problem. She would display an excessive need for attention getting in a negative way, attempt to use power to control the teacher and peers, and even become revengeful or—even worse—retreat into helplessness.

Indeed, social development is not like progressing up stairs; the child may typically advance up two steps but then regress one step in a forward-and-back process. If healthy development does occur, however, the child will always advance more than she regresses, and will gradually make real developmental advancement. Being in a strange school and new home causes Marcia stress and regression, but her solid foundation enables her to quickly return to her former cooperative self. Many other factors can cause behavior like Marcia's, including not feeling well, changing teachers, losing a best friend who leaves the school, negative family occurrences at home, and a host of others.

Chapter 13 will present assessment instruments to use to observe and score children, including misbehaving and properly behaving children, in the context of these social stages and the criteria for sociodramatic play. At the end of Chapter 7, examples will be given of the teacher intervening with a host of techniques from the Teacher Behavior Continuum. These techniques will facilitate sociodramatic play, helping the child acquire the necessary social skills. The teacher will be an active agent in this important process and will not leave the acquisition of these skills to chance.

The Worker

The young child between ages 2 and 7 years may be accurately called a player. He is still too egocentric intellectually and cannot place himself cognitively into another perspective, thus limiting his social ability. With proper development, the child moves through role-play to cooperative behavior, which must be solidly established to achieve true readiness for formal schooling. It is at the end of the preschool years and the beginning of formal schooling, near the age of 7, that most children become workers. A *worker* is a child who has advanced socially to a point where, unlike the toddler, he can inhibit his desires to follow selfish wants; he can inhibit his sense of rivalry and competitiveness and is able to carry out socially agreed-upon tasks with others. In short, he is well disciplined.

SUMMARY

The Confronting-Contracting techniques require the teacher to face misbehaving children with a demand to stop and, through questioning, get the child to reach an awareness of his actions, a clear memory of rules, and a plan for solving the problem through change. The teacher insists that an agreement be made, with a handshake to seal the "deal." If the child is flooded, the teacher uses a "relax chair" until the child feels he is ready to join the group and has contracted to do so. Most children who are misbehaving are motivated by four needs (attention getting, power, revenge, or helplessness) because they lack the social skills to obtain recognition and belonging. The teacher, by using the social stages, can assess developmentally how far the child has progressed in social skills, and can help the child move through the stages by using such techniques as the Most Wanted list and sociodramatic role-play. The teacher is supportive through the use of encouragement, but if the child breaks the contract, he will need to experience a logical consequence for his actions. Through the discipline techniques, the teacher attempts to help the child gain a social understanding of how his behavior affects others—an understanding that will enable the student to reach a more mature level of moral development.

Test Yourself

Test your understanding of the concepts related to the Confronting-Contracting face of discipline. Check one answer. Answers may be found at the end of this chapter, following the Endnotes.

A. ____ attention getting B. ____ power C. ____ revenge D. ____ helplessness	1. The child acting from this motivation makes the teacher feel inadequate.
A. ____ attention getting B. ____ power C. ____ revenge D. ____ helplessness	2. The child acting from this motivation makes the teacher feel annoyed.
A. ____ attention getting B. ____ power C. ____ revenge D. ____ helplessness	3. The child acting from this motivation makes the teacher feel hurt.
A. ____ attention getting B. ____ power C. ____ revenge D. ____ helplessness	4. The teacher asks the child to go to the "relax chair" and the child responds with, "No, you can't make me!" What is the probable motivation of this child?
	Check "true" or "false" for each statement as it would relate to the Confronting-Contracting face and philosophy.
A. ____ True B. ____ False	5. When contracting with a misbehaving child, the teacher clearly states the change of behavior that she wants from the child and promises there will be a punishment if the misbehavior is seen again.
A. ____ True B. ____ False	6. Time out for the Confronting-Contracting techniques is considered "not a punishment."
	Place a check next to the item that indicates whether the statement is a punishment or logical consequence, or a praise or encouragement.
A. ____ punishment B. ____ logical consequence	7. Juanita spilled an entire jar of red paint and was required to get a sponge and water and clean it up.
A. ____ punishment B. ____ logical consequence	8. Gary and Ivan were fighting over their favorite toy; the teacher placed the toy on a top shelf out of their grasp, and they were not permitted to play with it for two weeks.
A. ____ punishment B. ____ logical consequence	9. Randy threw grapes at snack time and was required to eat at a table by himself until he thought he could obey snack-table rules.
A. ____ praise B. ____ encouragement	10. "You shared your Legos, Martha. You must feel good that you have friends you can help."
A. ____ praise B. ____ encouragement	11. "That is the best block tower that was built this year!"
A. ____ praise B. ____ encouragement	12. "Ann, look how you used those scissors today. Remember last week how hard it was for you to do round circles?"
A. ____ associative play B. ____ onlooker C. ____ cooperative or organized D. ____ parallel activity E. ____ unoccupied behavior F. ____ solitary independent play	

Glossary

Clean Slate After the teacher and child complete the step of contracting, the child returns to the classroom activity as if nothing has occurred. The child has a "clean slate" whereby the teacher does not continually remind him of past misbehavior and is optimistic that the misbehavior will not be repeated.

Confronting The teacher responds to misbehavior with a verbal request to the child to stop the action.

Contracting The teacher demands from the misbehaving child that he reflect on his past behavior and come up with a way he will change to ensure that it does not occur again. The child must now commit himself to this as an agreement or contract, entered verbally and sealed by shaking hands.

Encouragement Action taken toward the child to permit him to evaluate himself and how he is becoming more effective, growing and changing. The focus is on the child's effort, not the product.

Irreversibility of Thinking Young children cannot intellectually reverse their thinking to review sequences of action from beginning to end. They recall the ending or last action occurring in a story or real-life event.

Isolation Placing the child spatially by himself for the purpose of having him become relaxed to the point that he can talk and negotiate with the teacher. This is not punishment. The child may return when a contract or agreement is established.

Locus of Control When children make decisions is it because *they* decided (internal locus of control) or because *someone else* (external locus of control) is insisting or coercing them to perform such action.

Logical Consequence A sanction directly related to the misdeed that permits the child to make restitution.

Most Wanted An agreement among all school staff to treat a difficult child whom they are having difficulty liking as if he were their honored guest for a two-week period. Every adult gives that child extraordinary positive attention throughout each day. During every time period, the child will be invited by an adult to be a part of the activities.

Motor Rules The unthinking behavior of performing daily actions (hanging up a coat when entering the classroom, putting waste paper in the trash can rather than on the floor, etc.) that are usually seen as appropriate in a certain room, space, or setting.

Relax Chair A place to put a misbehaving child in isolation to permit him to calm down; this may be a chair or some other comfortable space.

Social Stages Six stages (Unoccupied Behavior, Solitary Independent Play, Onlooker, Parallel Activity, Associative Play, and Cooperative or Organized Supplementary Play) that the child must go through as a precursor to becoming a cooperative social being.

Sociodramatic Play The social play involving taking on a role and carrying out make-believe stories like dramas; this is the highest form of social interaction seen in children's behavior from ages 3 to 7 years. True sociodramatic play involves the following elements: (1) imitate a role, (2) sustain a theme (script) for many minutes, (3) use gestures and objects to represent imaginary objects, (4) interact with others, and (5) use verbal exchange.

Water Power Crying for the sole purpose of getting one's own way.

"What" Questions Questioning language that confronts the misbehaving child to intellectually reflect on his past misbehavior or the rules, and to consider how he will change.

Related Readings

Dinkmeyer, D., & McKay, G. D. (1983). *Parenting Teenagers: Systematic Training for Effective Parenting of Teens*. Circle Pines, MN: American Guidance Service.

Dinkmeyer, D., & McKay, G. D. (1989). *The Parent's Handbook: Systematic Training for Effective Parenting*. Circle Pines, MN: American Guidance Service.

Dinkmeyer, D., & Dreikurs, R. (1963). *Encouraging Children to Learn: The Encouragement Process*. Englewood Cliffs, NJ: Prentice Hall.

Dinkmeyer, D., McKay, G. D., & Dinkmeyer, J. S. (1989). *Parenting Young Children*. Circle Pines, MN: American Guidance Service.

Dreikurs, R. (1964). *Children: The Challenge*. New York: Hawthorn/Dutton.

Dreikurs, R. (1968). *Psychology in the Classroom: A Manual for Teachers* (2nd ed.). New York: Harper & Row.

Dreikurs, R., & Cassel, P. (1972). *Discipline Without Tears: What to Do with Children Who Misbehave*. New York: Hawthorn.

Dreikurs, R., & Grey, L. (1968). *Logical Consequences*. New York: Meredith Press.

Glasser, W. (1969). *Schools Without Failure*. New York: Harper & Row.

Glasser, W. (1975). *Reality Therapy: A New Approach to Psychiatry*. New York: Harper & Row.

Glasser, W. (1986). *Control Theory in the Classroom*. New York: Harper & Row.

Glasser, W. *Glasser's Approach to Discipline*. Los Angeles: Educator Training Center.

Endnotes

1. Dinkmeyer, D., McKay, G. D., & Dinkmeyer, J. S. (1989). *Parenting Young Children*. Circle Pines, MN: American Guidance Service.
2. A child gets up from the snack table and begins to walk away. Suddenly he stops, looks back, and sees his chair sticking out in the aisle. He returns and automatically uses his lower body to push the chair in under the table. This is an example of one of the hundreds of small rules governing behavior that we follow without thinking each day. It is called a *motor rule*, and is explained in more detail in Chapter 4.
3. Isaacs, S. (1972). *Social Development in Young Children*. New York: Schocken.
4. Piaget, J. (1965). *Moral Judgment of the Child*. (M. Gabain, Trans.). New York: Free Press.
5. Dreikurs, R. (1968). *Psychology in the Classroom: A Manual for Teachers* (2nd ed.). New York: Harper & Row.

Answers to Test Yourself

1D, 2A, 3C, 4B, 5B, 6A, 7B, 8A, 9B, 10B, 11A, 12B, 13A-5, 13B-3, 13C-6, 13D-4, 13E-1, 13F-2

Manual for Social Competency Observation System (SCOS) by Charles H. Wolfgang

The Social Competency Observation System

SCOS is a time-sampling, data-gathering system whereby the teacher records the number of times a child performs within a category of behavior (one of the six social stages) at a predetermined time interval. The teacher defines a specific time interval (15 minutes is suggested) in which the behavior will be observed. Four children are listed on the scoring form and are then scored in a round-robin format with a single group member observed and recorded by placing a check mark within one of the six social categories on the Scoring Form (Figure A). After many observations, determined by the teacher, the total number of observations is counted and divided into the number found in each category to obtain a percentage score for that category. Finally, the percentage is graphed on the Child's Graph (Figure C) to create a visual display that permits comparison of social categories.

Procedures

1. Place the Social Competency Observation System (SCOS) Scoring Form (Figure A) on a clipboard (or some similar convenient location). Write the teacher's or observer's name in the appropriate space provided under the figure heading. This observation may be done indoors or on the playground, but in either place the child must be free to engage socially with other classmates in play, and the area must contain a sociodramatic play area that will permit the child to perform the highest social level of cooperative play.

   In column A, write in the names of the children who will be observed. The teacher may choose to record any number of children during this process if she is free of all other teaching responsibilities, but past experience indicates that four children may be easily managed by a teacher who is still supervising the entire classroom.

2. Set a timer for whatever time interval the teacher wishes to use (15 minutes is advised). When the timer signals, the teacher finds Child #1 in the classroom and observes him for 30 to 60 seconds, attempts to determine the social stage (such as unoccupied, solitary, onlooker, etc.), and then records a mark in the box to the right of the child's name under the appropriate category. The other children are observed and scored in a similar manner. The timer is reset for a second interval (must be the same number of minutes for each interval), and the teacher returns to her classroom duties.

3. When the timer signals the teacher again, she repeats step 2. It is advisable to observe and score at least two times per *observational event*, with four or more being ideal.

4. The teacher repeats the observational event at the same time of day, at the same location, and under the same conditions as much as is possible for a 5- to 10-day period.

FIGURE A Social Competency Observation System (SCOS) Scoring Form

Teacher's Name ______________

A	B Unoccupied	C Solitary	D Onlooker	E Parallel	F Associative	G Cooperative (Sociodramatic)
Total Score ____ #1. Child's Name __________	No___/tot___=___%	No___/tot___=___%	No___/tot___=___%	No___/tot___=___%	No___/tot___=___%	No___/tot___=___%
Total Score ____ #2. Child's Name __________	No___/tot___=___%	No___/tot___=___%	No___/tot___=___%	No___/tot___=___%	No___/tot___=___%	No___/tot___=___%
Total Score ____ #3. Child's Name __________	No___/tot___=___%	No___/tot___=___%	No___/tot___=___%	No___/tot___=___%	No___/tot___=___%	No___/tot___=___%
Total Score ____ #4. Child's Name __________	No___/tot___=___%	No___/tot___=___%	No___/tot___=___%	No___/tot___=___%	No___/tot___=___%	No___/tot___=___%

Recorded Event	Date	Time Started	Interval	Symbol or Color Code	Recorded Event	Date	Time Started	Interval	Symbol or Color Code
1					6				
2					7				
3					8				
4					9				
5					10				

5. The teacher now adds up all scoring marks in the entire row to the right of the child's name to get a total score, which is written in the space provided above the child's name in column A.

6. The teacher moves to each square under each of the categories and performs the following:

   a. Add the number of scoring marks within the square and place that number on the No___ (number) space at the bottom of the square.
   b. Write the total score, which was originally placed above the child's name in Column A, in the space to the right of tot____ (total). The number within that category is now divided by the total, and a percentage is determined and written in the space provided (No___/tot___=____%). Using the example in Figure B, notice that William scored as follows:
   B—unoccupied: He had 4 marks which, when divided by the total of 40 marks, results in a 10% score;
   C—solitary: He had 6 marks, resulting in a 15% score;
   D—onlooker: He had 24 marks, resulting in a 60% score;
   E—parallel: He had 6 marks, resulting in a 15% score;
   F—associative: He received no marks;
   G—cooperative: He received no marks.

7. At the bottom of the scoring form are spaces to document 10 recorded events (two or more observations per day), requesting the teacher to indicate the date it was done, the starting time, the interval, and the type of mark used. If the teacher wishes to do a finer analysis of any time changes over this period, a new mark (Xs, Os, /s, etc.) may be used for each event. Also, the same mark could be made with different colored pens, permitting the teacher to see how a category of play changes over all the scored events. In the example of documentation for William (Figure C), notice that event #1 was scored on March 1, 1994, at 10:00 A.M., and in 15-minute intervals. The symbol was a blue slash mark.

8. Refer to page 76. With the use of the Social Competency Level graph (Figure D), convert the child's percentage for each of the categories into graph lines. Continuing with the example of William, notice that Figure E shows 10% unoccupied, 15% solitary, 60% onlooker, and 15% parallel. Also notice that in item #1 an X appears after Stage #3 Onlooker because this was the highest social stage, reaching 60%. Thus, the teacher knows she must work or intervene to help William move on to Stage 4 and above. Also, after observing William's attempts at sociodramatic play, notice that the teacher has scored William on the five criteria as yes or no. In sociodramatic play, William successfully imitates a role, uses gestures/objects, and can sustain a theme, but he cannot interact with others or use verbal exchange. These last two now become the goal set by the teacher for William.

FIGURE B Example of Scored Form

A	B	C	D	E	F	G
	Unoccupied	Solitary	Onlooker	Parallel	Associative	Cooperative (Sociodramatic)
Total Score 40 #1. Child's Name William	////	//////	//////////////// ////////	//////		
	No 4 /tot 40=10%	No 6 /tot 40=15%	No 24 /tot 40=60%	No 6 /tot 40=15%	No___/tot___=___%	No___/tot___=___%

FIGURE C Example of Documentation for William

Recorded Event	Date	Time Started	Interval	Symbol or Color Code
1	March 1, 94	10:00 A.M.	15 minutes	/ -blue
2	March 2, 94	10:00 A.M.	15 minutes	/ -blue

Social Competency Level

FIGURE D Child's Graph (% of Time versus Social Stage)

% of Time		Unoccupied	Solitary	Onlooker	Parallel	Associative	Cooperative
	100%						
	90%						
	80%						
	70%						
	60%						
% of Time	50%						
	40%						
	30%						
	20%						
	10%						
	0%						

Child's Name: ____________________ Date ____________________

Teacher's Name: ____________________ School: ____________________

1. Based on the graph above, which is the highest social stage (defined as 30% or more) this child has obtained? (check) __ Stage 1: Unoccupied; __ Stage 2: Solitary; __ Stage 3: Onlooker; __Stage 4: Parallel; __ Stage 5: Associative; __ Stage 6: Cooperative (sociodramatic). *Note*: The intervention objective becomes the next social level beyond the one checked here.
2. Check each element of sociodramatic play that is missing from the child's skills and that needs to be facilitated.

   Imitates Role __

   Gestures/Objects __

   Sustains Theme __

   Interacts __

   Verbal Exchanges __

Social Competency Level (Example)

FIGURE E Child's Graph (Percent of Time versus Social Stage)

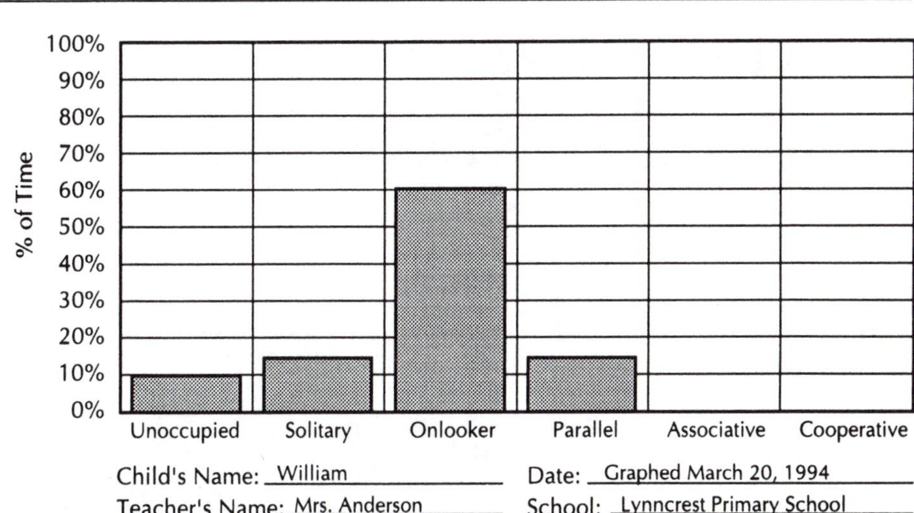

1. Based on the graph above, which is the highest social stage (defined as 30% or more) this child has obtained? (check) __ Stage 1: Unoccupied; __ Stage 2: Solitary; __ Stage 3: Onlooker; __Stage 4: Parallel; __ Stage 5: Associative; __ Stage 6: Cooperative (sociodramatic). *Note*: The intervention objective becomes the next social level beyond the one checked here.

2. Check each of the elements of sociodramatic play that is missing from the child's skills and that needs to be facilitated.

Imitates Role	Yes
Gestures/Objects	Yes
Sustains Theme	Yes
Interacts	No
Verbal Exchanges	No

4

The Rules and Consequences Face

The Three Faces of Discipline considers that the teacher can consciously be aware of and design the actions taken toward a misbehaving child. The Relationship-Listening face accepts that the misbehaving child is rational and may be made more purposeful and cooperative through a supportive nonjudgmental approach that requires the child to talk out his problem. The Confronting-Contracting face presents a clear use of power and demands verbal techniques by the teacher to stop the misbehavior and get the child to become cognitively aware of his action and how it mis-serves him socially. The child is permitted nearly total control in choosing how he or she will change, but the teacher engineers ways to help the child gain social skills.

The Rules and Consequences face, on the other hand, comes into play when the child is "flooded" and in a defensive stance. Even with the teacher's verbal questioning and mediation, the child cannot accurately view his own behavior, nor does he have the ability to change his actions of his own free will. To help such children requires strong intrusion and management techniques that demand that the teacher first be assertive and then plan a systematic shaping process to help the child gain self-control and a reawakening sense of trust.

Jimmy stands before the paint easel. Using a large, thick paintbrush, he dips the end into the paint pot. Soon the brush reappears, dripping with a large glob of paint. As Robert walks by, Jimmy turns and sticks out the brush as if it is a sword and attempts to "stab" his schoolmate. Robert screams and runs off, much to the delight of Jimmy. Smiling, Jimmy "El Zorro" dips his brush into the paint pot and looks about for a new target.

Robert huddles with two friends in the block corner to tell them of Jimmy's "paint stabbing." The three classmates smile broadly as they move as a group, much like a military assault squad, tentatively and defensively approaching Jimmy to see if they can get the same results. Jimmy eagerly

This chapter was cowritten with Mark A. Koorland, Professor of Special Education, Florida State University.

complies by dipping his brush into the red paint and stabbing out toward the approaching boys. The three boys gleefully scream and flee through the classroom, knocking over another child's block building. This creates a loud crash and screams of distress from the child using the blocks, as the boys take up a hiding position behind the block shelves.

The teacher quickly approaches "El Zorro" and orders, "Jimmy, behave yourself!" Jimmy drops his head before the easel and, placing the brush on the paper, makes circular scribbling actions as if he is painting. After the teacher returns to her previous activity, Jimmy—aware that he has four paint pots each with a primary color—begins to pump the paintbrush up and down in each pot. He rotates his paint-covered brush from one pot to the next until the colors in all four pots become a blended mess of muddy brown. The teacher reprimands, "Jimmy, look what you have done—you have mixed all four paints together. You have made them look like mud, and people can't paint with colors like this!" The teacher takes away the pots of muddy brown paint and replaces them with fresh pots taken from a nearby easel.

The teacher stresses, "Now, Jimmy, do not mix these colors!" The teacher then departs, leaving Jimmy with a supply of fresh colors. He watches closely to see that the teacher is involved with another child, and then moves his body so that his back is to the teacher, blocking her view of the paint pots. He dips his brush into the blue paint, then slowly sinks it into the yellow pot, making a blue swirl in the yellow paint. Giggling, Jimmy brings out the brush, inspects it closely, and reaches over to his neighbor's easel and makes a blue-and-yellow streak down the right side of the child's paper. The neighboring painter now screams at Jimmy, and the teacher once again appears before Jimmy.

Previous chapters have discussed how the techniques of the Relationship-Listening and Confronting-Contracting faces can modify routine misbehaviors in many cases. However, in some cases, certain children's misbehaviors call for further escalation along the Teacher Behavior Continuum. Through the techniques of the Rules and Consequences face, the teacher plays a more specific role in shaping appropriate behavior by these children.

How should the interaction between Jimmy and the teacher be viewed, and how could the teacher have more successfully intervened by using the Rules and Consequences face? This question calls for a two-step answer: First, the teacher should assertively demand that the misbehaviors desist and change to behaviors that the teachers wants. Then, through *behavior analysis*, the teacher begins to arrange consequences and to measure behavioral change to help the child acquire the more positive behaviors.

THE ASSERTIVE POSITION

The *assertive position* takes the view that you are the teacher and this is your classroom; you have a perfect right to get your needs as a teacher met. Misbehaving children are taking away your right to teach and other children's right to learn, and thus you must assert your control. You do this by determining the rules and behavior you want in your classroom and making them clear to the children. When children break these rules, you must take assertive action by stating clearly what behavior you want stopped and then demanding compliance from the child. If there is no compliance, you as the teacher have a plan and are prepared to take actions to decrease misbehavior and reward appropriate behavior.

An assertive teacher, as described by Canter,[1] is one "who clearly and firmly communicates her wants and needs to her students, and is prepared to reinforce her words with appropriate actions. She responds in a manner which maximizes her potential to get her needs met, but in no way violates the best interest of the students."

THE NONASSERTIVE POSITION

Adhering to Canter's definition, one can see that many seemingly assertive comments or actions by a teacher are actually *nonassertive* and are generally ineffective. The *passive* teacher ("Jimmy, behave yourself!") merely pleads and begs for children to behave and change their ways. This teacher appears not to be clear as to what behavior she does want and has no plan to acquire that behavior from the children. The *hostile* teacher screams at the children ("Shut up and sit down. I don't want to hear any more from you today!") or might grab, shake, or even strike the misbehaving child. The hostile teacher knows what she wants but her actions in attempting to get that behavior violate the best interest of the child.

Characteristics of Nonassertive Teachers

The Passive Teacher

1. Asks the child to accomplish an intermediate but nonspecific behavior goal
   Example: Asks the child to make an effort, such as, "Try to be good!"
2. Makes statements to the child about his behavior that do not communicate what she wants the child to do
   Examples: "Why are you doing that?" or "What is wrong with you?"
3. Says all the right words ("stop fighting") but does not back up the words with the necessary consequences to impress the child and influence the child to choose to eliminate the improper behavior
4. Demands the child to stop, and threatens to follow through but does not do so
   Example: "The next time you do that, you're going to time out!" A few minutes later: "I am warning you: One more time and out you go!"
5. May plainly ignore the behavior as if it never occurred, hoping it will go away

The Hostile Teacher

1. Uses a "you" statement that conveys a negative "put down" message, but in no way clearly communicates to the child what the teacher wants, leaving the child simply feeling guilty
   Example: "I am sick of your behavior. How many times am I going to need to tell you?"
2. Expresses her negative value judgment of the child and/or his behavior
   Example: "You are acting like a little monster this morning."
3. Threatens the child in an angry manner, with no evidence of consistent follow-through
   Example: "You just wait. I will get you for this!"
4. Utilizes follow-through consequences that are overly severe
   Example: "You are going to stay after school two weeks."
5. Physically responds to a child out of anger

Example: Pulling the child's hair, squeezing the child's arm, shaking or throwing the child, or hitting the child.

The Assertive Teacher

The *assertive* teacher is one who can state her wants and needs clearly to the child without violating the child's rights. This is done initially through the assertive command, which contains the following actions by the teacher:

1. Moves to the child, kneels down to make direct *eye contact*
2. *States the child's name*
3. *Gestures*
4. *Touches* the child
5. Verbally demands that the child stop (*demands a desist*)
6. *Demands change* for positive behavior by the child (tells the child what to do, rather than what not to do)
7. Promises a *follow-through* consequence

Note that nearly all modalities are used to communicate with this child in an assertive command: visual through eye contact and gesture; auditory by stating the child's name and demanding that he desist; and tactile through touching.

Let's look again at our example and see the teacher using the assertive command.

> *As Robert walks by, Jimmy "El Zorro" turns and sticks out the brush as if it is a sword and attempts to "stab" his schoolmate.*
>
> ***Teacher (makes eye contact):*** *"Jimmy (states his name in a nonthreatening but firm voice), stop that (verbally* demands a desist *and* gestures *by pointing to the brush and then the paper;* touches *the child by placing her right hand on Jimmy's left shoulder). Use the brush to paint on the paper (*demands a positive behavior *action). The rule is that we do not hit others. If you cannot follow the rule, I will take you out of the painting area and ask you to go to another area" (promises a* follow-through *consequence).*
>
> ***Jimmy:*** *"But Robert won't be my friend!"*
>
> ***Teacher:*** *"Use the brush to paint on the paper. The rule is that we do not hit others" (*broken record*).*
>
> ***Jimmy:*** *"No, this is my brush!"*
>
> ***Teacher:*** *"Use the brush to paint on the paper. The rule is that we do not hit others" (*broken record*).*
>
> ***Jimmy:*** *"No, I am going to hit you! You butt-head!"*
>
> ***Teacher:*** *"Use the brush to paint on the paper. The rule is that we do not hit others" (*broken record*).*
>
> *Jimmy physically pushes the teacher away and strikes out with the brush. The teacher removes the brush from Jimmy's hand and he is moved (*follow-through*) to a time-out room (normally used for storage). A timer is set for 6 minutes (this time may vary but it should always remain under 10 minutes).*

When it rings, Jimmy is permitted to return to the classroom to rejoin the other children in another area of the classroom (seclusionary time out).

Once the teacher has delivered this assertive command, she does not allow herself to be sidetracked by excuses or other discussions by the child. She repeats the assertive command two or three times as a "broken record" and then takes follow-up action if the child does not comply.

This strong assertive command is a very powerful intervention technique that may normally be used when the child is endangering himself or other classmates or is taking actions that may lead to property damage. For day-in, day-out classroom management, after the teacher has used the assertive command, she begins a consequence management process based on behavior analysis techniques.

BEHAVIOR ANALYSIS

Behavioral Objectives

When dealing with a child's misbehavior, it is imperative for the teacher to define clearly the behavior that she wants changed so that the teacher may be clear about the *target behavior*. A target behavior may be selected for change because it (1) is a behavioral deficit, lacking in the child's daily activities (e.g., using the paintbrush and paints incorrectly; pedaling the wrong way on the tricycle path) or (2) is a behavior that is correct in form or function but is displayed excessively or at the wrong time (e.g., asking so many questions at circle time that no one else has a chance to ask a question; talking during nap time; eating all the snack so there is nothing left for peers).

To decrease an inappropriate target behavior exhibited by a difficult child who seems not to respond to initial intervention efforts, the teacher must begin by choosing and defining *behavioral objectives* for this child and committing these objectives to writing.

In order to understand the behavioral changes that are desired and to communicate them to other staff members, the teacher must establish a behavioral objective that contains the following components (see Figure 4–1):

1. Identify the learner.
2. Identify the antecedent conditions under which the behavior is to be displayed.
3. Identify the target behavior.
4. Identify criteria for acceptable performance.

Returning to the example of Jimmy "El Zorro," with his repeated attempts at "stabbing" others, as a first step in a behavior change program, the teacher engages in *pinpointing*—specifying in measurable, observable terms a behavior targeted for change—by establishing a behavioral objective. "Jimmy (1. *identify the learner*), while at the easel, (2. *identify the antecedent conditions*) will use the brush by marking paint on the paper (3. *identify the target behavior*) for three of the next four times he uses the easel (4. *identify criteria for acquisition*) (see Figure 4–1). Now that the behaviors are pinpointed, the teacher may move to the next step of behavior analysis—collecting data to help the child acquire this behavioral objective.

FIGURE 4–1 Components of a Behavioral Objective: "Learner A-B-C"

Identify the Learner (answers "Who")	Promote individualization of instruction by specifying the targeted student or group of students.	Jimmy will... *(state action)* Children in the block corner will. . . *(state action)*
Identify the Antecedent conditions	Describe the preceding activity, condition, or stimuli (antecedent stimulus that sets the occasion for occurrence of the target behavior).	Jimmy, when using the paint easel, will place his paintbrush on the paper and paint. Debbie, when sitting at the table, will put her feet on the floor. Kevin, when finished at the snack table, will stand, pick up his trash, and place it in the wastebasket.
Identify the target Behavior	What will the student be doing when the desired change is achieved? The words chosen should lead to behavior that is observable, measurable/countable, and repeatable.	*Good verbs:* mark, remove, put on, label, place, say, cross out, take, put hand up, point *Poor verbs:* apply, appreciate, analyze, understand, select, perform, become competent
Identify Criteria for acceptable performance	Set the standard for evaluation and define what will be measured to determine the completion of the desired behavior. This may include how long the child will perform the desired behavior (duration) or the length of time from a start signal or cue before the child actually starts (latency).	*Acquisition criteria:* Four days out of five On each occasion Completes all five steps independently *Duration criteria:* Role-plays in sociodramatic play for 10 minutes Stays seated in circle time for 5 minutes *Latency criteria:* After waking up, the child will put on her socks and shoes within 3 minutes. Within 60 seconds after being seated, the child will place food in his mouth.

The following are some other examples of behavioral objectives:

Beth cries and has a temper tantrum (or becomes inactive and sucks her thumb) when her mother departs each morning.

1. Identify the learner (answers "Who").
   "Beth"
2. Identify the conditions.
   "when parting from her mother in the mornings"
3. Identify the target behavior.
   "will pick up toys or materials (or speak to another person)"
4. Identify criteria for acceptable performance.

   "within five minutes after her mother leaves." (*latency*)

Judy throws sand in her playmates' faces while playing in the sand box.

1. Identify the learner (answers "Who").
   "Judy"
2. Identify the conditions.
   "while in the sand box"
3. Identify the target behavior.
   "will pour and use sand without throwing it"
4. Identify criteria for acceptable performance.
   "for a period of 10 minutes." (*duration*)

Cal refuses to eat at lunch time.

1. Identify the learner (answers "Who").
   "Cal"
2. Identify the conditions.
   "during the lunch period"
3. Identify the target behavior.
   "will eat food from his lunch"
4. Identify criteria for acceptable performance.
   "in the amount of at least two bites for the next three days." (*acquisition criteria*)

Collecting Data

In the opening vignette, the hard-working, well-meaning teacher attempted to intervene with Jimmy "El Zorro" and stop his stabbing with the paintbrush. She reprimanded him, physically appeared before him, and changed the paint pots, even as the other children ran or became upset because of his actions. By closely examining exactly what is going on—in this case, understanding the technical concept and operation of positive reinforcement—one can discover that the teacher is actually a large part of the problem. The teacher's reinforcement, in conjunction with the reinforcement from classmates and the materials themselves, served to reward misbehavior. Unfortunately, this is not an isolated incident; it is rather typical of what, at times, is really occurring when misbehavior is repeated—the teacher's behavior is unknowingly exacerbating the situation.

For us as teachers, the classroom is a very dynamic situation, requiring attention to a host of stimuli coming from children and fellow staff members, as well as attention to safety concerns with the objects and materials being used. On top of all that, we have a child like Jimmy, who is like a hand grenade ready to go off at any minute. Time and again these overwhelming activities may require us to take some action. Unfortunately, the behavior and actions of others might be shaping and controlling our behavior when instead we should be in control of them. We will never know where this is really true until we collect reliable data that can give us a perspective on just what influential events are occurring in our classroom and school. But most importantly, data will tell us if our intervention is working. If it is not, then this is a signal to us to try to improve our intervention.

Consider the following example: It is the third week of the new school year and Jimmy "El Zorro" is a new child in the classroom. He has made these last three weeks a living hell for his teacher, Mrs. Anderson. She realizes that she cannot continue through an entire school year "putting out all the fires" and halting all the disruptions that Jimmy starts. She challenges herself to get on top of the "Jimmy problem" and really think through the situation. She makes a list of the misbehaviors she can recall from the first two weeks. She discovers the following:

- Four out of five days a week, there is a temper tantrum exchange between Jimmy and his parent (usually his mother) when he is dropped off in the morning.
- Jimmy has knocked over the block structures of a group of boys on four occasions. The boys involved are Mark, Robert, Walter, and Barry.
- Three out of five days Jimmy was part of a food-throwing activity that turned to aggressive biting during snack time. At the table were Barry, Carol, Robert, and Kevin.
- During one circle time, Jimmy began violently kicking Janet and Robert, who were sitting next to him.
- Nearly every playground period there is a fight over who can ride on the rickshaw, which carries three children, with Jimmy pulling the rickshaw and hitting other children. Those usually involved are Mark and Steven; Robert is always involved.

From this list, the teacher begins to see that the *antecedent condition* leading to some form of misbehavior, aggression, and disruption always involves Robert (who the teacher considers a generally well-behaved child) and involves an arrival period in which the mother brings Jimmy to school. Mrs. Anderson decides to attempt to collect reliable data on Jimmy's behavior for the following reasons: (1) she wants precise observations and measurements of behavior, which may enable her to determine the best way to change Jimmy's misbehavior and to give information about Jimmy to other teachers, Jimmy's parents, school administrators, and, if need be, school counselors or psychologists; and (2) the observation/data collecting will establish a *baseline,* which enables her to accurately determine if her particular intervention is really working over time.

Almost desperate, Mrs. Anderson decides that Jimmy "El Zorro" will be her special project for a one- to two-week period. She recognizes that the commitment of time to his problem is justified because Jimmy is already dominating her time as she tries to "put out the fires" that he causes, at the expense of time taken from other children. Therefore, for a one- to two-week period, she will give Jimmy her time and will focus on him proactively rather than reactively as she had before. On Friday, she meets with her aide, Ms. Walker, and they agree that together they will begin gathering data on Jimmy by using a number of measurements: (1) event recording, (2) an anecdotal report, and (3) the time sampling Social Competency Observation System that indicates social stages of play ranging from isolated to cooperative play (described in Chapter 3) conducted by the aide between 10:00 and 10:30 A.M. for five days.

Event Recording Since Mrs. Anderson works with an aide, at times the aide is required to intervene with Jimmy in dealings that are not seen by Mrs. Anderson. Therefore, a cooperative system is created to count and record Jimmy's disruptive actions (*events*) over an entire week. On a centrally located shelf out of the reach of the children, Mrs. Anderson and Ms. Walker place two plastic cups, one labeled "clips" (containing a supply of paper clips or some other readily available item) and the second marked "disruption." When Jimmy acts in a manner disruptive to

FIGURE 4–2 Event Recording Data Sheet

Student: Jimmy
Observers(s): Mrs. Anderson Ms. Walker
Behavior: disruptive behavior toward others and objects

	Monday	Tuesday	Wednesday	Thursday	Friday
Arrival to 10:00 A.M.	3	0	3	0	3
Snack to 12:30 P.M.	1	0	3	0	2
12:30 P.M. 3:30 P.M.	1	1	0	1	3
3:30 P.M. to departure	1	1	0	1	2
Total	6	2	6	2	10

his peers or destroys materials, the teacher or aide—whoever sees the event and is closest to the cups—takes a paper clip from the supply cup and puts it in the "disruption" cup. While on the playground, where the cups are not in easy reach, the adults simply move a paper clip from their right "supply" pocket to their left pocket, which serves as a temporary "disruption" container.

A *data sheet* is created with the five days listed and divided into four time periods: Arrival to Snack (10:00 A.M.), Snack to Beginning of Nap (12:30 P.M.), Napping to Midafternoon (3:30 P.M.), and Midafternoon to Departure. At the end of each of these time periods, Mrs. Anderson counts the number of paper clips in the "disruption" cup and writes that number on the data sheet (see Figure 4–2).

Graphing The total number of disruptive events for each day was then graphed (see Figure 4–3). Looking at the graph of disruptive events over the week, it is obvious that Monday, Wednesday, and Friday were very difficult days for Jim-

FIGURE 4–3 Graph of Daily Number of Disruptions

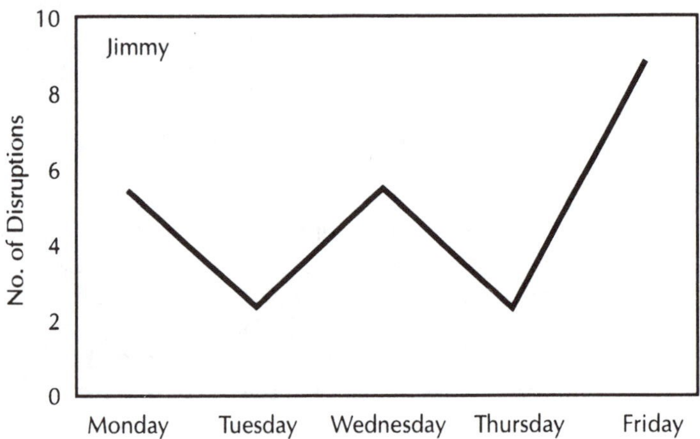

my, whereas Tuesday and Thursday were much easier days. Various kinds of graphic displays can be used to show a student's behavior. Often, line graphs with data points and connecting lines are used. Figure 4–3 shows an example of Jimmy's data in line graph form.

In addition, the child's behavior appears to get worse as the week progresses, with Friday being the worst day of the week for him. The question that arises in the teachers' minds is: What was different (the antecedent stimulus) that set him off into disruptive behavior on Monday, Wednesday, and Friday, as compared to the other two days of the week? The teachers could also tell from the four time intervals on the data sheet that Tuesday and Thursday mornings went quite well for Jimmy, with only two disruptive incidents—both after napping. His afternoon disruptions were nearly even across the days, with the exception of Wednesday, which presented no difficulties. What had changed—what antecedent stimulus was absent on Wednesday afternoon?

Anecdotal Report

To shed even more light on Jimmy's behavior, the teacher keeps an anecdotal report on Jimmy's behavior for these same five days. She focuses on arrival, snacking, circle time, napping, and outdoor play as she attempts to describe generally in writing the disruptive events. Because Robert appears to be a consistent peer associated with Jimmy's disruptions, Mrs. Anderson attempts to make note of Robert's location during any of Jimmy's misbehaviors. When possible, she also records her location and that of her aide, Ms. Walker.

For five days (Monday through Friday), Mrs. Anderson ends each day by writing a daily *anecdotal report* on Jimmy, focusing on any events of misbehavior. Her report is shown here.

Monday

Arrival

7:45 A.M. Mother brings Jimmy to school, carrying 6-month-old baby brother. Jimmy has a temper tantrum and pouts passively after mother leaves. He does not begin active play until 9:30. Note: He is passive for approximately 1½ hours.

Snack

10:00 A.M. Knocks over Andy's milk glass and screams and throws food at those children at his table. Complains that he is not seated by Robert.

Circle time

Kicks Carol, who is seated between him and Robert.

Nap

12:45 P.M. Makes noises and disturbs other children during nap time; is defiant when told to desist. Ms. Walker was supervising.

Playground

3:30 P.M. Fights over tricycle with Andy. Wants the red tricycle just like Robert's.
3:50 P.M. Goes the wrong way on the path and runs into other cyclists, who scream at him and finally knock him over for blocking their way.
4:00 P.M. After tricycle conflict, Jimmy cries, goes to tire structure, and sits in tire, sucking his thumb or biting his sleeve for 45 minutes.

Pickup

5:15 P.M. Reunites well with father.

Tuesday

Arrival

7:45 A.M. Mother brings Jimmy to school; no infant is in her hand. Jimmy arrives well and begins playing with Robert, building a block structure immediately after mother departs.

Snack

10:00 A.M. Eats well at snack. At his table are Mark, Walter, Carol, Andy, Matthew, Judy (no Robert).

Circle time

Handles himself well at circle time. Robert is seated at the farthest end of circle from him.

Nap

12:45 P.M. Naps well but awakens defiant and moody. Refuses to put on his shoes or put his blanket in the storage box. Ms. Walker was supervising.

Playground

3:05 P.M. Sits passively in the sand box, slowly digging with a small shovel in the sand. For no immediately apparent reason, throws sand in Mary's face. Runs to the opposite side of the playground and hides in bushes for 35 minutes.

Snack

4:00 P.M. Refuses to eat snack; sits and pouts.

Pickup

5:15 P.M. Reunites poorly with father by kicking at him when he attempts to put on his coat.

Wednesday

Arrival

7:45 A.M. Mother brings Jimmy to school, again carrying 6-month-old baby brother. Jimmy has a temper tantrum and pouts passively after mother leaves; does minor injury to his hand while hitting the front door as mother departs. Does not begin active play until 9:30.

Free Play Period

8:45 A.M. Using the paint easel and brushes, repetitively attempts to stab passer-by with the paint-covered brush. Paints on neighboring child's paper, to the displeasure of the classmate.

Snack

10:00 A.M. Is first at snack and grabs the snack basket; shoves much of the snack into his mouth and refuses to relinquish the basket so others may share the food. During this tussle, he knocks the gallon of milk from Ms. Walker's hand, spilling a white sea of milk over one-third of the dining area floor.

Circle time

Jimmy sits in a back corner off by himself; appears withdrawn and sucks his fingers.

Nap

12:45 P.M. Falls asleep quickly and is slow to wake up. Mrs. Anderson was supervising.

Playground

3:30 P.M. Spends most of outdoor time on a swing by himself.

Pickup

5:15 P.M. Reunites well with father without speaking, but appears flat and expressionless as father takes his hand to go.

Thursday

Arrival

7:45 A.M. Father brings Jimmy to school with no infant in hand. Jimmy departs well and begins building with Legos with Robert and three other boys immediately after father departs.

Snack

10:00 A.M. Eats well at snack; sitting with Robert at a two-person table.

Circle time

Handles himself well at circle time. Robert is seated beside him and they chat in a friendly manner.

Nap

12:45 P.M. Naps well but awakens defiant and moody. Refuses to put on his shoes or put his blanket in the storage box. Begins a game of "catch me if you can" by jumping dangerously from cot to cot out of Ms. Walker's reach. One cot he jumps to turns over and strikes him in the face (nosebleed quickly stopped when attended to). Ms. Walker was supervising.

Afternoon

Sits in the outdoor truck tires passively, sucking his thumb with a flat expression; participates in no activities.

Snack

4:00 P.M. Refuses to eat snack; sits and pouts.

Pickup

5:15 P.M. Reunites warmly with his father, indicating that he wishes to be carried "like an infant" to the car.

Friday

Arrival

7:45 A.M. Father brings Jimmy to school, carrying 6-month-old baby brother. Jimmy has a temper tantrum over who will open the classroom door. Refuses to hang up his coat, and lays on the floor crying as father departs.

Snack

10:00 A.M. Pushes another child out of the chair next to Robert, which develops into a hair-pulling fight between him and the other child. Calls the other children at his snack table "butt-face" and "fart breath." Takes a large bite out of a neighboring child's fruit, to the distress of that child.

Circle time

Pinches and pulls other's hair, makes noises to such a level that group activities cannot go on. He is removed from circle time and moved to another area of the room by the aide, whom he attempts to bite.

Nap

12:45 P.M. Makes noises and disturbs other children during nap time. Is defiant when told to desist. Refuses to put on socks, shoes, and coat. Ms. Walker was supervising.

Playground

3:30 P.M. Starts a game of "run and chase," putting himself into dangerous positions (attempts to climb over the school fence, runs into the path of children on swings, and jabs the pet rabbit viciously with a stick). When the aide approaches to intervene, he runs off quickly to the other side of the playground to start the same dangerous activity again.
4:00 P.M. Falls on the playground steps; scratches his knee and cuts his chin (both bleed slightly).

Pickup

5:15 P.M. Cries when father appears, and continues crying as father carries him to the car.

The anecdotal data, when added to the event recording accounts of daily disruptions, suggest a number of hypotheses to the teacher:

1. Generally, the arrival was difficult and would involve a temper tantrum or negative behavior if Jimmy's infant brother was in a parent's arms when the parent brought Jimmy to school. This suggests a series of antecedent events before Jimmy arrived at school in the morning, and sets a negative tone for him for the entire day. This possibly calls for a parent conference to show these data to the parents and perhaps suggest that a morning arrangement without the infant sibling might create a less disruptive process of departing home and arriving at school.
2. Waking up from nap was a difficult process for Jimmy, although the one day that Mrs. Anderson supervised his awakening (Wednesday) he had no trouble, compared to the awakening process when it involved Ms. Walker. More data are needed on this before any conclusions can be drawn.
3. Jimmy appears to want to be friends with Robert. Their relationship can be warm and cooperative at some times and hostile at others. More data and observation are needed on the Robert-Jimmy relationship, but at this early stage we might see the need for a goal of teaching the two boys how to work together.

Finally, the social competency level (see Figure 4–4) established through the time-sampling instrument (previously described in Chapter 3) shows that Jimmy's dominant social activity is onlooker activity (50%), and that he has some social skills indicated by associative play (10%), but more than one-third of the time he is engaged in the low social activities of unoccupied (15%) and solitary (20%). In the scores related to the ability to role-play as a part of sociodramatic activity, he can imitate a role, use gestures/objects, and sustain a theme in his play. He cannot interact or use verbal exchange well. The data at this early point would suggest that the teacher should set larger goals for Jimmy in terms of teaching him the social skills necessary for him to play more effectively with his peers.

After doing the event recording, the anecdotal record, and the time-sampling instruments, the teacher now has solid data related to Jimmy's level of functioning and events, *antecedent stimuli*, leading to Jimmy's misbehavior. With

FIGURE 4–4 Social Competency Level: Child's Graph (Percentage of Time by Social Stage)

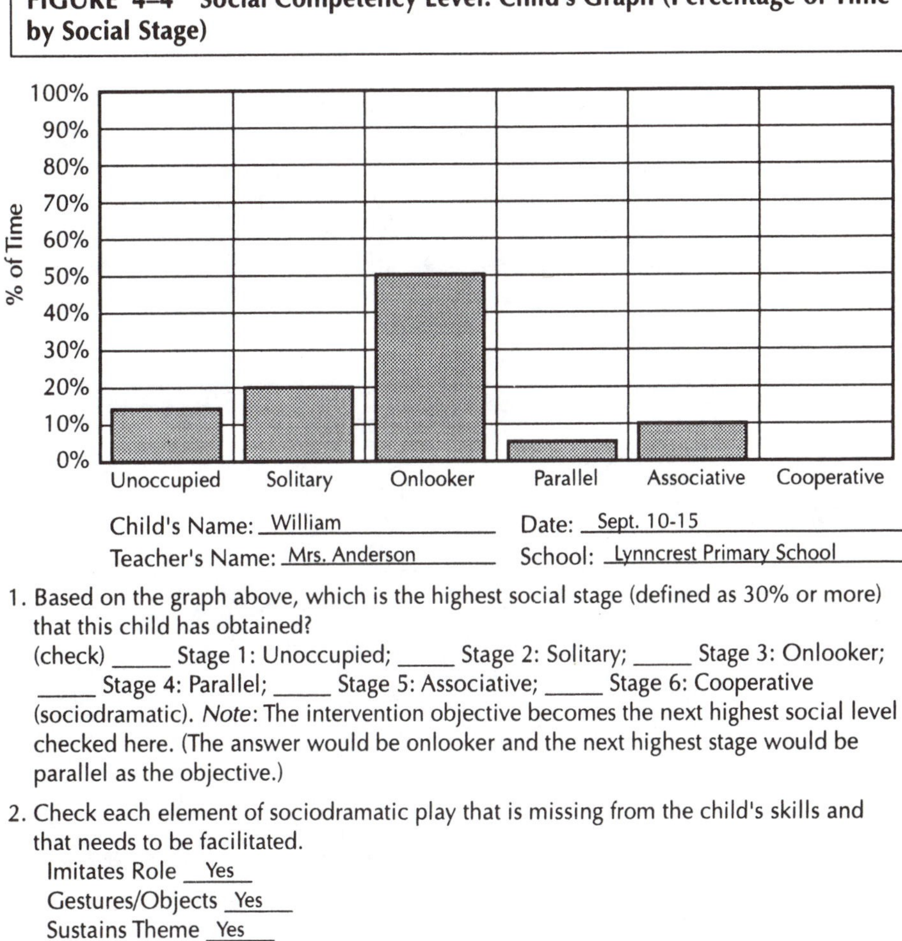

Child's Name: William Date: Sept. 10-15
Teacher's Name: Mrs. Anderson School: Lynncrest Primary School

1. Based on the graph above, which is the highest social stage (defined as 30% or more) that this child has obtained?
(check) _____ Stage 1: Unoccupied; _____ Stage 2: Solitary; _____ Stage 3: Onlooker; _____ Stage 4: Parallel; _____ Stage 5: Associative; _____ Stage 6: Cooperative (sociodramatic). *Note*: The intervention objective becomes the next highest social level checked here. (The answer would be onlooker and the next highest stage would be parallel as the objective.)
2. Check each element of sociodramatic play that is missing from the child's skills and that needs to be facilitated.
Imitates Role Yes
Gestures/Objects Yes
Sustains Theme Yes
Interacts No
Verbal Exchange No

this knowledge, she can establish goals for dealing with Jimmy, and out of these goals establish clear behavioral objectives. The following objectives (which should be stated positively) might involve helping Jimmy:

- Arrive at school more effectively
- Play and work with Robert
- Wake up from nap in a cooperative manner
- Acquire social skills as identified by social competency levels
- Acquire social skills related to sociodramatic play
- Follow group rules in group settings such as circle time and snack time

Understandably, the teacher cannot achieve all of these goals and objectives at once. But she can use her professional judgment to select the more immediate behavior to work on and then, over a period of many weeks, gradually make real and lasting growth gains with Jimmy by achieving each of the goals.

Mrs. Anderson should continue collecting and graphing data regarding Jimmy. Valuable insights may be obtained regarding the frequency of conflict with Robert; how long Jimmy can play with blocks (duration recording), paint, or engage in sociodramatic play; how long it takes him to wake up (latency recording) and become productive; how long it takes in the morning to begin productive activity after the parent departs (latency recording); the loudness of his nap-time noises that disturb others (measure of intensity); and whether he has acquired certain defined skills, such as tying his shoes, pouring juice at snack, and so on (simple yes-no measurement-criterion recording). All of these measurements can be graphed to display the data in a manner that enables the teacher to see if the behavior is changing in the desired direction over time.

Note: Generally, classroom teachers would rather have root canal surgery than comprehensively assess a child's behavior. This is most likely the case because assessment is time consuming, and most assessment has typically been for the simple purposes of awarding a letter grade. But the effective application of behavior analysis with the use of the Rules and Consequences face requires scientific and systematic data collection that enables the teacher to understand just what reinforcers or other stimuli are at work in the classroom; to display the data in ways that will suggest goals and objectives; and, finally, to show that the behavioral procedures are effective and behavior is really changing.

Reinforcement and Other Consequences

The basic view of behavior analysis is that human behavior—both *good behavior* and *misbehavior*—is learned. Jimmy's behavior occurs as a result of the consequences of his behavior. Behavior that is followed by a pleasant consequence, for that particular person, is a *positive reinforcer;* it tends to be repeated and thus learned. Behavior that is followed by an unpleasant consequence—a *punisher*—tends not to be repeated and thus one learns not to perform that behavior.

Jimmy's stabbing with the paintbrush, destructively mixing paint colors together, failing to follow the teacher's commands, and painting on the neighbor's paper were all a result of Jimmy having learned to do these destructive actions. The peers (Robert and the attack squad), the screaming neighbor, and—most importantly—the teacher have unknowingly reinforced Jimmy's misbehavior by giving him the attention he was seeking.

Reinforcement is a behavioral principle that describes a direct relationship between two real events: a *behavior* (any observable action: "Jimmy stabs at Robert with a wet paintbrush") and a *consequence* (a result of that act: "Robert screams and runs away"). There are two kinds of reinforcement: positive and negative. Care should be given in dealing with these terms, for positive reinforcement is not always good for a child and negative reinforcement is not always bad. The key to these behavioral principles is what kind of behavior increases when these different reinforcers are applied.

Positive Reinforcement *Positive reinforcement* is observed when a behavior is followed by a consequence that increases the likelihood of that behavior occurring again ("Jimmy looks for a new target for stabbing"). Jimmy draws a strong response by his actions, and his actions increase; thus, the actions have been positively reinforced and he is now likely to repeat them to get this predictable payoff.

In the preceding example, Jimmy was reinforced on at least 10 occasions in a very short time period. (The underlined statements in the examples below identify the reinforcer.)

- *Behavior*: Jimmy turns and sticks out the brush as if it is a sword and attempts to "stab" his schoolmate.

  Consequence: <u>Robert screams and runs off, much to the delight of Jimmy.</u>

- *Behavior*: Jimmy dips his brush into the red paint and stabs out toward the approaching boys.

  Consequence: The three boys gleefully scream and flee through the classroom, knocking over another child's block building and causing a loud crash.

  Consequence: The teacher quickly approaches Jimmy and orders, "Jimmy, behave yourself!" [This may appear to be negative statement, but Jimmy's continuing actions indicate the teacher has unknowingly reinforced his behavior by attending to him.]

- *Behavior:* Jimmy pumps the paint brush up and down in each color pot and rotates his paint-covered brush from one pot to the next.

  Consequence: The colors in all four pots become a blended mess of muddy brown.

  Consequence: The teacher reprimands (provides attention, a positive reinforcer for Jimmy), "Jimmy, look what you have done—you have mixed all four paints together. You have made them look like mud, and people can't paint with colors like this!" [Again, this may appear to be a reprimand, but Jimmy's actions indicate that the teacher's acknowledgment has unknowingly positively reinforced his behavior.]

  Consequence: The teacher takes away the pots of muddy brown paint and replaces them with fresh pots taken from a nearby easel. [By replacing the paints, the teacher has unknowingly positively reinforced and concretely rewarded Jimmy for his inappropriate actions.]

  Consequence: The teacher stresses, "Now, Jimmy, do not mix these colors!" [By talking and interacting with Jimmy, the teacher is rewarding him.]

- *Behavior:* Jimmy dips his brush into the blue paint, then slowly sinks it into the yellow pot.

  Consequence: He makes a blue swirl in the yellow paint and giggles. Jimmy brings out the brush and inspects it closely.

- *Behavior:* He makes a blue-and-yellow streak down the right side of the child's paper.

  Consequence: The neighboring painter now screams at Jimmy.

  Consequence: The teacher once again appears before Jimmy. [The neighbor's scream and the teacher's attention that follow are positive reinforcers for Jimmy.]

A reinforcer can only be judged as positive or negative based on its effect for an individual child in a specific time context and situation. One has heard the term *positive reinforcement* used widely by the general public, and may have heard it used to describe such common examples as "Clean up your toys and you will get a lollipop'" (with the lollipop supposedly being the positive reinforcer). However, if, unknown to the adult, the child has just eaten four lollipops, he will be satiated at that particular time by this taste and the consequence of the candy will not serve to reinforce the child. The adult will not get the desired behavior—cleaning up the toys—thus, the candy is not a positive reinforcer at the moment.

In another example, an adult may say, "Do your homework and then you may go outside for the playground period." However, if outside is a threatening place that the child wishes to avoid, then going outside is not a positive reinforcer—being indoors with the teacher is. In fact, the child might not do the homework specifically so he will not be made to go outside. Teachers may have to experiment and must clearly observe to truly determine whether their actions as offered consequences are in fact positive reinforcers, negative reinforcers, or punishers.

On the surface, all of the teacher's reprimanding statements ("Jimmy, behave yourself!" or "Jimmy, look what you have done—you have mixed all four paints together. You have made them look like mud, and people can't paint with colors like this!" or "Now, Jimmy, do not mix these colors!") may be seen as reprimands or punishing statements. For this particular child, however, they are really positive reinforcers. The true test for defining a consequence as a *positive reinforcer*, then, is if the behavior followed by a consequence increases in rate of occurrence over time.

Punishment A behavior is seen as being punished *only if it is followed by a consequence that decreases the behavior's future rate of occurrence.* It is best to keep in mind that any consequence to a behavior is defined by its effects on that behavior. Thus, paddling may be seen by the general public as punishment, but for some children getting paddled enables them to gain status in the eyes of their peers, so the action may actually be a positive reinforcer resulting in increased misbehavior. A child whose father rarely gives her attention might be very positively reinforced by a paddling for misbehavior, even though she cries during and after her father's actions. But if she continues the "punished" behavior, then punishment is really not taking place—reinforcement is actually occurring.

Note: *Negative reinforcement* (explained later) and *punishment* are generally confused by the wider public use of these two different terms. Remember that any time the term *reinforcement*—whether positive or negative—is used, it means some behavior will increase, and when the term *punishment* is used, it means a behavior will decrease. The punishment and negative reinforcement produce very different outcomes.

Behavior analysts use the word *punishment* as a technical term to describe a specific, observable, and concrete relationship: *punishment has occurred only when the behavior followed by punishment has decreased.* Again, just because one thinks one has responded with an unpleasant event or consequence, this may not be punishment. Much of the so-called punishment done in schools today is ineffective because it is judged by teachers and administrators as punishment, but little observation is being done to determine the real effects in terms of the child's actions.

The common use of time out, for example, can be considered punishment only if a functional relationship can be established between the child's behavior and the application of the consequence, resulting in a decrease in the behavior's rate of occurrence. In such a case, the action can be classified as punishment because the behavior that was followed by unpleasant consequences was not repeated or was repeated less and less over time.

Negative Reinforcement Punishment is said to occur only if behavior is followed by a consequence that decreases the likelihood of that behavior occurring again. The concept of *negative reinforcement* is a somewhat more difficult concept to define. Essentially, it involves getting the child to take an action (i.e., increase certain kinds of behavior) in order to escape or avoid an unwanted consequence. For example, Margaret is a child who, when she is awakened from nap time, is generally noncompliant and will refuse to leave her cot, put on her shoes and socks, go to the toilet, and move outside for the daily routine of playground period and snack. The teacher says, "Margaret, we are having juice popsicles (a favorite of hers) at the picnic table on the playground today. If you get up and move soon, the juice popsicles won't melt and be put away and you won't miss out on your treat today."

Negative reinforcement enables the avoidance or termination of an unpleasant situation if the behavioral goal is achieved. In technical terms, it is the *contingent removal* (if you get up and act, this will not occur) of an *aversive stimulus* (missing out on the treat) that increases the future rate or probability of the response (the child dresses, uses the toilet, and quickly moves outside). For negative reinforcement, there is an aversive stimulus—missing out on the treat—but the situation requires the child to behave or act to avoid that aversive stimulus. In this way, appropriate behavior (the behavior desired by the teacher) will increase in its rate of occurrence. In contrast, punishment is intended so that the consequences (e.g., time out) will *decrease* the future rate of occurrence of the inappropriate behavior (e.g., stabbing with the paintbrush). Another way to think of negative reinforcement is that the child does a behavior in order to subtract (avoid or escape) some undesirable situation in his environment.

Other examples of negative reinforcement are the following:

- The child is required to pick up his toys or materials (blocks, waste paper, puzzles, etc.) at the end of free play period and then move to circle time, where today the fireman is visiting. "Tommy, these are your (blocks, materials, etc.) to pick up and put away. If you move quickly, you won't miss out on seeing the fireman at circle time today."
- The child refuses to put on his coat to go outside in cold weather. "Coats keep us warm so that we will not get sick outside. If you put your coat on, you won't have to stay inside. We have a new sled outside for children to ride, and if you do not go outside, you will miss having your turn on the snow sleds. Inside toys are closed."
- The child refuses to wash her hands before snack. "Sarah, hands must be washed before snack to wash off germs so that we will not get sick. If you move quickly and wash your hands, you won't have to miss out on snack (or have to eat snack by yourself)."

Use Negative Reinforcement and Punishment Sparingly Suppose you, the teacher, describe the classroom behavior of a child who is causing you considerable difficulty (e.g., the child bites other children, willfully destroys other children's objects, and swears in very strong sexual language). If you ask for solutions from other adults, including teachers, many of their "answers" are likely to involve punishment. In some cases, these suggestions will involve a highly aversive stimulus following inappropriate behavior, such as rapping the back of the child's hands with a ruler, squeezing the child's neck muscle, verbally giving the child a "dressing down," or sending the child to an authority figure such as the principal or school director. When this aversive stimulus is used heavily, the child usually flinches when the teacher approaches or the principal appears.

Negative reinforcement and punishment in the short term are the easiest solutions to think up and they often get immediate results. But there are long-term side effects to the use of negative reinforcement and punishment. The negative consequences—especially if the actions are strongly aversive—are paired through *associative learning* with the teacher, the classroom, and the school itself.

The child who refused to awaken properly from her nap was dealt with by stating that she would miss a juice popsicle as a snack treat. She now watches to see what snack is going to be given that day; if it is something she likes, she refuses to take a nap, and may even refuse to remain in the room where the other students are napping. In the short run, a "cheap" quick victory was won by getting the child to get up from a nap promptly. But in the long run, the "campaign" has been lost because the child has learned a different lesson of avoiding a nap altogether. The child who refused to clean up the blocks before participating in a special activity refuses to play with blocks altogether; the child who refused to put on his coat now demands to wear his coat all day inside the classroom; the child who refused to wash her hands for snack now screams at the school door and refuses to come to school, seeking to avoid the place where she is required to wash.

Negative reinforcement can be an effective tool if it is used correctly with children, but it must be used sparingly and with an awareness of the degrees of intrusiveness associated with different aversive techniques.

Emphasize Positive Reinforcement A child learns more positive behaviors by seeing positive models from teachers or peers. These models teach the child, inspiring him to comply and follow these positive models. The classroom in which the process is one of 99 percent positive reinforcement creates a school where strong emotional attachment is given to the teacher and fellow classmates. The experiences and materials are welcoming and satisfying to the child, and the student wants and loves to come to school and be with teachers and peers. So, on balance, *positive reinforcement should dominate the classroom* behavioral procedures, with punishment and negative reinforcement used sparingly.

For the noncomplaint child who refuses to join activities after getting up from nap, one teacher may be freed up to stay with that child after nap time for a few days. During this time period, the teacher gives this difficult riser more time to really wake up, perhaps reading a favorite reinforcing story with her and cuddling with her on the floor near the child's cot. In subsequent days, the teacher moves to an adult rocking chair, and the child gets up and goes to the chair to be read to and cuddled. Next, the teacher takes the child to the toliet and then reads. Then, the child uses the toliet and goes outside for the teacher to read the story on the school steps. Finally, a shorter and shorter story is read and the book is phased out; the child can now follow the normal routine of getting up from nap. For the child who refuses to put on her coat, the teacher can make "putting on coats" a game accompanied by a humorous song. The child who refuses to wash her hands may be allowed to choose an attractively colored soap bar, which becomes a reinforcer for her to wash her hands.

Since negative reinforcement and punishment creep quickly and unknowingly into daily classroom procedures, teachers may be advised at monthly faculty meetings to make a list of all the punishment and negative reinforcement being used that month in order to design *shaping strategies* to teach the desired behavior through positive reinforcement.

Types of Reinforcers

Primary Reinforcers A child's natural, unlearned, or unconditioned reinforcers are called *primary reinforcers*. These include edible reinforcers (food and liquids) or sensory reinforcers that appeal to the child's five senses (the sight of a favorite character, the sound of music or mother's voice, the taste or smell of food, or the feel of the child's favorite silky blanket). These reinforcers are central to the child's basic and early survival need and life experiences and provide the child with pleasure, thus they are very powerful reinforcers for the child.

The strength of the primary reinforcer will depend heavily on the extent to which the child has been deprived of this reinforcer. The child who has been reinforced with a primary reinforcer (e.g., small sugarless candies) for 10 or 15 minutes will become *satiated*, a condition of nondeprivation. In other words, the reinforcer has lost its strength for the child at that particular time. This child will reject the candies or even spit them out, showing that these candies are weak as a reinforcer for now.

Both edible and sensory reinforcers can quickly satiate. In addition, they can be awkward and time consuming to deliver repeatedly, and may use up much of the time that should be spent on the learning activity. The overuse of small candy treats as a primary reinforcer has brought much criticism from behavioral professionals. The use of primary reinforcers is only a temporary measure to enable rapid acquisition of appropriate behavior, but the primary reinforcer quickly needs to be replaced by a secondary reinforcer.

Secondary Reinforcers *Secondary reinforcers* include *tangible reinforcers*, such as stickers and badges; *privilege reinforcers*, such as the opportunity to be first or to use a one-of-a-kind toy; *activity reinforcers*, such as the chance to help make cookies; *generalized reinforcers*, such as tokens, points, or credits; and *social reinforcers*, in which the teacher gives her attention and reinforces the child through such things as her expressions, proximity to the child, words and phrases, feedback, and similar social interaction. Social reinforcers may also be given by classmates in a similar manner.

Secondary reinforcers are not basic to the child's survival, and initially may be of little interest to the child. Their value needs to be learned. After some previously neutral event or stimulus is learned to have reinforcing value, it is said to be a *conditioned reinforcer* (conditioned means learned). In rewarding successful behavior, the teacher may state how successful the child has been, may gently stroke the child's back as she cuddles the child, and may place a sticker on the

SENSORY REINFORCERS

Taste	Smell	Sound	Sight	Touch
fruit juice	garlic clove	party blowers	flashlight	balloons
flavored gelatin	vinegar	push toys	mirror	breeze from electric fans
raisins	coffee	whistles	pinwheel	air from hair dryers (on low)
cereal	perfume	bells	colored lights	body lotion
honey	cinnamon	wind chimes	bubbles	electric massager
pickle relish	suntan lotion	tambourines	reflector	body powder
peanut butter	oregano	harmonica	strobe lights	feather duster
toothpaste	after-shave lotion	car keys	Christmas tree ornaments	water
lemon juice	flowers	kazoo	wrapping paper	sand
bacon bits	vanilla extract	bike horn	rubber worms	burlap
apple butter				silly putty

Source: From *Introduction to Mental Retardation* by D. L. Westling, 1986, in *Special Educator's Handbook* by D. L. Westling and M. A. Koorland, 1988, Boston: Allyn and Bacon. Copyright © 1988 by Allyn and Bacon. Reprinted by permission.

back of the child's hand. Soon the statements and the sticker will become a powerful secondary reinforcer.

Another approach to secondary reinforcement would be to have the child wear a filing card on his shirt, attached by a safety pin or ribbon around the child's neck. When the child is successful, he is permitted to reach into a fish bowl that contains trinkets and claim a reward. At the same time, the teacher uses a paper punch to make a hole in the child's card to serve as a "diary" of the successful behavior. The child is soon required to have two punched holes in his card before he can go to the treat bowl, then four punches, then eight; the number continues to increase, requiring a greater delay of gratification on the child's part.

Since the primary and secondary reinforcers have been *paired* in their early and repetitive presentation, the primary reinforcer can be gradually dropped. The secondary reinforcer is now conditioned and is just as powerful as the original primary reinforcers. If the secondary reinforcer begins to lose its effectiveness, it can be paired again with a primary every now and then. This is sometimes necessary until the secondary reinforcer again regains its strength for the child. See Figure 4–5 for types of reinforcers.

Thinning Reinforcement by Using Schedules

Let's now consider a case in which the teacher has established a target behavior (having the child complete a six-piece puzzle, drink all the milk at snack, or interact at the sand table by sharing toys) and has written a behavioral objective. The child does perform the behavior and the teacher has positively reinforced it, possibly with a primary reinforcer (edible or sensory) or secondary reinforcer (token or social reinforcer). As a result of the reinforcement, the child repeats the desired behavior. The teacher now reinforces again and again—but soon the process gets too time consuming and exhausting to keep up such a repetitive routine of reinforcement. However, if the reinforcement is abruptly stopped, the child's desired behavior will begin to weaken.

Instead, the teacher turns to the behavioral procedure of *thinning* the reinforcement. That is, the reinforcement is gradually made less available for a given behavior or is contingent on a greater amount of appropriate behavior, until eventually the need for the reinforcement is eliminated altogether. The teacher does not deliver or withdraw a reinforcer at whim just because she is busy or it just seems like the thing to do at the moment. The reinforcer must be thinned based on a scientific process involving various *intermittent schedules* where reinforcement is given following some, but not all, appropriate responses. See Figure 4–6 for further discussion about types of schedules.

Shaping

Behavior analysis is employed to bring behavior under the control of time, place, and circumstances. Outside on the playground, yelling with "outside voices" is perfectly acceptable, yet at nap time loud talking, even with "inside voices," is unacceptable. Varying types of reinforcers, punishment and negative reinforcers, as previously described in this chapter, can help bring children's existing behavioral skills under the control of the teacher and result in well-disciplined behavior.

A second part of behavior analysis is the teaching of new behaviors that are not in the child's existing repertoire. How, for example, can the teacher positively reinforce the skill of putting puzzles away into their rack if the child has never before used the rack or put the puzzles away? New behaviors are acquired often through a process called *shaping*. Shaping is much like the childhood game in

FIGURE 4–5 Types of Reinforcers

Class	Category	Examples
Primary Reinforcers	1. Edible reinforcers	Foods and liquids (e.g., pieces of cracker, sips of juice, pudding, juice popsicles)
	2. Sensory reinforcers	Exposure to controlled visual, auditory, tactile, olfactory, or kinesthetic experience (e.g., face stroked with furry puppet, the child's security blanket, taped music through headphones, mixing colors of paint)
Secondary Reinforcers	3. Tangible (materials) reinforcers	Certificates, badges, stickers, balloons, status clothing (e.g., a police hat)
	4. Privilege reinforcers	Being first to share at circle time, setting the table for snack, holding the teacher's big book while she reads, sitting near friends or on the teacher's rocking chair, being first to use a new toy
	5. Activity reinforcers	Play activities and special projects such as making cookies
	6. Generalized reinforcers	Tokens, points, credits, or reinforcers that can be traded in for other valuables
	7. Social reinforcers	Expressions, proximity, contact, words and phrases, feedback, seating arrangements

Source: Adapted from *Applied Behavior Analysis for Teachers* (3rd ed.) (p. 201) by P. A. Alberto and A. C. Troutman, 1990, New York: Merrill-Macmillan.

which one person is "it" and others hide an object, such as a coin under a chair cushion. The person who is "it" wanders around the room and when he moves in the direction of the hidden coin, all the children shout, "You are getting hotter!" (a positive reinforcer). When the person turns away, the response is, "You're getting colder!" The verbal feedback has now shaped the child to move in the correct direction. As he approaches the chair, everyone screams, "Hotter, hotter, hotter!" until he passes the chair and the screams change to "colder, colder." The person who is "it" turns around to a new chorus of "hotter, hotter," until finally the child locates the chair, moves his hands around the cushion (while being reinforced by repetitive statements of "hotter, hotter") and finds the hidden coin. The children's reinforcements have shaped a new behavior, leading the subject child to new positive actions.

Consider yet another example: After saying good-bye to her parent in the morning, Adrienne spends an hour or even two hours doing nothing but sucking her thumb, her behavior flat and expressionless. When the teacher goes to her and attempts to "dazzle" her with good cheer to perk the child up, Adrienne only sucks her thumb more vigorously and withdraws further. The teacher's target or pinpointed behavior is to get Adrienne to leave her parent and go to activity objects and materials or to classmates and be playfully active. When shaping, it is very important for the teacher to choose a clearly stated terminal behavior, in the form of a behavioral objective. "Adrienne (1. identify the learner), when departing from parents in the morning (2. identify the conditions), will go to materials and objects and begin to use them or will verbally interact with a classmate

FIGURE 4–6 Types of Schedules

Name	Description/Example	Advantage/Disadvantage
Fixed-ratio schedule	The number of times the child *does* the target behavior will determine when he will receive the reinforcer (e.g., for every four worksheet math problems completed, the child is reinforced; every third time the child hangs up his coat he is reinforced). Thinning may now occur by increasing the number of times the child must perform (e.g., from four math problems to six).	Since time is not critical, the child might take far too long between tasks (e.g., complete a puzzle and then pause for an hour before starting the next puzzle). If the number of tasks, given the schedule of reinforcement, is too large, then the child may even stop responding. The key is to seek the right amount of work given the reward schedule. Normally, a ratio schedule produces consistent work.
Variable-ratio schedule	The target response is reinforced on the average of a specific number of correct responses—sometimes after the 3rd, 5th, 9th, 10th, 13th, 17th, or 20th, but on the average of once for every 10 times. This makes the reinforcement unpredictable for the child.	A child operating under a fixed-ratio schedule may realize that it will be a long time between reinforcers, and may therefore work slowly. The variable-ratio schedule is done in such a manner that the reinforcer is not predictable, so the child maintains or increases the pace of his output. Normally, behavior is persistent under this kind of schedule.
Fixed-interval schedule	The child must perform the behavior at least once, and then a specific amount of time must pass before his behavior can be reinforced again. The child is reinforced the first time (e.g., does one puzzle) and then a specific time must pass (e.g., four minutes); on the very next puzzle completed after the four-minute wait, the child is again reinforced. This reinforcement arrangement will be thinned by increasing the wait to six minutes, then eight, and so on.	The student can become aware of the time length and, knowing he has to perform just once, will wait for the time schedule to almost run out before beginning his next task. This kind of schedule is easiest for teachers to use, since it is based on the passage of time. A teacher does not have to monitor each piece of work, but only the clock and the work performed at the moment.
Variable-interval schedule	The interval between giving reinforcers will vary and be unpredictable to the child, with the interval differing but maintaining a consistent average length.	The child's behavioral performance is higher and steadier because he cannot determine the next time interval that will be used to make reinforcement available.

(3. identify the target behavior), within a five-minute period" (4. identify criteria for acquisition). With the terminal behavior stated in the form of a behavioral objective, the teacher is ready to reinforce Adrienne as her behavior gradually changes step by step into the specific target behavior (touching objects or speaking to playmates).

The shaping process unfolds in successive approximations of the terminal behavior as follows:

1. Adrienne leaves her parent but is in tears and sits passively.
2. She stops crying (the teacher socially reinforces).
3. Her eyes drop and she turns her face to the wall (the teacher withdraws her presence and stops reinforcement).
4. Hearing children laugh, Adrienne turns and looks intently at what is occurring (the teacher catches her eye and smiles, stating, "Friends are doing fun things."[social reinforcer]).
5. Adrienne stands to get a better view of the classmates' activities (the teacher stands by the play activity and holds out her hand [social-reinforcer]).
6. Adrienne walks across the room and grasps the teacher's hand with both of hers and buries her face behind the teacher's back, away from the classmates (the teacher stands still and does not reinforce the "looking away").
7. Adrienne stands erect, still holding the teacher's hand, and takes a sustained look at the play of the classmates. (Teacher: "Ah, see what they are doing—Carol is a nurse, Jane is the doctor, and Mary is the patient, and they are pretending to wrap Mary's injured arm.") At the same time, the teacher drops Adrienne's hand and affectionately strokes her head; the child cuddles into her as the teacher sits herself on a small chair nearby (social reinforcement).
8. Adrienne runs to the play area, picks up the stethoscope and runs back to the teacher, attempting to crawl onto the teacher's lap. The teacher subtly closes her lap, denying Adrienne the use of it, and places her hand in her pocket—differentially stopping reinforcement that would continue to permit Adrienne to be dependent.
9. Finally, Adrienne moves into the play area, picks up a toy doll, pretends to listen to its heartbeat with the stethoscope, and plays *parallel* with the classmates. The teacher catches her eyes, smiles warmly (social reinforcement), looks on at Adrienne, and then moves to another area of the room to help another child (the natural reinforcement of playing with others takes over—the target or terminal behavior has been obtained).

The skills needed for the use of shaping are to (1) clearly state a behavioral objective with a target (i.e., terminal) behavior, (2) know when to differentially deliver and withhold reinforcement, and (3) be able to shape the child in gradual successive approximations toward the target behavior. It is important not to move too quickly or too slowly when shaping. The experienced teacher eventually can anticipate the steps of successive approximation, but for the newer teacher attempting to use shaping, it might be helpful to attempt to write out the steps on a Shaping Planning Worksheet (see Figure 4–7). It is important to keep in mind that although these steps are likely to be followed in a shaping process, they may not develop in this exact form.

DECREASING MISBEHAVIOR: STEPS AND PROCEDURES

We now realize that when we want to *increase* a child's behavior, we present a positive reinforcer after the behavior. In contrast, when we want to *decrease* a child's misbehavior, we present an aversive stimulus after the behavior occurs and, if that stimulus is aversive for that child, the behavior will stop or decrease. Aversion associated as punishment or negative reinforcement can have its fallout

FIGURE 4–7 Shaping Planning Worksheet

Space is provided below to help you determine what gradual step-by-step actions a child might take toward acquiring target behaviors. Go first to Step 7 and write a behavioral objective, then retum to Steps 1 to 6 to project shaping steps that the child might take. Also write at the bottom the types or reinforcers you will use. As an alternative, it often helps to work backwards and think of the behavior that comes just before the last one that you want. Continue this process untill you are at the child's current behavior.

Shaping Steps:

1. ____________________

2. ____________________

3. ____________________

4. ____________________

5. ____________________

6. ____________________

7. Behavioral Objective

   a. Identify the learner ____________________

   b. Identify the conditions ____________________

   c. Identify the target ____________________

   d. Identify the criteria for acquisition ____________________

What Reinforcer(s) Will Be Used? (Describe)

1. Edible reinforcers

2. Sensory reinforcers

3. Tangible (materials) reinforcers

4. Privilege reinforcers

5. Activity reinforcers

6. Generalized reinforcers

7. Social reinforcers

effects (e.g., a child who must eat alone because he didn't pick up the blocks quickly now refuses to play with blocks at future times), thus we are required to cautiously limit the use of any form of aversion. To acquire guidelines in applying the various procedures in an attempt to decrease a misbehavior, we may establish a continuum consisting of five steps, moving from the use of minimally intrusive procedures to the use of maximally intrusive procedures (see Figure 4–8).

The first level of intrusiveness is Step 1: Extinction, in which any positive reinforcer that is being given to an inappropriate target misbehavior is abruptly withdrawn or stopped. Next along this continuum, using minimum procedures, is Step 2: Differential Reinforcement, in which the teacher seeks to lower the rate of the misbehavior by reinforcing an alternative or incompatible behavior to replace the child's misbehavior. The next escalation on the intrusiveness continuum is to Step 3: Response-Cost Procedures, in which reinforcing objects and stimuli are removed. This is followed by Step 4: Time Out, in which the child is removed from a stimulating environment. Time out can be performed itself along a continuum from nonseclusionary time out to contingent-observation, followed by exclusionary time out, and finally seclusionary time out. The final location on the degrees of intrusiveness continuum is Step 5: Aversive Stimuli, involving the application of some form of discomfort directed at the child who is evidencing a dangerous behavior to himself.

Step 1: Extinction

Extinction is the stopping of positive reinforcers that have been maintaining an inappropriate target behavior.

> *Peggy fails to raise her hand and cover her mouth at circle time, which is the proper procedure for being called on by the teacher. Instead, she shouts out the answer. During the first few days of school, the teacher mistakenly accepts Peggy's shouted answer. Without realizing it, the teacher is positively reinforcing Peggy's behavior. By the fourth day of school, the teacher understands her mistake and decides to use extinction to stop Peggy's shouting out. The teacher will not provide any reinforcement when Peggy shouts, and instead will call on those with their hands in the air, then state the rule and reinforce those complying. When Peggy shouts out, the teacher acts as if the child does not exist. When the teacher's reinforcement stops, Peggy's shouting gets louder and she pushes her way to the front of the circle. When the teacher continues to ignore her, Peggy even goes to the extreme of using her hands to move the teacher's head so the teacher is forced to look at her. The teacher physically but gently moves her aside and out of her view. Peggy drops to the floor and has a full-blown temper tantrum. The teacher continues to ignore Peggy's tantrum and moves her own chair to another section of the circle, so that all the children are looking at the teacher and their backs are to Peggy and her tantrum on the floor.*

Extinction is most effective to decrease classroom behavior when the child finds the teacher's attention and approval to be reinforcing. When extinction—the abrupt stopping of reinforcement—is used, a number of behaviors may occur, including the following:

1. The child's behavior will get worse before it gets better. When Peggy did not get the teacher's attention, she escalated her shouting and behavior into a full-fledged tantrum.

FIGURE 4–8 Degrees of Intrusiveness

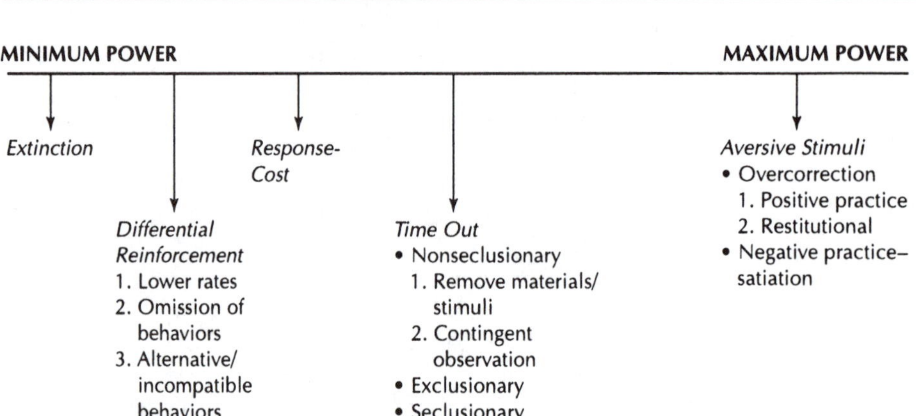

2. Extinction can induce aggression by some children. The next day, Peggy again fails to follow the rule of raising her hand to speak, and the teacher withholds all attention or reinforcement. Peggy walks forward and strikes the teacher (or a classmate).
3. Other children might begin to imitate the very misbehavior the teacher is ignoring, thinking, "If Peggy can get away with it, so can I." Normally, dealing with these "copycat" children through an assertive command will desist the copied behavior quickly.

One of the criteria for determining if the teacher can use extinction is whether she can put up with this increased disruption for a period of time. Extinction will be effective only if the teacher perserves and does not give in.

Step 2: Differential Reinforcement

Differential reinforcement employs the procedure of reinforcing certain dimensions of behavior selectively. This process can utilize three techniques: (1) reinforcing lowered rates of the misbehavior, (2)reinforcing the omission of the misbehavior, and (3) reinforcing incompatible behavior or alternative behavior.

Reducing the Rate of the Misbehavior One method of differential reinforcement is to reinforce lower rates of misbehavior.

> *The school rule for children's safety is that young children remain seated while eating, especially when chewing a mouth full of food. Event recording done by the teacher shows that Kevin was out of his seat at snack time 15 times in a 30-minute period, and nearly every one of those times his mouth was full of food. The teacher decides to use the Step 2: Differential Reinforcement procedure involving the reduction of the rate of the misbehavior. The teacher establishes a specific objective: "While at the snack table, Kevin will leave his seat five times or less during the 30-minute period."*
>
> *Since the teacher has identified a baseline of 15 out-of-seat behaviors in 30 minutes, she knows that requiring Kevin to stop out-of-seat behavior completely is not practical. She begins a system in which Kevin obtains a positive reinforcer—being able to take the large plastic trash bags to the back*

of the school with the janitor—if he gets out of his seat five times or less. Every time Kevin leaves his seat, the teacher makes a mark on a 3 × 5 filing card she keeps in her pocket. She also reinforces Kevin every 5 minutes for being in his seat by commenting on how he is remembering the rule, touching him on the shoulder and smiling. At the end of the 30-minute snack period, the janitor appears—and so does Kevin.

The teacher has Kevin count the marks that indicate the number of times he was out of his seat. On Monday, he counts five marks, on Tuesday nine marks, on Wednesday four marks, on Thursday six marks, and on Friday three marks. As a result, on Monday, Wednesday and Friday, Kevin is permitted to help the janitor. During the second week of the differential reinforcement process, the teacher drops the number of out-of-seat behaviors allowed to three, and the third week to one. At the beginning of the fourth week, the teacher does not need to count any out-of-seat behaviors because Kevin is now able to follow the rule, getting out of his seat only for appropriate reasons and frequency, and never with his mouth full of food. This method requires the child to reduce the behavior to a set number of times in a preestablished time period.

At times, we do not totally wish for all forms of a target behavior to be reduced.

On the playground, Mary appears before the teacher and breathlessly begins to tell the teacher whatever is going though her mind at the moment: what she did in the past, what her parents have done, a list of trivial items of interest to her, and more. She does not stop to permit an interchange or give-and-take with the teacher. Mary keeps up this verbal barrage for the entire recess period. The teacher would not wish to totally eliminate Mary's enthusiasm for talking, but would want to bring it to a more reasonable level. Therefore, the teacher uses the strategies of differential reinforcement.

The teacher says to Mary, "Mary, you have lots of wonderful things to tell me at recess, but sometimes I get tired and I need to talk to other children. (Teacher holds up five fingers.) You may tell me five things that interest you today, and then I will need to be with other children and you will need to go off and play." As Mary speaks, the teacher closes one finger at a time, visually counting off all five items Mary tells her. Two days later, the teacher holds up four fingers, and listens only to four of Mary's tales. In the following days the limit changes to three and then finally to two. The teacher verbally reinforces Mary when the girl stops herself when no more fingers are up. From then on, when Mary appears to be going off into one of her self-centered monologues, the teacher simply holds up two fingers and says, "Two, Mary, two!" Soon, the teacher does not need to speak but gains Mary's compliance simply by holding up two fingers. Finally, Mary can come to speak to the teacher in a normal fashion, without any finger prompts from the teacher.

Omission of the Misbehavior A second method of differential reinforcement is omission of the misbehavior. Applying this method to our earlier example, the teacher could establish set time intervals of 5 minutes each over the 30 minutes of snack time. The teacher lightly tapes a 3 × 5 card to the table in front of Kevin and places a check mark on the card if he has *not* gotten out of his seat (omission of the misbehavior) for that 5-minute time interval. The child turns in the card to the teacher at the end of the snack period; if there are two checks on the card during the first week, he earns the activity reinforcer. The next week, the criteria changes and Kevin must have three checks; later the standard is four, until finally Kevin stays in his seat for the entire 30 minutes of snack period.

One difficultly is that in requiring the child to omit a behavior, the teacher can create a problem if the child does not have a repertoire of other behaviors he can perform instead. For example, Jimmy comes to the edge of the block area and watches for most of the morning (social stage of onlooker; see Chapter 3) as Robert and his friends build a structure with blocks. Finally, without provocation, Jimmy kicks out and knocks over the blocks (or grabs a particular block most needed by the boys). He then runs off to hide in the corner. Jimmy has just shown a behavioral vacuum. Differential reinforcement of omission can be applied, but Jimmy is still left without an understanding of how to behave to join Robert and the other boys in the block construction. He needs not only to know how to stop kicking, snatching, and running but also how to make social overtures to be an associative player.

Both these methods accept the position that the child cannot stop his misbehavior immediately and completely. However, by changing the criteria, the teacher can place more and more demands on the child until the final terminal behavior is reached.

Incompatible Behavior and Alternative Behavior In the use of differential reinforcement of incompatible behavior, a response is chosen and reinforced to make it physically impossible for the student to engage in the inappropriate behavior. In differential reinforcement of alternative behaviors, an appropriate behavior is reinforced. This behavior is not one that when performed eliminates the physical possibility of exhibiting the target behavior. An example of incompatible and alternative behavior involves the teacher's practice of requiring the children to raise a hand to be called on after the teacher asks a question. This "wait time" permits all children to have a few seconds to think about the answer. However, Peggy impulsively shouts out the answer again and again. In response, for a few weeks the teacher gives the children new instructions: When they have the answer and want to speak, they are to cover their mouth with their left hand (incompatible behavior making it impossible to speak) and raise their right hand (alternative behavior). The teacher ignores anyone who does not have their mouth covered and hand raised—including impulsive Peggy. In her desire to be heard, Peggy quickly learns the proper procedure, and soon her impulsive responses are less frequent and then, finally, stop. Before long, the requirement for the left hand over the mouth will be dropped and the class will return to simply raising hands. Often, alternative behaviors are differentially reinforced since there is not always a physically incompatible behavior available for every target behavior. Figure 4–9 further discusses examples of incompatible and alternative behaviors.

Step 3: Response-Cost Procedures (Removal of Desirable Stimuli)

Paul, a most unruly child, treasures wearing the school's police officer outfit consisting of a hat, a badge, and a large thick belt on which is snapped a set of handcuffs. The teacher tells Paul that police officers are bosses and that he needs to be the boss of his own behavior—no hitting, no destroying others' products, and obeying the school rules. If he cannot be the boss of his own behavior, he will lose the privilege of wearing the police outfit. By 9:30 A.M., Paul has taken another child's toy. The teacher removes the handcuffs from Paul's belt and states, "If you want to wear these items—the belt, the badge, and the hat—you must obey school rules." By 10:00 A.M., he has kicked a neighbor during circle time. As a result, the belt is taken by the teacher. At

FIGURE 4–9 Examples of Incompatible Behaviors/Alternative Behaviors

Target Behavior	**Incompatible/Alternative**
When traveling through a large museum (or zoo, etc.), the children wander off and don't stay with the group.	A soft 1½-inch rope is used with a "train engine" (leading child) at the front of the rope and a caboose" at the end. All children are taught to be a "train car" by holding the rope with one hand—a practice that is incompatible with wandering off.
The children are screaming at the top of their voices on the field trip bus.	The teacher leads the children in soft singing of familiar songs. Singing is an alternative to screaming.
Susan reunites poorly with her father at the end of the day, kicking and refusing to put on her coat.	The teacher gives Susan a small envelope containing a surprise. It is her father's job to open this envelope, which contains a sticker Susan treasures. The father places the sticker on Susan's coat after the child is wearing it (alternative behaviors).
The boys are throwing stones over the school fence at passing cars.	The teacher brings out a basket and ball and sets up a target at the opposite side of the playground. She encourages the boys to throw the balls at the target (incompatible/alternative behaviors).
Some of the boys, when urinating, are having much fun aiming everywhere but into the toilet bowl.	The teacher adds some liquid soap to the "residual water" in the toilet bowl and when the boys aim properly, bubbles appear. Over time, liquid soap is only occasionally placed in the bowl; eventually it is phased out completely.
Some of the children have been seen playing with the pet gerbil too vigorously.	The children are shown how to pet the gerbil slowly and softly. They are permitted to handle the gerbil more if they pet it gently.
Mike comes to school and immediately goes to Ms. Smith, the aide. He follows her and remains close at all times, not interacting with any other adults.	Ms. Smith is seated with Ms. Seay at the start of class. When Mike first approaches, Ms. Smith and Ms. Seay conduct the morning's activities together while Mike follows along. Ms. Smith is called to the school director's office. Ms. Seay now engages Mike in a new activity and reinforces him with verbal and eye contact while Ms. Smith is away. Ms. Smith now interacts with Mike only if he is with other caregivers.
At meal times, Jeanne constantly demands to be served first.	The teacher tells Jeanne that if she uses an inside voice to ask, "May I be served first today?" she might be served first. However, the teacher also points out that someone else who asks with the same inside voice might be first instead.

snack time he throws food; he loses the badge. While washing his hands to get ready for lunch at 12:00 noon, he is found throwing water at peers; he loses the police hat. This produces a temper tantrum. After nap time, all four items are given back to Paul, but the process of removing this desirable stimuli can be repeated if necessary. It is important that the teacher also reinforces Paul by "catching him being good" and reminding him to be the boss of his own behavior (like the police officer). During the afternoon, Paul loses no items. The second morning only one piece of the police outfit is taken from him, and in the afternoon he is able to go the entire time without losing one item.

The teacher in this vignette is removing a desirable stimulus. This requires that the child has within his possession and control certain tangible items he treasures and that serve as reinforcers for him. The question or dilemma for the child is how much is he willing to pay—in terms of losing these reinforcers—in order to continue with his misbehavior. In technical terms, this is called a *response-cost procedure,* in which the teacher has the ability to take away a reinforcer once given. Here is another example of using response-cost procedures.

All the children have five tokens pinned to their shirts as they depart on the field trip. The children are taught rules of desirable behavior for the trip, and remaining tokens will be redeemed for a treat. The teacher removes one token each time a child breaks a rule. If a child has all his tokens taken away, he is unable to receive a treat through token redemption.

Step 4: Time Out and Time-Out Procedures

Time-out procedures serve as punishment by denying a child, for a fixed period of time, the opportunity to receive reinforcement. This removal of stimuli is actually time out from positive reinforcement. Time out generally is used when the social context is so reinforcing that the teacher's application of other reinforcers is ineffective. In the illustration of Jimmy "El Zorro," this can be seen in the approach of Robert and the "attack squad" or the lure of the multicolored paint pots. The next option for the teacher is to remove the child from some or all reinforcement. There are three categories of time out: nonseclusionary, exclusionary, and seclusionary.

Nonseclusionary Time Out To deal with a minor disturbance, the teacher takes some physical intervention to deny the student reinforcement by removing the materials that are being used inappropriately (e.g., eating utensils at snack time, water play toys, or paints and brush), or by having the children put their heads down on their desks and turning off classroom lights. This time out is called nonseclusionary because the misbehaving child is not removed from the classroom or immediate environment.

After a visit by a local police officer, a police hat is donated to the classroom's dress-up corner. Paul, the most aggressive and difficult child in the class, clearly desires to wear the hat. Paul is given a second police hat with his name taped in it, and the teacher tells him, "Police officers are bosses. If you want to wear the police officer's hat, you must be the boss of your own behavior. If you hit, destroy, or disrupt the activities of other children, then you will lose your hat" (If-then statement: If you do X behavior, then Y consequence will happen).

In the first two or three days, when Paul forgets and is disruptive, the teacher takes away his police hat, places it within his view on a hook too high for him to reach, and sets a timer for three to five minutes. When the bell rings, the hat is returned to him. On the first day, Paul loses the hat (nonseclusionary time out) on six occasions, on the second day it drops to two occasions, and in the remaining three days of the week the hat is removed only once.

Another form of nonseclusionary time out is contingent observation. The child is removed to the edge of an activity so he can still observe the other children being reinforced.

The school has a narrow circular tricycle path with painted arrows pointing the direction in which the children are to ride (visual prompt). The arrows guide the children so they will not collide with each other by going in opposite

> *directions. The rule has been explained and taught to Harold, but he repeatedly seems to enjoy going in the opposite direction and colliding with playmates who then complain in the strongest of terms. The teacher pulls Harold and his tricycle to the school steps at the edge of the cycle path, removes Harold from his tricycle, and requires him to sit passively and watch others obeying the rule and having fun. The teacher reinforces the other children (models) as they correctly obey the direction rule. After four minutes, she asks Harold, "Do you now see how our rule works, and can you ride your tricycle following the direction of the arrows?" If he says yes, he is permitted to return to his tricycle; if he says no, he stays on the steps (the time out) for another two minutes and is again asked whether he is ready to comply.*

The contingent observation is nonseclusionary because the child is not removed totally from the environment, such as being required to go inside the school or leave the section of the playground. Instead, he is placed at the edge of the activity so he may observe others being reinforced. Other examples include the following:

> *Jonathan is splashing others while he is supposed to be washing his hands. He is removed to the side to watch others washing. When the line of children is complete, he is then allowed to wash his hands.*
>
> *Kim's behavior is disrupting her peers at the snack table. Her chair is pulled away to approximately four feet from the table and out of reach of her food. After four minutes, she is able to return to snacking.*
>
> *Maria is being reckless on the tire swing (or slide, or any other playground equipment). She is removed from the apparatus and asked to sit nearby and watch. After four minutes, she is allowed to return.*
>
> *While seated on the floor at circle time, Timmy repeatedly disturbs others seated nearby. He is removed from the circle and seated on a chair in the doorway. After three minutes, he is allowed to return.*

Note: The criterion for returning or being released from the contingent observation nonseclusionary time out, such as those just described, is contingent on the child maintaining nondisruptive behavior for a minimum time requirement. Normally, the child is asked, Do you know and understand the rule and will you obey it when you return?

When the techniques of nonseclusionary time out have been tried but have failed, the teacher may recognize that the child's behavior is so serious that it demands a stronger form of response. Two other forms of time out are available in such a situation: exclusionary and seclusionary.

Exclusionary Time Out This involves the removal of the child from an activity as a means of denying access to reinforcement but generally not access to the classroom. Whereas contingent observation and modeling were used in the nonseclusionary time out, these procedures are *not* used in exclusionary time out. The child may be placed near a corner facing the wall or in an area of the classroom that is screened off from the room activities so the child's view is restricted.

Seclusionary Time Out This is the complete removal of the child from the classroom or environment to a time-out room because of the child's misbehavior, usually aggression or noncompliance. This denies the child access to any reinforcement from the classroom, including peers, adults, objects, or activities.

Note: The justification for the use of any of the forms of time out is not for purposes of retribution as a moral level of punishment (see Chapter 3 for an explanation of moral levels; see also Figure 3–4) based on the idea that the child has failed morally or has not lived up to the adult's values and expectations. From a behavior analysis standpoint, the justification is that the environment and social context are so strongly reinforcing the children to continue their misbehaviors, and the objective is to remove that reinforcement, that the only way to accomplish this is to use one or more forms of time out. Time out and time-out rooms have historically been misused or mismanaged by teachers, causing great distrust of this technique by parents and the general public. Children of any age are not to be put in time out for a long period. The child should be in time out for 1 to 6 minutes; it is clearly doubtful that any period beyond 10 minutes would be effective for the young child. A time-out record form documenting the procedure (giving witness names, circumstances, times and dates), such as the one in Figure 4–10, should be required for each staff member who uses time out.

It should be remembered that when a child is told that time out is over and that he or she may return to the classroom activities, the teacher should do so in a calm and low-key manner. No anger or extended conversation should take place or the teacher may actually set up a chain of events in which the child learns to misbehave and then be placed in time out in order to get into a conversation with the teacher when time out is over. Some teachers use a bell timer to indicate when time out is over, and the child is informed that he or she can rejoin the group when the bell sounds. The teacher interacts minimally with the child. The bell "tells" the student it is time to rejoin the class. From that point forward, the teacher should treat the child the same as any other child.

GUIDELINES FOR THE TIME-OUT ROOM

The following are basic requirements for the space and procedures for a time-out room.

1. The room must be at least 36 square feet (approximately 6 × 6 feet).
2. The room must have adequate lighting (never a darkened or unlit room or space).
3. The room must be properly aired (not an enclosed space, such as a large refrigerator box or closet).
4. The room must be void of objects and materials that the child may use when angered to hurt himself.
5. The adult must be able to see and hear the actions of the child at all times.
6. Locking the room door is forbidden.

Source: Adapted from *Applied Behavior Analysis for Teachers* (3rd ed.) by P. A. Alberto and A. C. Troutman, 1990, New York: Merrill-Macmillan.

Let's now relive the opening vignette and see the teacher correctly using the Rules and Consequences face, with positive reinforcement and punishment provided under the control of the teacher.

> *Jimmy stands before the paint easel. Using a large, thick paintbrush, he dips the end into the paint pot. Soon the brush reappears, dripping with a large glob of paint. As Robert walks by, Jimmy turns and sticks out the brush as if it is a sword and attempts to "stab" his schoolmate. Robert screams and runs off, much to the delight of Jimmy. Smiling, Jimmy "El Zorro" dips his brush into the paint pot and looks about for a new target.*
>
> *The teacher moves to Barbara, who is painting at a nearby easel, and states, "Good painting, Barbara, I see you have remembered our rule about keeping the paint on the paper." (The teacher gently touches Barbara's back and smiles at her warmly. The teacher gives no sign of acknowledgment or awareness to Jimmy. The teacher is using positive social reinforcers with Barbara, who is modeling the appropriate behavior that the teacher wishes Jimmy to perform. She ignores, or gives no reinforcement of any type for, Jimmy's misbehavior, attempting through the removal of reinforcement to place Jimmy's destructive actions on extinction.)*
>
> *Robert huddles with two friends in the block corner to tell them of Jimmy's "paint stabbing." The three classmates smile broadly as they move as a group, much like a military assault squad, tentatively and defensively approach Jimmy to see if they can get the same results. The teacher steps in front of the "assault squad" and tells them in a soft voice that Jimmy cannot hear, "Boys, do you see that box on the shelf? In that box are new outdoor sand toys, and I believe you might find some new cars and trucks in that box. I want you to choose one of our inside toys to play with now, and after you play inside when we go out to the playground today, you may open the box and be first to select one of the new sand toys." The boys move to the block area and begin cooperatively building a castle. (The teacher has established a contingency [if-then statement] with the boys and diverted their attention from*

FIGURE 4–10 Time-Out Record

<table>
<tr><td>Student's Name</td><td>Date</td><td>Time of Day</td><td>Total Time in Time Out:
_________ number of minutes</td></tr>
<tr><td colspan="3">Teacher's Name

Other Adult Witness</td><td>Type of Time Out (check one):
____ Contingent Observation
____ Exclusion
____ Seclusion</td></tr>
<tr><td colspan="2">Description of the Situation</td><td colspan="2">State Behavioral Change Wanted</td></tr>
</table>

Jimmy's "brush stabbing," thus preventing Jimmy from receiving social reinforcement from the boys.)

Jimmy stands holding his paintbrush "sword," waiting for a new victim. The teacher again moves to Barbara, touches her warmly and smiles, "Barbara, you sure have been working hard on your painting today. I would like to invite you to bring your painting to circle time today to share it with the other children." (The teacher positively reinforces the model, Barbara, who is correctly performing the behaviors that the teacher wishes Jimmy to perform, and at the same time gives no reinforcement to Jimmy in an attempt to place his inappropriate behavior on extinction.)

Jimmy touches the brush to his easel and paper and makes a red circle. The teacher quickly moves to him, places a hand gently on his shoulder and smiles warmly, "Jimmy, you have chosen red, an exciting color. It looks like you are also on the way to making a painting that we may all wish to see. Let me know when you have completed your picture and I will come back to see it." (The teacher has "caught" Jimmy being good, and when he has performed the desired behavior she immediately provides social reinforcement. She also has established an if-then statement: "When you finish a painting [behavior] I will come back to see it [consequence].")

Jimmy adds a mouth, eyes, nose, and ears to his circle and calls it a "doggie." He looks around and catches the teacher's eye. The teacher moves quickly to his side and states, "Great job, Jimmy!" (social reinforcer). She writes his name and date on the back of the paper and includes his description of a dog. "You may use the clothes pins and clip your painting to the rope line until it dries (activity reinforcer). We must remember to have you bring that painting to circle time to share today." (The teacher promises another social reinforcer.)

Jimmy begins a second painting with a clean sheet of paper. He now holds the brush as one would use a knife and slashes up and down, heavily matting paint over the paper and slightly tearing the paper. With this same knife-like grip on the handle of the brush, he begins to pump the paint brush up and down in each colored paint pot, rotating his paint-covered brush from one pot to the next until the colors in all four pots become a blended mess of muddy brown. The teacher removes all but one "mud"-colored paint pot from Jimmy's easel, applies a strip of masking tape on the remaining pot, and labels the pot by writing the boy's name on the tape. "Jimmy, this is the color you have chosen to make and use for painting. I have written your name on it, and we will save it when you are done today for you to use tomorrow." (By removing the three paint pots, the teacher has used nonseclusionary time-out[2] procedures to deny the student access to reinforcers through a temporary manipulation of the environment—removing the materials, herself, and her attention for a brief period contingent on the inappropriate behavior.)

The teacher turns to Barbara, who is still painting next to Jimmy, and states, "Barbara, let's see what you have painted. (The teacher gently touches the child and smiles.) Great, I can clearly see that you are giving this second painting much care! (social reinforcer). And look (points to the child's fingers holding the brush)—you have remembered the rule of how to hold the brush and use it correctly. (The teacher's pointing is a visual prompt to clearly show what behavior is desired by the teacher. At the same time, the teacher socially reinforces the model Barbara.) It looks like you're going to have a second painting to share with us this morning!"

Jimmy also begins his second painting in a similar manner, creating a circle with two eyes. Suddenly, he stops and dips his brush into the paint pot.

He brings out his brush, inspects it closely, and then reaches over to Andy's easel and makes a mark down the right side of this child's paper. Andy screams at Jimmy, and the teacher appears. Without saying a word, the teacher takes away Jimmy's brush and paint pot, but permits him to continue wearing his smock.

Jimmy is placed on a small chair at the edge of the painting area and told to watch and see how others paint. Four minutes later, the teacher approaches and asks Jimmy if he feels he can now return to painting and use the brush for painting only. He says he can, and is permitted to return to the painting (nonseclusionary time out with contingent observation).

What we have just seen is the teacher reinforcing those children who were models of the correct use of materials, attempting to reinforce Jimmy while he was exhibiting "cooperative behavior" and using punishment in the form of time out to control the reinforcement Jimmy was receiving after a misbehavior.

Step 5: Aversive Stimuli

Overcorrecting Consider the following scenario:

When Johnny is through the classroom door, he seems incapable of stopping himself from running down the hall and stairs to the playground. This practice is dangerous and should be stopped. Once the teacher has deposited the other class members safely on the playground under another teacher's supervision, Johnny's teacher takes him by the hand and walks him back to the classroom. The teacher verbally states the school rule to "walk in the halls and on stairs" and, still holding his hand, walks Johnny out to the playground in a correct manner. She then returns him to the hallway, repeats the rule, and now makes Johnny walk down the hall and stairs without holding her hand. He is made to walk the hall and stairs three more times, each time returning to the classroom.

This demand for rewalking is a behavioral procedure called *positive-practice overcorrection*. It is educational because it teaches the child how to perform correct behavior through an element of aversion. Another example would be a child who drops her coat on the floor when she comes in instead of putting it on her hook; the child is now required through positive-practice overcorrecting to repetitively "come in and hang up" three or four times as the teacher repeats the rule.

Mark has just finished eating his juice popsicle and discards the used stick by simply dropping it on the playground. He has a history of dealing with nearly all waste materials in such a manner. The teacher now takes him by the hand and states, "When we have trash, we throw it in the waste can," and she has him pick up the stick and throw it in the can. She now walks him to a second piece of trash laying about and has him pick up this trash and throw it in the trash can. The teacher then takes him around the playground, requiring him to pick up trash on six more occasions as she verbally states the rule.

This procedure, called *restitutional overcorrection*, requires the child to make amends by restoring the object, materials, or environment he may have destroyed or disrupted back to its original and proper condition and then going beyond that to do more—thus, overcorrecting. See Figure 4–11 for additional examples of evercorrection.

Negative Practice-Stimulus Satiation Here is another vignette example:

Lisa has a problem with spitting at inappropriate times. When she does not get her way in most matters with classmates and teacher, she will predictably spit at them. The teacher decides to use negative practice-stimulus satiation to deal with Lisa's spitting. She takes Lisa to the toilet and gives her a large cup filled with water, then asks her to take a large mouthful and spit it into the toilet. The girl does that compliantly and with a little giggle. She is then asked to continue taking water from the cup and spitting, until the cup is empty. A second cup of water is then presented to her, and her demeanor changes to reflect a sense of drudgery. At this point, the teacher begins each discharge by stating, "Spitting is against school rules."

With the use of negative practice-stimulus satiation, there is no intent to be educational or to teach new behaviors; instead, the idea is to have the child repeat the inappropriate behavior over and over until the act becomes tiresome and punishing, and the child becomes satiated and does not wish to do this action again. Figure 4–12 gives additional examples of negative practice stimulus satiation.

Sensory Insult In the vast majority of cases, the techniques previously discussed will be sufficient to put an end to most forms of misbehavior. However, there are occasional extreme cases that call for extreme measures. These measures will not be necessary for most children; when they are required, they must be used with the utmost care and with the full participation and approval of the parents of the child with the problem behavior.

Martha is a new child in the classroom. In the first two weeks of her attendance, the teacher discovers that Martha will bite and chew her right hand until the flesh is actually torn and bleeding. This self-abusive act occurs repeatedly throughout the day and creates a serious physical danger to the child. The teacher determines that the self-abusive behavior occurs for six to seven hours per day over a five-day period, and Martha's behavior of biting herself is on the increase. The teacher attempts a host of positive reinforcers, as

FIGURE 4–11 Examples of Overcorrection

Positive Practice	Restitutional Overcorrection
Child urinates on floor; child must help clean up.	Child puts inappropriate or dirty object in mouth; child must brush teeth.
Child bites; child must practice kissing.	Child bites; child must wash affected area, apply antibacterial cream, and dry surrounding area carefully.
Child steals; child must return object and practice borrowing.	Child steals; must help gather all misplaced objects and retum them to proper place.
Child throws food; child must help clean up and must practice proper eating techniques.	Child throws food; child cleans up spills and wipes all tables after snack.

FIGURE 4–12 Negative Practice-Stimulus Satiation

Target Behavior	Example
Child runs down stairs.	Child must repeatedly run up and down stairs.
Child hits playmate.	Child must repeatedly hit a pillow.
Child kicks over other's block construction.	Child must assemble simple block structure, then kick it down and repeat.
Child will not share toy.	Child must play only with that toy the rest of the period, as well as the next play period.

well as the first three steps of the degrees of intrusiveness process (extinction, differential reinforcement, and response-cost) without success.

A meeting is called, bringing together Martha's classroom teachers, a school administrator (or director), the child's parents, a special education teacher (when possible), and a local psychologist (or school counselor or social worker). The teacher passes out records she has kept on the aversion steps attempted, including various forms of time out and positive reinforcement, and graphs she has made to track Martha's biting. Also, with the permission of the parents, a videotape of Martha's typical self-abusive biting behavior is shown to this committee of professionals. The group recommends approval of the final component of Step 5: Presentation of Aversive Stimuli—sensory insult. The group, including the parents, approves and signs an Individualized Educational Plan (IEP), stating a new goal: the reduction of self-abuse. The members of the group permit the teacher to use such aversion stimuli as (1) putting a lemon into Martha's mouth when biting (aversive taste stimulus); (2) using bright food coloring to paint the area of her hand that she tends to bite (possible visual aversion); (3) painting her hand with a quinine liquid, which would create an aversive taste when she puts her hand in her mouth; and/or (4) if necessary, putting the hand into a leather glove she could not remove, which would protect her from most of the force of the biting. The IEP indicates that any or all of these aversion techniques may be used for a period of 10 days, with the teacher recording data and graphing the results. A second IEP meeting is set for the end of this 10-day period.

The classroom teacher has come to the point where she feels required to deliver an aversive stimulus, in the form of sensory insult, in order to stop a child's behavior that is endangering herself and others. However, this teacher is considering a dangerous series of strategies with a high risk of being accused of child abuse or being exposed to possible legal assault charges. When allegations of aversive procedures (see Figure 4–13) are brought into court and possibly circulated by the news media, the general public might be shocked and feel as if the teacher is being inhuman and using excessive punishment. But in reality, it would be no less inhuman to permit Martha to suffer the potential physical pain and health risks of repeatedly abusing herself by biting her hand and disfiguring her body, which will likely cause the need for expensive medical care. It is highly recommended that if a teacher is faced with the need to utilize such aversive activities, the child should immediately be referred to a psychologist or behavioral specialist, as this child's needs might be beyond the skills and abilities of the classroom teacher.

The teacher observes Martha constantly for three days, and when biting occurs, the teacher uses the lemon and issues a sharp verbal "No!" Martha stops her biting for approximately 2 minutes the first day. When these events are played out again on the second day, the no-biting period increases to 45 minutes. On the third day, the lemon and command are needed on only two occasions. On the fourth day, since the sharp verbal "No!" has been paired with the sour taste, the teacher needs only to say "No!" to Martha and she stops the biting. (Note that these time periods are for purposes of illustration; reaching this level of progress may take more or less time, depending on the individual learner.)

By the end of the second week of intervention, Martha can go an entire day without biting herself. Finally, during the following four weeks there are two occasions when the sharp command "No!" and the use of lemon stop Martha's biting. Since it was previously paired with the lemon as an aversive consequence, the sharp verbal "No!" has now become a learned or conditioned aversive stimuli. For the remainder of the school year, with the exception of returning after long holidays, Martha almost completely stops the biting as a

FIGURE 4–13 Examples of Sensory Insult Aversion Procedures

Target Behavior	Sensory Insult	Procedure
Head/self injury: • Striking own head with hand or object • Pulling out large amount of own hair	Hearing Touch	Blow a whistle to distract the child. Apply and require wearing of restraining devices (plastic or leather helmet).
Limbs/self injury: • Biting hands or feet or other parts of body	Touch Smell Sight Taste	Apply and require wearing of restraining devices. Apply ice cube or cold water. Touch smelling salts to child's nose. Paint the area being bitten with bright food coloring. Put lemon into child's mouth.
Climbing poles or support beams to dangerous heights on the playground	Touch	Cover reachable area with axle grease.
Eating materials such as clay, modeling dough, paints, etc.	Taste	Add or spray quinine to the materials.
Sucking or biting play objects	Taste	Spray objects with diluted water and tabasco sauce.
Kicking others	Touch	Remove the child's shoes on rough or textured floor surface.
Scratching oneself to the point of bleeding	Touch	Cover the area with heavy petroleum jelly.
Repetitive behaviors (excessive head rocking, repeating nonsense phrases, etc.)	Hearing Touch	Blow a whistle to distract the child. Apply and require wearing of restraining devices (plastic or leather helmet).

daily occurrence. When it does appear, only the conditioned aversive stimuli ("No!") is needed to stop the target behavior of self-biting. The collected data and graphing (described earlier in this chapter) clearly demonstrate the effectiveness of the aversive stimulus to help Martha reach the goal of reduced self-abuse. Success! But not all stories, of course, have such a pleasant or simple ending. See Figure 4–13 for additional examples of sensory insult aversion procedures.

To summarize, strong aversive stimuli should be used rarely, and only when adhering to strict guidelines that require the following:

1. The failure of alternative nonaversive procedures to modify the target behavior is demonstrated (possibly through videotaping) and documented (data collection and graphing).
2. Informed written consent is obtained from the student's parents or legal guardians, through due process procedures and assurance of their right to withdraw such consent at any time.
3. The decision to implement an aversive procedure is made by a designated body of qualified professionals.
4. A prearranged timetable for reviewing the effectiveness of the procedure is established as soon as possible.
5. Periodic observation is conducted to ensure staff members' consistent and reliable administration of the procedure.
6. Documentation of the effectiveness of the procedure and evidence of increased accessibility to instruction are maintained.
7. Administration of the procedure is performed only by designated staff member(s), who should be knowledgeable and skilled in behavior analysis.
8. Incompatible behavior is positively reinforced whenever possible, as a part of any program using aversive stimuli.[3]

Important Note: Never use aversive stimuli as punishment techniques without strictly following all of these guidelines as well as any adopted by school administrators.

SUMMARY

When the teacher feels it necessary to use the techniques of the Rules and Consequences face, she typically is faced with very serious and difficult inappropriate behavior, usually including aspects of aggression or destruction and a general disruption of the ongoing classroom activities. In applying these techniques, the teacher would begin with an assertive command, making quite clear the behavior she wishes to see. If that command does not work, the teacher would begin a behavior analysis process based on data gathering, positive and negative reinforcement, and perhaps various steps in the application of the escalating use of reduction procedures.

Application of behavioral principles requires the teacher to state a target behavior and behavioral objectives, and the target behavior must be observed through a variety of assessment processes (with event recording the method of choice due to ease of implementation). The teacher uses a host of positive reinforcements with children who demonstrate or model proper behavior, catching them acting appropriately. This increases the likelihood of obtaining desired appropriate behavior, while at the same time documenting behavior changes by repeated observations through various methods. If the behavior does not change in the desired direction, the teacher must modify the intervention.

For very destructive behavior that the teacher wishes to stop, various steps involving increased degrees of intrusiveness may be used—but only with much caution and preparation to minimize the potential negative side effects of punishment.

Additionally, the teacher can use shaping to teach new behaviors to children while gradually thinning the use of reinforcers until little or no teacher-delivered reinforcement is needed. The experiences of life itself then become rewarding to the well-adapted child and the child is reinforced naturally.

Test Yourself

Read each of the numbered descriptions in the right column and place in the space before it the letter of the concept word listed in the left column. Answers may be found at the end of this chapter, following the Endnotes.

A. anecdotal reports B. assertive command C. aversive stimulus D. baseline data E. behavior F. broken record G. conditioned aversive stimulus H. conditioned reinforcer I. consequence J. contingency K. deprivation state L. differential reinforcement M. duration recording N. event recording O. extinction P. sensory insult Q. frequency R. functional relationship S. interval recording T. latency recording U. modeling V. negative practice W. negative reinforcement X. overcorrecting Y. pairing Z. permanent product recording a. pinpointing b. positive reinforcement c. primary reinforcer d. prompt e. punishment f. reinforcer g. response-cost h. satiation i. schedules of reinforcement j. secondary reinforcers k. thinning l. time out	____ 1. "Carol, I need your feet to be on the floor. (No response) I need your feet to be on the floor. Feet on the floor!" ____ 2. Lollipops are given to all children when a new student arrives. A new student arrives, and the children cheer. ____ 3. Children are attempting to climb a telephone pole guide wire found on the playground. To stop this, the wire is covered by axle grease. ____ 4. An if-then statement. ____ 5. Date: 2/23/94. Today, Jane cried for 4 minutes when her mother departed. She then stopped, went to the book corner, and turned pages in a book. Later she did two puzzles. ____ 6. Using a stop watch, the teacher timed Sally's actions and found that she sucked her finger for 20 minutes today. ____ 7. Billy hurries to finish his puzzle so he won't have to stay inside. ____ 8. After observation, the teacher decides that she will begin reinforcing Martha for "staying in seat behavior" at lunch time. ____ 9. After saying how to put the blocks away, the teacher now shows the actions desired. ____ 10. Sugarless lollipops are given after everyone has their outside coat on. ____ 11. The children who run in the hall are required to return and walk the hall five times over and over. ____ 12. Suzanne has had a very large dessert. As a primary reinforcer, a snack fails to reinforce her behavior when it is offered. ____ 13. An event recording procedure shows that Carlos was out of his seat 15 times during a 15-minute period. ____ 14. An event recording procedure shows that after her mother departed, it took Melissa 20 minutes to begin to play. ____ 15. Yesterday the teacher awarded a reinforcer once for each five times Brian performed the desired behavior. Today the ratio is 1 to 8, and tomorrow it will be 1 to 14.

Glossary

Anecdotal Reports A descriptive, sequenced written record of behavioral events generally focusing on identified time periods, interaction among individuals, and use of objects and materials. This record is then used primarily to develop a hypothesis regarding the events in the environment that appear to increase, decrease, or maintain behaviors.

Antecedent Stimuli The stimuli or events that precede or set the occasion for a behavior or series of behaviors. There may or may not exist an influencing relationship between these stimuli and the subsequent behaviors.

Assertive Command A command used to communicate to the child the direct behavior that the teacher wants, incorporating the following elements:

1. State the child's name.
2. Gesture, in which the teacher signals through hand movement and/or nodding of her head.
3. Eye contact, whereby the teacher positions herself in front of the child, close enough to ensure that they are looking into each other's eyes.
4. Touching, whereby the teacher touches the child to make him tacitly aware of her presence and her need for his attention.
5. Demand that the child desist the improper behavior.
6. State the consequence, whereby the teacher tells the child what punishing action will occur if the child does not perform the desired appropriate behavior (or continues to perform the inappropriate behavior).

Aversive Stimulus An unpleasant stimulus applied as a consequence to an inappropriate behavior, to decrease the rate of the behavior or the chances of it being repeated.

Baseline Data The early collection of data on an event or behavior that provides a measurement of the behavior's typical occurrence prior to any intervention.

Behavior An action by a person that is both observable and measurable.

Behavioral Objective A statement of the desired change to occur after intervention; includes the child's name, the conditions under which the behavior will be performed, and the criteria (normally quantifiable) for evaluating success.

Broken Record The process by which, after a child fails to act on the teacher's request for a particular behavior, the teacher repeats the command over and over in a controlled manner (as if a "broken record").

Conditioned Aversive Stimulus A stimulus, such as saying "No," that has been paired with an aversive stimulus of pain or discomfort and that has become effective as a form of punishment.

Conditioned Reinforcer A learned reinforcer in which previously neutral stimuli are learned ("conditioned") through pairing with a natural or primary reinforcer.

Consequence An action taken or stimulus delivered immediately following the child's behavior.

Contingency An arrangement (through if-then statements) through which if a behavior is performed then a consequence will follow.

Deprivation State A psychological or physical state (e.g., being hungry for sweets) in which the child lacks a desired reinforcer (e.g., candy).

Differential Reinforcement A process of selectively reinforcing a particular dimension of behavior such as the type of behavior or high or low rates of a behavior. Includes the following:

1. Lowering the rate of misbehavior, in which reinforcement is used to gradually lower the rate of occurrence
2. Omission of the misbehavior, in which the child earns a positive reward for the demonstrated absence of an inappropriate behavior
3. Incompatible behavior or alternative behavior, in which the child is guided and reinforced for actions that make it difficult or impossible for him to perform a misbehavior or that reinforce him to perform other, more appropriate behaviors.

Duration Recording The recording or measurement of the time that passes from the beginning of a behavior or event until its conclusion.

Event Recording An observational recording process whereby the teacher makes tally marks or counts in some other manner to indicate how often a behavior occurs over a predetermined observation period.

Extinction The abrupt cessation or withholding of reinforcement from a previously reinforced behavior resulting in a very low or zero rate of targeted misbehavior.

Frequency The number of times, within a predetermined observation period, that a countable behavior occurs.

Functional Relationship A cause-and-effect relationship between two events.

Interval Recording A observational process in which a large time period (e.g., the school day) is divided into small periods, and the presence or absence of the target behavior within the smaller intervals is marked.

Latency Recording The measurement in minutes or seconds of the time delay between the stimulus or request for the child to perform an action and the start of the actual performance of that task or behavior.

Modeling A demonstration by the teacher or a peer of a behavior or group of behaviors that the teacher wishes the targeted child to imitate.

Negative Practice The forced requirement of a child to repeat an inappropriate behavior over and over until the child tires or becomes satiated and does not choose to repeat the behavior.

Negative Reinforcement A negative event or stimulus that is removed as a consequence of the child's behavior (e.g., if the child does three math problems correctly, he gets to skip the fourth one).

Overcorrection A process requiring the child to repeat an action again and again in order to teach him to do it properly or to eliminate the inappropriate behavior; includes the following:

1. Positive practice overcorrection, in which the child is forced to practice, over and over, a correct behavior he has failed to perform in the past
2. Restitutional overcorrection, in which the child is required to correct the environment he has disrupted and to go a step further to improve the setting beyond how he originally found it.

Pairing The linking of a natural primary reinforcer and a secondary stimulus (e.g., verbal statements or tokens) so that, through association, the secondary reinforcer acquires the same stimulus power as the primary reinforcer.

Permanent Product Recording The scoring or counting of tangible items or effects produced by the behavior of the child.

Pinpointing Specifying an observable and measurable target behavior that the teacher wishes to change.

Positive Reinforcement Any stimulus, following a behavior, that increases the likelihood of the behavior occurring again, whether that behavior is desirable or not.

Primary Reinforcer A stimulus that appeals to the child's natural, unlearned desires, including edible and sensory reinforcers.

Prompt A signal, cue, or sign used by the teacher to assist the child in knowing when or what form of a behavior is correct to do.

Punishment The delivery of an event or stimulus, often physically or psychologically discomforting for the student, after a behavior that results in a decrease in rate or elimination of that behavior.

Reinforcer A stimulus following a behavior that increases the likelihood that the behavior will be repeated and will increase in rate in the future.

Response-Cost The removal of a positive reinforcer following an inappropriate behavior, resulting in a reduction or stopping of that behavior, similar to being fined for a particular act.

Satiation A state whereby the child no longer is in deprivation of a particular stimulus and consequently is no longer motivated to obtain that stimulus.

Schedules of Reinforcement The preestablishment of time between occurrences or number of occurrences necessary for the child to receive reinforcement for an appropriate behavior; includes the following:

1. Fixed-ratio schedule—the awarding of a reinforcer after the child performs the desired behavior a fixed number of times
2. Variable-ratio schedule—the reinforcer is delivered after a varying number of occurrences of appropriate behavior, so the child cannot predict the schedule and maintains the pace of his output steadily or at a high rate
3. Fixed-interval schedule—the awarding of a reinforcer after the child performs the desired behavior and a predetermined time period passes
4. Variable-interval—the reinforcer follows an appropriate behavior but not at fixed intervals, so that the child cannot predict when the reinforcer will come and must continue to repeat the desired behavior

Secondary Reinforcers Stimuli (e.g., verbal statements or tokens) that become reinforcers when paired with primary reinforcers.

Shaping Teaching a child new behaviors by reinforcing small and gradual behaviors that are the successive steps toward acquiring a larger final target behavior.

Social Reinforcers Learned secondary reinforcers that come from the teacher or peers in the form of facial expressions, proximity, contact, privileges, words, and phases.

Terminal Behavior A clearly stated or predetermined behavioral goal.

Thinning Delivering reinforcers less frequently than before while at the same time maintaining the performance of an appropriate behavior or increasing the behavior the child must perform to obtain the same amount of reinforcement required as before.

Time Out Reducing inappropriate behavior by physical removal of the child or objects, so that the child will not be reinforced for his inappropriate behavior; includes the following:

1. Nonseclusionary time out—objects or other reinforcers are denied to the child within the setting, but the child is not removed from that setting
2. Seclusionary time out—the physical removal of the child to an isolated part of the environment after exhibiting an inappropriate behavior so that the setting and those in it are less likely to reinforce the child for those behaviors
3. Exclusionary time out—the removal of the child from the classroom or general area so he will not receive any form of reinforcement or stimulation from that setting, as a result of his inappropriate behavior

Unconditioned Aversive Stimuli A stimulus that gives the child physical pain or discomfort. This is only known by the effect on behavior of that stimulus (i.e., behavior followed by that stimulus is reduced or stimulus is actively avoided) .

Related Readings

Canter, L., & Canter, M. (1976). *Assertive Discipline: A Take-Charge Approach for Today's Educator.* Los Angeles: Lee Canter & Associates.

Alberto, P. A., & Troutman, A. C. (1990). *Applied Behavior Analysis for Teachers* (3rd ed.). New York: Merrill-Macmillan.

Endnotes

1. Canter, L., & Canter, M. (1976). *Assertive Discipline: A Take-Charge Approach for Today's Educator.* Los Angeles: Lee Canter & Associates.
2. Alberto, P. A., & Troutman, A. C. (1990). *Applied Behavior Analysis for Teachers* (3rd ed.). New York: Merrill-Macmillan.
3. From Alberto, P. A., & Troutman, A. C. (1990). *Applied Behavior Analysis for Teachers* (3rd ed., pp. 276–277). New York: Merrill-Macmillan.

Answers to Test Yourself

1F, 2H, 3C, 4J, 5A, 6M, 7W, 8a, 9U, 10c or b, 11X, 12h, 13Q, 14T, 15k

SECTION II

Helping Aggressive and Passive Young Children

The earlier chapters, which presented The Three Faces Of Discipline, stated the position that the teacher can consciously be aware of and design the actions taken toward a "misbehaved" child. Those actions can be categorized into three schools of thought, or faces, along a power continuum from minimum use of power (Relationship-Listening), through increased power (Confronting-Contracting), and then finally to maximum use of power by the teacher (Rules and Consequences).

The Relationship-Listening face accepts the view that the misbehaving child is rational and may become more purposeful and cooperative through a supportive, nonjudgmental technique requiring the child to "talk out" his problems. The Confronting-Contracting face presents a clear use of power and demands the use of verbal techniques by the teacher to stop the misbehavior and then get the child to become cognitively aware of his action and how it mis-serves him socially. The child is permitted nearly total control in choosing how he or she will change, but the teacher does engineer ways to help the child gain social skills. The Rules and Consequences face comes into play when the child is "flooded" and has assumed a defensive stance. Even with the teacher's verbal questioning and mediation, the child cannot accurately view his own behavior, nor does he have the ability to change his actions of his own free will. The use of Rules and Consequences techniques can be effective to deal with a child who has a life-stance position toward others and toward life itself as being revengeful (physically and verbally aggressive) or as a sense of helplessness (passive).

Having read all the previous chapters, we as teachers and professionals are now familiar with most of the techniques for solving discipline problems. The chapters in Section II will now apply these methods and add new constructs related to play facilitation to permit the teacher to be an active agent in helping the child move out of such a life-stance position of aggression or passivity and become a more developmentally effective person.

Chapter 5 describes the levels of crisis through which a child will progress during incidents of assault and violence. Discussion will also focus on how to restrain a child nonaggressively during displays of violence and raw aggression, and how to reassure the child's classmates after they witness violent behavior. Chapter 6 presents a theoretical framework for viewing aggressive and passive children that can be used to justify various techniques for intervening with such children. Chapter 7 introduces a step-by-step intervention process for helping these problem children through developmental play techniques.

5

Restraining the Violent Child

Revengeful, assaultive, and violent children are simply "reflex" beings, their negative behavior automatically triggered by external stimuli or situations and by internal fears. To help such children requires strong intrusion and controlling techniques that demand the teacher first to be assertive and then to plan a systematic shaping (behavioral) process to help the children gain self-control and a reawakening sense of trust. In order to keep a violent child and others safe from the child's assaultive and aggressive actions, the teachers may need to nonaggressively restrain the child. Let's look at an example of such a child and the teacher's response with the use of Rules and Consequences techniques.

LEVEL OF CRISIS

Crisis Level 1: Potential Crisis[1]

Jimmy stands before the paint easel. Using a large, thick paintbrush, he dips the end into the paint pot. Soon the brush reappears, dripping with a large glob of paint. As a peer walks by, Jimmy turns and sticks out the brush as if it is a sword and attempts to "stab" his schoolmate. The peer screams and runs off, much to the delight of Jimmy. A second child unknowingly wanders by and Jimmy positions himself for a second attack.

Teacher: *"Jimmy (name), stop!" (The teacher points to Jimmy's brush and then to the paint pot [gesture], then moves face-to-face [eye contact]. "Put the brush in the paint and go to the block room and find something to do there."*
Jimmy: (Stands, still holding the brush tightly with both hands, glares directly at the teacher, and then looks down at the floor.)

Teacher: *"Jimmy (name), stop!" (The teacher points to Jimmy's brush and then to the paint pot [gesture], then moves face-to-face [eye contact] and places her hand gently on his shoulder [touch]. "Put the brush in the paint and go to the block room and find something to do there" (broken record).*

Crisis Level 2: Developing Crisis—Ventilation and Defiance

Jimmy: *(screams) "You bitch! You bitch! Keep your bitch hands off me! Keep your bitch hands off me! No, let me go—don't touch me!"*

Teacher: *(lets 45 seconds pass) "Jimmy (name), stop! Put the brush in the paint pot! (broken record) If you cannot, then I will need to take the brush from you" (preparatory). (The teacher moves toward Jimmy.)*

Crisis Level 3: Imminent Crisis (Assault)

Jimmy turns and with both hands—including the one still holding the brush—forcefully pushes the teacher at waist level, causing a large green streak of paint on her skirt and knocking her back three full steps. The teacher quickly catches her balance.

Teacher: *"Jimmy (name), stop. Put the brush in the paint and go to block room" (broken record).*

Jimmy: *"No—let me go!" (Jimmy screams at full volume and again attempts to push the teacher with both hands; the teacher grasps both his arms at the wrist to prevent him. He drops the paintbrush and attempts to bite the teacher's right hand, which is holding his left wrist. To prevent this, the teacher pulls both of Jimmy's arms above his head and moves her hands away from his mouth. He now lashes out with his right leg in three quick kicking motions, one of which strikes the teacher squarely on the shin, causing her definite discomfort.)*[2]

Teacher: *(Holding both of Jimmy's wrists in one of her hands, she uses the other to pull off his shoes. He kicks barefooted, again making contact with the teacher's shin, but his expression shows that the contact has hurt his toe. Seeing that a small side room is empty, the teacher visually signals a co-worker that she is departing, and pulls Jimmy into the room and closes the door.) "Jimmy, I am not going to hurt you, and I am not going to let you hurt me. You are safe—I will keep you safe, I will not hurt you!" (seclusionary time out).*

The teacher now releases Jimmy to see if he will quiet down; instead, he runs to the door to pull it open and run out. The teacher physically prevents this by holding the door. He kicks the door, to his discomfort, and runs his arm across the block shelf, knocking most the blocks to the floor with a great crashing noise. He now moves to the window and violently strikes it with a fist; it cracks, but the window pane stays intact. This action carries the real potential for Jimmy to injure himself. Before a second blow lands, the teacher again grasps his wrists and pulls and partially carries him to a chair, where she seats herself before an upright mirror. The teacher is now forced to use nonaggressive restraining techniques for Jimmy's own safety.

Being seated and located behind the child, the teacher puts her arms around Jimmy, grasping his right wrist with her left hand and his left wrist with her right hand, and pulling toward her in a way that causes Jimmy's arms to cross over the front of his body (see Drawing 1). The teacher moves her body sideways to the child, at a 45-degree angle, while seated on a small chair in front of an upright mirror. This places the child's back or hip on the teacher's right thigh, and she then pull his arms back toward her and lightly lifts up. This causes the child's heels to come slightly off the floor, forcing him to stand on his tip-toes with his weight supported by her thigh, thus preventing him from kicking, biting, or struggling free from her.

DRAWING 1 Single Basket Technique Restraint

While holding Jimmy in the basket restraining hold,[3] *the teacher parallels her physical action with accompanying verbal explanation and reassurance to Jimmy.*

Teacher: *(whispering) "Jimmy, I am not going to hurt you, and I am not going to let you hurt me. You are safe—I will keep you safe, I will not hurt you!" (broken record). I am the teacher, I keep children safe; I will not hurt you! Jimmy, I am holding you with my hands to keep you safe. These hands will not hurt you. See... see... see in the mirror? You can see in the mirror that I am not hurting you; you are safe. See my hands? They are holding you but they are not hurting you (broken record). (Jimmy attempts to struggle free but the teacher holds him firmly.) See in the mirror? You can see in the mirror that I am not hurting you; you are safe. See my hands? They are holding you but they are not hurting you (broken record). You need to be here on my lap until you can relax. I am holding you but I am not hurting you."*

Jimmy attempts to bite the teacher again, but she moves to prevent this; he screams a list of profanities at the teacher. The teacher continues to speak to him in a whisper.

Teacher: *(whispering) "I am not going to let you hurt me, and I am not going to hurt you. See in the mirror? You can see me and you can see yourself—I am not hurting you. These are helping hands that do not hurt children! You are safe; I am going to keep you safe. I am the teacher. I am the boss and I can keep children safe. I am going to keep you safe!" (Jimmy now begins to cry and slowly stops struggling.)*

Crisis Level 4: Reestablishing Equilibrium

Teacher: *(Points to Jimmy's image in the mirror) "Jimmy, that is you, and I can see by your face that you are very angry. But look, here are my hands and they are holding you to keep you safe. I will not hurt you—you are safe now." (Jimmy's body goes limp in the teacher's lap. The teacher permits Jimmy to cuddle in her lap, and she reaches to the shelf to retrieve a children's book, which she reads to him in a soft gentle voice.)*

We have just witnessed one of the most demanding teacher-child interactions—one that involves a clear assault on the teacher and a danger to the child. As teachers dealing with such a child, our hearts are pounding and the adrenaline is pushing through our bodies, pushing us to a state of hyper-alertness and creating a defensive stance for our own protection and secondarily for the child's safety. Out of our own understandable fright, we ourselves may emotionally flood, thus causing ourselves real difficulty in thinking correctly and acting constructively as these sudden and quick actions are unfolding.

Experts who have studied such violent actions by children recognize a general level-by-level progression in the child's behavior and actions. If we as teachers understand these levels of crisis progression, when the sudden developments do occur, as above, they can be better understood and thus less frightening. Previous *thought rehearsal* will permit us to respond constructively.

There are generally four levels of crisis development leading to possible violent acts by the child: Level 1: Potential Crisis; Level 2: Developing Crisis (ventilation and defiance); Level 3: Imminent Crisis—Assault/Revengeful; and Level 4: Reestablishing Equilibrium. (These levels parallel the passive-aggressive construct explained in Chapter 6 and in Figure 6–1.)[4]

LEVEL 1: POTENTIAL CRISIS

In Level 1: Potential Crisis, the child, as a result of some source of frustration, appears as if he is a tightly wound spring ready to snap; inner emotional energy and tension are mounting. His hands may be clenched into a fist with white knuckles, and he may drop his eyes or glare intently, his gaze either focusing sharply on a peer or teacher or, instead, alternately focusing on his subject and then darting away. He may become physically restrictive, pulling inside of himself and turning away, or actively pacing like a caged cat and exhibiting nervous ticks. His actions clearly attract the attention of peers and observant adults. Children will ask, "Why is Jimmy acting funny?" whereas adults will say, "It looks like Jimmy is going to have one of his bad mornings."

If caught quickly, the child is still rational enough to respond to the teacher's use of language. The goal is to take this built-up internal energy and have the child ventilate it externally in representational form in two ways: through the use of language (talk it out) or through the use of symbolic play (play it out).

"Talk It Out" (Verbal)

If possible, we as teachers bring into use all the Relationship-Listening techniques we have learned. We use *door openers:* "Jimmy, I can see that you are very unhappy this morning. Tell me what is bothering you." If the child does speak, we use *acknowledgments* and *active listening,* and encourage the child to externalize

FIGURE 5–1 Levels of Crisis, Child Behavior, and Teacher Techniques

Crisis Levels	Child Behavior Characteristics	Teacher Goals and Techniques
#1: Potential Crisis (Attention Getting)	As a result of some frustration, the child appears as if he is a tightly wound spring ready to snap. His hands may be clenched into a fist with white knuckles, and he may drop his eyes or glare intently, his gaze either focusing sharply on a peer or teacher or, instead, alternately focusing on his subject and then darting away. He may become physically restrictive, pulling inside of himself and turning away, or become active, pacing like a caged cat and exhibiting nervous ticks. His actions clearly attract the *attention* of peers and observant adults.	If caught quickly, the child is still rational enough to respond to the teacher's language. Have the child ventilate representationally through language (talk it out) or redirect the child to symbolic play (play it out). Redirect the child away from fluid materials and social interaction, giving him his "personal space." If possible, make few or no demands. With the use of teacher's language, employ Relationship-Listening techniques. With symbolic play, channel the child's energy and aggression from the body to the toy, from the toy to play, and from play to work. Provide "lap time" if possible.
#2: Developing Crisis (Ventilation and Defiance)	In order to maintain his *power* over a teacher or peer, the child now screams or shouts verbal aggression in the form of swearing, name calling, and similar verbal outbursts that appear as a release or ventilation of stored-up tension. This may quickly escalate to threats against peers and the teacher and/or definite defiance of the teacher.	The teacher positions herself in an alert *supportive stance* and permits the child's ventilation through verbal aggression. If the verbal aggression turns to defiance, the teacher moves to provide an *assertive command* (assuring the student of potential consequences) and promises of safety. Give the child time and space to ventilate, and do not physically intervene if possible.
#3: Imminent Crisis (Assault/Revengeful)	The child now becomes totally *revengeful* and nonrational, and cannot control his own actions. He physically strikes out in a direct *assault* toward peer or teacher by choking, biting, hitting, or throwing.	In response to the assault, the teacher defends herself with restraining techniques (head down, basket hold) and accompanies her physical actions with an assertive command, sending two messages: an order to desist action in a way the teacher desires, and verbal reassurance through a promise of safety and nonaggression toward the child. Restrain the child in front of a mirror if possible.
#4: Reestablishing Equilibrium	After the violent action, the child is deflated and becomes passive with little energy. He has feelings of guilt and feels *helpless* as to how others might respond to him.	Intervene by mirroring both body referencing and motor imitations if the child retreats too deeply into passivity (e.g., sleep) or begins physically self-abusive activities. Help by cognitively recapitulating the happenings for the child, first by having him verbally talk about it with the teacher using Relationship-Listening techniques, and then, if unsuccessful, advancing to Confronting-Contracting techniques.

or ventilate these strong pent-up feelings through language and words, keeping in mind that some of these words may be aggressive and hostile. If this "talking it out" is effective and we begin to hear the child tell us the root cause of his heightened emotional condition ("Andy won't let me play with him!"), we might use the Six Steps to Problem Solving to help him resolve his problem or dilemma.

Here is a repeat of the teacher-child example:

Teacher: *(nondirective statements) "Jimmy, paints can be scary and sometimes hard to control. That is fun and exciting for you, but other children are frightened by the paintbrush."*

Jimmy "El Zorro": *"I don't like him!" (meaning the peer, Walter, who just passed by and was the target of Jimmy's latest attempt to stab with the paintbrush).*

Teacher: *"You're angry with Walter?" (active listening)*

Jimmy: *"He is mean!"*

Teacher: *"Walter has been mean to you?"*

Jimmy: *"Yes, I am his best friend, and he let Robert sit beside him at snack!"*

Teacher: *"You're angry because you were not able to sit by your friend" (active listening).*

Jimmy: *"Yes, could I sit beside Walter?"*

The teacher's efforts to determine the cause of Jimmy's sword play have exposed a deeper problem that Jimmy is facing, and she can begin dealing with it from a new perspective.

The Six Steps to Problem Solving The example continues:

Teacher: *"Ah, you have a problem, and that problem is, 'How can you get to sit beside Walter at lunch?' (Step 1: Defining the Problem) Let's think together of ways that you might solve this problem. What are your ideas?" (Step 2: Generating Possible Solutions)*

Jimmy: *"I could get to the table first."*

Teacher: *"That may work, but let's think of a lot of other ways, too."*

Jimmy: *"I could ask Walter to sit by me. But Robert always gets there first. I could sit at the little table (which has only two seats) and ask Walter to sit with me. But Robert would come and push me out of my seat. I could push him back or tell the teacher on him!"*

Teacher: *"Robert wants to eat with Walter, too." (active listening)*

Jimmy: *"Yes, could he eat at the little table? We could have three chairs, and be best friends."*

Teacher: *"Which one of your ideas is best?" (Step 3: Evaluating the Solutions)*

Jimmy: *"Having three chairs."*

Teacher: *"Is that what you will do at lunchtime today?" (Step 4: Deciding Which Solution Is Best)*

Jimmy: *"Yes."*

The next day, the teacher watches as Jimmy adds a third chair to the table and invites both Walter and Robert to eat with him. (Step 5: Implementing the Solution) After lunch, the teacher talks to Jimmy.

Teacher: *"Was your solution to your problem a good one?" (Step 6: Evaluation the Solution)*

Jimmy: *"Yes, it was* great, *and I figured it out all by myself!"*

With quick and early intervention, the teacher has headed off an aggressive situation with this child by having him talk it out through language, with the teacher using Relationship-Listening techniques.

If the root of the child's stress is beyond the immediate and manageable confines of the classroom setting, such as having been paddled by daddy at breakfast that morning, we would not be able to turn to the Six Steps to Problem Solving, but would instead continue with active listening or move to the second method of ventilation through symbolic play (play it out).

"Play It Out" (Motoric to Symbolic)

With the use of the play materials, we may redirect and encourage the child to vent motorically (body) stored-up excessive internal energies, which later will lead to symbolic play. This follows a line of development from the body to the toy, from the toy to play, from play to work.

Body to Toy[5] The child in Level 1: Potential Crisis, actively pacing like a caged cat, is directed to a free space where others will not interfere with his actions. "Jimmy, I see this morning that you are going around and around—use this toy car (wheeled toy)[6] and make it go around and around." We barrier or section off this zone, possibly by movable partitions or chairs, to give Jimmy private space, and encourage him to externalize his pent-up energies into "car pushing"—from the body to the toy. This car pushing will be initially aggressive, with the car smashing into things. The barrier of private space has clearly defined a zone where the aggression is acceptable. Also, a child in Level 1: Potential Crisis becomes overly sensitive when others, peer or teacher, move into or invade space around him within a zone of three to six feet. We prevent classmates from going into this space because the flooded child will feel threatened by the spatial approach of others and may assault the unsuspecting peer.

This aggressive car play is exactly what we want because it gives a motoric outlet to Jimmy's internal emotional energy, and the child might play aggressively with the car for minutes, hours, or even days. The teacher continues to monitor and maintains modality cueing with the child, indicating nonverbally to him that she approves of this aggressive play. If the child takes his aggressive car play outside of the defined area preestablished for him by the teacher, she redirects him back to the defined space; if he again fails to stay within this space, the teacher is now required to stay in the space with him. The child may *not* use the toy, such as the car, to take aggressive action against others but must play in the make-believe miniature world of toys (microsymbolic play).

Attempt to move the child who is a biter from biting (from body) to an alligator puppet (to toy), a miniature lion or tiger, or some similar toy that has an open mouth and teeth. Encourage him to play motorically, performing the act of biting within the miniature world of toys (micro) but not with peers (see Figure 5–2).

Spitting is considered as an aggression or assault with the mouth (from body), and the same aggressive mouth-and-teeth animals (to toy) and channeling should be used as with the biting child. Often, the spitter is frightened by fluid materials, so fluids with less degree of freedom such as clay and modeling dough will be effective with them.

A behavioral technique called *satiation* may also be used. Take the spitting child to the toilet and, using a nonbreakable quart container, encourage the child to take a large mouthful of drinking water and spit it into the toilet. This should be done again and again until the child tires of spitting. Repeat this satiation technique each time spitting occurs. (*Note*: This technique will work well with attention-getting and power-motivated children who use spitting, but the revengeful and crisis-assault potential child that is described here will not comply and may assault the adult when such a request is made. Therefore, *do not* make a satiation demand on a violent child.)

For the child who hits and kicks (from body), channel his energy into motoric action of carpentry construction (to toy) play (pounding a nail into an old log, sawing discarded wood pieces), or more controlled fluid construction (pounding clay or modeling dough).

Indeed, these techniques actually encourage the child to bite, hit, and be outwardly aggressive—but that energy and action is channeled through a socially acceptable outlet as motoric play, and it is confined in the miniature world (micro) and in a clearly defined and sectioned-off space where this play aggression may occur. Thus, the aggression is channeled.

Lap Time There are certain times when the teacher may offer her lap to the child for purposes of cuddling. This is especially useful if the child is caught at the early point of flooding or after the one-to-one intervention techniques outlined in Chapter 8 begin to be effective.

> *Jimmy has awoken at 6:00 A.M. Confusion reigns in the home of his large family; he fought with his sister in the car on the way to school this morning and has been spanked by his mother. He enters school (or the center) "wired,"*

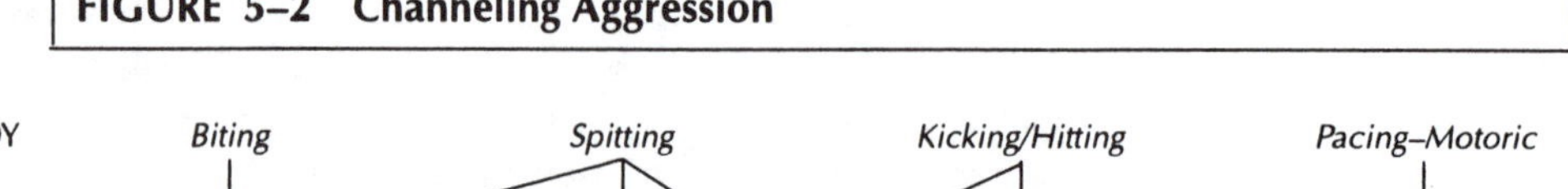

FIGURE 5–2 Channeling Aggression

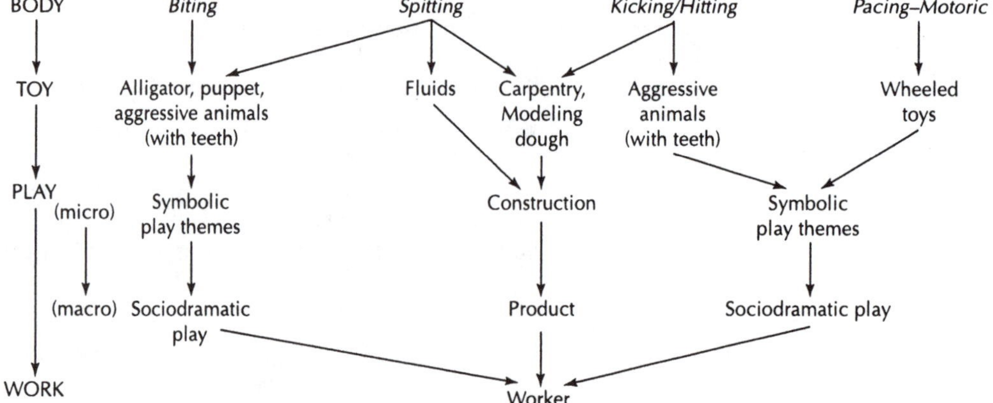

definitely within the realm of Level 1: Potential Crisis. The teacher offers, "Jimmy, I can see by your face this morning that you could use some lap time; come sit here on my lap and let me read you your favorite book."

Lap time or cuddling permits the child to positively regress into himself and relax, thus getting out of this tense hyper-alert defensive frame of mind. However, many children cannot be touched while in Level 1: Potential Crisis and will assault the teacher if she approaches and invades their private space. With such children, the teacher should extend open arms to the child and invite him to come be cuddled; if instead the teacher goes to the child, he may see it as a potentially hostile or aggressive approach and react negatively.

Toy to Play The teacher closely watches a child's aggression or similar actions by other children who are biting and hitting. Micro toys (e.g., wheeled toy, alligator or tiger puppet, modeling clay) are used first and then the Teacher Behavior Continuum is employed to channel the aggressive toy action into real symbolic play—toy to play.

The Teacher Behavior Continuum

- Modality Cueing. By looking on approvingly, we signal that the child is encouraged to play aggressively with the toys and materials, but within the established space. We may accompany the child's strong emotional ventilation by using *non-directive statements.*
- Nondirective Statements. "Jimmy, I see that your car (alligator puppet, tiger-aggressive animal, modeling dough, or hammering) is very angry and it crashes (bites, is squashed, hits) into everything" (active listening). This verbal encoding of the child's nonverbal actions applies emotional words to the child's actions with toys and materials, and the teacher may repetitively mirror the child's motor actions and ventilation with active listening for minutes, days, or weeks. Judging by the amount of energy expended, ventilated, or expelled, we move to a more intrusive intervention as we use questions and attempt to have the child move to play.
- Questions. "Jimmy, I see you going around and around. Where is the road for your car? (The teacher pushes unit blocks toward the child.) Where is a garage for your car? Where is the gas station for your car to get gas?" Questions such as these attempt to have the child mentally reflect on more positive play and dramatic themes as he plays with the vehicle. For the alligator puppet play or aggressive animal play, the teacher may ask, "Could your alligator (tiger) keep the people safe and be a mommy or daddy to the other toys?" For the pounding of carpentry or using fluids such as clay, the question might be, "Could you make something with your hammer and nails (clay, etc.)?" When the child responds by stopping the aggressive use of the toys and materials and appears interested, we may give him some "wait time" to see if he can produce symbolic play on his own. If it becomes apparent that he cannot play but is interested in our suggestion, we move to directive statements.
- Directive Statements. "Jimmy, pick up the blocks and move them to create a road for your car! Use these small blocks to make a gas station. Make a story happen with your toys!" (For the carpentry, "Make an airplane," or for clay, "Make an egg for a bird's nest" or similar object.) If there still is a lack of direction and initiative but an apparent interest, we now move to *physical intervention.*

- Physical Intervention. By doing physical intervention, we actually take the toys and model the play activity for the child. "Jimmy, watch what I am doing. I am putting these long blocks in line to create a road and we can run the car down the road like this (teacher demonstrates). Now, we will use these little blocks to make a house for the car to live in—a garage for the car." The teacher physically handles and moves the objects about, performing the play that she is verbally describing.

The teacher now begins to retreat down the power levels of the Teacher Behavior Continuum. "Jimmy, you play what I played" (directive statement). What else can you do with the toys? (questions). Oh, I see, you are pretending to fill the car with gas" (nondirective statements). Finally, with the child engaged in successful play, the teacher retreats to visually looking as she modality cues her approval of the child's play actions.

Further guidelines to follow while the child is partially flooded and in the Level 1: Potential Crisis stage are: (1) redirect the child *away from* highly fluid materials, such as sand (especially in large sand boxes), water play, and painting (Chapter 8 includes techniques for introducing these more expressive fluids to the difficult children); and (2) prevent or limit social interaction with others, giving the child his "private space." With symbolic play, the child's energy and aggression are channeled from the body to the toy, from the toy to play, and from play to work.

If we are *unsuccessful* in resolving the problem in Level 1: Potential Crisis because we caught it too late or because the intensity of the child's emotional flooding was excessive, most likely the child will regress to a more severe Level 2: Developing Crisis, with its two substages of ventilation and defiance.

LEVEL 2: DEVELOPING CRISIS—VENTILATION AND DEFIANCE

In order to maintain his power over a teacher or peer, the child enters Level 2: Developing Crisis. He uses ventilation, screaming or shouting verbal aggression in the form of swearing, name calling, and similar verbal outbursts, which appear as a release or ventilation of stored-up tension. This verbal aggression, no matter how it frightens the teacher and classmates, is a good release or ventilation. We as teachers *do nothing*. We *do not* challenge his display of power as the child screams, shouts, and swears, because after many minutes of doing so the child will have no anger energies left for a more physical assault. So the longer the child ventilates by being verbally aggressive, the better—because he is simply wearing himself out and dispersing his stored-up tension. Do not be frightened by the verbal aggression but do be cautious. This verbal aggression may quickly escalate into threats to peers and teachers and/or definite defiance toward the teacher.

> *Jimmy:* (screams) "You bitch! You bitch! Keep your bitch hands off me! Keep your bitch hands off me! No, let me go—don't touch me!" (ventilation)
>
> *Jimmy:* "No, my brush! I am going to kill you!" (defiance)

In this Level 2: Developing Crisis situation, the child is not rational, but a defensive reflex has set in and he is not capable of controlling his own behavior. While in this state of hypertension, the child will have much difficulty in hearing our words, but will depend visually and auditorily in assessing our nonverbal actions for any hint of action toward him, which he will interpret as hostile and aggressive. Once the defiance and threats are heard, the teacher should signal to a fellow adult or send another child to get the assistant teacher, the teacher across the hall, or the principal—in short, *get help*. This second adult is helpful both in restraining the assaulting child and as a later witness to any actions that may occur in the event of any administrative evaluation.

Also, the teacher should take actions to remove onlookers by either having the other children moved to another room, sectioning the area off from the view of other children, or, if possible, moving the child to another room. Witnessing an outburst by the revengeful, flooded child can be very frightening for classmates, and witnessing our restraining actions on the assaulting child can appear to young children as if we are hurting this child. "Mrs. Anderson was hurting Jimmy!" Later in this chapter will be a description of how to explain the assaulting child's behavior and our restraining actions to onlooking children through a problem-solving class meeting.

When the Level 2: Developing Crisis event does occur, we as teachers have two ways of responding: assertive demand with its parallel assertive stance, and supportive demand with its parallel supportive stance.

Assertive and Supportive Demands

The *assertive demand* and stance should be used with children whose behavior is a problem because of their need for attention or to maintain power over the teacher or other children. The *supportive demand* and stance are used with flooded, revengeful children who may pose a danger to themselves or others or to objects. Both the assertive and supportive commands are made up of two parts: a verbal directive statement and a follow-up preparatory command if the child does not desist. In addition, one more important verbal statement is said repetitively as a broken record: a promise of safety: "Jimmy, I am not going to hurt you, and I am not going to let you hurt me. You are safe—I will keep you safe. I will not hurt you and I will not let others hurt you. I want to help you be safe!"

The nonverbal actions that are a part of the assertive and supportive stances differ dramatically, but the manner in which we deliver our verbal commands should have certain common characteristics. When issuing an assertive or supportive command, use a well-modulated voice (controlled tone, volume, and cadence)—neither too fast nor slow, neither too loud nor soft. In the most normal voice possible, the teacher tells the child the motor actions or behaviors that she wants performed. Remember: Do not tell the child what *not* to do.

Assertive demand can be seen as: "Jimmy (name), stop! (points to Jimmy) Put the brush in the paint pot. (gesture) (moves face to face [eye contact]) Put the brush in the paint pot and go to the block room and find something to do there" (broken record). The parallel nonverbal behavior, or stance, of the teacher to accompany the assertive verbal command is to (1) say the child's name, (2) gesture with hands and fingers, (3) move squarely in front of the child and make fixed eye contact, and (4) touch the child. When accompanying the verbal assertive demand, these actions are most confrontational. By these actions, the teacher challenges the child's power directly (see Figure 5–3).

This assertive demand, with its accompanying stance, may be used effectively with the child who is motivated by attention getting and power seeking, and who may be having an uncontrollable moment. However, this approach will be disastrous with the revengeful child who is flooded and has taken this general life-stance position toward his world. *Do not* use an assertive demand with a flooded, revengeful child at Level 2: Developing Crisis. The challenge will set him off and he will become assaultive, especially if his personal space is violated. The teacher technique to use with a child at this level of crisis is the supportive

FIGURE 5–3 Rules and Consequence Face

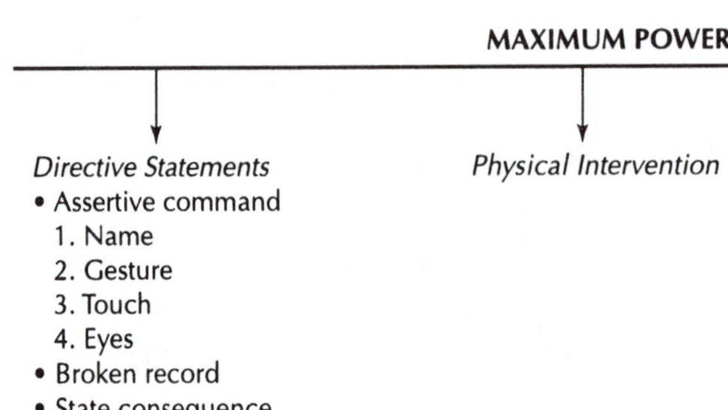

demand, with the verbal techniques described previously, and its accompanying stance. The nonverbal behavior, or stance, used for the supportive demand includes the following:

1. The teacher stands still and does not get closer than three feet from the child, nor does the teacher touch the child, for this would be considered an invasion of his private space, or "bubble." All people have a circle of space around them, a hypothetical "bubble," and they feel unsafe if others close into this space. When others do close into this space, it is typically for purposes of expressing intimate affection (cuddling) or for purposes of aggression. The hyper-alert Level 2: Developing Crisis child will clearly interpret closing space as an aggressive act, which will arouse his aggressive instincts. This is why the teacher beckons the child in Level 1: Potential Crisis to come cuddle rather than approaches the child to cuddle.

2. The teacher turns her body at an angle, with her preferred foot pointed toward the child (see Drawing 2) and the other foot at a 45-degree angle. The teacher should not put herself squared shoulder-to-shoulder with the child. This angled stance toward the flooded child is interpreted as nonhostile, whereas a squared shoulder is a position one would choose for confrontation and fighting. The foot pointed toward the child may be raised to deflect or block the kicking action of a child's foot. The other, angled foot can be used for temporary balance; a stance with parallel feet leaves the teacher flat-footed and prone to being knocked off balance by any minor assault.

3. Eye contact by the teacher should not be fixed or glaring.

4. The teacher should place her hands behind her back but be ready to use them to block an assault (she should not gesture or make any threatening moves with the hands, such as pointing). If assault appears imminent, the teacher should hold both hands open, one at stomach level and the other in front of her chin, with the palms open and showing their flat face to the child. The teacher also does not put her hands on her hips, clench her fist, or point.

While employing the supportive stance, the teacher states a supportive verbal command and repeats it two or three times (broken record), attempting to have the child hear her. If the teacher does not get a change in the child's behavior, she clearly states a preparatory directive statement for possible consequences followed by a promise of safety: "Jimmy, lower your voice, put the brush in the paint pot, and go to the block room (supportive command;

DRAWING 2 Supportive Stance

teacher is also in a supportive stance). Lower your voice, put the brush in the paint pot, and go to the block room (broken record). If you do not, I will need to (teacher chooses one): call your mother and father and tell them of your behavior/have you go to the time-out chair/keep you from going out to the playground with us today/say you will not be permitted to use the paints again. Jimmy, I am not going to hurt you, and I am not going to let you hurt me. You are safe—I will keep you safe. I will not hurt you and I will not let others hurt you. I want to help you be safe!"

The stand-off between the flooded Level 2: Developing Crisis child and the teacher's supportive demand and stance should not be rushed. Do not be in a hurry; what we are trying to do is prevent an assault by the child. We may permit many minutes to go by in the hope that the child will desist, back down, and comply. If he does not and instead regresses further, the next action is likely to be physical flooding and an assault.

LEVEL 3: IMMINENT CRISIS (ASSAULT/REVENGEFUL)

The child now becomes totally revengeful and nonrational, and cannot control his own actions. He physically strikes out in a direct assault against a peer or teacher by choking, biting, kicking, grabbing, hitting or throwing. In response to the assault, the teacher should defend herself with restraining techniques (described below), using the help of a second adult if one is nearby. The teacher should accompany her physical actions with an assertive command, sending two messages: a directive to desist the unwanted action and a promise of safety and nonaggression toward the child. Perform the restraint in front of a mirror if possible.

Assault by Choking [7]

When a child assaults by a front choking—placing his hands around the teacher's throat and squeezing—the teacher responds by standing erect, thrusting both arms upright above her head, stepping back one step to put the child off balance, and turning suddenly to the right or left so the child's hands will be pulled. The teacher should not try to grab the child's hands and pull them off her throat; this will simply be inefficient or ineffective, and the child might dig his fingernails into her throat (see Drawings 3 and 4).

Assault by Biting

If the child has caught the teacher off guard and has sunk his teeth into her (most likely an arm), she can get herself free from the biting hold by putting the edge of a flat free hand under the child's nose and against his upper lip and quickly vibrating her hand up and down with sufficient force to free herself without injuring the child. The teacher should not pull away from the bite but lean into it, as her pulling can cause more damage than the bite itself. If the child has turned in such a manner that the teacher cannot immediately get to his lip-nose area, she should take the fingertips of her flat free hand and push it firmly into his cheek, finding the teeth between upper and lower jaw and again vibrating her hand in an up-and-down motion to free herself (see Drawing 5).

DRAWING 3 Front Choke Release

DRAWING 4 Back Choke Release

DRAWING 5 Bite Release

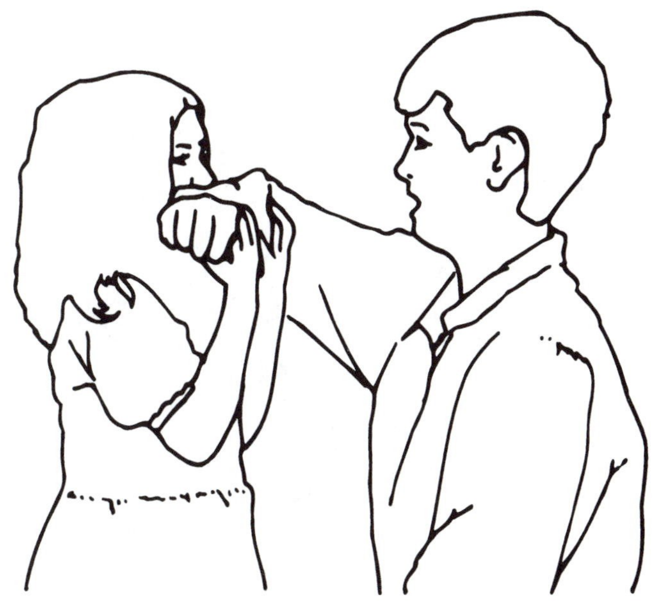

Assault by Kicking

From a supportive stance with her feet at a 45-degree angle, the teacher is able to lift the foot pointing toward the child while balancing on the other foot. While holding up her foot as a barrier, she attempts to block the kick with the back of her foot or shoe. If the teacher has a strength advantage over the child, she can remove his shoes and he will desist or else feel the natural consequences of his action. If this kicking continues, a restraining hold might be required (see Drawing 6).

Assault by Grabbing

The assault by grabbing will usually be the child doing a one- or two-handed grab of either the teacher's arms or hair.

One- and Two-Arm Grabbing Release When the child uses either one or two hands to grab the teacher's arm, there is a weak link in the grab between the child's thumb and forefinger. The teacher should simply take her free hand, lock the fingers of her two hands, and pull in the direction that the child's thumb is pointing, normally up (see Drawings 7 and 8).

One- and Two-Hand Hair-Pulling Release If the child grabs the teacher's hair, either with one hand or two, she should clasp his hand and push it into or against her head, while at the same time turning toward the student and bending her upper body down in a 45-degree angle. The child's wrist is bent backwards,

DRAWING 6 Kick Block

DRAWING 7 One-Hand Wrist Grab Release

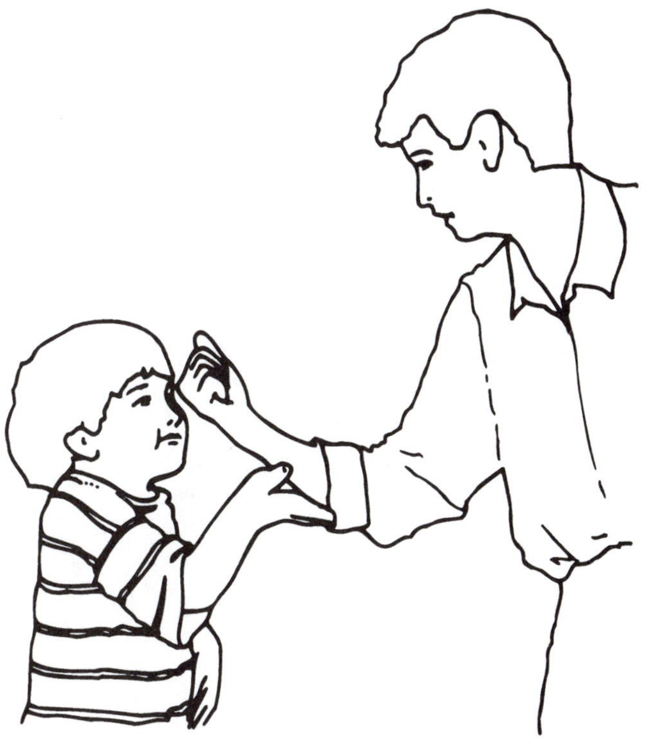

DRAWING 8 Two-Hand Wrist Grab Release

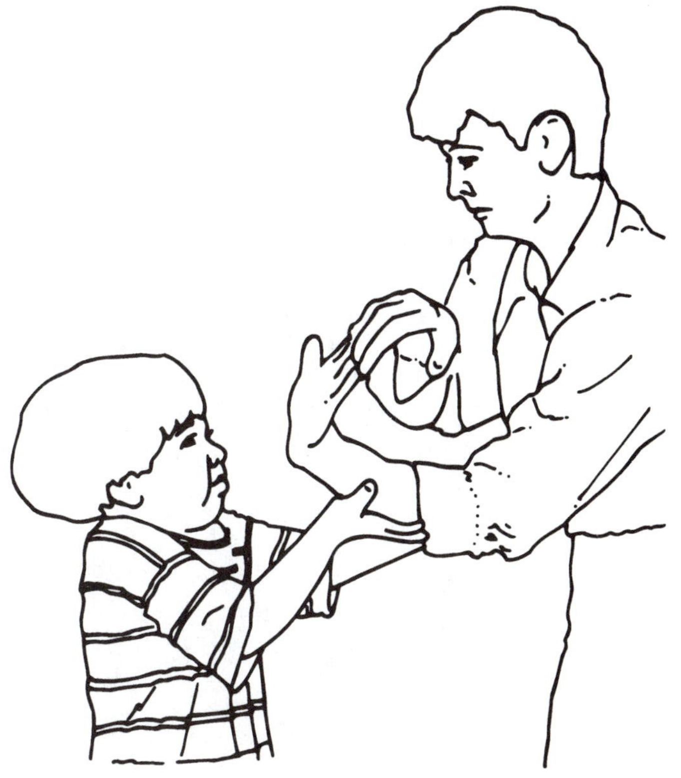

causing a loss of strength in his hands and enabling the teacher to break free. The teacher then physically moves away (see Drawings 9 and 10).

DRAWING 9 Hair Pull Release

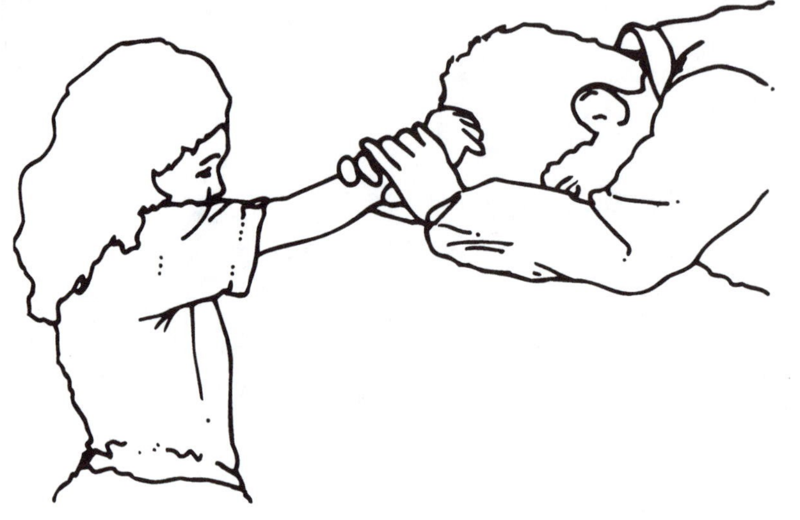

DRAWING 10 Two-Hand Hair Pull Release

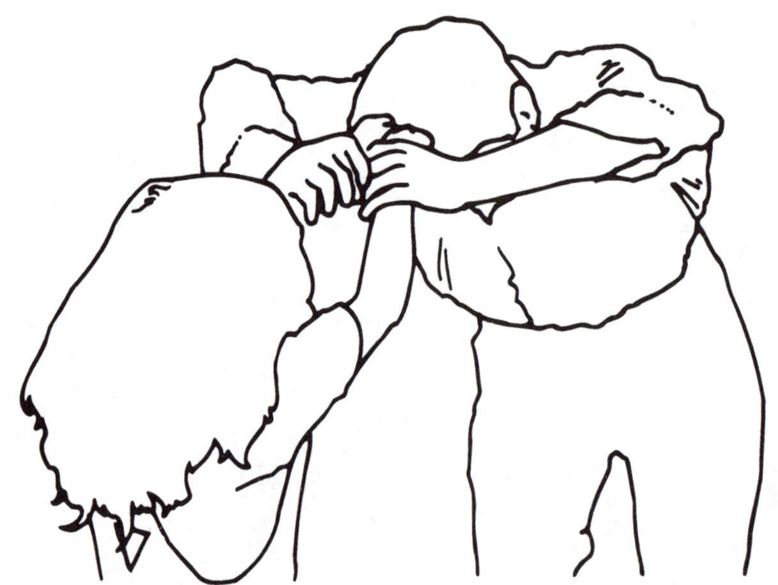

Assault by Hitting and Throwing

With hitting and throwing, the teacher has two ways of handling an object moving toward her with the potential to do bodily harm. She can either move out of its path and dodge or block and deflect the object. If there is time and the child is strong enough to do serious harm, the teacher may pick up an object—such as a book or small chair (used like a "lion tamer")—and use it to block and deflect the blow or object thrown. The three-foot spacing in the *supportive stance* may give the teacher the room to use such an object. If the child catches the teacher off guard and has closed in on her, striking with his right fist, the teacher would block and deflect this blow with the edge of her right arm by holding it across her body (the reverse would occur with a left-hand blow).

If, after an incident of choking, biting, kicking, grabbing, or hitting and throwing, the child retreats and moves to a protective corner or space out of the way of classroom activities, presenting no danger to himself or others, the teacher simply leaves him alone. We consider him to have moved to Level 4: Reestablishing Equilibrium, and we use the techniques explained below. However, if the child still is endangering others, property, or himself, we must now use nonviolent restraining techniques on him.

Nonviolent Restraining

Basket-Weave Hold Restraint[8] If the child is small enough and the teacher has the advantage of strength over him, she may choose to use the basket-weave hold. This is a preferable restraining technique because mirror techniques may be employed from a seated restraining position. This hold is accomplished by the teacher getting behind the assaulting child and putting her arms around him and grasping his right wrist with her left hand and his left wrist with her right hand. The teacher then pulls toward her in a way that causes the child's arms to cross over the front of his body (see Drawing 1). As the teacher stands, she moves her body sideways to the child, her feet at a 45-degree angle. This places the child's back on the teacher's right hip; she then pulls his arms back toward her and lifts up. This causes the child's heels to come slightly off the floor, forcing him to stand on his tip-toes with his weight supported by the teacher's thigh. The teacher also may hold or restrain the child in a seated position. Remember: Use only the minimum amount of force needed, so that no injury is done to the child. The basket-weave restraining hold is the much more preferred hold with very young children because of the reduced likelihood of doing injury to them.

Important Note: The teacher should accompany her physical restraining—with the basket-weave hold—with parallel language of supportive command, preparatory directive statement, and promise of safety. "Jimmy, I want you to stop hitting and relax (supportive command), and when you do so, I will let you go! (preparatory) You are safe. I am not going to hurt you and I will not let you hurt me" (promise of safety). Also, the entire verbal sequence should be repeated over and over as a broken record and as an attempt to get the child to hear the teacher from within his state of flooding.

Some early childhood teachers state that when they are hit, kicked, or bitten by a child, they hit, kick, and bite back, so that the child "knows how it feels." *WARNING: Never*, under any circumstances, hit, kick, or bite a child who has done this to you. This could rightly be defined as child abuse, and you could properly be charged under the law. When a young child is flooded and carries out an assault, he is no longer rational and capable of stopping himself; returning his aggression does not teach him "how it feels" but simply confirms his unreasonable concern that you are a person to fear. When we use nonviolent restraining techniques and parallel supportive demands and promise of safety, and we do not return their aggression, children gradually learn to trust us and give up this aggression and fears. Remember that during each of these levels of crisis—and especially during the assault action—the child is terribly frightened. He actually scares himself when he is out of control.

Again, if the child becomes passive or introverted after an assault, retreats to a protective corner or space out of the way of the classroom activities, and now presents no danger to himself or others, the teacher simply leaves him alone. We consider him to have moved to Level 4: Reestablishing Equilibrium.

LEVEL 4: REESTABLISHING EQUILIBRIUM

After the violent act, the child is deflated and becomes withdrawn, with little energy. He has feelings of guilt and feels helpless as to how others might respond to him. Some children will retreat so far back into passivity that they fall asleep or begin self-abusive activities such as pulling out their hair, biting themselves, or some similar act of physical abuse on themselves. We will intervene with mirroring both body referencing and motor imitations if the child retreats too deeply into passivity as sleep or begins physically self-abusive activities. (See Chapter 8 for details of how to do mirroring.)

Since the child is now rational, we wish to help him cognitively recall what has happened, for he may not actually remember what started the flooding incident or what occurred once it began. We will primarily use the Confronting-Contracting techniques.

Jimmy "El Zorro": (Slouches down into the chair, drops his eyes, pouts with a frowning face for a period of 4 to 6 minutes, and then begins to sit up in the chair watching other children.)

Teacher: (approaches) "I need to talk to you about the painting. What did you do?" (Step 2—confronting: "What" question)

Jimmy "El Zorro": "I don't know." [or the child might say, "I painted people!"]

Teacher: "Well, I saw what you did, and you were using the paintbrush to paint Mark. What is the rule of how paints are to be used? (Step 2—confronting: "What" question requesting a verbal statement of the rule) You got so angry that you wanted to hit and bite, but I stopped you and kept you safe."

Jimmy "El Zorro": (eyes drop) "A-a-h, keep the paint, ah—paper."

Teacher: "Yes, when paints are used, our rule is to keep paint on the paper. Also the rule is that hitting and biting are not allowed, and when someone is angry they need to use words to tell the other person. When you got angry and did hit and bite, I needed to hold you tightly to keep you safe and I did not hurt you and I didn't let anyone hurt you. I kept us both safe. These are helping hands, not hurting hands, and these hands keep children safe.[9] (Teacher restates the rule so it is very clear.) Now you and I must work this out. (Step 3—contracting) We must have an agreement. (Teacher moves to Jimmy, takes him gently by the hands, and makes eye contact.) What will you do to change? When you use the paints again, how will you use them?" (Step 2—confronting: "What" question, requesting change)

Jimmy "El Zorro": "Keep the paint on the paper."

Teacher: "Yes. Do we have an agreement on this? Can I depend on you to remember the rule?" (Step 3—contracting: verbal agreement)

Jimmy "El Zorro": "Yes." (Jimmy looks up and makes eye contact with the teacher.)

Teacher: "What will you do when someone makes you angry?"

Jimmy "El Zorro": "Words."

Teacher: "Yes. Do we have an agreement on this? Can I depend on you to remember the rule?" (Step 3—contracting: verbal agreement)

Jimmy "El Zorro": "Yes." (Jimmy looks up and makes eye contact with the teacher.)

Teacher: "Good, we now have an agreement. If you agree, I want to shake hands to show a special agreement between us." (The teacher holds out her hand to Jimmy and smiles warmly.) (Step 3—contracting)

Jimmy "El Zorro": (Returns the teacher's smile and shakes her hand.)

Teacher: "Good, we now have an agreement! If you can now remember the painting rules, you may paint. But if you forget the painting rules, your behavior will say that you do not know how to use paints and you will not be able to use the easel. (Step 3—consequence) Now, you may feel free to come back to work and play with us when you feel that you are ready." (handling isolation)

Jimmy "El Zorro": (Hops up, takes off the paint smock, hangs it on the appropriate hook, moves over to the puzzle shelf, and selects a puzzle.)

It is recommended that during Level 4: Reestablishing Equilibrium, the child and teacher be eye-to-eye in a very close, intimate space. This can be done by seating the child on an adult chair, with the teacher sitting on a small child-size chair, or by placing the child on a countertop with the teacher standing, thus bringing them eye-to-eye.

To summarize, during this level, it is important that the child be able to cognitively state—or for the teacher to describe—the events that have occurred in a way that imparts no guilt, and for the relationship between the teacher and child to reach a new emotional equilibrium free of hostility. Both the child and the teacher need this reunion.

Caution should be taken by the teacher in forcing a verbal apology that requires the child to say, "I'm sorry." The verbal statement may be something the teacher needs, but if forced, the child will begin to have feelings of guilt. Children, if the equilibration goes well, will have feelings of remorse and wish to apologize, but they may express it in a nonverbal form. There is a feeling of warmth and the child physically leans into the teacher for a small cuddle, or the child meets the teacher's eyes, saying nothing but smiling affectionately. We as teachers must also learn during the interaction to nonverbally express our "forgiveness" back to the child through similar cuddling and smiling, but we must also do it in the form of verbal expression as a statement of promise of safety.

CLASSMATES AS ONLOOKERS TO THE ASSAULT

It has been suggested previously that steps should be taken to remove onlookers by either having the other children move to another room, section an area off from the view of other children, or, if possible, move the child to another room. Witnessing the revengeful, flooded child is very frightening for classmates, and seeing the teacher's restraining actions on the assaulting child may appear to young children as if the teacher is hurting the child.

It is quite important to deal with the classmates who were onlookers to an assault by a revengeful child. Witnessing such aggression can cause an individual child or an entire group of children to move to level 1: Potential Crisis, whereby they become highly anxious with accompying behavior that might escalate through these crisis levels. This may be handled by using the ventilating techniques previously suggested in working with Level 1: Potential Crisis children. After a violent incident, the teacher should view the entire class as being in Level 1: Potential Crisis; thus, she will want them to "play it out" or "talk it out." The "play it out" technique involves having the children take the inner tension and disperse it from the body to play, whereas the "talk it out" technique involves holding one or more class problem-solving meetings, using the Relationship-Listening techniques.

Body to Toy (Motor Ventilation)

When dealing with many children who have begun flooding and are experiencing fears and inner tension, we as teachers simply stop our close socially demanding indoor play and instead take the entire class outside. This permits them plenty of space to be motorically active with much running. It would be advisable *not* to take children to activities that immobilize their bodies or demand close cooperation such as the snack table, nor should we want them to be able to lay on their cots or mats soon after viewing these frightening actions. If we take the flooded children into these activities without permitting a opportunity for ventilation, we will find large numbers of these young children unmanageable.

The "running off" of this inner tension will work with most children, but the outdoor supervision will require extra vigilance because of a dramatic increase of fantasy role-play related to aggressive roles. Play with such characters as Ninja Turtles and Batman will often be seen. These roles are acceptable outlets for the children in a large outdoor space, but there must be close supervision by the teacher to make sure the "pretend" aggression does not take over the children and they begin to kick and strike each other while playing within these violent roles. Just as the teacher was required to use the Teacher Behavior Continuum to facilitate the play of an individual child progressing along the construct of body to toy, toy to play, and play to work, this outdoor play may need to be channeled from negative aggressive theme play to more positive constructive role-play. Although this intervention may be needed, we do want to permit as much harmless "bang, bang, shoot-em" motoric "pretend" aggression as possible because it provides good ventilation. We should intervene only with those children who overstep and cannot control the aggressive play to the point where they actually do become aggressive. We can also expect to witness much silliness and nervous giddy laughter among the children as they appear to "run wild" on the playground.

Class Meetings (Verbal Ventilation)

The entire class is seated on child-size chairs along a circular line (for control of error) on a rug or the floor. The assaulting child is included in the meeting, and should preferably be seated in the lap of an aide or assistant teacher. Just as the Confronting-Contracting techniques were used for Level 4: Reestablishing Equilibrium to enable the teacher to establish an emotional equilibrium with the previously assaulting child, this equilibrium will also need to be reestablished with the child's classmates. They have seen or heard the frightening event and have identified themselves as a part of the action. Through verbal ventilating in the class meeting, we attempt to reach the point where the teacher and students have gotten rid of any feelings of hostility. If we do not do this, the classmates—out of their fear of the acting-out child—will begin to make him an outside aggressor. Let us watch the meeting unfold. Notice that the teacher techniques begin with the teacher wearing a Relationship-Listening face with its accompanying techniques, and then the teacher moves to Confronting-Contracting:

Teacher: (opens the meeting) "Friends, I would like to talk about some scary and frightening things that happened this morning." (door opener)

Children: (No one speaks for a few minutes, but then a discussion begins.)

Harriet: "Jimmy was mean!"

Paul: "He hits people."

Teacher: "Jimmy was very angry. And when he gets angry, he hits" (active listening).

Diana: "I don't like him; he is mean!"

Teacher: "When people hit, it is hard to like them."

Jeffrey: "You hurt Jimmy's arm."

Teacher: "When I held Jimmy, you thought I was hurting him" (active listening).

Paul: "You didn't hit Jimmy."

Teacher: "What else did you see and feel?" (door opener)

Nancy: "I saw Jimmy hit you and bite your arm. He cried and screamed naughty words."

(This verbal ventilation may continue for 5 to 10 minutes, with the teacher maintaining a Relationship-Listening face and techniques. Now the teacher moves to Confronting-Contracting and does not hesitate to deal with the realities of the situation and explain misinformation.)

Teacher: "What happened first? Harriet?" (Confronting: "What" questions)

Harriet: "Jimmy was splashing people with paint—he wasn't using the rules for painting."

Teacher: "What happened next?" (Confronting: "What" questions)

Jeffrey: "You told Jimmy to stop painting, and he pushed you and got paint all over your dress."

Teacher: "What happened next?" (Confronting: "What" questions)

Diana: "Jimmy screamed and hit, and you took him into the block room. And there was a big crash."

Teacher: "What happened next?" (Confronting: "What" questions)

Paul: "You hurt Jimmy's arm."

Teacher: "No. Because Jimmy got so mad that he could hurt me, he could hurt others, and he could hurt himself, I needed to hold him tightly to keep him safe. I am the teacher and boss but I do not hurt children. I am a friend. But when children get very angry, I need to hold them tight to keep them safe" (a reality explanation and promise of safety).

Paul: "You hurt Jimmy's arm."

Teacher: "No, Paul. I was holding his arm and hands tightly so that his hands would not hurt me. I did not hurt Jimmy; I was keeping him safe. Come up here, Paul. (Paul stands before the teacher.) Let me show you how safely I was holding Jimmy." (The teacher now demonstrates the basket-weave restraint on Paul and two other children. Paul giggles as if it is a game, and now a number of other children want a chance. The teacher demonstrates the basket-weave restraint on all children who have requested it—including Jimmy, who has left the assistant teacher's lap.)

Teacher: "When friends get very angry, they sometimes try to hurt other people. I am the boss, and I keep people safe. And no matter how mean people are, I will not hit them, I will not hurt them, I will not kick them, and I will not bite them. I am the teacher and I hold children to keep them safe (reality explanation and promise of safety). Now we need to make some promises—we need to have an agreement. What should we do when others make us angry?"

Nearly the entire class, in unison: "Use words."

Teacher: "Yes. When others make us angry, the rule is, 'we do not hit, but we tell that person with words,' and we can come to the teacher to get help. Hitting, biting, kicking, and spitting are against the rules. Also, how can we help Jimmy when he gets mad?"

Diana: "We can share with him."

Jeffrey: "We can let him play with us."

Teacher: "We now all have an agreement. We are going to use words when we are angry, and we are going to invite Jimmy to be our friend and play with us" (contracting).

This vignette, of course, is for purposes of modeling teacher techniques and is certainly somewhat artificial. The ventilation process and the confronting and contracting might take many minutes, or even many meetings, and may need to occur throughout the year if aggression is high in the classroom. But the techniques to be used, and the general attitude and processes to be employed, should develop in a direction much as the one demonstrated in the vignette.

This class meeting will serve a number of purposes:

1. It ventilates any pent-up anxiety and feelings that any child might have after witnessing such aggression.
2. It helps both Jimmy and his classmates to reestablish an emotional equilibrium, potentially preventing Jimmy from becoming an outside aggressor.
3. It helps children understand that if they, too, should become angry (and they will), the teacher will not take aggressive action against them but instead will help.
4. It dispels any misinformation and misperceptions the children might have (e.g., "You were hurting Jimmy's arm").

VERBAL AGGRESSION

Verbal aggression is defined as any vocalization, such as crying to get one's own way, shouting, whining, swearing, name calling, verbal threats, and similar actions. We as teachers can decide what action we should take toward such verbal aggression by asking the question, What is the motivation of the child for such verbal aggression? The answer will be one of the following: attention getting, power, or revenge.

Swearing

When dealing with children who are swearing, we can apply the Three Faces of Discipline.

Relationship-Listening "Harold, when that swear word is said, I am afraid that other children will begin to say those words, and those are not school words that I can permit children to use in our classroom." Before delivering such an I-message, we take Harold by the hand and move him out of the hearing and possibly the vision of the other children.

Confronting-Contracting If the I-message fails to work, we may move to Confronting-Contracting techniques. "Harold, come with me (take him out of the hearing of classmates). I need to talk to you about these silly words. What are you doing? Well, I think what you are doing is trying to get other children to see you when you use those words so you can have everyone look at you (attention getting), or these words can make you the boss (power) and feel strong. The rule is that they are not school words, and if you say them again I will need to have you go to the bathroom and close the door to say that word all you may want."

Rules and Consequences We approach the attention-getting or power-seeking child who is swearing, take him off to the side out of the hearing of others, and deliver an assertive demand. "Harold (name), stop (holds Harold's hand—touch). This is not a school word (eye contact). If this word is said again, I will need to call your mother and I will send you to time out" (preparatory).

As an alternative, we may take a behavioral analysis response to Harold's swearing. If the child is motivated by attention getting or power seeking, he may use the "Big F" word or similar swearing so that others will see him and respond in a way that makes him the center of attention. In such an instance, we may behaviorally deal with this by *not* giving attention and by acting as if we do not hear it. We refuse to give our attention (extinction by withdrawing social reinforcement); thus, the child has no payoff. When we do withdraw our attention, a number of actions will occur. The attention-getting and power-seeking child will intensify the action, since his motivational payoff is to get attention and experiencing the opposite prompts him to escalate the swearing action. We may be able to persevere by refusing to respond to the swearing. After it gets worse, it will dissipate (extinction).

At times, we as teachers might observe unwanted reinforcement and attention for the swearing child from classmates who might giggle and begin saying the same word. This provides the swearing child with a very powerful social reinforcement. We then isolate the child (time out) in such a space that classmates will not socially reinforce him by requiring him to go to the bathroom, close the door, and swear all he wants—out of the range of our hearing and that of the other children. We enforce this isolation each and every time the attention-getting child acts out through swearing. The power-seeking child will usually refuse to stay in this isolation, and it might require us to restrain him in the isolated, screened off space; it certainly will require that we remain with him in this space. When we are restraining in time out, we do not speak to the child or give him any other form of verbal or nonverbal acknowledgment. It is helpful to set a timer for 3 to 5 minutes, and once it goes off, the child is permitted to return to classroom activities. (See Chapter 4 on Rules and Consequences and the guidelines for the use of time out.)

One of the difficulties of an ignoring approach is that swearing is contagious—other children imitate and begin to use these explosive words for the purpose of gaining attention. One technique often used by teachers is to "silly-it-out" as a form of saturation. When many children are using such words, we may teach them to do a host of similar rhyming words to take the attention away from the swear words and away from the attention-seeking child.

> *Attention-getting Caroline is going about the classroom saying, "F--k it, f--k it, f--k it." The children nearby begin a "monkey hear, monkey say" behavior of repeating, "F--k it, f--k it." The teacher brings together the children involved (not the whole class if all are not involved) and states, "That sounds like you are saying a silly word to make us laugh at you. Friends, let's see if we can think of other silly works like this. I know some—*truck, muck, buck, cluck, wuck, ack, mack, clack, pack, wack! *Friends, what silly words can you think up?"*

If a child swears, "Sh-t," "silly-it-out" by making and saying words similar in sound—*hit, mit, bit, fit,* and so on. When using "silly-it-out," the teacher turns her body in such a manner as to isolate and not reinforce the original attention-getting or power-seeking child who started the swearing. The teacher literally turns her back to him, taking away his attention/power and putting him out of this new game that we control. She focuses on the "contagious" children who were picking up these words to repeat, thus taking the audience away from the first child. When a great volume of rhyming words is heard (saturation), the original swear word is "washed out" in the contagious children's hearing and memory and they actually forget the original word that started all the nonsense. The teacher has snatched the attention, taking away the game the attention-getting child was attempting to play; she took control by subtly isolating the swearing child, while at the same time using saturating sounds to wash out the impact of the swear word being said.

Swearing is a very different matter for the revengeful child who is regressing through the levels of crisis. When such a child is flooded emotionally in Level 2: Developing Crisis, his verbal aggression in the form of swearing, threats, and other hostile verbal actions is considered ventilating. As odd as it might seem, the more verbal aggression, the better, because it means that the child's internal anger, anxiety, and related energy are being ventilated.

Crying to Get One's Own Way/Whining

Crying to get one's way, sometimes called "water power," and whining are both auditorily abrasive expressions that grate on the nerves to such a point that teachers often give in to the child's demand just to get these sounds to stop. To deal with these ploys, the teacher again may follow the escalation of power techniques of the Three Faces of Discipline continuum.

Relationship-Listening The I-message contained in the Relationship-Listening face is a particularly helpful technique to use both for the "water-power" crying and for whining.

Crying: "When I hear crying, I cannot understand what the person wants, and crying hurts my ears."

Whining: "When I hear a squeaky little voice, it bothers my ears, and I have a very difficult time listening to what the squeaky voice wants. People who want me to hear them must use a big boy's (or girl's) voice for me to hear."

We do not give the child what he wants while he is crying as a use of water power or whining. As a result, the behavior will soon dissipate.

Confronting-Contracting If the I-message fails to work, we move on to the Confronting-Contracting face. "What are you doing? What is the rule?" (The teacher uses words to state her needs.) Possibly we may apply a logical consequence: "That 'squeaky voice' bothers our ears and we are not able to be comfortable at snack. If that 'squeaky' voice is used again, it is showing us that you do not know the rules for being with us, and I will need to ask you to eat at a table by yourself where that 'voice' will not bother other's ears."

Rules and Consequences We may choose to reinforce another child who is not crying or whining, use extinction to attempt to withdraw reinforcement given to these acts, or use forms of time out. "Conchita (name and gestures), stop (eye contact, touches). Move now to choose a place to play, and begin."

SUMMARY

At times, teachers are faced with a child who is so flooded that he acts out in an assaultive and violent manner that endangers himself and others. Teachers are required to understand the levels of crisis through which the child will move and first make attempts to get the child to ventilate his inner tension through language or play that will move from body to toy, from toy to play, and then through play to become a cooperative worker. Teachers will also be required to mediate for classmates who have witnessed violent behavior through classroom meetings. Any of the techniques previously learned in the Three Faces of Discipline may be used to deal with many forms of verbal aggression such as swearing, whining, and crying.

Test Yourself

Test your understanding of the concepts related to the Teacher Behavior Continuum (TBC), by writing your answers in the column on the left. You will find the answers at the end of this chapter, following the Endnotes.

A. ____ developing B. ____ imminent C. ____ potential	1.–3. Rank the terms to indicate an increase in the seriousness of these three crisis stages.
	Select one answer for each of the following questions, choosing from the answers on the left.
A. ____ promise of safety B. ____ symbolic play C. ____ reestablishing an equilibrium	4. After a violent act, the child feels guilty and remorseful. The teacher approaches the child to reestablish friendly relations and dispel these negative feelings.
A. ____ restraining B. ____ ventilation C. ____ basket-weave restraint	5. What term is used for the shouting or motor activity that externalizes pent-up emotions?
A. ____ outside aggressor B. ____ play it out C. ____ wait time	6. When the classroom of 3-year-olds is told that a new child will join the class, the children state, "I don't like him (or her)!"even though they have never met the new child.
A. ____ work B. ____ body C. ____ toy D. ____ play	7.–10. Place a number from 1 to 4 before the steps through which the teacher would progress in channeling a child's aggression with the use of play.

Glossary

Assertive Command A forceful, nonaggressive method of stating to the child to desist his misbehavior and change to behaviors desired by the teacher. The command must contain the child's name, gesture, eye contact, and a clear statement of the behavior wanted.

Basket-Weave Hold A nonaggressive restraining technique of holding young children so they will not hurt themselves or others.

Body Referencing During a time that a child is violent or having a temper tantrum, she loses a sense of self and her own actions; the teacher brings the child before a mirror and verbally begins reassuring her by naming her body parts and telling her that she is safe.

Developing Crisis As the child is beginning to become violent and may lose self-control, his behavior passes through three levels of crisis. The first is potential crisis; with increased intensity, the child moves to a stage of developing crisis; and finally, with loss of control, the child is in a stage of imminent crisis.

From Body to Toy A process for channeling aggression for the young child that moves that aggression from the body (biting, hitting, or striking) to a toy (make-believe biting with an alligator puppet) as a way of ventilating stored-up hostility and anger.

From Play to Work Aggressive energy is ventilated into the active use of objects and make-believe play; other children then join in this activity, permitting the child to be cooperative. Or the child uses the materials to make products, thus becoming a worker (able to carry out agreed upon social tasks with others).

From Toy to Play Once the child has ventilated pent-up aggressive energies with the toy (hitting with hammer and nails, biting with the alligator puppet), the teacher wants the aggressive themes to dissipate so the child can now move to productive make-believe play.

Imminent Crisis As the child is beginning to become violent and may lose self-control, his behavior passes through three levels of crisis. The first is potential crisis, then moving to a stage of developing crisis, and, finally, with loss of control, the child is in a stage of imminent crisis where he is actually violent.

Lap Time Cuddling the child in the teacher's lap to enable the child to relax.

Life-Stance Position A ritualistic, stereotypical manner of behavior, normally with elements of passivity or aggression, done by a poorly adjusted child as a way of dealing with any of life's demands and tensions.

Mirroring Helping the child either gain control of herself or gain an awareness of herself by bringing her before a large upright mirror.

Motor Imitations The enactment of a behavior that shows the child knows a label or concept. The child cups his hands and puts them to his mouth as if drinking.

Motoric Ventilation Dispersing stored-up emotional tension through large-muscle/physical activities.

Outside Aggressor Groups of children, out of a sense of fear or rivalry, project their hate (real or as fantasy play) to a child who is not a member of the group.

Personal Space An area of approximately three feet around the child; when others invade this space, the child feels frightened or threatened.

Play It Out Taking pent-up inner emotional tension and energy and expelling it into the active use of toys and materials in the form of make-believe play or creating products (painting, clay, etc.)

Potential Crisis As the child is beginning to become violent and may lose self-control, his behavior passes through three levels of crisis. The first is potential crisis, where the child shows nervousness; this is followed by a stage of developing crisis; and, finally, with loss of control, the child is in a stage of imminent crisis.

Promise of Safety Once the child has been violent, the teacher repetitively tells the child that she is not going to return that violence (hit) and that the child is safe with her.

Reestablishing Equilibrium After a violent act, the child feels guilty and remorseful; the teacher approaches the child to reestablish friendly relations and dispel these feelings.

Restraining Techniques Nonviolent methods of holding children so they will not hurt themselves or others.

Supportive Stance When a child is about to be violent, the teacher approaches to get him to calm down and faces him at a 45-degree angle; without gesturing, the teacher attempts to communicate that she is not going to physically confront or assault the child.

Symbolic Play Enacting make-believe fantasy activities either with toys or gestures.

Ventilation Dispersing pent-up feelings of aggression either by physical activity, play, or talking it out.

Verbal Ventilation Talking out pent-up emotional feelings.

Wait Time After making a demand of children or asking them questions, the teacher must be prepared to give them ample time to comply.

"Water Power" Crying for the purpose of getting what the child wants and controlling others.

Related Readings

Freud, A. (1968). *Normality and Pathology in Childhood: Assessments of Development*. New York: International University Press.

McMurrain, T. (1975). *Intervention in Human Crisis*. Atlanta: Humanics Press.

Nonviolent Crisis Intervention for the Educator: Volume III: The Assaultive Student. Brookfield, WI: National Crisis Prevention Institute.

Wolfgang, C. H., & Wolfgang, M. E. (1992). *School for Young Children: Developmentally Appropriate Practices*. Boston: Allyn and Bacon.

Wolfgang, C. H. (1977). *Helping Aggressive and Passive Preschoolers through Play*. Columbus, OH: Charles Merrill.

Endnotes

1. McMurrain, T. (1975). *Intervention in Human Crisis*. Atlanta: Humanics Press.
2. *Note*: After reading the full explanation to follow, we will see that the teacher in this example made a number of mistakes in handling this incident and dealing with a revengeful child. She should have used supportive demand and stance rather than assertive demand and stance (soon to be explained). However, if the teacher has had little past experience and does not know the history of this child, she might judge his actions as an attempt to grab attention or power, and then might find herself handling the revengeful incident as best she can once it begins.
3. *Nonviolent Crisis Intervention for the Educator: Volume III: The Assaultive Student*. Brookfield, WI: National Crisis Prevention Institute.
4. This is also a reconceptualization of the Crisis Development Behavior Levels as developed by the National Crisis Prevention Institute. Training videos and training workshops by the institute are highly recommended.
5. Freud, A. (1971). *The Ego and the Mechanisms of Defense*. New York: International University Press.
6. The size of the wheeled toy will depend on the amount of space available to be sectioned off as a private space for the child. Very large wooden trucks and cars (six to eight inches or bigger) might be effective in a large-muscle room or playground, but generally not in a well-balanced indoor space. A very small wheeled toy could be confined to a very narrow space such as a table top or large cafeteria tray with raised edges, which helps establish control of error.
7. National Crisis Prevention Institute.
8. National Crisis Prevention Institute.
9. Often it is adult hands that *do* hurt children and create great fear in them.

Answers to Test Yourself

1C, 2A, 3B, 4C, 5B, 6A, 7B, 8C, 9D, 10A

6

Aggressive and Passive Children

Explanations and Expectations

Four-year-old Brandon is the only son of a rugged, athletic, chain-smoking father and an attractive high school teacher mother. Because of recent moves, Brandon has been in and out of a number of early childhood centers, with some speculation that he was "requested" to leave those other centers. He is a thin-featured, pale-complected (to the point of looking anemic), tense child who appears as tightly coiled as a spring and who rejects any supportive touch by the teacher. Brandon never uses the school toilet but often shows many indications of needing to do so, such as holding his stomach and carrying himself as if he is experiencing stomach cramps. He often wets himself during nap time and rarely relaxes or falls asleep.

At lunch or snack, where he refuses most foods, he seats himself with the more excitable boys, and uses "bathroom talk" in a whispered, covert manner. His words whip the boys into a giggling frenzy, which usually ends with their throwing food at each other. When the teacher approaches to stop this behavior, Brandon puts down his head, smiles slightly, and acts as if he is totally innocent.

During play periods in the classroom, Brandon is like a caged tiger, typically crouched in a protective corner in the block room, wanting to use the materials but not feeling free to do so. His attitude is one that says, "If I begin a block structure, someone will destroy it." This fearful and untrusting view of his peers causes him to lash out with sharp fingernails, sometimes directly at the other children's eyes, and to repeatedly bite peers for the most minor contact. After his act of aggression, he tells the teacher that the other child was hostile to him; however, investigation or close observation usually shows that the other child merely bumped Brandon accidentally or inadvertently stepped on one of his toys. He cannot look the teacher directly in the eyes, and usually turns away when invited to join activities.

On those rare occasions when the father picks Brandon up at the end of the school day, the man seems impatient to get in and out of the school. Brandon complicates this by refusing to come when called and running to the opposite side of the playground. This causes his father to move after him and forces the father to play a game of "run and chase," which Brandon seems to enjoy. The frustrated father, on one occasion when he felt no teacher was looking, struck Brandon sharply on the backside. He then departed with Brandon crying and being dragged by the arm. Brandon also refuses to permit his mother to leave in the mornings and refuses to reunite or depart with his mother at the end of the day. Whispering in his ear, she offers bribes of candy or gifts that she has for him in the car. During conferences, his mother refuses to discuss aggressive behavior or adjustment difficulties, changing the topic to Brandon's performance in more academic curriculum. She implies a dissatisfaction that the teacher is not teaching Brandon to read.

YOUNG AGGRESSIVE AND PASSIVE CHILDREN

Once the young toddler is able to walk, she no longer needs to remain in her parents' arms as a "lap baby." The 1- and 2-year-old is consumed with active movement as she begins to explore her new physical world. Now that she can walk away from her parents, she does so with reckless abandon, unaware of what dangers may exist in her increasingly interesting world. We have all seen the toddler at the local grocery store who has "escaped" from her mother or father and comes toddling around the corner and down the aisles with a large nervous smile on her face as she breaks all speed limits. Moments later, we see the parent in hot pursuit, a look of near-panic etched in her or his face.

Parents and caregivers now must become quite active in intervening with the highly physical toddler. The first step is to "child-proof" the space in which the child is living so the toddler is active but safe from objects or dangers that might injure her. The caregiver's second step is to serve the role of limit setter. This is the stage at which we must begin to stop toddlers from a wide variety of actions that might endanger them—getting into the stereo equipment, running across parking lots, or playing near dangerous stairs—and to make demands for more mature socially acceptable behavior ("Eat your potatoes with a spoon, not your fingers").

When we use a physical action or verbal "No!" to stop these children from a behavior they have started (e.g., stopping them from grabbing the candies at the check-out counter), we have in varying degrees frustrated them. As infants, all they had to do was emit a small cry or whimper and we, as caring adults, rushed to discover the problem and give comfort to them. This exchange makes an infant very powerful; she is the center of her world and can make that world serve her. Now, no longer restricted as a lap baby and able to travel considerable distances away from us as caregivers, the toddler requires us to teach her what is safe and to make increasing social demands for more mature behavior. By setting limits, such as saying "No!" or physically intervening in a skilled manner, we help the toddler channel her behavior into safe and proper actions. When these limits are set skillfully, the young child comes to understand that we are helping her be safe. She may thus internalize the "No!" messages or limits,[1] resulting in a fully developed conscience near the age of 6 or 7. (Remember tattling on the first-grade playground?) Let's take a look at two mothers setting limits with their toddlers.

Mother-Skilled is spending the holidays at grandmother's house, which is not a child-proofed space. Jonathan, her toddler son, spies a treasured breakable knickknack of grandmother's on a low end table. His eyes widen and he bolts to get ahold of the sparkling object, unaware that it is a priceless heirloom.

Mother also arrives at the table at the same time—experience having taught her to keep an eye on her son. "Oh, Jonathan, I see you have found grandma's Hummel figurine. Let's take a look at it together." Mother gently and in a very slow and dramatic manner picks up the figure and moves it to the floor in front of Jonathan, who is now seated. He reaches out and fingers the object with great interest as mother verbally explains it. She uses a wide variety of adjectives to describe the object. After a period of seven to eight minutes, the child begins to lose interest. He stands up to leave and set out for another object to interest him. Mother states, "Look, Jonathan, this is grandma's very special figurine, and now let's put it back in its safe place. If you want to see it again, come and get me and I will help you look at it safely." Jonathan never shows any further interest in the item and does not touch it again.

Mother-Nonskilled's child bolts toward a similar precious object. "No, Chanta, no! Do not touch that—that's grandma's and it's not a toy." The toddler remains interested and again moves toward the object. Mother repeats, "No! Don't touch that!" Chanta reaches out in a manner of pointing at the object. Mother moves quickly to Chanta and slaps her smartly on the hand, stating, "You heard me. I said no!" Chanta throws herself to the floor in a full-blown temper tantrum, crying intensely and flailing her arms and legs.

These and 1,001 similar instances of limit setting, from the age of 12 months through 6 years, communicate to the young child that this *is* or *is not* a safe and interesting world to be enjoyed, understood, and managed. For Chanta, exploring the new world open to her as a toddler is like walking into a minefield. Things that she will do but as yet cannot understand—the importance of grandma's figurine, for example—will trigger a spanking or other harsh action from adults that will cause her physical pain or great stress. Add to this the accumulation of the natural daily accidents that normally befall a developing toddler, and we gain a picture of the world of frustration for the Chantas of this world. Gradually, her demeanor and actions will make it appear as if she is suffering "battle fatigue." She is learning to mistrust the world, to feel guilty for her actions and behavior, and to have a growing doubt in her own abilities. If this continues, we will hear from her future teachers that Chanta "has a poor self-concept." Limit setting is one of the central variables in helping a young child acquire a healthy self-concept.

In Defense of Mothers

The vignette about Chanta and her mother, presented for purposes of example, appears to put a heavy burden and the blame on mothers; this is not the intent. There are many children who are very difficult, if not impossible, to "mother." Thus, one may see negative interaction between mother and child but may not understand the past history of incidents and circumstances that led to the interaction. A number of different factors could contribute to such a history, including prenatal variables (genetic temperament, prenatal effects of medication, etc.), the birth process (use of forceps causing early injury, lack of oxygen in the first minutes of life), or early neonate factors (prematurity accompanied by difficulty in maintaining temperature or breathing, intestinal difficulties). In addition, early development trauma (severe accidental burns, accidents, need for major operations) could lay a foundation for negative interactions.

Any of these factors might have destroyed the infant's basic trust in the world, producing very demanding and difficult behavior for mother to handle. For some mothers, there may be no good solution or methods to protect the growing young child from life's harsher experiences. With an awareness that many variables might contribute to the child's difficult behavior at ages 2 to 7, three classifications may be made:

- As teachers, we must be very careful in early childhood centers and in school not to make harsh value judgments and hastily assign blame to mothers and fathers. The negative behavior that we see in a child might have been far beyond the parents' abilities and sphere of skill in managing and handling. However, if we see a cycle of negative parent-child interaction, such as abuse, we should take all necessary steps to encourage parents to enroll in parenting skill classes or obtain the counseling of child experts and professionals, as well as take any actions dictated by law (see Chapter 11).
- We will spend little or no time speculating as to what early factor might have caused the child to be as he or she is today as a 3- to 7-year-old. The process of human growth and development is not like an automobile engine, where if it is running poorly we can identify the source of the problem (e.g., a misfiring spark plug) and make a change so that all will run well again. We simply take the child as he or she is and, through the developmental principles, work with that child over many months to see true growth and improvement in the child's behavior.
- Having said that generally there is not one "spark plug" that we may change to help the child, we make one exception. That is, we should encourage—and if in our power *require*—the child to have a complete physical examination to determine if there might be some physical basis for the child's actions.

As an example, consider the case of a kindergarten child whose teacher called the parents to a conference and raised the plausible possibility that their daughter was hyperactive and needed to be placed on Ritalin, a medication often prescribed to help hyperactive children better focus their attention. This was a surprise and shock to the parents, who felt their child was quite normal. When they took their daughter to the family doctor, they found that the doctor was making the same recommendation for medication. The parents were not convinced, removed the child from school, and took her to two more experts without getting advice they considered acceptable. The teacher described the child as one who would become very intense and would hit her fist against her head repeatedly. The girl would "froth at the mouth" and was not able to focus on instruction. Finally, a school counselor gave the child a hearing screening and discovered that she had a 60 percent hearing loss. Later, a doctor trained in ears, nose, and throat matters confirmed the hearing loss. The doctor suggested a minor operation to insert small rubber tubes in the child's eardrum to permit the inner and outer ears to reach a pressure balance. The child simply had inner-ear pressure similar to what we as adults feel when we fly in an airplane. By striking her head with her fist, the girl was trying to ease the pressure and pain that the ear was causing her. The simple ear tube, once in place, eliminated the difficulty and the child's "hyper" behavior stopped. In this case, it would have been a serious problem and hindrance to the child's development if she had simply been placed on medication for the next two to three years of her life and the hearing difficulty had not been identified.

So, it is highly recommended that children whose behavior difficulties in a classroom setting are so severe as to require deliberate and planned intervention should be screened at a developmental clinic. This clinic should have specialized knowledge of young children and should focus on hearing, vision, dietary problems, or similar physical variables. Once the child is medically examined by experts, we may then feel more confident in moving forward with our intervention.

Note: The techniques described in this book are for children who are experiencing school adjustment difficulty but who can still be considered "normal." If a child suffers extreme emotional difficulties that suggest pathology, that child might be classified outside the "normal" category and a psychologist or psychoanalyst with expert knowledge may be needed. A child with emotional disturbances would be considered outside of the teacher's skills and abilities, and the techniques that follow might not be effective with such children.

LIMIT SETTING AND IMPULSE CONTROL

Young children from ages 2 to 7 go through developmental phases as they attempt to deal with limits set for them by adults, internalize these limits as a conscience, and gain impulse control over their own behavior. These phases are passivity, physical aggression, verbal aggression, and control through the use of language.

Phase 1: Passivity (Helplessness)[2]

The child's process of mastering his own impulses and gaining control[3] of himself appears to progress through predictable phases. When the child first experiences limits, even done in a highly skilled or sensitive way, he feels a degree of frustration and his first response is *passivity,* or helplessness. When stopped from throwing food across the table or sticking objects in the electrical outlet, the child is frustrated by adults' physical intervention. He simply pulls back into himself in a passive manner, a flat expressionless look on his face. Remember, again, that in the first year of life as a lap baby the child was constantly receiving and was rarely denied anything. In normal behavior among young children, this passivity lasts for a very short period, sometimes only seconds, and then the child's actions change to physical aggression (see Figure 1–2 and Figure 6–1).

FIGURE 6–1 The Passive-Aggressive Construct

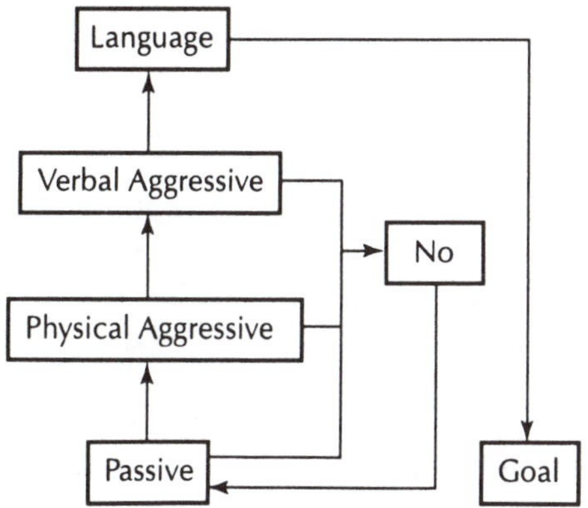

Phase 2: Physical Aggression (Revengeful)[4]

Now the passive child responds to being stopped from throwing food across the table or sticking items into electrical outlets by striking back. He throws the spoon or other hand-held objects at the adult and might strike, kick, scream, and cry at the adult who is frustrating him (setting a limit). This physical aggression will vary in intensity from a quite mild aggressive response to a full-blown temper tantrum. Whereas the frustration appeared to be dammed up in the behavior of the Phase of Passivity, for the Phase of Physical Aggression the frustration or feeling of anger and revengefulness felt by the immature child is dispersed through the body as outward aggression.

Note: In many instances, the actions of physically aggressive children have their roots in physiological causes, such as Attention Deficit Disorder and chemical imbalances. Many of these children are placed on medication by their doctors to help control this behavior. Although these children are not the primary focus of this text, the Appendix at the end of the book provides a general description of the most common types of medications given to such children.

Phase 3: Verbal Aggression (Revengeful or Powerful)[5]

The next behavior seen occurring after the Phase of Physical Aggression is the Phase of Verbal Aggression. When the child is confronted by an adult who sets limits, the child responds by screaming or shouting "No" back at the adult. The child, in anticipation of a demand from the adult, attempts to assert herself with the verbal aggressive "No" and tries to maintain control of the situation by a global "No!"[6,7] to every encounter with her caregivers, even when she truly wants what is being asked of her. ("Karen, would you like some ice cream?" Karen replies, "No!" at the same time she digs into the ice cream with great gusto.) This is the age period that has commonly been called the "terrible twos" because the child is naturally globally defiant as a form of almost automatic response to everything and everyone. The child is making her first attempts at asserting her own personality to obtain wants and desires but is still not yet sure what these desires are, thus the global "No!" Later in the preschool years, this verbal aggression will also change to bathroom talk, swearing, and the forbidden four-letter words. Instead of striking out physically as in the previous phase, the child strikes out with aggressive words.

Phase 4: Beginning Use of Language in Conflict Mastery

One final phase remains in the internalization of "No" as a beginning conscience and gaining control over these childish impulses. This phase involves the ability to use language in a situation that is causing frustration or preventing the child from obtaining a desired goal. John takes a possession from Robert. Robert responds passively (pouts and thumb sucks), responds with physical aggression (bites), or responds with verbal aggression (swears). But now, at Phase 4, Robert is able to say to John, "No, that is mine. I was using it; give it back!" Now the child has gained great power with language to effect his world. It has taken much time, help, and instruction by caregivers for the child to obtain this level of maturity. With the skill of using language to express needs to adults and peers, the child is well on his way to becoming a socially well-adjusted, mature person.

THE HIDDEN LANGUAGE OF SYMBOLIC PLAY

In life's experiences as a child (and as an adult), one cannot always positively resolve life's frustrations by achieving a desired goal, even with the skills of verbal language. The child is often left with the feeling of raw frustration and anger. However, a second hidden language is built into the child's cognitive and emotional system, and that is fantasy and symbolic play. Let's begin with an adult example. Your boss, friend, spouse, neighbor, or parent has taken some action you consider extremely unfair—one that blocks you from obtaining a goal or desire. You are perhaps even enraged, and you express this to the offending person, but with no positive results. That evening, as you drive home through traffic or as you begin to fall asleep at night, you fantasize and relive the incident. In your "daydream," you see yourself "telling off" the offending person or empowering yourself to change the outcome and obtain the goal you wanted. You may simply keep having this fantasy, reliving the incident over and over until you tire of it, repress it, and rarely think about it again.

In such a situation we are performing self-therapy. We, in our symbolic fantasy, (1) become the *fantasy aggressor* and do unto others as we feel they have wrongly done to us, or (2) *piecemeal digest* the "bad" experience by replaying this "tape" over and over until we tire and repress it, or (3) *change the outcome* in fantasy to make it more acceptable.[8] Nature has given young children (ages 2 to 7) this same built-in, self-healing fantasy system to enable them to externalize their raw frustration and anger.

For young children, however, the fantasizing is overt and still not hidden inside their heads as thoughts.[9] We as adults think our angry thoughts and fantasize in our own minds, where others cannot hear them. We keep these most private thoughts secret, for we might be embarrassed if others should know that we have "dreamed" such hostile thoughts and feelings, or we may share them but only with a trusted friend. For young children, these thoughts, feelings, and fantasies are clearly overt for us to observe in their symbolic play. Let's look at some examples.

Becoming the Fantasy Aggressor

The young child has just returned from the doctor's office where he was probed, examined, and injected with a vaccine. This caused him pain and great fear turning to anger, and he used language to attempt to stop this strange frightening experience. "No, don't! I don't like you to do that to me." After returning home, the child turns to gain emotional relief from his symbolic fantasy play by making one of his dolls or animal figures the "doctor" and, using a toy stick as a hypodermic needle, gives the "doctor doll" hundreds of "shots."

The child in symbolic fantasy play becomes the aggressor rather than the helpless victim—as he was in the doctor's office—to gain active control by doing to the "doctor doll" what was done to him in reality. In this way, the child may digest the "bad" experience in a piecemeal fashion. Giving the doctor doll "shots" may continue for days or weeks, until the intensity goes out of this repetitive play. Fuller elements of doctor role-play include undressing the doll, conducting an examination, taking its temperature, inspecting its throat, and giving a diagnosis. It appears that the child has become comfortable with playing doctor, and "giving shots" has become only a minor element in the role-play.

Thus, we find that this symbolic play is a built-in, self-healing process for the young child. When children have negative or traumatic experiences, it is as if the experiences are too large emotionally to accept or digest at one time. This is much like a large apple that is too big to eat in one bite, so the child must repeatedly nibble on the apple, bite after bite, until it is gone and digested. The doctor experience is too large an emotional experience to digest in one "bite." Therefore, the child replays—or piecemeal digests*—the "bad" experience gradually, until it is emotionally digested and out of his emotional system of concern. He is then able to stop playing doctor.*

Changing the Negative Outcome

Let's take a look at another child who uses play to emotionally handle the frustrations of daily 3-year-old life, adding the passive-aggressive construct (see Figure 6–1).

Three-year-old Amanda sees mother bringing in the groceries at 4:00 P.M. On top of the grocery bag is a gallon of her favorite ice cream.

Amanda: *"Mommy, can I have ice cream?" (Phase 4: Use of Language)*

Mother: *"No, not now dear. You will spoil your appetite for dinner. After dinner, you may have ice cream for your dessert."*

Child: *"No, Mommy, now. I want it now."*

Mother: *"After dinner, dear."*

Child: *"Now! Mommy, now! Now! I hate you, Mommy!" (screaming; child has regressed to Phase 3: Verbal Aggression)*

The child goes to the gallon of ice cream and attempts to open it; mother intervenes, takes it away, and puts it in the freezer. Amanda kicks at the refrigerator door and performs an all-out temper tantrum (further regression to Phase 2: Physical Aggression). The child now becomes quiet, sticks her thumb into her mouth, and sits on the floor, with a flat facial expression as if looking off into space (Phase 1: Passivity). Since the child is underfoot, the mother opens the patio door and gently nudges her daughter outside to her sand box.

If we watch this child's actions over time in the sand box, we begin to see the young child "bounce back" and actually progress up through these phases again. The child drops to her knees in the sand box, still sucking strongly on her thumb (Phase 1: Passivity). Soon she stands, looks back into the house and glares at her mother in anger. Walking aimlessly about, she kicks a sand bucket (Phase 2: Physical Aggression). She drops to her knees in the sand and gives one final shout, "I hate you, Mommy!" (Phase 3: Verbal Aggression). She now begins to rub her hands in the sand, and this leads to vigorous and intense activity on her part. Once she has finished, it is obvious that she has made 10 "ice cream cones" out of sand and small cups. She now picks one up, looks inside the house to see if mother is looking, and with a deep guttural laugh, pretends to eat every one of the ten ice creams cones. She casts great victory glances toward mother (Phase 4: Language [hidden language of symbolic play]). Through symbolic play, we have seen the child harmlessly fantasize a new ending to a reality experience that serves her need for self-healing of her anger and negative feelings. Haven't we as adults done the same in our secret fantasies?

UNCONTROLLABLE MOMENTS

From ages 2 to 7 years, young children are gradually gaining the ability to master their own impulses. They are able to move thorough sequential phases of passivity, physical aggression, verbal aggression, and the ability to use language—both spoken language and symbolic-fantasy play language—as a response to life's frustrations and as a means to obtain goals and needs. We must not think of each phase as simply a "room" where a child opens a door, moves into another, and closes that door behind. These phases and related behavioral characteristics will be seen in the behavior of one child over a very short time period as he or she progresses and regresses through these behaviors, as in the ice cream sand box incident. But with the help of caregivers and skilled methods of limit setting, the less mature behaviors of passive and aggressive actions will dissipate over time and the young child will gradually be able to handle frustrations and use language as a powerful tool to socially interact with others.

Even when children (or adults) have obtained much control over their own impulses, we will all have little "uncontrollable moments." At 7:00 A.M. on a cold winter's morning, we turn our car's ignition key only to discover that the battery is dead. We swear (Phase 3: Verbal Aggression), perhaps pound the steering wheel or slam the door (Phase 2: Physical Aggression), and sit frustrated in a living room chair feeling sorry for ourselves, "I don't need this aggravation this morning," and we do not respond to our spouse's question, "What's wrong, dear?" (Phase 1: Passivity). We have just experienced one of life's frustrations and our response has reflected an uncontrollable moment. We will quickly bounce back and begin actively solving our immediate problem. Adult behavior is not mechanically unemotional and "mature," but we will have hundreds of little uncontrollable moments to deal with daily through our lives.

Due to their immaturity, young children also will have many small uncontrollable moments in which an immediate frustration causes them to momentarily regress to more immature behaviors of verbal aggression, physical aggression, and passivity. We should expect this in their behavior and learn effective skills to deal with actions that might be labeled expectable and normal "misbehavior" in school settings. We, of course, will see that children will have more of these losses of control when they are tired, sick, or in a strange and unfamiliar location.

Although small regressive moments and the short loss of self-control leave both adults and young children embarrassed and feeling guilty, this negative behavior becomes a serious problem for the child, especially when it increases with intensity, duration, and repetitiveness. Slamming a toy to the floor as a result of a mild frustration is one degree of intensity. But if the child at age 3, 4, or 5 sinks his teeth into a peer, and the aggression increases in duration and becomes a constant repetitive action that might occur hourly, we now have a very difficult child who needs our help through planned intervention.

LIFE-STANCE POSITION

The child who has not progressed through these phases, such as the earlier example about Brandon, appears to be stuck in a life-stance[10] position where his day-in and day-out manner of dealing with life is that of passivity (flat, expressionless, inactive, no range of emotions) or of aggression in which, like a tightly wound spring, the child repetitively does physical and verbal aggressive behavior (defiant, tense, impulsive, and uses raw aggression of hitting, biting, kicking, swearing). In the case of the aggressive life-stance position, the actions may be

GENERAL CHARACTERISTICS OF THE AGGRESSIVE (REVENGEFUL) CHILD

- The child is in motion, even when seated; arms and legs are overly active.
- While moving about as unfocused behavior, the child's eyes fall on some object and he seems unable to stop a motor response of picking up the object and then quickly discarding it.
- The child may exhibit run-and-chase behavior, putting himself or herself in a dangerous position or disrupting (leaving the school grounds, climbing to the top of shelving, pulling the cap on the indoor water table) and forcing adults to run after him.
- He may hate quietness (such as rest time) and will fill the void with tapping sounds or his own voice.
- He runs (never just walks) or walks stiffly like a robot (as if using effort to stop and control himself).
- His facial expression is wrinkled brow of seriousness and intensity; his vision darts from one object to another without staying power.
- He has a quick and intense interest in new or focused activities, and appears to push to be first.
- He appears to be fearful of not getting a turn, but when activities take real committed focus, he will state angrily, "I can't", and go off to something new; "I can't!" is the dominant phrase.
- When peers accidentally bump him, he responds with, "So and so hit (or hurt) me," and responds with physical or verbal aggression.
- He describes and is convinced that others are trying to hurt him, especially other active children to whom he or she is attracted.
- He will take an aggressive action toward others without provocation (he is so fearful that others will hurt him, he "hits back first" even when not hit).
- When using fluids (finger painting/water play), he loses control and the materials take control of him, or he loves fluids and water play and does it over and over as if to practice control.
- He eats ravenously at snack time and will hoard food as if he is not sure he will get enough.
- He cannot stop his body in order to fall asleep at rest time.
- He may be overly sensitive to stimuli, as shown by his use of senses (he cannot meet adults eye to eye, he cannot be touched—especially for cuddling, and sounds trigger increased fear and motor action).
- He is a light sleeper.
- He does not choose or enjoy structured materials (blocks/puzzles) that demand thinking to complete.
- When fearful or angry, he may "pepper" adults with strong adult sexually aggressive words.
- He gets silly and uncontrolled in the toileting area and will urinate on others.
- He is feared and rejected by peers.
- He plays power games with parent(s) at departure times.
- He cannot maintain himself in groups (circle time and snack time) and will annoy or take an aggressive action toward peers.

CHARACTERISTICS OF THE PASSIVE (HELPLESS) CHILD

- The child is lethargic.
- He has a flat expression; appears dull and lifeless.
- He rarely laughs or smiles.
- He has little to no attention span; drifts off into an inner world of thought.
- He rejects expressive materials such as paints or clay.
- He cannot be a co-player with others.
- He chooses structured items such as simple puzzles and does them over and over, as if tending to hide behind the material.
- When cuddled, he does not physically cuddle back (feels limp like a wet noodle).
- At times he quietly loses bowel and bladder control (unable to read inner body signal of need).
- He refuses to eat or chooses a narrow range of food to accept.
- He spatially wanders about without direction.
- He may or can do self-abusive activities, such as pulling out small amounts of his hair, biting his skin or fingers, and similar actions.
- He has difficulty awakening after nap time.
- He may cover his ears from all sound (as if sound can hurt).
- He may masturbate at various times during the day, especially during story time or at nap time.
- He generally goes unnoticed by adults.

triggered by minimal interference, or at the time the reason for the aggression may not be apparent. The child is frozen in the passive or aggressive life-stance position, unable to grow developmentally.

Passive and aggressive children ages 2 to 7 are frozen in their development and are not progressing through phases of passivity, physical aggression, and verbal aggression as they attempt to gain control of their impulses. The passive or aggressive life stance toward others and toward play materials in the classroom is the central manner through which they deal with their world on a day-to-day basis.

The aggressive child, by the destructive nature of his behavior, draws attention and it is quite easy to see that there is a problem. However, the passive child can go unnoticed as a "shadowy" child who lives in the background of the classroom and does not cause difficulties or make demands. Teachers may therefore overlook the needs of the passive child. However, based on the passive-aggressive construct (see Figures 1–2 and 6–1), the passive child is to be considered the child with the greatest need—only one step away from needing true psychological or psychoanalytic help. The aggressive child may be considered actually less "in trouble" because the aggression at least is focused outward, obvious in its detrimental effect on the climate of the classroom. But the passive child has turned that aggression inward, spending long periods of time preoccupied with worrisome dreams and fears. This child will do self-abusive body defacing, such as pulling out small quantities of hair, biting himself, and similar self-abusive actions.

THE CHILD'S THREE WORLDS

When a baby is born, her perception and focus is inside herself. She is not aware that this is her own hand passing before her eyes or that it is the mother who appears before her. The infant simply lives internally in a gray area of being awake and sleeping. Gradually, with maturity, the child's perception moves outward and she does discover her hands and body. Then, near the age of 1 year, the child has fully moved into her body world. The toddler is full of large body movement, and, when put down to nap, her legs and body may keep pumping. The child cannot seem to relax or move back into her inner world to relax and sleep. Finally, near the age of 2 years, the child moves into the world of toys and actively spends large amounts of time focused externally, attempting to discover new objects and her social world.

So, we may say that a child lives in three worlds (as do we as adults): the inner world of thought and feeling, the body world of large motor activity, and the external world of work and play with objects and with others. The young child gradually "hatches" outwardly, psychologically breaking from the inner shell, to the body, and then to the outer world of toys and play.

If we place the child's three worlds and the passive-aggressive constructs together, we may say that the passive child has not "hatched out" or has retreated back into the inner shell or world, and is unable to fully use objects and perform with others in the body world or the external world. The aggressive child has "hatched" outwardly to the body world but seems to be frozen in the body activity, much like a toddler, and can neither positively regress back inside himself to relax nor move developmentally forward to the external world in order to play and work with others.[11]

The child on the passive-aggressive construct has then fully hatched and can deal and interact with others through verbal language and play language. If we accept this approach, we see that the passive child is in the greatest difficulty because he is still locked in his inner world. We may also hypothesize that when we begin to intervene with the passive child and begin to have success, we will see a period in which the passive child moves to physically aggressive behavior. Although this physical aggression may appear nonsocial and causes us difficulties in the classroom, the aggression we are beginning to see from the passive child is a positive step forward because the child is now turning those energies outward and is "hatching." Our role as teachers will be to channel this energy into productive activities. In contrast, if we have this child placed in the time-out chair after an aggressive act, we tend to immobilize his body and possibly push him back into passivity with the accompanying self-abusive activities of biting himself or pulling out his hair.

Continuing with the "hatching," the child begins using harsh verbally aggressive language at us or at peers. Again, we must recognize that this is a step up from raw physical aggression. We would all agree that we would prefer to have the child swearing at us than sinking his teeth into himself by biting. The verbally aggressive child has focused the energy into outward verbal aggression, which on the surface looks nonsocial but through which the energy is now channeled through language. If we punish this verbal aggression, we will push the child repressively back to physical aggression. Our role as teachers, again, is to have that child move forward from nonsocial verbal aggression to the effective use of language to deal with frustrations, wants, or needs.

EMOTIONAL FLOODING

With an understanding of the (1) inner world, (2) body world, and (3) external world, we may now understand a concept often seen in young children's behavior. This concept is often called *emotional flooding*. The young child sees an insect he fears or the nurse approaching with a hypodermic needle. This produces internal fear that causes adrenaline to begin pumping in the child's body, which in turn causes the child to actively cry and flail his body about to disperse this energy or to avoid the external stimuli. At this point, the child is so emotional that he is unable to hear the verbal reassurances we wish to give. Instead, our message only adds to the "flood."

This example is one in which flooding occurs as a result of external stimuli, but flooding might also occur as a result of such internal stimuli as thought and dreams. We as adults might have undergone a highly negative experience, such as an automobile accident that had the potential of being very serious and costly. Since it has had such an emotional impact on us, we relive it in our mind over and over, and the fear and unpleasant feeling is just as real as the actual experience. In fact, this reliving can cause us to dwell on the accident for days; we seem unable to get it out of our system or to concentrate on anything else, and our work might suffer. Our outward behavior, whether passive and depressive or aggressive or verbally hostile, might be the result of these internal concerns and our tension.

This is also true for young children, who as yet do not have a strong grasp of reality. The passive and aggressive child's mind is often dominated by internal fears produced by mentally "replaying tapes" of past experiences—seeing a drunken daddy beat up mommy, seeing himself hit, or the many other negative experiences that might be a part of that child's history. The passive child might be emotionally flooded, living inside a shell of inner fear and thought and unaware of the many happenings of school life around him.

For the aggressive child, similar negative "tapes" are being mentally played; they may be triggered by an external stimuli or by a fearsome image that effervesces in the mind until the child strikes out in defense at anything or anyone nearby. Thus, we may see the aggressive child bite another without any provocation by the victim. What caused this aggression? It is possibly the result of an effervescing of the child's internal fears. A peer picks up what looks like a harmless toy—a tiger with teeth—and the aggressive child sees the peer approaching with the "tiger teeth" coming. The teeth might quickly evoke in the child a memory of being bitten by his big brother or aggressed upon by another. The aggressive child therefore fears the peer based on his own internal fear, not on a reality that the peer intends any harm.

The aggressive child fears and anticipates harm and then hits out in defense—he "hits back first."[12] We arrive to stop this aggression and as teachers we say to the aggressive child, "Why did you do that? Tommy was not hurting you or doing anything to you. Why did you do that?" The child's fearsome internal fantasy is now gone as he is forced to deal with us in reality, and he might not actually know why he did this. Or he still may believe that Tommy meant him harm. With so many competing emotions, he now will be flooded with guilt and fear. He now has a new fear of us, the adult, because like other adults in the past, we have "injured" him because of his aggressive actions.

IMMINENT PUNISHMENT

Developmental psychologists have demonstrated that the moral reasoning of right and wrong for the child age 2 to 7 is very different from that of an adult. Young children are too egocentric to understand motive and place themselves in other people's perspective, so their concept of right and wrong is tied to what their parents punish or do not punish. Young children's overriding goal is to maintain their parents' love, so their biggest fear when they are punished or reprimanded is that they might lose that love. At this age, if they break a rule, they expect to be physically and harshly punished; this fear or expectation exists even among children who have been raised without physical punishment. The concept of imminent punishment[13] is that the child age 2 to 7 expects or fears physical retribution for failing to obey adults.

One can imagine the intensity of fear felt by children at this age who have been raised with harsh physical discipline as a daily occurrence. After a misbehavior, such as an aggression toward another, the imminent punishment phenomenon leads the aggressive child to expect us as adults to physically return this aggression. Therefore, we see children flooding when we confront them, attempting to run away from us, or aggressing against us. Believing that we will hit them, they "hit back first." Chapter 7 will describe techniques of verbally reassuring children that we will not take an aggressive action toward them, including bringing children before a mirror to permit them to see themselves and that no harm is coming to them.

SUMMARY

Aggressive and passive children are not deliberately "naughty" and do not need to be punished for this misbehavior. "Misbehavior" such as biting, hitting, spitting, or passive refusal is simply learned behavior from the child's past experiences. With the use of the developmental passive-aggressive verbal-aggressive construct (Figures 1–2 and 6–1), we see that all children between the ages of 2 to 7 progress through these acting-out stages of behavior. With many growth experiences, they gradually move to the development of self-control over their own impulses. We accept this construct as a universal "railroad track" of development on which all children must travel as they develop. All children will have uncontrollable moments, but the child who is not progressing well developmentally through these passive-aggressive stages is stalled on the railroad track of development. He is stuck in a life-stance position of meeting the world day-in and day-out with aggression or passivity. It is our goal to help the child gain great expressiveness through language and self-control and progress to more mature levels of true social cooperation.

Test Yourself

The following questions or statements will permit you to test your understanding of the concepts in this chapter. The answers may be found at the end of the chapter, following the Endnotes.

A. ____ language B. ____ passivity C. ____ aggression-physical D. ____ aggression-verbal	1–4. With an understanding of the limit-setting process and the phases through which children move as they internalize these limits, number the terms on the left from 1 to 4, from the least mature behavior to the most mature response.
A. ____ inner world B. ____ body world C. ____ outer world	5. Susie is making ice cream cones out of the sand as she is seated in the sandbox. Identify in which of the child's three worlds she is functioning.
A. ____ life-stance position B. ____ uncontrollable moment C. ____ imminent punishment	6. John has had his peanut butter and celery snack taken by a classmate. He screams and strikes the peer. Minutes later, he is playing "cars and trucks" with this same classmate. Select the concept that explains this behavior.
A. ____ emotional digesting B. ____ egocentrism C. ____ emotional flooding	7. John's screaming and hitting in question 6 may also be called ________? (Select one)
A. ____ life-stance position B. ____ egocentrism C. ____ the child's three worlds	8. Colleen shares a book brought from home at circle time. She points to each picture, describing it for her classmates, but they can see only the cover of the book. Select the concept that explains this behavior.
A. ____ emotional digesting B. ____ verbal aggression C. ____ imminent punishment	9. During snack time, Walt knocks over the milk container and white milk floods the table top. Three-year-old Angela, seated three tables away, stands and screams, "I didn't do it! I didn't do it!" and begins to cry. This action is produced by a phenomenon called ______? (Select one)
A. ____ physical aggression B. ____ passivity C. ____ uncontrollable moment	10. Harriet has been a passive child for the first four months of her attendance in the classroom, and the teacher has begun to intervene with her. Harriet is beginning to change and has taken several aggressive acts against Martha. She is moving to the _______ phase as gains impulse control. (Select one)

Glossary

Aggressive Child Chacteristic A life-stance defensive position in which the child is in a constant panic regarding others and disperses this tension though constant body movement and varying degrees of violence toward other people or objects that make any demands on him.

Child's Three Worlds A construct that describes the positive aspects of regression, through which the child who is tired and lacks energy may perceptually relax and become unaware of the outside world or her own body. The three worlds are the inner world, the body itself, and the outer world in which the child plays with others and with objects.

Egocentrism Children under the age of 7 cannot cognitively place themselves into another person's position and "look back" in order to understand how others might perceive their actions.

Emotional Digesting The fantasy seen in young children's make-believe is a built-in, therapeutic, or "self-healing" process in which the child can transform himself from a victim of emotional trauma by actively repressing the emotional fear and tension by symbolically playing over and over ("biting off") positive and negative experiences until they are repressed ("digested").

Emotional Flooding A condition in which the child's inner tension—whether caused by inner fantasy fears or outside stimuli and demands—causes the child to become so overwhelmed by feelings that he cannot act or can only disperse this emotional energy through a temper tantrum.

Imminent Punishment Because the young child (2 to 7 years) is preconceptual and has a strong attachment to primary caregivers, her idea of what is right and wrong is defined by what parents reprimand; she believes that if she violates one of the adult prohibitions, she will be physically punished.

Life-Stance Position A condition whereby the child deals with life's experiences in a ritualized defensive manner and is unable to use his energies for productive social experiences with others.

Limit-Setting The process of saying no or denying a child a desired object or action (the desire usually motivated by an inner need) because it may be harmful to her; or the process of making a demand that the child act in a more mature manner.

Passive-Aggressive Construct A construct that permits us to view the child's reaction to limit setting or frustration by suggesting that children will progress through the phases of passivity, physical aggression and verbal aggression before being able to deal with others through language.

Passive Child Characteristic A life-stance defensive position in which the child has retreated to an inner world of emotional fantasy and lives in a constant state of being lethargic, nonactive, and nonintuitive toward life's experiences.

Uncontrollable Moment Short-lived emotional flare-up from which the child quickly recovers her emotional equilibrium but now may feel some guilt because of her actions.

Related Readings

Curry, Nancy. University of Pittsburgh, personal communication.

Fraiberg, S. H. (1959). *Magic Years: Understanding and Handling the Problems in Early Childhood.* New York: Charles Scribner's Sons.

Freud, A. (1969). *Normality and Pathology in Childhood: Assessments of Development.* New York: International Universities Press.

Harris, T. A. (1969). *I'm OK, You're OK: A Practical Guide to Transactional Analysis.* New York: Harper & Row.

Peller, L. E. (1959). Libidinal Phases, Ego Development and Play. In *Psychoanalytic Study of the Child,* # 9. New York: International Universities Press.

Piaget, J. (1965). *The Moral Judgment of the Child* (M. Gabain, Trans.). New York: Fee Press.

Spitz, R. A. (1957). *No and Yes.* New York: International Universities Press.

Spitz, R. A. (1957). *The First Year of Life.* New York: International Universities Press.

Vygotsky, L. S. (1962). *Thought and Language.* New York: MIT Press and John Wiley.

Wolfgang, C. H. (1977). *Helping Aggressive and Passive Preschoolers through Play.* Columbus, OH: Charles Merrill.

Wolfgang, C. H., & Wolfgang, M. E. (1992). *School for Young Children: Developmentally Appropriate Practices.* Boston: Allyn and Bacon.

Endnotes

1. Spitz, R. A. (1957). *No and Yes*. New York: International Universitites Press.
2. See Chapter 3 for the parallel construction of helplessness, revenge, power, and attention getting.
3. Spitz, R. A. (1957). *The First Year of Life*. New York: International Universitites Press.
4. See Chapter 3 for the parallel construction of helplessness, revenge, power, and attention getting.
5. See Chapter 3 for the parallel construction of helplessness, revenge, power, and attention getting.
6. Fraiberg, S. H. (1959). *Magic Years: Understanding and Handling the Problems in Early Childhood*. New York: Charles Scribner's Sons.
7. Spitz, R. A. (1957). *The First Year of Life*. New York: International Universities Press.
8. Peller, L. E. (1959). Libidinal Phases, Ego Development and Play. In *Psychoanalytic Study of the Child, #9*, New York: International Universitites Press.
9. Vygotsky, L. S. (1962). *Thought and Language*. New York: MIT Press and John Wiley.
10. Harris, T. A. (1969). *I'm OK, You're OK: A Practical Guide to Transactional Analysis*. New York: Harper and Row.
11. Freud, A. (1969). *Normality and Pathology in Childhood: Assessments of Development*. New York: International Universities Press.
12. Nancy Curry, University of Pittsburgh, personal communication.
13. Piaget, J. (1965). *The Moral Judgment of the Child* (M. Gabain, Trans.). New York: Free Press.

Answers to Test Yourself

1–4: A4, B1, C2, D3; 5C, 6B, 7C, 8B, 9C, 10A

7

Intervening with Passive and Aggressive Young Children

THE PASSIVE (HELPLESS) CHILD

Larry was a small, thin child with an automatic smile that he used in responding to any intrusion. He came into the classroom on the first day holding his body rigid and looking about as little as possible. His favorite spot was a lone chair next to the record player, where he enjoyed watching the disc spin; he would often look off into space for long periods of time.

Larry rarely used language, except when questioned or prodded by his teacher. When he could not put a puzzle or manipulative toy together, he would just sit with it in front of him, making no motion to seek help or to try another solution. When the other children had snacks, Larry often had to be persuaded to eat just one piece; otherwise, he would eat nothing at all. At rest time, he delighted in shutting his eyes and lying quite still. His mother reported that when she scolded him at home, he would run to his room and fall fast asleep on his bed.

Larry's favorite art activities were coloring with crayons and making repetitive-stereotypic strokes with magic markers. During both of these experiences, he would visually check adults' response for signs of approval. Larry hated fingerpaints and water play. His first response to these experiences was to call out "No, no, no" while holding himself rigidly, and on one occasion he wet his pants. He refused to play with blocks for fear that they would fall and create a crashing noise that appeared to assault his hearing.

In the dress-up corner, Larry's participation consisted only of being dragged in by some of the bossier children and made the "baby" or "prisoner" or some other character with whom they could do what they wanted; even then, Larry couldn't maintain such subservient play.

At home, Larry was the younger of two children. His mother valued the early mothering role and enjoyed his babyish needs and behaviors. This loving family was against "strict punishment" and set few firm limits against which Larry would have to clash.

THE AGGRESSIVE (REVENGEFUL) CHILD

During classroom play periods, Brandon is like a caged tiger, normally crouched in a protective corner in the block room, wanting to use the materials but not feeling free to do so. His attitude is one that says, "If I start a block structure, someone will destroy it." This fearful and untrusting view of his peers causes him to lash out with sharp fingernails, sometimes directly at the other children's eyes, and to repeatedly bite peers for the most minor contact. After his act of aggression, he tells the teacher that the other child was hostile to him, but upon investigation or when observed closely, it usually turns out that the other child merely bumped him accidentally or inadvertently stepped on one of his toys. He cannot look the teacher directly in the eye, and usually turns away when invited to join activities. Brandon is a child who seems to be fearful of all others and who maintains himself as if everyone intends him harm—so he "hits back first."

THE THEORETICAL BASIS FOR INTERVENTION

The theoretical foundation of the intervention techniques that follow is built on the premise that there is a universal "railroad track" of development that all children must follow in the first three years of life as they gain the ability to become cooperative, socially skilled individuals. Difficult children such as Larry and Brandon have been unable to progress developmentally down this "track" and/or are stalled or frozen in their development, performing ritualized response behaviors to their world—a life-stance position—of passive or aggressive behavior. The steps and techniques that follow are drawn from the interaction between the child and caregiving adult (usually the mother) during the early stages of development through which most children normally progress[1] and gain social skills. In a very broad sense, the techniques attempt to "re-mother" the child, helping to create the security and behavior that will launch the child's development.

The plan of action for helping passive and aggressive young children—such as Larry, the introverted passive (helpless) child, and Brandon, the aggressive (revengeful) child—will generally progress through the following steps:

- Step 1: Bonding (basic body trust)
- Step 2: Causal Actions toward Others
- Step 3: Causal Actions toward Objects
- Step 4: Expressing Fears and Ideas through Symbolic Play
- Step 5: Becoming a Co-Player

Note: As mentioned earlier, some physical aggression by children has a medical cause, and these children are placed on medication by their doctors to help control this behavior. Although these children are not the primary focus of this book, the Appendix at the end of the text provides a general description of the most common types of medications given to such children.

STEP 1: BONDING (BASIC BODY TRUST)

Trust versus Mistrust (Birth to 8 Months of Age)

It is from birth to age 8 months that a newborn child gains a basic sense of trust about his world and himself as adults care for him. Through caring, we as parents bathe the child in sensory experiences related to modalities of touch (caressing), hearing (singing and play speaking), seeing (peek-a-boo games), smell (a pleasing perfume or cologne) and taste (feeding). All of these modalities result in close physical bonding and attachment. Because they are the channels to experiencing the real world, these same sense modalities can be "punished" as a result of negative sensory experiences, developing a sense of mistrust. The child whose hands are smacked when he touches safe items that are nonetheless forbidden by the caregiver[2] will come to mistrust his world. The act of touching and being touched emotionally floods or panics the child, and he withdraws from the physical cuddling or the touching of sensory materials such as fingerpaints and clay (see Figure 7–1).

A child who is screamed at incessantly by adults may panic when hearing various sounds and will cup his ears with his hands to shut out the sounds of the world. Or he may need to fill his world with sound and cannot stand quiet, as with the child who continues to make odd noises at rest time. A punished vision modality may also be evidenced, as seen by a child who cannot meet adults or peers eye-to-eye, possibly the result of having been confronted by adults and told to "look me in the face" but are then slapped with a warning of, "Don't you look at me that way, young man!" (See Chapter 6 for a more in-depth theoretical discussion.)

In contrast, most children have a strong modality or cluster of modalities that can be used to give them comfort and reassurance. Some children can relax at nap time by having their back rubbed, others are comforted by being talked to softly, and still others want to be held firmly and cuddled. If the interaction between the child and the primary caregiver is monitored, especially as the child is learning to first adapt to the new and strange classroom, one will see the child's mother "cueing" in the child's best modality (looking, talking, or touching) to give the child comfort. The teacher may now cue with the child in a similar

FIGURE 7–1 Normal Development and Reestablishing Intervention Steps

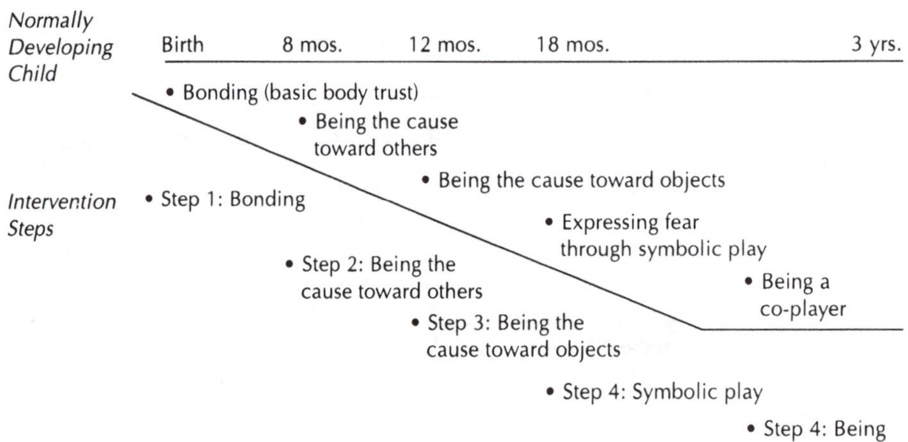

manner and modality. In contrast, if the child cannot relate physically and his new teacher pushes herself on this child in an attempt to comfort him—especially approaching the child in his weak or punished modality—the child will flood, panicking at the physical intrusion or advance. (From the Rules and Consequences constructs, these modalities may be seen as primary sensory reinforcers that have been positively reinforced or punished.)

In Step 1: Bonding (basic body trust), questions such as these are asked: Can the child meet a person eye-to-eye and communicate verbally or nonverbally? Can the very difficult child physically cuddle with the teacher? Does this child socially-emotionally attach and interact confidently with the teacher and peers? For the misbehaving aggressive or passive child, the answer is clearly no.

For most normally developing children, this bonding is well established during the first year of life. When a newborn baby is hungry, cold, and in a general state of displeasure, a caring adult (usually a parent) appears visually before the child to feed, diaper, cuddle, and emotionally comfort her. These pleasurable or comforting feelings enable the young infant to become attached and bonded to the adult, and especially to the adult face.[3] The typical social-emotional interaction between the infant and the primary caregiver is eye-to-eye facial play that can be seen in games of peek-a-boo, "this little piggy went to market," blowing "raspberries" on the child's tummy, and a host of similarly joyful facial play, all of which involves eye contact between the child and the significant caregiver. It is felt that the misbehaving child is not bonded; therefore, the first step is to reestablish eye contact with the child and reestablish a bonding relationship between the teacher and child.

Reestablishing Eye Contact (Visual)

The procedure for reestablishing eye contact with a target child who is not capable of relating to us as teachers in such a manner is to bring the child before an upright mirror and look over the child's shoulder as both child and teacher face the mirror, meeting eye-to-eye in the mirror. This is part of a shaping process that will help or reestablish the child's ability to relate to the teacher. Normally, this child—whether an aggressive or passive child—will have a flat, unemotional facial expression that does not show unhappiness or joy; he will refuse to meet us eye-to-eye or communicate in any manner. This child especially has an inability to use language. Hopefully, this expressionless child will become able to smile and laugh at the end of this fun mirroring activity.

Procedures Bring the child before a large upright mirror, having him stand between your legs or sit on your lap to cuddle (if the child will not cuddle, the following techniques will teach the child to cuddle). You and the child both face the mirror. The child's back is to you and you are looking over his shoulder, able to see him in a face-to-face and eye-to-eye contact via the mirror. The mirror might be positioned approximately two to three feet away from the child and then, with success, the mirror is gradually moved closer and closer to the child, thus narrowing the personal space.

Stick-on Note You will now use a token reinforcer (in this example a "stick-on" note will be used, but any item that will stick to the surface can be used) paired with a primary reinforcer (an edible). In using a stick-on note as a token, start with bright and dramatic colors such as hot pinks and then fade to lighter or less dramatic colors, ending up with white or tan (fading of intensity). Place the stick-on note anywhere on the mirror and atempt to get the child to take the note and give it to you in exchange for an edible (possibly a raisin or piece of cookie). It is, of course, important that the edible be a positive reinforcer for the child, and it may take some experimentation to find one that will work. The edible must also be something that is easily handled, takes only seconds to consume, and will not saturate or quickly fill the child up. The process of taking and giving the stick-on note to you requires the child to visually stand in front of you, and sets up a behavior-reinforcement sequence.

The process now becomes a game—play it with great animation and drama as if this is the greatest game ever invented. You place the stick-on note on the mirror and the child physically retrieves it, gives it to you (secondary reinforcer—token), and then receives the edible (primary reinforcer). Thus, the mirror game is paired with the reinforcers. You may even initiate a game of hide-and-seek by placing some stick-on notes behind the mirror, enabling the child to easily find them. The interval of awarding the edible is at first one to one: Each time the child retrieves a note and gives it to you, an edible is given. After establishing this behavior four to six times, begin thinning the reinforcement by only giving the reinforcer after two and then three retrievals. The task has taught the child to "look out" and visually find and locate an object.

Child-Body Referencing Next, the game is replayed with you placing the stick-on note on the child's body, first on his extremities and then gradually moving toward his face. Encourage the child to locate the token by looking in the mirror at his own body. For example, you may wish to use the following sequence:

On his feet (shoes)
On his knees
On the back of his hands
On his elbows
On his shoulders
On his chest
On top of his head
On his forehead
On his cheeks
On his chin
On his nose

It is important that each time the child pulls the stick-on note from his body part (or your body part, as suggested in the next procedure), you label this body part for the child: "Oh, Larry, you found it! It's on my *nose*!" Many of these difficult children have a limited or absent true concept of self, and this verbal encoding or labeling of their body is a beginning step in helping them gain an understanding of themselves. Also, the child is learning body parts that will be words and labels that you will wish them to use in later steps in the intervention process, when the aspects of causality are taught. This task has taught the child to visually scan and locate an object related to his own body through the mirror.

Teacher-Body Referencing The game is now played for the third time with you placing the stick-on note on your own body. Begin with body parts that are in front of the child (feet, hands, and knees—remember that the child is either in your lap or standing between your legs), and then gradually move to parts of your body behind the child that he can see only by looking through the mirror. Finally, place the notes on your face. Places to put the stick-on note on your body might progress as follows:

On your shoes
On your knees
On top of your head
On your forehead

On the back of your hands
On your forearms
On your elbows
On your shoulders
On your cheeks
On your chin
On your nose

This mirroring game may need to be played with the child—especially the passive child—for many weeks. Again, as the child's token-body-labeling game is carried out, you should begin thinning the primary reinforcer. You should also fade the token (stick-on note) by gradually cutting the paper into a smaller and smaller size and moving from bright colors, such as hot pink, to lighter and lighter colors, finally ending with white or light tan (fading intensity). The target or terminal behavior in Step 1: Bonding (basic body trust) is to use many days or weeks of shaping, through the use of facial play with the mirror, to get the child finally comfortable with looking at your face and making eye contact. In this way, one of the first steps toward having the child bond will be achieved.

Touching and Cuddling

Most normally functioning young children can cuddle and give and accept platonic physical affection from significant adults in their lives, such as teachers. But what is most likely seen with a physically aggressive (revengeful) child is that when he is touched, the teacher will feel his muscle system become rigid and tense and he will physically reject the teacher's affection. It is as if his tactile-body trust is missing, and he acts as if physical touch is punishing or hurting him. Later, after some intervention with this child, he will appear as if he is "sticky," needing to constantly be on the teacher's lap and constantly be physically comforted. In essence, after intervention, it will appear as if the child is making up for "lap time" he may have missed during earlier stages.

For the passive (helpless) child, his cuddling with the teacher generally can be described as the "wet noodle." When a person hugs or cuddles with another, one usually feels that person affectionately cuddling back physically, but the passive child does not give back. He responds as if he is a rag doll or wet noodle. It is as if the child is living in the "inside world" not even connected to his own body. It is through cuddling and a host of other interactions with the child's primary caregiver (mother/father) that the child attaches or bonds with the first significant adults in his life. This bonded intimate relationship with meaningful adults in the child's life is basic to his development, but the passive or aggressive child has not bonded or has bonded poorly. The teacher's goal in Step 1: Bonding (basic body trust) is to intervene through modalities to build on nonverbal communication with the difficult child and then take actions to desensitize those punished modalities, permitting the child to fully experience his world in a relaxed, trusting manner.

Helping a Child Learn to Cuddle

The Shaping Planning Worksheet (Figure 7–2) shows the possible steps in a shaping process where the teacher uses primary reinforcers (such as juice popsicles, the child's favorite) and, through associative learning, pairs the primary reinforcer with the social reinforcers of being read to, being touched and cuddled, and hearing the teacher's words and phrases. Through the pairing of primary and secondary reinforcers, the child is learning to be comfortable, or bonding, with the teacher and learning to cuddle and be touched. This is only one example, demonstrating how to desensitize the touching or tactile modality. In similar

FIGURE 7–2 Shaping Planning Worksheet

Directions: To plan for a shaping strategy, go to the final step (11) and write a behavioral objective first, and then project the shaping steps from 1 to ? (whatever number is needed) that the child might take prior to reaching the final step. At the bottom, write the types of reinforcers you will use. Note that the shaping steps occur over many days.

Shaping Steps (Behavioral Objectives)

1. Peter, while being read to, permits the teacher, for a period of three minutes, to be seated on the floor three feet from him. (The child is eating his favorite juice popsicle—primary reinforcer.)
2. Peter, while being read to, permits the teacher, for a period of five minutes, to be seated on the floor three feet from him.
3. Peter, while being read to, permits the teacher, for a period of five minutes, to be seated on the floor six inches from him. (The child is eating his favorite juice popsicle—primary reinforcer.)
4. Peter, while being read to, permits the teacher, for a period of three minutes, to be seated on the floor and touch shoulder to shoulder.
5. Peter, while being read to, permits the teacher, for a period of five minutes, to be seated on the floor and touch shoulder to shoulder. (The child is eating his favorite juice popsicle—primary reinforcer.)
6. Peter, while being read to, permits the teacher, for a period of three minutes, to be seated on the floor with the teacher's arm across his back in a cuddling position. (The child is eating his favorite juice popsicle—primary reinforcer.)
7. Peter, while being read to, permits the teacher, for a period of five minutes, to be seated on the floor with the teacher's arm across his back in a cuddling position. (The child is eating his favorite juice popsicle—primary reinforcer.)
8. Peter, while being read to, permits the teacher, for a period of five minutes, to be seated on the floor with the teacher's arm across his back in a cuddling position.
9. Peter, while being read to, permits the teacher, for a period of three minutes, to be seated on the floor with the teacher's arm across his back in a cuddling position and Peter seated on the teacher's lap. (The child is eating his favorite juice popsicle—primary reinforcer.)
10. Peter, while being read to, permits the teacher, for a period of five minutes, to be seated on the floor with the teacher's arm across his back in a cuddling position and Peter seated on the teacher's lap.
11. (a) Identify the learner .... Peter,
    (b) Identify the conditions .... when having a story read to him,
    (c) Identify criteria-acquisition ..... permits the teacher, for a period of 10 minutes,
    (d) Identify the target .... to be seated on the floor with her arm placed around him and physically cuddling.

What reinforcer(s) will be used?		
(Check)		(Describe)
x	1. Edible reinforcer	Juice popsicles
	2. Sensory reinforcer	
	3. Tangible (materials) reinforcers	
	4. Privilege reinforcers	
	5. Activity reinforcers	
	6. Generalized reinforcers	
x	7. Social reinforcers	Verbal reinforcement such as story reading, physical proximity

*The judgment as to whether to give a primary reinforcer will depend on the techer's analysis of the responsiveness and effectiveness of the procedures, but the teacher will quickly initiate a goal of thinning and withdrawing reinforcers. The teacher may choose to use a different edible or primary reinforcer.

manner, any other modalities that the child appears to be incapable of or uncomfortable in using freely or in a trusting way can also be reinforced (see Figure 7–3 for suggested sensory reinforcers) in the same manner.

The Shaping Planning Worksheet is given as a model of how the teacher may plan elements of the intervention strategy. A Shaping Planning Worksheet could also have been completed to guide the teacher on the mirror activity or any of the following techniques to be described.

STEP 2: CAUSAL ACTIONS TOWARD OTHERS

"Being the Cause" (8 to 12 Months of Age)

The difficult child—passive (helpless) or aggressive (revengeful)—ritualistically acts the way he does as a defensive stand toward a world of which he is afraid. The passive child has regressed to the inner world and the aggressive child to the body world (see Chapter 6 for a description of the three worlds), and when

FIGURE 7–3 Suggested Primary/Sensory Reinforcers

The teacher may need to do desensitizing activities with a difficult child who may have a punished modality. This list of items has been successfully used in the desensitizing process by other teachers.

	Modalities				
Step	Sight (visual)	Touch (tactile)	Hearing (auditory)	Smell (olfactory)	Taste (gustatory)
Step 1: Bonding (basic body trust) (desensitizing modalities)	• Direct visual cueing: Mirroring Flashlight Mirror Pinwheel Colored lights Bubbles Reflector Strobe lights Christmas tree ornaments Wrapping paper Rubber worms	• Cuddling at lap-time • Tactile training: Balloons Wind fan Electric fans Air from hair dryers (on low setting) Body lotion Electric massager Body powder Feather duster Water Sand Burlap Silly Putty	• Soft verbal words • Mother's voice on audiotape Auditory training: Party blowers Push toys Whistles Bells Wind chimes Tambourines Harmonica Car keys Kazoos Bike horns	• Mother's smell (perfume) • Olfactory training: Garlic clove Vinegar Coffee Perfume Cinnamon Suntan lotion Oregano After-shave lotion Flowers Vanilla extract	• Teacher/ child eating • Taste training: Fruit juice Flavored gelatin Raisins Cereal Honey Pickle relish Peanut butter Toothpaste Lemon juice Bacon bits Apple butter

Source: Adapted from *The Special Educator's Handbook* by D. L. Westling and M. A. Koorland, 1989, Boston: Allyn and Bacon.

objects and people make any demand from these children, they are not confident and do not know how to "be the cause" or make the world meet their needs. Therefore, they have a *behavioral vacuum* [4] of not knowing how to perform appropriate behaviors, to "be the cause" of actions in and upon their world. The life-stance position of the passive child is one of helplessness and a feeling of unworthiness, whereas the motivation of the aggressive child is revengefulness—"The world has hurt me, and it is a frightening place; I will fight back and hurt others before they hurt me." In Step 1: Bonding (basic body trust), the teacher has begun to reestablish trust in these children at the very basic body level by having them attach to her and to desensitize modalities that may have been "punished." With minimal trust beginning to be established, we may now begin techniques found under Step 2 by beginning to teach the child to initiate and take action—to be the cause of actions that will occur and affect himself and others.

Procedures Continue with the mirroring activity as described in Step 1, with the child in your lap or between your knees while you are both before an upright mirror. There are three new goals in this step: (1) to have the child gain an awareness of self through motor action and labeling of his body parts, (2) to have the child learn to imitate your actions, and (3) to teach the child to initiate actions to get you to follow, thus "being the cause." (Normally, older infants ages 8 to 12 months are learning these goals of self-awareness and causality.)

During the stick-on note reinforcer game, you verbally encoded by labeling the child's body parts as well as your own. Now ask the child to show you *your* foot (knee, arm, elbow, shoulder, etc.) by having him touch that part. If the child fails to respond, you will need to use some form of reinforcer, either an edible or a stick-on note token that he can turn in for an edible. Alternatively, you may need to back up and do more of the procedures described in Step 1. Use your judgment and the learning reinforcement procedure until the child can effectively show, through touching, that he knows all the parts of your body mentioned in Step 1. Next, perform a similar process with the child's body as a reference, having him touch his own body parts: "Larry, show me your chin (knee, shoulder, head, etc.)." The same behavioral teaching and reinforcers may be used if necessary.

Through the mirror activity, you now begin to teach the child to imitate. In all of the imitative games that follow, certain actions will occur:

- First, you will provide the lead or model for the child as to how to perform the imitation, using your body. Employ imitative activities (open/close your mouth, open/close your eyes, shake your head to the right, shake your head to the left, touch the top of your head, open and close your hands, and a host of any other imitative body actions you may devise.) Then teach the child to imitate these simple actions. Again, reinforcers may be used to get the child to perform this behavior, and a shaping planning form (Figure 7–2) may need to be used for guidance.
- Second, have the child perform the behavior (open/close his mouth, etc.) while you imitate the child's actions. At a very basic level, he is nonverbally being the "cause" through imitation of the teacher.
- Third, teach the child to imitate by model using traditional hand games often used in early childhood classrooms. The "Ten Little Indians" or "Thumbkin" are examples (see other examples in Figure 7–4). Again, the child is further developing the skill of learning to be the cause with these games, which require language output accomplished by motor actions.

FIGURE 7–4 Imitative Body-Hand Games

Little Boy
Here's a little boy
(child makes fist with thumb extended)
That's going to bed.
(cover fist with second hand)
Down on the pillow
He lays his head.
He wraps the covers
(second hand closes around fist, letting thumb be exposed)
Around him tight.
And that's the way
He sleeps all night.

Grandma's Glasses
Here are grandma's glasses
(fingers make glasses over eyes)
Here is grandma's hat.
(two index fingers make pointed hat)
Here's the way she folds her hands
(fold hands and lay in lap)
And lays them in her lap.

Grandpa's Glasses
Grandpa lost his glasses
(fingers make glasses over eyes)
Before he went to bed.
Guess where grandma found them?
Right on top of grandpa's head!
(move glasses on top of head)

Pig
I had a little pig
(fist with thumb up)
And I fed it in a trough
(make cup of left hand)
He got so big and fat,
(make circle of arms)
That his tail popped off!
(clap both hands and knees)
So, I got me a hammer
(one hand is hammer)
And I got me a nail
(hammer on thumb of other hand)
And I made the pig
(continue to hammer)
A wooden tail!

Five Little Astronauts
Five little astronauts
(hold up fingers of one hand)
Ready for outer-space.
The first one said,
(hold up one finger)
"Let's have a race."
The second one said,
(hold up two fingers)
"The weather's too rough."
The third one said,
(hold up three fingers)
"Oh, don't be gruff."
The fourth one said,
(hold up four fingers)
"I'm ready enough."
The fifth one said,
(hold up five fingers)
"Let's blast off!"
10, 9, 8, 7, 6, 5, 4, 3, 2, 1
(start with ten fingers and put one down with each number)
(clap loudly with "Blast Off")
BLAST OFF!!

Mr. Bullfrog
Mr. Bullfrog sat on a big old rock
(fist with thumb up)
Along came a little boy
(left hand walks)
Mr. Bullfrog KERPLOP!
(both hands slap knee)

Touch and Clap 1-2-3-4
Hands on your hips, hands on your knees
Now put them behind you if you please!
Then on your shoulders, then on your nose
Touch your eyes, then touch your toes
Hold your hands high up in the air
Then down at your side, now touch your hair
Hold your hands high up as before.
Now let's clap 1-2-3-4.

(continued)

FIGURE 7–4 Imitative Body-Hand Games (continued)

Thumbkin
(hold both hands behind back)
Where is Thumbkin? Where is Thumbkin?
Here I am, here I am
(bring out one hand showing thumb; bring out the other)
How are you today, sir?
(wiggle other thumb)
Very well, I thank you.
(wiggle other thumb)
Run away. Run away.
(put one hand behind back, put the other hand behind back)
Where is Pointer? Where is Pointer?
(bring out index fingers—one at a time)
Here I am, here I am
How are you today, sir? Very well, I thank you.
Run away. Run away.
Where is Tall man? Where is Tall man?
Here I am, here I am.
How are you today, sir? Very well, I thank you.
Run away. Run away.
Where is Ring man? Where is Ring man?
Here I am, here I am.
How are you today, sir? Very well, I thank you.
Run away. Run away.
Where is Pinkie? Where is Pinkie?
Here I am, here I am.
How are you today, sir? Very well, I thank you.
Run away. Run away.
Where is the family? Where is the family? Here we are, here we are.
How are you today, sir? Very well, we thank you.
Run away. Run away.

Open, Shut Them
(holding both hands in front of chest)
Open, shut them; open, shut them
Let your hands go clap.
Open, shut them; open, shut them
Lay them in your lap.
Walk them, walk them, walk them, walk them
(making walking motions up legs and trunks toward head)
Right up to your chin
Open up your little mouth—but
Do not let them in!
(quickly pull hands away from chin and hide behind back)

Ten Little Indians
(begin with two hands in front of chest with all fingers closed)
One little, two little, three little Indians.
(raise left little finger, left ring finger, left middle finger)
Four little, five little, six little Indians.
(left forefinger, left thumb, right thumb, etc.)
Seven little, eight little, nine little Indians,
Ten little Indian boys (girls, children)
Ten little, nine little, eight little Indians.
(reverse)
Seven little, six little, five little Indians.
Four little, three little, two little Indians
One little Indian boy *(girl/child) (allow left little finger to stand)*

Five in the Bed
There were 5 in the bed
(hold up 5 fingers of one hand)
And the little one said,
(wiggle little finger)
Roll over, Roll over
(make rolling motion from little finger towards thumb—twice)
So, they all rolled over
(roll hand around in circular motion)
And one fell out
(fold thumb down)
There were 4 in the bed
(hold up 4 fingers)
And the little one said,
Roll over, Roll over
So, they all rolled over
and one fell out
There were 3 in the bed
(etc.)
And one fell out.
There was 1 in the bed
And the little one said,
Good night, Good night.
(fold little finger down)

- Fourth, the child now plays imitative games (Figure 7–4) to get you to follow or imitate him. With the attainment of this skill, a large gain has been made in teaching and reestablishing a sense of causality for the child.

What is important in the mirroring and imitative activities is to have the passive and aggressive child initiate the game, or be the cause, while the teacher follows. It is important that these games be a fun and joyful activity, and the hope is that the child gets caught up in the fun of the activity like most well-functioning children would. What might appear to be a nonsense game is in fact an initiating activity for the child, allowing him to be the cause with language and, symbolically, with his hands (e.g., pretending to wear grandma's glasses).

Being the Cause through Language We may now return to the body-labeling mirroring game by asking the child to choose one of the teacher's body parts while she says its name (using reinforcers if necessary). This simple activity requires the child to initiate this simple action motorically—the first rudimentary acts of causing an action by the teacher. The game of "you point and touch, and I say" now moves to the child's own body, with the child providing the initiation and lead in the game while the teacher follows. (*Note*: Discussion from this point on will not mention reinforcers, although if they are necessary to obtain the desired actions, the teacher may use reinforcers or the shaping planning form, shown in Figure 7–2.)

The next target behavior is to have the child use words to "be the cause" of actions by the teacher. The teacher initiates a game in which the child states the name of a body part (knee, chin, etc.) and the teacher points, using her body first and then moving to the child's body. With this accomplished, we now have the child using words to be the cause. We should now begin to see the child's face becoming more animated, with the beginning of a smile and signs of enjoyment.

STEP 3: CAUSAL ACTIONS TOWARD OBJECTS

Learning to Touch

Through mirroring, a bonding process between the difficult child and the teacher has begun. The child gradually comes to enjoy making eye contact with the teacher. The teacher has taught the child to cuddle, and now he uses his entire body for a sense of pleasure and comfort as he nestles into the laps of significant adults. Now the child, just as the infant did during the first year of life, needs to reach out into the world and begin to have an effect on his world—"being the cause toward objects." (Normally this begins in the infant at age 8 to 12 months and dominates toddler ages 12 to 18 months.) This is typically done by the child's hands through the sense of touch.

If the child's act of touching and extending his hand into the world has been punished, one will see him withdraw from touching and panic or flood when such demands are made. (Normally it is the young toddler age 12 to 18 months who has learned to be the cause toward objects from a developmental perspective.)

The teacher now attempts to bring Larry, the passive child referred to earlier in this chapter, to the fingerpainting area or the water table to enjoy these activities. Larry appears to panic, refuses to put his hands into the fingerpaint or other fluids, and wishes to flee from the activity. The aggressive child, on the other hand, is magnetically drawn to such fluid materials; the materials seem to seduce him in stereotypic play, until he loses control (throwing the water aggressively at others or tearing the fingerpainting paper). It is as if the passive child is dramatically overcontrolled and turned inward (inner world), unable to use his hands outwardly with creative materials, whereas the aggressive child is turned outward (body world) and enjoys full use of these materials. The aggressive child's enjoyment, however, is only for the sensory experience and not for creating products, and he is likely to become controlled or overwhelmed by these materials. That is why aggressive children will literally climb into the water table or totally cover themselves with fingerpaint. In Step 3: Causal Actions toward Objects, the target behavior is to have the child use his hands to actively manipulate and use materials, first for the sensory pleasure and later to create a product—but always, and especially for the aggressive child, with control.

Procedures Sit on a small chair in front of previously prepared fingerpaints, with the child on your lap or standing between your legs. (For the passive child the fingerpaints should be on a very small cafeteria-type tray [as small as 4 × 6 inches]; with success, the process will advance to larger and larger trays, eventually to as large as 2 × 3 feet. For the aggressive child, the fingerpainting will occur on the large 2 × 3 cafeteria tray, gradually moving to smaller and smaller trays. The tray's raised edges communicate clear boundaries for the child—a message that is not conveyed by fingerpaints simply laid on a table. [See the concepts of control of error and degrees of freedom in Chapter 9.])

Encourage the child to experiment by placing his hands into the fingerpaints and smearing it to enjoy the sensory experience. (It is advisable that you and the child wear aprons or smocks to protect yourselves from paint. Difficult children can become quite upset if paint gets on their clothing, and the apron or smock enables the child to feel much freer in doing such activities. You should experiment with various colors, beginning with light shades of white or yellow, and then move to more dramatic shades of red, orange, or black. Make a mental note as to which colors are more upsetting for the child and then make a special effort to introduce these colors gradually.)

Generally, a passive and restricted child will panic at your first request to smear paint with his hands. You should first model the "smearing with hands" behavior as a way of introducing the fluid medium to the child. As you hold the child in your lap at the table in front of the fingerpaints, bring your arms around the child, place your hands into the paints and begin to smear the paints, covering the entire surface of the tray. Sing or talk, rocking yourself back and forth to give all indications that this is a fun and safe activity.

Next, manually prompt the child by asking him to place his hands on the back of your hands as you repeat the smearing action. With the child's hands still on the back of yours, smear with a wooden object such as a pencil, stick, or paintbrush. Next, eliminate the object and use one finger of each hand, and then, finally, use your entire hands. Now ask the child to repeat the modeled sequence, first smearing with a wooden object (paintbrush), then one finger on each hand, and finally with full hands. The speed at which the child will be able to progress through this lead-in manual prompting will vary greatly, and you must be sensitive to the child's growing anxiety. Over a number of sessions, make demands but do not rush the child too quickly. Ultimately, the child will reach a point where he has gained the freedom to engage in fluid painting and he begins to find joy in the activity. Fluids, especially fingerpaints, show immediate response to even the most minimal action by the child and they give the child the immediate feedback of its sensory feel.

In working with passive and aggressive children as they learn to be the cause with objects (fingerpainting), teachers will find very different results. The passive child will reject the attempt and we may again need to use reinforcers and shaping. The passive child is described as living in an inner world cut off from his own body and outside happenings. The purpose of the chosen medium is to have the child become physically more expressive. The sensory experience with the fluids, which may be initially frightening for the overcontrolled passive child, is just the medium that is needed to enable him to become freer and more relaxed and to enjoy such experiences, which are highly attractive to most well-functioning children.

The aggressive child, on the other hand, will only minimally hesitate to engage with such materials. He will tend to dive right in and become more and more active and excited, until the materials begin to take over and he floods, losing control of the materials and himself. He will begin to smear outside the boundaries of the tray, smearing paint up his arms, on nearby tables, or even on the walls. At worst, the child might become aggressive and attempt to smear the teacher and frighten her with the sticky materials. It is the teacher's job to not permit the aggressive child to lose control while fingerpainting. She may bring her hands around the child, placing her hands on top of his, and manually and verbally help him slow down and control the medium. If the loss of control is extremely dramatic, she might have to remove the child from the materials for a short period, and then reintroduce him a short time later.

Fluid materials such as fingerpaints actively permit the teacher to turn the passive child expressively outward, whereas for the aggressive child—who is already "out"—this fingerpainting becomes a context for learning control. Once the child has developed the expressive freedom to use such materials freely—but under control within the body world of sensory experience—he will gradually gain the parallel freedom to be expressive in the real world with others.

With this success through fingerpainting with these children, a full curriculum of fluid play materials (sand play, easel painting, clay, modeling dough, and various drawing materials) may be presented to build on the expressive nature of these materials. (See Chapter 13 on the value of play.) Soon, the child's sensorimotor use of the fluid materials will change to create recognizable symbolic products (e.g., instead of merely smearing, the child will paint a picture of a dog).

STEP 4: EXPRESSING FEARS AND IDEAS THROUGH SYMBOLIC PLAY

Near the age of 2, young children begin to show the cognitive capacities to play symbolically. They begin to use toys or even household items to express their fantasy ideas related to their age interest and emotional concerns. (The toddler, for example, uses domestic play themes of "being like mother.") Passive and aggressive young children, possibly ages 3 to 6, still may not demonstrate this ability to express themselves symbolically or ventilate inner emotional feelings. During Step 4: Symbolic Play, the teacher attempts to reteach the children to play, and their first attempts might show strongly aggressive themes.

Procedures Bring the child to a rug or floor area with a collection of small miniature toys (micro-symbolic toys), such as rubber people, animals, toy furniture, and similar items. Encourage and ask the child to use these toys in make-believe fantasy play.

Depending on the amount of time you can get free from total classroom supervision, the play facilitation might be done (1) in a small empty room, office,

SUGGESTED MICRO-SYMBOLIC TOYS

Rubber animal families
Rubber wild animals
Rubber farm animals
A collection of small blocks
Small wooden transportation toys (cars, trucks, etc.)
Miniature playhouse with furniture

or end of hallway; (2) during other children's nap period; (3) in the block room space while encouraging similar play with other children under your supervision; or (4) while other children are on the playground.

The goal of such symbolic-fantasy play is to have the child gain the ability to use the world of play and toys to externally express the fears, ideas, and thoughts that reside in his internal world. Initially when the child does play these themes, this play might be full of aggressive content, and again one might see the child (1) become the "aggressor" and do unto others as he feels has been wrongly done to him; (2) digest the "bad" experience piecemeal by replaying this "tape" over and over until he tires and represses it; or (3) change the outcome in fantasy to make it more acceptable. (See Chapter 13 for a full explanation of the value of play.)

The teacher's facilitation or intervention to help the child play symbolically will gradually progress up a continuum from an open, noncontrolling position to gradually becoming more closed or controlling (see Figure 7–5). The general techniques, moving from open to closed, are looking on, nondirective statements, questions, directive statements, and physical intervention; this, of course, is the Teacher Behavior Continuum. Let's see how this process might develop:

Mike is a passive child with whom the teacher has been intervening, using methods found in Steps 1 through 3 for a number of weeks. She is now attempting to begin techniques in Step 4: Symbolic Play. The teacher and Mike are seated facing each other on the rug in the block section of the classroom, while the remaining children are outside with the classroom aide.

FIGURE 7–5 Play Facilitation Continuum

OPEN (NONCONTROLLING) → **CLOSED (CONTROLLING)**

Looking On	Nondirective Statements	Questions	Directive Statements	Physical Intervention
1.(a) Nonverbal acknowledgments	2. Active listening	1.(b) Door openers 3. "What" questions	4. Tell what to do	5. Teacher plays

Between them are a toy rubber farm and wild animals, small bendable people, and house furniture.

Mike quickly glances at the toys. He takes a toy tiger, holds it in both hands on his lap, drops his eyes, and takes no other actions.

Teacher Facilitator: *(Looks on at Mike and the toys and smiles [nonverbal acknowledgments].) "Mike, these are safe toys for you to play with. I would like you to take the toys and make any story you would like to make" (teacher states goal).*

Mike: *(Reaches out and takes a bendable "father" toy, now holding the tiger in the right hand and the "daddy" doll in the left hand.)*

Teacher Facilitator: *(Smiles [acknowledgment] and simply looks on for a period of four to six minutes.)*

Mike: *(After a long period of silence and inactivity, Mike brings both of the toys up to his face and appears to visually inspect them.)*

Teacher Facilitator: *"Ah, you have a 'daddy' and a 'tiger'"(nondirective statement as active listening).*

Mike: *(Takes the male doll and tiger and brings them together in a controlled manner; the tiger is biting the male doll on the foot.)*

Teacher Facilitator: *(Smiles, looking on as a nonverbal acknowledgment.)*

Mike's tiger now gently bites the male doll's other foot, then the doll's hand, a second hand, and then the stomach. All of these biting actions are carried out by Mike as if in slow motion and without any sound or change in his facial expression. Suddenly, the biting becomes vigorous as Mike breaks into a quick smile and accompanies the tiger's biting action with "growling" noises; finally, the tiger bites the male doll's head. Just as suddenly as this intensive "biting" started, it now stops and Mike places both toys behind him, out of view.

Teacher Facilitator: *"Ah, the tiger can bite" (nondirective statement as active listening).*

Mike's facial expression becomes expressionless again, and he drops his eyes and becomes inactive. Three to four minutes pass with no action.

Teacher Facilitator: *"Mike, would you like to tell more of the story?" (question as door opener).*

Mike does not respond to the door-opener question. He now slides himself over to the small blocks and quite actively builds two uprights with a cross-piece, creating a doorway. This construction is done with the same controlled slow-motion action. Now Mike places a toy baby lamb in the opening of the blocks and gives a partial smile. Next, all remaining toy animals and people, with the exception of the tiger and daddy behind him, are lined up like a train behind the baby lamb, as if they are in line to pass through the doorway. Mike stops, drops his head, and becomes inactive again for three to four minutes.

Teacher Facilitator: *"Mike, what will happen next in your story?" ("What" question).*

Mike looks for the first time directly at the teacher, making eye contact, and then leans over on his elbows and knees and rapidly builds a full house structure with four walls, using the "door" as the opening to the "house." This work is accompanied by many grunting noises from Mike and is done with considerable speech—quite a change from the slow-motion action of all previous activities.

Teacher Facilitator: *"You have built a house and all the animals and people are waiting to go in" (nondirective statement as active listening).*

Mike now drops his eyes and becomes inactive again for a two-minute period. (The teacher simply looks on.) Suddenly, Mike reaches behind him, and his right hand appears with the tiger, which advances to the "house" and the lined-up animals and people, and proceeds to make the tiger crash and destroy the house and line-up. Mike then throws the tiger behind him and across the room, looks intently at the teacher, and again drops his eyes and assumes his previous inactive position.

Teacher Facilitator: *(Waits approximately 30 seconds, then smiles in nonverbal acknowledgment) "Would you like to tell me the story?" (question as door opener).*

Without looking up, Mike slowly nods his head yes but remains inactive.

We may now see the teacher encourage Mike's play to continue, with the teacher providing nonverbal acknowledgments and asking "What" questions, such as, "What else would happen in your story?" Later, the teacher might tell Mike through a directive statement, "Build your house again, and put in furniture," or she may actually pick up the toys and physically intervene and model a make-believe play sequence and theme for Mike. The teacher's play modeling might be putting the people in their beds and having them awaken, eat breakfast, and go off to work. Then the teacher retreats down to directive statements and tells the child to "play what I played." If the child is able to carry out this structured play, the teacher moves back along the Play Facilitation Continuum (figure 7–5; also these techniques are explained in much detail in Chapter 13) to more open facilitation through questions: "What is going to happen next?" She then retreats to active listening and acknowledgments. The preferred facilitation method is the open (noncontrolling) technique of simply looking on, but if the child does not play, the teacher may advance up and down the continuum (from open to closed, from closed to open) until the child is free to play under his own ideas and initiation.

Generally, a symbolic play facilitation in a one-to-one (teacher-to-child) situation lasts for a period of 30 to 60 minutes. The teacher must take the initiative to determine whether the child is tiring and to judge the amount of time to use, as well as how controlling to be. The most effective intervention requires sessions every day or every other day for a two- to three-week period. Each child will be different, however, and the teacher will need to make a judgment as to how well the symbolic play is progressing. When the child is truly able to play themes with a well-developed story line, he is ready to have other children join him in this fantasy place. The child would finally have reached Step 5: Becoming a Co-Player.

The classroom teacher who does not have an extensive level of psychoanalytical training should not attempt to draw conclusions from the projected themes expressed by children in these play sessions. When Mike takes the tiger doll and bites the "daddy" doll, one could incorrectly jump to the conclusion that Mike has strong negative feelings toward his father and that some family-child counseling is needed. What is more important, however, is that the child becomes free to do symbolic play. As mentioned earlier, certain themes might appear when the child first becomes free to express his strong feelings in play, such as (1) becoming the "aggressor"; (2) digesting the "bad" experience piecemeal; or (3) changing the outcome in fantasy to make it more acceptable. Generally, after one or more of these dimensions of expressing strong feeling is used, the themes move toward more reality-oriented themes, playing out parallel adult roles and behavior.

Becoming Comfortable with Facilitating Fantasy Play

Some teachers, especially those who are accustomed to direct instruction classrooms and may have had little or no experience closely observing or facilitating young children's fantasy play, may feel uncomfortable with the onlooker role. It is as if the teacher is spying into the child's personal and emotional world, and she may not know what to expect as the play unfolds. Therefore, it is recommended that teachers who are new to young children's fantasy play read one or more of the classic texts on play facilitation. Virginia Axline's *Dibs: In Search of Self*[5] is an easy-to-read case study of one child, Dibs, progressing through nondirective play therapy conducted by the author. Also, Axline's *Play Therapy*[6] provides many observations and anecdotal descriptions of children's actions during play sessions, with a discussion of procedures for doing such facilitation. Two books by Clark Moustakas[7] provide many play examples of child behavior and guidelines presented in "how-to" methods. *The Authentic Teacher* is written expressly for the classroom teacher, with some examples of the play of kindergarten children but a greater focus on older children. These older books, which may be out of print, are more likely to be found in larger libraries.

Both Axline and Moustakas work from a Rogerian theory, a total Relationship-Listening approach of nondirective facilitation first developed by the esteemed Carl Rogers. They give nearly total freedom for the child to begin play, primarily using only looking on and active listening, and would probably reject the more controlling techniques of questions, directive statements, physical intervention, and modeling (see Figure 7–5). However, the difficult children in most classrooms are not pathological or emotionally disturbed, and we as teachers are not doing therapy. Instead, we are teaching and facilitating our nonplaying children in order that they will play; thus, more controlling or intrustive techniques are justified.

STEP 5: BECOMING A CO-PLAYER

The steps for intervening with passive and aggressive children are based on the idea that the young child may be taken through activities paralleling the early stages of development (i.e., basic trust with cuddling and modality training [birth to age 8 months], asserting actions toward others [8 to 12 months], asserting actions toward objects [12 to 18 months], and expressing fears and ideas through symbolic play [18 months to 3 years]). If the teacher has been successful with this intervention, she may now begin helping these beginning players learn to express themselves with others as co-players, a stage normally reached shortly after age 3.

To state this clearly, the goal is to have the child learn to be a co-player by learning to do sociodramatic play. When one thinks of social behavior by young children, such things as waiting in line for one's turn, showing social graces by saying "please" and "thank you," and similar social demands come to mind. But the way the young child becomes truly social is by gaining the ability to act out *scripts* in role-play with others.

For instance, a 3-year-old stands in an early childhood classroom wearing a man's hat and a woman's skirt and sucking on a toy baby bottle. This is a 3-year-old who is about to learn to become a role-player. This image represents a pivotal time for the 3-year-old. He is experimenting with a role that he is not (woman's skirt) and the role he will become (man's hat), while still tentatively clinging to the role of infancy (baby bottle) that he must give up.

The make-believe role-play, as sociodramatic play, and playing such things as mommy, daddy, firefighter, police officer, doctor, and similar roles enables the child to acquire the give-and-take abilities to co-play with peers. This will eventually lead to the ability to become a worker with others.

Sociodramatic play can be defined as:

1. Imitative role-play: The child undertakes a make-believe role and expresses it in imitative action and/or verbalization.
2. Make-believe with objects: Toys, unstructured materials, movements, and verbal declarations are substituted for real objects or gestures.
3. Make-believe with actions and situations: Verbal descriptions are substituted for actions and real situations. This consists almost entirely of make-believe with situations in which the child says, for example, "I'll save you, come back, I'll pick you up," or "So that's what's wrong with her—her heart goes 'whoosh,' not 'thump-thump.'"
4. Persistence in role-play: The child stays with a single role or related role for most of a five-minute time period.
5. Interaction: At least two players interact within the framework of a sociodramatic play episode.
6. Verbal communication: There is some verbal interaction related to a sociodramatic play episode.[8]

In Step 5, the intervention process for the passive or aggressive child is begun by using the dress-up corner in the regular classroom when the classroom is empty, perhaps when the other children are outdoors. The teacher can bring together the beginning player and two "star" players. The star players are those children who have already demonstrated their ability to engage in elaborate sociodramatic play and would not be threatening to the beginning player. The beginning player and the star players should have shared a common experience in which they actually observed adults engaged in some form of role activity. This common experience might be one of viewing a film or visiting a post office, police station, fire department, or grocery store—perhaps as part of a class trip. Within a day or two after the shared experience, appropriate props and materials to support role-play should be added to the dress-up corner, and the children can be asked to play with the materials and create a make-believe story.

The teacher should partition off the play area so that the children are in close proximity and then seat herself on the periphery of the group to lend her visual support. Initially, there is a "tooling up" period when the children declare and agree on their role preferences; the teacher must make sure the beginning player

SUGGESTED ROLES FOR SOCIODRAMATIC PLAY

Doctor	Astronaut
Nurse	Pilot
Postal worker or Letter carrier	Railway engineer
Ship's captain	Cowboy
Bus driver	Beautician
Electrician	Firefighter
Teacher	Farmer
Police officer	Restaurant cook or Waiter
Grocer	Store attendant

is included. Generally, the ideas should come from the children. During initial attempts at play, it is common for the beginning player to take a subservient role, such as playing the "baby" or the "victim." As subtly and as unobtrusively as possible, the teacher should help the beginning player maintain his role by providing props or even making modeling statements to aid the novice player, who may either forget or be unable to think of what to say. The teacher may continue with many sessions involving these children, and, in time, add new props, provide new common experiences for roles, and give the beginning player considerable experience with the star players.

If the beginning player is not successful in this first attempt at sociodramatic play, the teacher must demonstrate more structured forms of behavior by modeling (see Figure 7–5). The Play Facilitation Continuum was previously used to facilitate micro-play, and now may be used to facilitate sociodramatic play or macro-play. Notice that the teacher is using the most controlling behaviors of modeling but will gradually move across the continuum to more open techniques.

The teacher may ask the beginning player, previously the difficult child, to watch as she "plays" with the star players. After they carry out a short sequence of sociodramatic play, the exact sequence can be replayed or expanded with the beginning player taking over the modeled part that the teacher had played, while the teacher provides both visual and verbal prompting support. The teacher may continue to support the play of the nonplayer with verbal directions ("Lay down and pretend that you are a sleeping firefighter. When the alarm rings, jump up and put on your hat and get on the fire engine") and then move to the less controlling verbal questions ("What will happen to the injured man?"). The teacher may then move to nondirective statements ("I see that all the firefighters are now on the fire engine ready to leave"), finally retreating to a position of looking on as a nonparticipating observer.

The teacher may now ask the three children to make up their own story. When this is carried out, with increased participation and performance by the beginning player, the teacher can become more open in the use of the techniques on the Play Facilitation Continuum, moving to nondirective statements and looking on. As the teacher finds more classroom time to facilitate the play of the beginning player in sociodramatic play during normal classroom play times, these individualized sessions will be needed less frequently. With the attainment of the ability to engage in sociodramatic play, the previously difficult child will become a well-integrated member of the class and a productive player to the fullest extent of his or her abilities.

VIOLENT ACTS

The passive-aggressive to language construct (more fully explained in Chapter 6; see Figure 6–1) accepts the position that the child's attainment of the capacity and ability to use language to negotiate socially with others is a major goal in the child's development. Conversely, when children cannot use language, they are left with nonproductive and nonsocial options of verbal aggression, physical aggression, and passivity. Thus, the use of language is the key to the final resolution for helping the nonplayers express their needs and acclimate themselves to others. With many aggressive children, this is the last productive step; on the way to that step through the intervention process, the teacher must deal with many violent acts that may endanger other children and the aggressive child himself. The teacher's general line of intervention is to gradually move up the Play Facilitation Continuum (Figure 7–5) to become more structured by establishing limits of safety for both the child and the classroom.

If the teacher has good organization of space and time (see Chapters 9 and 10) and has permeated the room with a "zone of safety and control," she will be free to give the aggressive child direct help. The teacher will begin by observing the aggressive child in closer detail to determine if there is a pattern of consistency to his outbursts of aggression. Is the aggression directed only toward certain children? Does it occur at certain locations in the room? Does it occur during a particular time of day, such as transitions? As the teacher begins to know the aggressive child, she develops a feeling or understanding as to when the child is about to become flooded with emotion and lose control.

When she sees the flooding about to occur, she can move physically close to the child (looking on) to enable him to use her presence to help him control himself. If the child is "lost" in the activity, the teacher might need to cue in the child's strongest modality (i.e., say his name softly [hearing], place a hand gently on his shoulder [touching], or move to get eye contact with the child [seeing]). (See Chapter 1 and the Teacher Behavior Continuum [TBC] shown in Figure 1–1.) Let's consider an example.

FIGURE 7–6 Play Facilitation Continuum II

OPEN (NONCONTROLLING)				CLOSED (CONTROLLING)
Looking On	**Nondirective Statements**	**Questions**	**Directive Statements**	**Physical Intervention**

Continuum	Teacher's Actions
1. Looking On	Move physically close to the child; cue in the child's strong modality.
2. Nondirective Statements	"Paints are hard to control."
3. Questions	"Do you need my help?"
4. Directive Statements	Tell the child exactly what to do (not what *not* to do).
5. Physical Intervention	Channel from body to toy, from toy to play.

Jimmy "El Zorro" has a large paintbrush at the easel and dunks it into the paint pots. He then holds the brush out like a sword toward other children, causing them to scream and run away. The teacher moves to Jimmy, places a hand on his back (cueing—touch), makes eye contact (cueing—seeing), and watches the child's activity (TBC Step 1: Looking On, or Modality Cueing). Jimmy continues to get more and more active and excited with the paints, approaching the point of flooding, and points the brush-sword as if to stab the teacher.

Teacher: *"Paints are sometimes exciting and hard to control "(TBC Step 2: Nondirective Statement).*

Jimmy giggles, again dips his brush in the paints and looks about; he sees Tommy approaching and signals clearly that he intends to "stab" the classmate with the sword-paintbrush.

Teacher: *"Do you need my help to control the paints?" (TBC Step 3: Questions; this is a sincere offer to help the child while still giving him ample time to control his behavior himself.) "Where do the paints go when you use them?" (TBC Step 3: Questions; the teacher attempts to focus the child's activity on the correct motor use of the brush and paint.) (See Figure 7–6.)*

UNCONTROLLED AGGRESSION

Unbridled aggression such as biting, striking, kicking, spitting, and similar actions are common and will often be seen coming from young children. This aggression understandably frightens a teacher, but she must intervene to keep other children safe, to protect herself and school property as objects of that aggression, and to help the aggressive child gain control of his own behaviors and move away from this destructive behavior. The traditional methods of responding to such aggression have been to put the child in time out, make him apologize to the person toward whom he was aggressive, or otherwise punish him in some manner. Most of these traditional methods are old standbys that the teacher produces from her "bag of tricks," but generally they lack any conceptual basis and most times are simply ineffective.

From the discussion of *the child's three worlds, flooding,* and the *passive-aggressive constructs,* one may see that after an aggressive act, if the teacher puts the aggressive child in a time-out chair, for example, (1) he will not stay there and the teacher will be required to physically hold him in the chair and (2) if the child does stay on the chair, the teacher is forcing him back into passivity, which is a more immature and potentially emotionally destructive response. This makes the child flooded with fears of imminent punishment and feelings of guilt, and may result in the child appearing flat, expressionless, and depressed, or beginning some form of physically destructive behavior on himself (striking himself in the head, pulling out his hair, or literally biting himself to the point of bleeding).

From Body to Toy, From Toy to Play, From Play to Work

The construct for intervening with children before, during, and after aggressive behavior is from the body to the toy, from the toy to play, and from play to work,[9] as described in Chapter 6.

This inner emotional tension, energy, anger, and stress must be externalized, ventilated, and channeled. The teacher intervenes to transfer this energy from the body (e.g., the child biting himself or others) to an outside object (e.g., a toy). The teacher thus channels the aggressive action of the child into a socially acceptable outlet. In working with the child who has attempted to bite or has actually bitten, the teacher might say, "I cannot let you bite others, and I won't let others hurt or bite you." She will then add, "Here, you may use the alligator puppet to pretend to bite these toys." The teacher then gives the child an alligator puppet with a large, fierce mouth and encourages him to demonstrate his aggression in the microcosm of toys. Examples of how to channel aggression around biting, spitting, kicking, and hitting are provided in Chapter 5 and Figure 5–3.

The mastery of aggression is a developmental line from the body to the toy, and then from the toy (or materials, such as clay) to play or construction activities. The child's aggression has already been directed into the sharp-toothed puppet; now the teacher encourages the child to use the alligator puppet in some form of positive play. Thus, one moves from microcosmic to macrocosmic play in the form of sociodramatic play. By mastering aggression through play, the child can become a cooperative socialized child who may be called a worker. If the child finds an outlet in toys and play, it will result in a direct improvement in his ability to master the larger lifespace of others.

The first themes with this miniature toy play (puppet tiger or lion, etc.) will be violent and aggressive: The tiger or alligator puppet "eats up the world." Remember the definition of the value of fantasy play as a form of self-therapy and self-healing process as the child (1) becomes the "aggressor" and does unto others as he feels others have wrongly done to him, (2) digests the "bad" experience piecemeal by replaying this "tape" over and over until he tires and represses it, or (3) changes the outcome in fantasy to make it more acceptable. First, the teacher got the aggressive child to externalize this aggression onto toys (from the body to the toy); she then moved the child's energy from the toy to play.

To repeat, aggression is a step up from passivity (see Figure 6–1). Admittedly, this is a difficult concept to accept when one has just been bitten by an aggressive child, but aggression can be defined simply as energy misdirected. The teacher's approach to handling that aggression is to redirect it through diversion (from the body to the toy, etc.).[10]

Mirroring

When the teacher must resort to the last step on the Teacher Behavior Continuum and physically intervene to restrain an aggressive child, both for his safety and the safety of others, the child often expects to be physically struck (imminent punishment) and becomes flooded. By using the basket-weave restraint (see Chapter 5) with sufficient firmness to prevent more aggressive actions, the teacher brings the child before a large upright mirror and, if possible, sits in a small chair holding the child in front of the mirror.

If the aggressive child cannot accept the channeling to the toy and continues to be uncontrollable, the teacher may scoop the child up and take him to the large upright mirror. This will enable the child to see himself as the teacher talks softly to reassure him that he is all right and that the teacher will not let anyone or anything (including herself) hurt him.

The teacher reassures the child with words such as, "I can see by your face that you are very angry and frightened. I am not going to hurt you. You can see in the mirror that these are friendly hands that are not hurting you (promise of safety) but are keeping you safe. I wouldn't hurt you, I wouldn't let others hurt you, and I wouldn't let you hurt me or other children. I am keeping you safe. I am the teacher. I am the boss. I keep people safe here." (The teacher may need to repeat this like a "broken record" over and over for the revengeful child.)

When the child is flooded, he has lost a concept of self or body boundaries and he cannot determine whether it is external stimuli or internal fantasies that frighten or anger him. By bringing him to the mirror, the teacher is helping him reestablish a visual image of himself. Many children have never seen their own face when they are angry. For some, it will surprise them and they will quiet quickly. For others, it will take many physical interventions—including the reassuring statements such as above—before the child gradually gains an awareness that the teacher will not return his aggression by striking him and that she can be trusted as someone who will help him control his frightening behavior.

Beginning Toy Play

If the aggressive child cannot respond to the body to toy or the mirroring intervention processes and remains unable to control his rage, thus constituting a danger to himself and other children, the teacher may pick him up, hold him firmly, and take him to an area that is partially screened off from the rest of the classroom. The teacher may have already sectioned off an area of the room, approximately 8x8 feet, by using movable partitions or simply lining up chairs where the teacher and the difficult child may confine themselves.

This designated area within the classroom is preferable to taking the child out of the classroom, because it will permit the child to move back easily into the classroom space by his own choice. Once the teacher and child are partially isolated, the teacher may say, "This is a safe space for you and me. We will stay here until you think you can go back into the room, or you might want another child to join you here. I have picked some toys for you to use in this safe space." Physical spatial boundaries give children a feeling of protection.

The teacher supplies the child with a toy to assist him in the movement from the body to the toy and on to play. The teacher also begins to visually look on, thus becoming nonintrusive. Most children will become passive for a few minutes and, once calmed, will begin to talk or play. Finally, with delight, they will ask another child to join them in the "safe space" or they will want to return to the general classroom. When the child asks to return, the teacher can ask him to select what activity he wants to engage in, and will assist him in getting started in this pursuit. Usually, the child will select structured materials, such as puzzles, Legos, or blocks that are predictable and easy to control.

Some children will demonstrate a severe form of passivity (see Figure 6–1) after such negative acts and will mentally disengage themselves from the present by appearing to daydream. At the same time, they begin to do such regressive body actions as rocking their body, sucking their thumb, or masturbating. Some children will actually fall into a deep sleep. It is with this regressive form of passivity that the teacher should intrude or become more structured in her actions. The teacher may bring the passive child onto her lap and begin mirroring activities and games to arouse the child and attempt to force him to return to the world of reality. After the teacher has obtained a high level of attentiveness, she should attempt to get the child to play with the toys.

In handling the aggression of the violent child, the teacher should make no value judgment regarding the "goodness" or "badness" of the child or the child's actions. Instead, she must accept the premise that if the child had the internal capacity to control his own behavior, he would have done so. The teacher should not ask the young child to evaluate his actions within a moral or social context as to how it has affected others. Statements such as "See, you have made Johnny's head bleed; you hurt him" or "If you continue to act like that, you will have no friends and no one will play with you" are a form of guilt inducing and simply heighten the anxiety of the child who is already flooded. Guilt inducing is a most destructive form of discipline because it provides the child with no solution to his behavior problems and adds to his feelings of guilt.

The teacher may view the behavior of all children, including the difficult child, on a growth continuum running from passivity to physical aggression to verbal aggression, to the attainment of expressive, adaptive control (see Figure 6–1). It should be our goal in working with young children to help them advance through this growth continuum by using the structure of objects (fluid to structured) and the teacher's structuring of her intervention (the Teacher Behavior Continuum) as the two tools for helping all children, particularly those with problem behaviors.

The final key to the intervention is to have the child turn his aggression to the external world of toys. Once into the toys, such aggressive children will, for example, violently push a miniature auto, thus providing a beginning point from which the teacher can help the child expand this action into dramatic play.

After first visually looking on, the teacher now moves up the continuum of teacher behavior to nondirective statements ("Ah, I see that your car can go really fast and crash into lots of things") to questions ("Where is your car's road? Here are some blocks. Can you make a road for your car? Can you make a garage for your car? What is going to happen in your make-believe story with your car?") to directive statements ("Move your car to the fueling station and put some gas in your car") to modeling ("Let me show you how we may play with these toys." [The teacher physically takes the toys in hand and plays out a dramatic play sequence, verbally describing the make-believe happenings for the child.])

Finally, if the child does begin to play symbolically, the teacher moves along the continuum to less and less structured behavior. ("Now, you play what I played" [*directive statements*]. "What else will happen in your story?" [*questions*]. "Oh, I see that you are driving your car into the garage" [*nondirective statements*].) Finally, she retreats to simply looking on as the child plays.

Once the problem child begins to play symbolically, other children are added to the play environment until the child can experience the highest form of symbolic play: sociodramatic play. It is through the use of role-playing, as a part of sociodramatic play, that children learn to interact with each other within a social context. After many experiences playing with others, children learn their own play potential as well as that of each peer. Through sociodramatic play, the child learns to move dynamically in and out of various roles to maintain social interaction with others. This is much like the game of life in which adults are wife or husband, son or daughter, teacher, customer, car driver, and so many other roles that enable us to be adaptive socially. Thus, if we acknowledge aggression as simply misdirected energy, our role as teachers is to channel that energy into healthy, valuable means of expression for the maturing young child. If we help the child attain mastery through the vehicle of play, he can become a worker and a cooperative, productive person.

MASTURBATION

It may surprise many adults to learn that large numbers of young children masturbate. Generally from a developmental standpoint, this is expectable and quite normal as the young child begins to explore his or her body and discovers that certain sensations feel better than others. But if this masturbation is dramatically more intense and repetitive, especially among passive or aggressive children, the explanation may lie within the three worlds of the child construct (inner world, body world, and external world with others). The passive or aggressive child who exhibits an excessive preoccupation with masturbation may be viewed as a child who cannot externalize inner tension and stress, and so turns these energies back on his or her own body (body world) as self-stimulation. The use of fluid play with clay or paint, mirroring, and channeling from the body to toy—all of which permit an outlet for the child's tensions—are techniques that will externalize these tensions. The masturbation will then gradually subside in intensity and frequency. If the child is punished or shamed, this will simply increase the child's inner tensions, and the teacher is likely to observe more masturbation rather than less.

TIME OUT AND THE "GET-RELAXED" CHAIR

Time out is a widely used practice in schools or centers for young children, as well as by parents at home. Most teachers were not taught the theory behind time out, including the conditions under which it should be applied and how it should be carried out. They simply pick up the practice as a technique they believe is widely accepted. However, for effective discipline action with young children, teachers must be very clear on the terms used to describe the isolation (as punishment) of children (time out) and the idea of the "get-relaxed" chair.

Time out is a technique that belongs to the behavioral analysis discipline (see Chapter 4 for a fuller explanation). These systems consider that children's behavior takes its form because the children have knowingly or unknowingly been reinforced for that behavior, and it is therefore repeated. This reinforcement—of both desirable *and* undesirable behavior—can take place in the classroom, and when it does, time out is used to separate the child from the people or objects providing that reinforcement.

The concept of the "get-relaxed" chair is that the child—especially the passive or aggressive child—is overwhelmed by the external stimuli and flooded by internal feelings, and needs a protective space to relax and quiet down. This is not a form of punishment, but is rather an opportunity for the child to avoid the rush of stimuli. A beanbag chair, a sectioned-off floor space, or something similar is used to give the child a place where he may be alone and have time to relax. Once the child is under control of his own feelings and behavior, he can now begin to play with toys or materials (the body to the toy, the toy to play, etc.). The risk when these children are permitted isolation is that some children may retreat into passivity and actually begin to fall asleep or do self-abusive activities such as biting or marring their bodies or performing such stereotypic behaviors as head rocking or doing the same motor action over and over. These children have retreated to the inside (body) self. If these behaviors occur, the teacher would intervene by conducting mirroring activities and gradually move the child to constructive play.

JUNGLE SAFARI

The question arises as to how to handle the classroom when there are two to four highly aggressive children. A technique called "Jungle Safari" may be employed. If possible, a small storage room or even an area partitioned off in the classroom is stocked with puppets and rubber animals, representing both passive animals (sheep, cows, etc.) and aggressive animals (lions, tigers, alligators, etc.). An upright mirror is also placed in this space. (One school converted a small storage area under the stairs into a Jungle Safari room, hanging jungle motif wallpaper and stocking it with various animal toys.) The teacher may begin with two or three of these aggressive children, bringing them into the Jungle Safari space and facilitating their play with the use of mirroring and the Teacher Behavior Continuum. A fourth or fifth child may be added to the group whenever the child has made an advance toward these children. The purpose of using the small room or sectioned-off space is to keep the aggressive children within arm's length so the teacher can physically intervene quickly if necessary. If the aggressive children learn to play in the Jungle Safari space, they can later use these same skills within the open classroom setting.

SUMMARY

Intervention with aggressive or passive children generally is a facilitation process of one-to-one intervention with a very difficult child who is stalled in his social-emotional development. The steps of this intervention process bring together many of the techniques and theoretical constructs developed in chapters throughout this book. The teacher will need to understand the passive-aggressive construct whereby children will respond to life's demands and frustrations by developmentally moving from passivity to physical aggression, verbal aggression, and then expressive language. The "problem child" is stalled in one of these aggressive-passive life-stance positions, and an intervention process will help facilitate the child's development.

That facilitation is carried out by working to get the child to bond with the teacher, learn to be the cause toward others, learn to express his inner tensions through fluids and symbolic play, and finally—through the use of expressive language—become a co-player with other children. Central to this intervention is the value of play as a process essential to normal growth and development. When the child cannot play, his energy is either turned inward as passivity or outward as aggression. Thus, the teacher attempts to turn out the passive child and channel the aggressive child, through the construct of the body to the toy, the toy to play, and play to working with others. It is when the child can attain sociodramatic play that he has reached the high level of functioning socialization desired in these early years. With the ability to do sociodramatic play, the child now becomes fully adaptive. We should now have a well-functioning child who exhibits little or no passivity and physical or verbal aggression. The Intervention Criteria Checklist (see Figure 7–7) will provide a documentation of the preceding procedures.

FIGURE 7–7 Intervention Criteria Checklist

Child's Name ______________________________
Teacher's Name ______________________________
School ______________________________
Dates (write date)
1st Week ______
2nd Week ______
3rd Week ______
4th Week ______
5th week ______
6th week ______
7th week ______
8th week ______
At the end of each week of intervention, rate the child on the following variables:

Behavior Criteria	**Yes**	**No**	**Sometimes**
Step 1: Bonding			
1. Looks, finds, gives token from mirror	[ ]	[ ]	[ ]
2. Looks, finds, gives token from teacher's body	[ ]	[ ]	[ ]
3. Looks, finds, gives token from child's body	[ ]	[ ]	[ ]
4. Looks at teacher's face when spoken to	[ ]	[ ]	[ ]
Step 2: Causal Action toward Others			
5. Permits teacher to be seated nearby (within 3 feet)	[ ]	[ ]	[ ]
6. Permits teacher to be seated side by side	[ ]	[ ]	[ ]
7. Permits teacher to place her hand on back	[ ]	[ ]	[ ]
8. Permits teacher to place her arm around him	[ ]	[ ]	[ ]
9. Will sit in teacher's lap	[ ]	[ ]	[ ]
10. Feels relaxed when seated in teacher's lap (cuddles)	[ ]	[ ]	[ ]
11. Touches most body parts (teacher) upon command to do so	[ ]	[ ]	[ ]
12. Touches most body parts (self) upon command to do so	[ ]	[ ]	[ ]
Child knows:			
feet (shoes)	[ ]	[ ]	[ ]
knees	[ ]	[ ]	[ ]
back of hands	[ ]	[ ]	[ ]
arms	[ ]	[ ]	[ ]
elbows	[ ]	[ ]	[ ]
shoulder	[ ]	[ ]	[ ]
top of head	[ ]	[ ]	[ ]
forehead	[ ]	[ ]	[ ]
cheeks	[ ]	[ ]	[ ]
chin	[ ]	[ ]	[ ]
nose	[ ]	[ ]	[ ]
13. Can imitate teacher's body actions (open/close mouth, blink eyes, etc.)	[ ]	[ ]	[ ]
14. Can imitate hand actions to "Thumbkin"	[ ]	[ ]	[ ]
15. Can say and imitate hand actions to "Thumbkin"	[ ]	[ ]	[ ]
16. Says name of body part to get teacher to point	[ ]	[ ]	[ ]
Child knows:			
feet (shoes)	[ ]	[ ]	[ ]
knees	[ ]	[ ]	[ ]
back of hands	[ ]	[ ]	[ ]
arms	[ ]	[ ]	[ ]

(continued)

FIGURE 7–7 Intervention Criteria Checklist (continued)

Behavior Criteria	Yes	No	Sometimes
elbows	[ ]	[ ]	[ ]
shoulder	[ ]	[ ]	[ ]
top of head	[ ]	[ ]	[ ]
forehead	[ ]	[ ]	[ ]
cheeks	[ ]	[ ]	[ ]
chin	[ ]	[ ]	[ ]
nose			
Step 3: Causal Action toward Objects			
17. Can place hands on back of teacher's hands while teacher paints	[ ]	[ ]	[ ]
18. Smears with object (stick) in finger paints	[ ]	[ ]	[ ]
19. Smears with one finger of each hand	[ ]	[ ]	[ ]
20. Smears with full hands	[ ]	[ ]	[ ]
21. Can smear over surface area larger than 1 x 2 feet with control	[ ]	[ ]	[ ]
22. Paints a symbol	[ ]	[ ]	[ ]
23. Is comfortable (not overly sensitive) with:	[ ]	[ ]	[ ]
classroom sounds (auditory)	[ ]	[ ]	[ ]
smells (olfactory)	[ ]	[ ]	[ ]
sight (vision)	[ ]	[ ]	[ ]
touch (tactile)	[ ]	[ ]	[ ]
Step 4: Symbolic Play			
24. Does dramatic (fantasy) play with:			
miniature life (micro-toys)	[ ]	[ ]	[ ]
gestures, sounds, or verbal	[ ]	[ ]	[ ]
a theme (nonaggressive)	[ ]	[ ]	[ ]
Step: 5: Becoming a Co-Player			
25. Can do:			
onlooker	[ ]	[ ]	[ ]
parallel	[ ]	[ ]	[ ]
associative	[ ]	[ ]	[ ]
cooperative	[ ]	[ ]	[ ]
26. Sociodramatic: imitates a role			
makes believe with objects	[ ]	[ ]	[ ]
makes believe with actions/situations	[ ]	[ ]	[ ]
persists in the play (10 min.)	[ ]	[ ]	[ ]
interacts with others	[ ]	[ ]	[ ]
verbal exchanges	[ ]	[ ]	[ ]

Glossary

"Hits Back First" Child The aggressive child who fears all peers and adults around him believes they will hurt him, and so tries to defend himself by striking out at them first—even though they were not actually going to harm him.

"Star" Players Peers of the difficult child who can perform sociodramatic play with great skill and therefore can serve as models to engage the difficult child in beginning play.

"Tooling Up" A process through which children become prepared for a new play experience, either by engaging in touching and sensorimotor use of new toys and materials to determine how they can best be played with or by determining which children will assume various roles for symbolic play.

Zone of Safety and Control The sensation of safety radiated to children by the teacher's looking into a play area or zone; the children are made to feel safe, that they can control their own behavior, and that others will not be aggressive toward them.

Related Readings

Alberto, P. A., & Troutman, A. C. (1990). *Applied Behavior Analysis for Teachers* (3rd ed.). Columbus, OH: Merrill.

Axline, V. M. (1971). *Dibs: In Search of Self.* New York: Ballantine Books.

Axline, V. M. (1971). *Play Therapy* (6th ed.). New York: Ballantine Books.

Freud, A. (1968). *Normality and Pathology in Childhood: Assessment of Development.* New York: International University Press.

Mahler, M. S. (1970). *On Human Symbiosis and the Vicissitudes of Individuation.* New York: International Universities Press.

Mahler, M. S., et al. (1975). *The Psychological Birth of the Human Infant.* New York: Basic Books.

Moustakas, C. (1971). *The Authentic Teacher: Sensitivity and Awareness in the Classroom.* Cambridge, MA: Howard A. Doyle Publishing Co.

Moustakas, C. (1974). *Psychotherapy with Children: The Living Relationship.* New York: Ballantine Books.

Smilansky, S. (1968). *The Effects of Sociodramatic Play on Disadvantaged Preschool Children.* New York: Wiley & Sons.

Smilansky, S., & Shefatya, L. (1990). *Facilitating Play: A Medium for Promoting Cognitive, Socio-Emotional and Academic Development in Young Children.* Gaithersburg, MD: Psychosocial & Educational Publications.

Wolfgang, C. H., & Wolfgang, M. E. (1992). *School for Young Children: Developmentally Appropriate Practices.* Boston: Allyn and Bacon.

Wolfgang, C. H., Mackender, B., & Wolfgang, M. E. (1981). *Growing & Learning Through Play.* Paoli, PA: Judy/Instructo.

Endnotes

1. Mahler, M. S. (1970). *On Human Symbiosis and the Vicissitudes of Individuation.* New York: International Universities Press. Mahler, M. S., et al. (1975). *The Psychological Birth of the Human Infant.* New York: Basic Books.
2. *Caution*: These limited examples describe parental activities, but there could be many reasons outside the control of the parent for the same punished modality. For example, a 2-year-old child at a restaurant accidentally pulls a coffee pot off a counter and burns himself, causing second- and third-degree burns; as a 3- and 4-year-old, he demonstrates much fear in fingerpainting or water play. The accident happened beyond the control of the parents, and they are not the cause of this behavior.
3. Mahler, M. S. (1970). *On Human Symbiosis and the Vicissitudes of Individuation.* New York: International Universities Press. Mahler, M. S., et al. (1975). *The Psychological Birth of the Human Infant.* New York: Basic Books.
4. Alberto, P. A., & Troutman, A. C. (1990). *Applied Behavior Analysis for Teachers* (3rd ed., p. 256). Columbus, OH: Merrill.
5. Axline, V. (1971). *Dibs: In Search of Self.* New York: Ballantine Books.

6. Axline, V. (1947). *Play Therapy*. New York: Ballantine Books.
7. Moustakas, C. (1966). *Psychotherapy*. Cambridge, MA: Howard A. Doyle Publishing Co. Moustakas, C. (1971). *The Authentic Teacher: Sensitivity and Awareness in the Classroom*. Cambridge, MA: Howard A. Doyle Publishing Co.
8. Smilansky, S. (1968). *The Effects of Sociodramatic Play on Disadvantaged Preschool Children*. New York: Wiley and Sons.
9. Freud, A. (1968). *Normality and Pathology in Childhood: Assessment of Development*. New York: International University Press.
10. *A word of caution*: This theory of the cathartic effect of externalizing aggression is not universally accepted and has been criticized based on a few controlled studies. In those studies, elementary school children were tested on an aggression measure and then deliberately frustrated. They were then required to shoot dart guns and strike punching bags (from the body to the toy), after which they were posttested on aggression. The channeling into the toy was shown to produce more aggression than in a control group that did not strike punching bags or shoot dart guns. The major flaw in these studies is that they failed to progress to the next essential step by having the children move from the toy to play. Shooting dart guns and striking a punching bag by their nature are aggressive activities and were dead-ended. This may move the aggression from the body to the toy (punching bag), but it does not lead to play and therefore does not permit the child to "play out" the strong feelings and anger. Therefore, we do not recommend the practice of merely having children strike a punching bag; this would be woefully unproductive in the absence of the final step in the process.

SECTION III

Preventing Misbehavior by Skilled Organization

In the first few chapters, a wide variety of new techniques were presented to deal with misbehaving children, clustered around three orientations or "faces." However, some children will be well-behaved in the block area of the classroom but aggressive and acting out when in the housekeeping area or when dealing with paints. How a child behaves in any given space will vary dramatically. Therefore, properly organizing space and materials is critical for preventing misbehaviors from occurring.

Time—early in the morning, late in the day, or during periods such as snack or circle time—will affect many children's behavior. Some will be highly influenced by these time periods, and the skilled management of time and the activities within time periods will go a long way in preventing misbehavior.

In this section, it is suggested that large numbers of children are not coming to early childhood centers, and especially to later formal schools, with the values of "how to behave"; this is because of a value disequilibrium between children, teachers, and schooling. If the values elaborated on in Chapter 8 are not a part of the children's behavior, then how can we, as early childhood teachers, help teach these values and proper behavior and conduct? Children rarely learn values related to positive behavior by being lectured to or talked to, but at this age, these values are learned in the "hidden" curriculum of daily home and classroom practices.

In Chapter 9, the teacher learns how to arrange and organize space and materials for preventing misbehavior and for teaching values through playing within this space. Chapter 10 provides the teacher with concrete techniques for handling misbehavior during critical time periods.

8

Today's Student and Misbehavior

Space and time "speak to" or *prompt* us, and what we unknowingly hear, see, and even smell controls our behavior. Let's take a look at two examples from the adult world.

> *We walk into Happy Harry's Crab House, a coastal sports bar and restaurant that specializes in steamed crabs. The hostess, dressed in short shorts, leads us across a sawdust-covered floor and seats our party at a long picnic table covered with newspapers. The room is dominated by large TV screens hanging from the ceiling broadcasting an athletic event, and country-and-western music blares from the jukebox. Let's step back to watch our behavior, as if we were peeking through the window like a modern-day Scrooge under the direction of the Ghost of Christmas Past.*
>
> *What we see would make an etiquette expert gasp. We eat with our hands, pulling the whole crab apart and cracking it with a large pair of pliers and a hammer. We chug heartily from tall mugs of beer or sweet iced tea, which our companions quickly refill from a large community pitcher. Our conversation is boisterous and animated, at times even shouting. We cheer loudly and join in a "war chant" when we see a replay of our favorite team scoring. We even throw peanuts at the TV screen when the umpire makes a mistake. When we are done, the waitress clears our table debris by simply rolling up the newspaper "table cloth" and throwing it away.*
>
> *Now let's move down the street to a very different restaurant, one that also specializes in crab. The occasion may be a birthday, a wedding anniversary, or a date with that "special person," and so we are dining at Chez Expensive. The maitre d' is formally dressed. He escorts us across a deep plush carpet to an intimate corner table adorned with a heavily starched linen tablecloth and matching napkins. The menu looks like the Magna Carta, and the prices would make a substantial dent in the national debt. We sip very slowly at our glass of wine poured from the $45 bottle of Chateau Nu De*

This chapter was cowritten with Karla Lynn Kelsay, Associate Professor of Elementary Education, Florida State University.

Bubbly. With a collection of cutlery that would make a world-class brain surgeon jealous, we daintily dissect and eat our crab as we relax to the soothing classical background music and speak softly to our dinner companion.

These are two wholly different spaces, with their accompanying furniture, equipment, and objects arranged is such a manner that what is acceptable behavior in one would be unacceptable in another. The space "speaks" to, or prompts us, and we behave in a rather predictable, defined manner. We could defy convention and return to Chez Expensive with a "boombox," which we would play at full volume to listen to the "big game" and shout at the top of our lungs when our team scores. But our actions would be an obvious distraction to the other diners, and we would now be a "discipline problem." In this case, we would have failed to understand the behavior required by reading the special cues or prompts and the context in which we find ourselves. In fact, if we act at Chez Expensive as we did at Happy Harry's Crab House, we might actually get arrested for disorderly conduct.

TODAY'S STUDENT AND DISCIPLINE

Children live and learn within homes and families long before they come to us as students. Early family life and parenting embeds in them a basic sense of values, which they use to guide their actions and behavior as they mature and progress through their schooling. This occurs in the earliest and the most formative and critical years. Schools and teachers, especially elementary and secondary teachers, have always depended on the child's home life to establish such basic values as a concept of timeliness, an understanding of basic rules governing appropriate behavior for the situation and context, and a respect for materials that will be used and the property rights of others. Teachers in the elementary and secondary schools have historically never seen their roles as mothering or fathering. Most teachers of older children consider that parenting belongs in the home—that teachers were not trained to "parent" but rather to teach.

What clearly has changed in recent years has been the family, with the explosion in the number of single parents and households in which both parents work. Large numbers of the recent generation of students that we have been receiving into our schools and early childhood centers have *not* spent their early formative years in the kind of "traditional" families that many of today's teachers experienced in their own childhood. As a result of economic realities, many children essentially have been raised in a child-care environment—far too many of which are unlicensed, untrained, and totally inadequate. It is not unheard of for some of today's children to be cared for in the first year of life by a dozen or more different caregivers. Unfortunately, in many cases, these caregivers are in reality poor teenage girls whose lack of skills keeps them from getting other jobs. These unskilled child-care workers typically stay at this job 8 to 10 months. The literate, brighter ones are "promoted" out of child care by getting a job as a waitress, factory worker, or some other repetitive assignment. This, of course, is a worst-case situation; we must also recognize that there are many good centers and qualified personnel serving early childhood needs very well—though these are too much in the minority.

Childhood for vast numbers of students has changed fundamentally. When we consider that many children spend 10 hours a day in child care, and then count the host of caregivers the child has gone through in the most formative early years, we can see the lack of a consistent emotional attachment and basic relationship with a significant adult in their lives. We may then ask, What values were taught or *not* taught?

Television shows of the 1950s presented romantic views of the "ideal" model of how families should function. This early family life, as characterized by such shows as "Leave It to Beaver," "Father Knows Best," and "Ozzie and Harriet" was heavily dependent on one person—the mother—to be at home. She made sure the house was clean and orderly, meals were on the table on time, homework was done, and the children were playing with trusted friends. We have now transformed to a world of slow cookers and microwave dinners, permanent-press clothing, and, in many instances, an exhausted parent or parents who do not want to be disturbed as they sit in front of the TV at the end of a particularly hard day at work. The modern family, whether headed by a single parent or two working parents, is highly likely to be living in stress just to maintain itself economically.

Through the experiences of the traditional family, children:

- Spent most of their first four years of life at home with adults, joined by only a few selected playmates
- Enjoyed a home environment rich with the exchange of verbal language between adults and children
- Were subject to many prohibitions and rules for daily living—eating times, bed time, how to take care of their possessions and those of the family, ways of speaking to show respect, and so on
- Were expected to produce high levels of achievement and do a job well
- Learned to prepare for the future, saving their pennies for the proverbial "rainy day"
- Learned healthy competitiveness through family activities and games, and later through youth league sporting events
- Recognized that the flow of communication was from adult to child[1]

This traditional early childhood family experience sent students off to first grade with an embedded sense of values, which they used to guide their actions and behavior as they matured and progressed through their schooling. Schools and teachers have always depended on children having certain basic values already in place from the home—things such as a concept of time, an understanding of basic rules governing appropriate behavior for the situation and context, and a respect for materials that will be used and the property of others. The traditional elementary school teacher, dealing with large numbers of children during the school day, maintained an emotional distance from her students. She felt little need for deeper affection and emotional investment with her students because this was implicitly the role of the parents.

It is blatantly evident that times have changed. In the elementary and secondary schools and classrooms, however, the teacher's role has changed very little during this same period of dramatic family change. This has produced a value disequilibrium between the children and their formal classroom schooling, and the teachers must attempt to do their best with students who appear disinterested in learning and appear bent on disrupting the classroom. The traditional reprimands, classroom discipline, or sanctions seem not to work with poorly motivated children. If we accept that students are different because of this change in the nature of early child rearing, we must determine how these differences create such difficulties in order for formal schools to deal successfully with these students. These value and behavior differences relate to concepts of (1) an urgency to work with regard to timeliness, (2) spatial rules, (3) possessions or property rights, and (4) effective relationships with teachers. The value differences must be understood if we are to help students in early childhood centers so that they may be effective later in more formal classroom settings.

Timeliness

Schools have historically been driven by time. Secondary schools were built around 55-minute class periods, with the entire student body moving to the sound of bells. Homework needed to be done at specific times. Semesters or quarters were based on time, and even subject credits are based on time ("credit hours"). Though elementary schools were not as controlled, subject areas such as reading, math, physical education, and so on were based on a set number of minutes per week. Again, time was the steam that powered and moved the machine called schooling. Most of the recent school reforms focused on time, such as adding more periods to the day and equating "time-on-task" in the classroom with "successful" teaching of children. In comparing U. S. education with foreign systems such as Japan's, the media point out that these countries have their children in school six days a week for longer hours. Here again, the focus is on time.

The successful student of today—the one who takes maximum advantage of formal school experiences—comes with a well-embedded concept of time. This student can get organized to be timely in producing classroom work and assignments under the rigorous demands of time. Where did this child acquire this concept of time? The answer is in the home—or possibly today in a *good* early childhood center.

In the traditional family, time has long been a driving factor. Constant and well-defined times were set for awakening, eating meals, completing chores, and organizing the activities of the day or week. In the traditional family of the 1950s, the child was in serious trouble if he or she was not home, washed, and ready for the family meal at 6:00 P.M.. Noncompliance was a serious infraction, and disciplinary sanctions were given to teach the child how inconsiderate and irresponsible it was to be late.

What about the family today? Researchers suggest that far too often the family meal is a thing of the past. Family members eat separately, often in front of the TV, with little or no communication taking place. "Mealtime" may be during any evening time period. Because modern parents work under the stress of time demands all day at their jobs, they see their own children for only a limited time in the evenings or on weekends, when they themselves need rest and relaxation. As a result, they have little desire to place time demands on their own children. Large numbers of today's children are growing up without developing a concept of time as a variable for organizing their lives.

In too many instances, children today place a different value on the importance of time than do their elementary and secondary school teachers. Homework does not get done on time, and children come to class late (or not at all). When this occurs and the student is reprimanded for untimeliness, he or she feels little or no guilt about these actions and cannot understand why the teacher and principal are "making such a fuss" about it. The teacher and school authorities respond by attempting to reason with these students about how this lack of responsibility will have long-term negative effects on the child, including the prospects that they will fail school or will not learn such basic tasks as reading, writing, and arithmetic. There is an inherent futility in the appeal of the school authorities: They are projecting their own values regarding time and concepts of the future, while the child has no concepts of urgency or time. The child is here-and-now oriented and fails to understand the adult warning or advice. The school and the child are speaking two different languages, and no communication occurs. We have a disequilibrium in values, an imbalance between what the child brings and what the formal school historically demands for success.

Spatial Rules

A child in middle school is seated in the cafeteria eating lunch. She finishes, stands up, picks up her tray, and takes four steps toward the disposal window. Suddenly she stops, turns, and returns to where she was seated. Still holding the tray in both hands, she uses her lower body to push her chair back under the table. Without even realizing what she has done, the girl has obeyed a *motor rule.* Sometime earlier in her life, this child learned the rule that "when you leave a table, you push in your chair." This child is well socialized, and therefore there will be hundreds of small motor-rule behaviors such as this one that she will automatically perform daily at school. When teachers or school officials observe these behaviors, they will make a judgment that this is a well-behaved girl, and thus a nonthreatening, likable student. A growing problem for these teachers and school officials is the increasing number of students who do *not* have this girl's sense of appropriate motor rules. Motor rules determine how one behaves at school assemblies, at school athletic events, on playgrounds, moving through the halls, and in classrooms. It is the challenge facing early childhood educators, in this time of changing families, to help young children acquire these motor rules.

Motor-rule actions are performed in an unthinking, automatic manner as one goes through daily life, but they are spatially or contextually based. In other words, they are controlled by the location or circumstances in which a person finds herself or himself. Our behavior would be different at a football game than in a church or synagogue; we act one way at Happy Harry's Crab House and another at Chez Expensive; we behave one way in public and another in the privacy of our own bedroom. The concept applies in any other space in which we find ourselves. Those who have not incorporated these appropriate behaviors as motor rules and do not use them in the right spatial context are considered ignorant, ill-bred, or inconsiderate of others. The mood of a theater or concert hall can be spoiled by those seated behind us talking or giggling throughout the performance. They do not know how to behave because they have not learned the motor rules for the theater.

Let's consider another example. As a funeral procession moves through the cemetery, one mourner is playing rock music on his car radio at such a high volume that all can hear it. At a subdued gathering later that evening, the offending driver is descending upon by the other mourners and berated for his lack of consideration and his disrespect during the funeral, as shown by his playing of such music during this solemn and painful experience. The driver is shocked, for he had been totally unaware of his actions. He was insensitive to spatial and contextual factors (the cemetery during a funeral) and the appropriate motor rules, thus he was seen as lacking the normal social understanding. As a result, he was ostracized. It would not be surprising to know that this adult was constantly a discipline problem throughout his schooling.

When and how is this spatial rule sensitivity developed and the understanding of spatial motor rules acquired? The answer is in the first years of life in the home or, increasingly today, in an early childhood center.

Parents and teachers of the "Baby Boomer" generation can hear June Cleaver, mother of the 1950s "Leave It to Beaver" family, reprimanding her child with a stern, "Young man, get your feet off the coffee table now—and I mean *now*!" We learn such spatial motor rules in our traditional families. Did we use furniture as footrests? No! Was it permissible to bounce a ball in the house? No! Did we eat in the living room? No! We were taught motor rules as they related to context and space from the earliest age. Every room or space in our house had a well-defined use, and children were taught that certain behavior was appropriate in these rooms and other behavior was clearly *not* appropriate. It was insisted that these rules be obeyed. We also learned to "shift gears" as we moved from space to space or room to room, changing our behavior appropriately. We were taught the appropriate behavior to use outside the home when we visited friends' homes with our parents, or when we went to church, theaters, and the host of other places we visited. When our feet were discovered on the living-room coffee table, or when we bounced the basketball in the house, this was seen as a serious transgression and we were disciplined for such misbehavior—often with the plaintive question, "What could you be thinking of, young man (lady)?"

In increasing numbers, today's parents, if they are available, are too tired or are not with the child enough during the first five years of life to make such spatial rule demands. Where does the child eat today? In too many instances, the answer is not the kitchen table; the eating is done almost anywhere—most likely in front of the TV. In many of today's homes, there is no substantial distinction drawn between child space and adult space, with different motor rules for each.

Today, many children and their tired parents use the home space and rooms in any manner, with few adult-imposed rules regarding where certain behaviors are appropriate or inappropriate. The child has free range with no structure. Thus, many children are growing up without a concept of spatial motor rules. When these children go to a school assembly, their teachers see the "misbehavior" as appalling. "These children don't have a shred of common sense when it comes to simple appropriate behavior. My goodness, didn't their parents teach them better?" The answer may be, no. Large numbers of children are arriving at formal elementary school lacking a concept of spatial motor rules. To today's adults, these rules seem so basic that the teachers are shocked by what they see—and what they see missing. Because the teachers were well-socialized, they hold strong values of what is appropriate behavior, while many students appear to have no understanding of why teachers or school officials disapprove of their actions. The students without a concept of spatial motor rules simply come from a different world than the teachers, and so we have a disequilibrium of values producing much tension and frustration in the very teachers who must deal with such children on a day-in, day-out basis.

Concept of Property

Matthew, a kindergarten student who lives with a single parent and a large number of brothers and sisters, comes to school. He is given the usual allotment of books, crayons, paper, and a pencil. As time goes by, Matthew loses his pencil, which leads to a problem when the teacher instructs, "Take out your pencil, everyone." Matthew, unable to locate his own pencil, sees another on a neighbor's desk. It is similar to the one he originally possessed, so he reaches over and takes his neighbor's pencil. The neighbor shouts, "He stole my pencil!" When questioned by the teacher, Matthew states, "It is mine, I have it."

A concept of property rights is not born but must be learned in the first few years of life. In some large families in which little parenting is provided, children are left to sort out property rights for themselves. These children learn a property rule that says if you get it first and can hold onto the property by physical power, it is yours. These children lack a concept of property rights. Matthew is simply displaying his early concept of property, which the other child may see as "stealing."

In traditional families, the mother kept the houseful of objects and possessions organized, and each child had his or her own room (or at least his or her own identifiable portion of a room). All family members knew where everything belonged, and there was a clear delineation of property rights.[2] In large unsupervised families today, there is a form of shared property. If you can't find your own item, you simply find a sibling's and use it as your own. You need it, you find it, and you use it; property ownership is irrelevant. In poorly run day-care centers staffed with young workers who have this same perspective, toys and classroom materials are unorganized and not cared for, thrown into any containers to get them out from under foot. When children from these centers enter elementary school, they will bring these same values to govern their behavior. The teacher is likely to be a product of an earlier time and culture, living in another world from the realities of such children. The teacher will label this taking of others' possessions as stealing, while the child has no such concept of property rights or stealing. The attitude of "I found it, I have it, it is mine" has up to that time permitted the child to survive.

This absence of a concept of property rights has been observed for some time in lower-class settings. However, as a result of the changing nature of family life, even affluent children today are beginning to show behavior characteristics of economically poor children who have never done well in middle-class schools. One can see why many elementary and secondary teachers are frustrated and confused as they attempt to run their classrooms. The very concept values that are needed to be successful in school—the concept values in which teachers believe so strongly—are now missing in many of today's children. The school response is to get tough with discipline, creating more rules and harsher punishment. Children have responded with returned violence toward teachers and schools or have retreated into helpless passivity through which they make no waves—and engage in little learning—until their earliest opportunity to drop out. This is a sad state of affairs, with the schools doing more of what they have always done but with no success amid many indicators of declining effectiveness for more and more children.

AUTHORITY AND LOVE: EFFECTIVE RELATIONSHIPS WITH TEACHERS

Child development research and theory have given us an understanding of how children gain a concept of right and wrong as they grow and develop, and how they view authority. The young infant comes into this world totally dependent on her mother[3] or some other significant person who is consistently there to meet her basic needs, who serves to assure that the child is fed, kept secure, and given large amounts of affection and stimulation. After these basic needs are met and the child is in a pleasurable state of comfort and alertness, she looks up to see this mother or significant person in her life and begins to love by associating that person with the good healthy feelings the child now enjoys. Early love suggests a mother's permanence in the child's world. With her limited intellectual abilities, the young child begins to feel that all things come from and are under the control of her significant caring parent. The child holds a romantic view of parents as god-like, as with the child who watches the sun set beneath the horizon and pleads, "Do that again,

FIGURE 8–1 Development Stages of Authority

Ages

0	1	2	3	4	5	6	7	8	9	10	11	12	13

------mother-------/-----romantic family-----/-----------peer---------/peer/opposite sex

daddy. That was nice." Because of this binding affection, attachment, and dependency, the child first develops a sense of authority that focuses on parents, mixing strong feelings of love and fear. The term *vertical authority* describes this relationship in which the child sees the parents as being above her (vertical), holding power over her life, needs, and actions. The mixture of feelings includes love because the child can depend on the parents for her needs, but also fear that if she makes the parents angry they might deny her their affections.

In the normal development of children raised in traditional families, the mother is the focus of the child's emotional investment from birth to age 3 and is clearly installed as the figure of authority. From ages 3 to 6 or 7, the investment now expands to include the father in the triad that defines mother-father-child as the romantic family. Children tell each other, "My daddy can beat up your daddy," a boast founded in the message that my daddy is god-like and all-powerful. Beginning with age 7, the emotional investment now moves to be focused on the peer of the similar sex (i.e., all boys together or all girls together). Children at this age and older will stand against parent authority, which they would be too fearful to do during the romantic family preschool age, in order to enhance their status with peers. The peer-oriented school-age child wants more than anything to find peer friendship and acceptance in a group.

Finally, in adolescence, the slavish attention to the peer group continues but the child also begins to move out of the same-gender groups of all boys or all girls; the child now wants to be found socially acceptable by those of the opposite sex. The developmental progression (see Figure 8–1) has thus shifted over time from vertical (focused on a higher, more powerful figure) to horizontal or democratic, to focused on peers (see Figure 3–4). Let's look at this in another way.

WHY DO PEOPLE OBEY RULES?

Why do people obey rules, and what authority asserts itself in our moral decisions regarding right and wrong? If we are driving down the street and come to a traffic light, why do we stop when it turns red? Generally, there are two answers to this question. The first reflects the concept of vertical authority: We stop out of fear of getting a ticket from the higher authority (the police)—we are afraid of receiving a fine or losing our license (i.e., punishment). The second reflects horizontal authority or reciprocity: We realize that in order to be safe while driving, some "rules of the road" are necessary. Therefore, we give up our selfish desire to get home first or to beat others; we obey the light signal because we depend on others to obey in a similar manner, thus contributing to the safety goal shared by all (reciprocity).

For children *younger* than age 7, the abstract idea of reciprocity—"for the good of all"—is intellectually beyond their ability to understand. Therefore, their first moral position on concepts of right or wrong, or naughtiness, is vertical. "My daddy is stronger than your daddy" is a boast that indicates that the child sees the parent-adult as god-like and all-powerful, and as a person who must be obeyed. The young child obeys out of the two-edged sword of love and fear of the parent (vertical authority figure). This will be true for all developing children at this early age, no matter how "nonpunishing" their upbringing has been.

During the school years (age 6 and older), the child is bridging out of vertical moral thought into horizontal reciprocity. If all goes well in development, the child firmly establishes this horizontal attitude near the age of 11 or 12.[4] The elementary school years are the transitional period, standing between home and family and the wider society. The position of discipline in the early childhood center, then, would be to lay a foundation that will enable the later school to help the child grow morally to a full understanding of reciprocity. We must use care, for our school discipline methods may either retard this moral growth or fully facilitate it. The question for the early childhood educator teaching children ages 3 to 7 is: Can we use discipline and classroom management techniques to help the child reach this more mature moral goal? The answer is an unequivocal yes, and the purpose of The Three Faces of Discipline is to provide a model to guide teachers along the path toward that desired result.

Educational Practice

The premise is that large numbers of today's children are growing up differently from the childhood experiences of their own teachers and that early childhood experiences of the past were geared to better preparing children for work within the school structure. Thus, today most children and their schools live in two different cultures, or value structures, and this difference can be seen dramatically in the excessively large numbers of students who drop out. The lasting positive effect[5] that early childhood programs such as Head Start have had on economically poor children is a result of these programs' ability to teach self-discipline and a sense of values to these children. If we accept this premise, it now becomes our role as early childhood teachers to serve these new needs of today's children by recognizing and addressing certain realities:

1. The values and related behaviors of motor rules related to the urgency of time, spatial rules, possession of objects, and reciprocity of relationships are still basic and needed in today's adult world and should be taught to students.
2. Early childhood classrooms and teachers must teach, or aggressively find ways of helping students learn, these values and related behaviors.
3. Using, and even increasing, the role of punishment in the name of discipline might be adding fuel to the fire for a large number of today's students, who cannot or do not understand our expectation that they comply with the demands of schools and schooling.

SUMMARY

The young child, who will be in an early childhood center for much of his early formative life, comes to the elementary teacher still in the role of "becoming." It is as if he is still "clay" to be molded. Our practices—especially involving the basic aspect of setting limits and taking actions when misbehavior occurs—will have a life-long educational effect on these children. If we do not succeed in fostering these values, elementary schools will continue to find large numbers of today's children arriving without concepts of (1) timeliness of work, (2) spatial rules, (3) possessions or property rights, and (4) effective relationships with teachers.

Glossary

Effective Relationships The ability of the child to work independently from nurturing adults, while still at times seeking them out for appropriate exchanges of affection.

Property Rights The value and understanding of property ownership.

Spatial Rules The motor-rule behavior used unthinkingly as a person acts in a socially acceptable manner, as defined by the spatial cue and social context.

Timeliness This is a learned value seen in children's behavior when they can work and produce results with in a defined time frame.

Related Readings

Ben-Peretz, M., & Bromme, R. (Eds.). (1990). *The Nature of Time in Schools: Theoretical Concepts, Practitioner Perceptions*. New York: Teachers College Press.

Erikson, E. H. (1963). *Childhood and Society*. New York: W. W. Norton.

Freiberg, S. (1973). *In Defense of Mothering*. New York: Basic Books.

Mahler, M. S. (1970). *On Human Symbiosis and the Vicissitudes of Individuation*. New York: International Universities Press.

Mahler, M. S., et al. (1975). *The Psychological Birth of the Human Infant*. New York: Basic Books.

Piaget, J. (1965). *The Moral Judgment of the Child* (M. Gabain, Trans.). New York: Free Press.

Endnotes

1. Bereiter, C., & Engelman, S. (1971). *Teaching Disadvantaged Children in the Preschool*. Englewood Cliffs, NJ: Prentice Hall.
2. It is interesting to note how, in recent years, an increasing number of young two-income families are attempting to return to the 1950s model. They are trying to find the economic means for one parent to stay at home, in order to provide their children with the kind of upbringing they enjoyed some three or four decades earlier.
3. The word *mother* is used here to denote the significant person who consistently cares for the child and with whom the child forms a first strong attachment.
4. Piaget, J. (1965). *The Moral Judgment of the Child* (M. Gabain, Trans.). New York: Free Press.
5. Lazar, I., Hubbell, V. R., Murray, H., Rosche, M., & Royce, J. (1977). *Summary Report: The Persistence of Preschool Effects* (Washington, DC: U.S. Department of Health, Education, and Welfare). OHDS 78-30129.

9

Preventing Misbehavior

Organizing Play Materials and Classroom Space

A group of four 3-year-olds is seated at a round table. The teacher places eight large markers and a collection of art paper in the middle of the table for their use. A marker rolls across the table and falls to the floor, and all four children pursue it. They are now out of their chairs and underneath the table, scrambling on hands and knees to find the lost marker. Two children find it at the same time, and now fight over who it belongs to. A third child hits his head on the underside of the table when he forgets where he is and tries to stand. The fourth child is still crawling on hands and knees, until he gets his fingers stepped on by a passing classmate.

Chaos, conflict, and total class disruption are seen here! Whose fault is this? The fault lies with the school and the teacher, because they do not understand the "concept of classroom."

When children are in a direct instruction classroom "bolted" to a desk and chair for long periods of time, and when they must ask permission before they may get up and move about or do any other task, the classroom can be organized with little care of classroom concepts. But when 15 or more young children are freely moving about in a fairly limited space with a host of play centers and a wide variety of equipment, this space and materials must be planned with scientific precision.

We as adults have all had to deal with space that for one reason or another was disrupted and temporarily disorganized. Having the flooring redone in our home can force us to spend unusual amounts of time in different rooms, and we can have trouble finding our checkbook or car keys minutes before we must depart for an important outing. Street repairs disrupt our normal patterns of traveling, and the quick trip to the store now takes three times as long—and we have not budgeted this extra time. Our favorite grocery store remodels and changes everything around, making us learn where once-familiar items are now located. Chaos, life pattern disruption, and real tension and stress are felt by us as mature adults. Space, objects in that space, and how they are arranged can all shape and control our behavior for better or worse.

MATERIALS FOR THE PLAY ACTIVITY CURRICULUM

Characteristically, it is the misbehaving child who cannot play and use play materials. One of the basic assumptions for teachers of young children is that children learn best by active learning through play. Play is the central way in which young children acquire knowledge and skills, especially social skills, in the early childhood years. In Chapter 13, play is defined and defended, and an attempt is made, in an abbreviated form, to show its value for the growth of young children. (For a more detailed explanation of play curriculum, see C. H. Wolfgang and M. E. Wolfgang (1992) *School for Young Children: Developmentally Appropriate Practices*, Allyn and Bacon.)

It is generally accepted among early childhood educators that there are three types of play basic in the early childhood classroom: sensorimotor (practicing fundamental movement patterns); symbolic, including micro (miniature life-like toys) and macro (child-size furniture, dress-up props, etc.); and construction, including fluids (painting, clay, etc.) and structured (blocks, puzzles, etc.).

Materials and equipment are selected based on the view that they support the larger categories or definitions of play (see Figure 9–1). With the exception of the fact that materials to support sensorimotor play of necessity are mostly confined to the outdoor playground area or indoor mini-gym ("large muscle" room), the indoor classroom must contain materials to support *all* of the play forms (symbolic-micro and macro, construction-fluids and construction-structured) in order to have a well-balanced environment. (Again, see Wolfgang and Wolfgang [1992] if further explanation is needed.) It is the arrangement and organization of these materials that produces a well-organized play environment; conversely, a poor arrangement produces dramatically more discipline problems, aggression, and conflict among classmates. Simply rethinking the classroom arrangement with regard to the principle of *concept of classroom* and changing this space can and will eliminate a large number of discipline demands on the teacher.

It is imperative that the teacher who wishes to create a supportive classroom, with a minimal amount of the kind of conflict seen in the scenario at the beginning of the chapter, actually create a paper floor plan/map[1] of the school

FIGURE 9–1 Play Form and Materials/Equipment

Play Form	Materials/Equipment
Sensorimotor Play	Slides, tricycles, balls, and similar items
Symbolic Play	
Microsymbolic Play	Miniature life-like toys (replicas of furniture, people, animals, vehicles, etc.) and puppets
Macrosymbolic Play	Child-sized furniture, toy eating utensils and food, dolls, toy telephones, and similar items
Construction Play	
Fluids	Clay, easel paintings, drawing tools, etc. (fluid materials that have a high sensorimotor quality generally have little or no form and easily transform their shape)
Structured	Carpentry material, interlocking blocks, and puzzles (maintain their shape and have a more work-like quality); an extensive collection of Montessori math manipulative items (includes computers)

SPACE

Question: What if too many children want to use one particular area, such as the block area? Should a limit be placed on the number permitted to go into that space?

Answer: Limiting the number of children permitted in an interest area may be one solution to be used for a short period of time when a new area or new materials are added and are novel to the children. "Overstacking" in one area usually means that there is an imbalance of the play interest areas. If everyone wants to play with blocks, there must be a competing interest area of housekeeping, a fluid area with sand play, painting, and so on, and/or a manipulative area cluster near a table. Generally, when children stack up in one area it is because the room does not contain adequate materials supporting other play forms.

area. It is suggested that at the end of each day for the first 10 days after creating a new classroom or starting a new school year, the teacher mark the floor map with a small mark indicating where some difficulty has occurred.

Many city traffic departments maintain a bulletin board map of the streets in their city, and place straight pins on the map where accidents occur. After a short period of time, it can clearly be seen on the street map that a handful of intersections account for an overwhelming percentage of accidents. The solution: Physically alter the intersection with an understanding of traffic flow to prevent accidents from happening, thereby saving the considerable costs of accident damage and possibly saving lives. The teacher will be surprised to discover that the same process will occur on her classroom map. The children may literally be falling over the equipment or each other. The check marks, indicating conflict and difficulties, will begin to cluster at key spots on the map, possibly near the easel or at one particular art table. The solution: Alter the space, moving equipment and materials around, thus eliminating large numbers of incidents that call for discipline action or that require the teacher to "put out a fire."

UNDERSTANDING SPACE

Space can be divided into zones of *natural units* or *arranged units*. Natural play units might include a corner of the playground where the building's walls mark a particular enclosed area, space beneath a climbing tower, or an alcove area indoors. Children will be drawn into this space and begin play and social activities. An arranged unit is *not* barriered off but can be constructed or arranged from materials and objects by the teacher, again to draw children into a defined area for productive play activity. This might be a table with four chairs and an array of art materials. Placing a double paint easel together on a plastic floor covering creates another arranged unit. In other words, play unit space partially or fully walled in, with two or more sides of obvious barriers to define it, may be called a *natural unit*,[2] whereas items clustered together to make a play zone with no obvious and particular barriers are called an *arranged unit*.

Either type of zone or unit, arranged or natural, has the potential for attracting young children within its space. But what happens in that space can be productive activity or—because of lack of materials or improper arrangement of those materials— conflictive activity. Three central variables may be used to understand whether a zone will be a productive area for play and free activity or whether it will be prone to conflict among children. These variables are the *complexity* of the materials and play items, the *number of children* in the zone, and the level of *teacher involvement*.

Kritchevsky has created a helpful complexity classification system using the categories of *simple, complex*, and *super-complex*. A play kitchen can be easily made by taking wooden boxes, child-size chairs, an old tablecloth, and some discarded pots, pans, cups, saucers, and plates, and adding some plastic utensils, sand or water for pouring, and men's and women's shoes. These objects can be clustered together either in a natural unit zone or an arranged unit zone. Because of its *super-complex* arrangement and collection of materials, it will attract and absorb a large number of children for a long duration of play time. In contrast, one puzzle, one easel, or one tricycle—each of which can be used by only one child—will not attract others and the child using this *simple* complexity item will be absorbed for a very limited period of time before boredom sets in. Between these two extremes is a play space arranged as a *complex* unit with two to three items, such as a sand table with pouring cups and plastic containers. This will absorb more children and engage them for a longer period of activity than the simple unit, but it is not as socially absorbing as the super-complex.

Each unit may be thought of as a social sponge, able to hold children in varying degrees of absorption. A scoring system can be used to rate the number of children each unit and the entire classroom may absorb productively. Each unit would receive a score equal to the number of children it can absorb productively, so a simple unit would receive a score of 1, a complex unit might rate a 4, and a super-complex unit might earn an 8. A table with six chairs, with a puzzle in front of each chair, can be thought of as six simple units, absorbing one child per unit and making a total score of 6 for the entire table.

Once the total classroom space is arranged to contain a balance of simple, complex, and super-complex units, the teacher may add up the number for each unit to get a total score for the classroom. For this discussion, let's say our classroom has a total of 50 potential play points (ppps). Kritchevsky's research indicated that there should be 2½ potential play points per child who uses this classroom space. Using the example of 50 ppps, and dividing by 2½, we would see that our hypothetical classroom would ideally be designed for 20 young children. If we enroll a greater number of children (the second variable for determining effective classroom arrangement), aggression and misbehavior will increase dramatically.

Kritchevsky made a helpful analogy between the popular game "Musical Chairs" and the play units or zones. In Musical Chairs, there may be 10 children circling 9 chairs; when the music stops, everyone scurries to find a chair, and 1 child is left out and must leave the game. In the play-oriented classroom, where children are free to move about, we want our zones to play the role of "chairs" in a game of Musical Chairs, but in reverse. Instead of having a child left out, we want that child to find a play space in which to be productively absorbed. We depend on the complexity of our arrangement, with the scoring of the ppps, to assure us that a child will always find a place to play and that the space is adequately complex.

The potential play points method is a scoring system that permits the teacher to judge complexity by established criteria, but the number of children (second variable) and teacher involvement (third variable) must also be considered. For instance, take a minimally complex play unit or zone, such as a table with paper and crayons for five children, and seat the teacher at the table where she can become involved with the children. If the teacher does not act, the children may do some coloring but will soon tire of it, and will either wander off or begin teasing and harassing activities against each other. This will lead to a discipline situation. But if the teacher observes the drop of interest, she can demonstrate how to make a flower from paper or how to combine two colors to make a third, new color. This will stimulate the children, enabling them to continue to be absorbed and work parallel to each other for a much longer period of time. Now, if 15 additional children are coloring and cutting paper at tables with one teacher, the second variable (number of children) has been increased dramatically. This teacher will find it extremely taxing, if not impossible, to maintain these children's interest in this minimally complex activity for a long period of time. Misbehavior requiring disciplining action will soon occur.

Understanding these three variables leads to the following conclusions:

1. If we have only one teacher (variable: teacher involvement) then, in order to make a play classroom work effectively, we must either drop the number of children (variable: number of children) or increase the complexity of the play units and zones (variable: complexity—ppps).
2. If we are required to have a large number of children in the space, this can only be done effectively if we add to the complexity or add more teachers. Some poor-quality day-care centers attempt to use television to compensate for this problem by having the children seated passively. The television set comes to dominate classroom space, overwhelming more productive areas.
3. If we have limited complexity, possibly because money is not available to purchase equipment, we must increase the number of teachers or decrease the number of children, since all three variables interact to create an effective, well-organized, and functioning classroom.

By considering the teacher-child ratio as a formula for how much it costs to run an early childhood program successfully, one can see the long-term cost effectiveness of purchasing quality equipment in more than adequate quantities, which permits an increase in play complexity.

The final point to be made is that when these three variables—complexity, number of children, and teacher involvement—are out of balance, the result is aggression, misbehavior, conflict, and an unhealthy classroom climate. A teacher's natural tendency when aggression and misbehavior increase is to impose on the children "more teacher rules"[3] to attempt to stop this aggression and misbehavior. But what is really required is to analyze the classroom and bring these three variables into balance. Adding more and more rules takes freedom from children, and the classroom changes from a child-centered space to an institutionally controlled teacher space. An understanding of the power of these three variables gives us, as teachers, an understanding of a *concept of classroom*. These same principles and concepts would also hold true for outdoor space, such as playgrounds, and great and equal care must be taken for these outdoor zones. This includes "mapping" the playground space, especially when it entails a large number of children, more than one class at a time using the playground, and many teachers supervising.

Degrees of Freedom

Within each zone or play unit, there are two new concepts to guide the teacher: *degrees of freedom* and *control of error*. Let's take a look at a complex play unit involving water play on the outside playground. A galvanized water tank (the kind normally used for watering lambs on a farm or ranch) is solidly anchored to the ground and sits in a boxed-in bed of gravel to permit quick drainage of water that spills to the ground. The tank, 6 × 2 feet wide and 15 inches deep, is filled with four inches of soapy water. It also contains hoses, siphons, pouring devices, and a collection of miniature rubber real-life toys, including boats and similar "sailing" vessels. On a hot summer day, the children are wearing their swimming trunks.

Let's contrast this outdoor water play with indoor water play in a typical Montessori classroom. One child has picked up an oval-shaped metal tray (12 × 6 inches) from the shelf on which it was stored. The child has taken the tray—which is designed to be used only by one child—and carried it by its two handles to a small child-size table and chair. The child seats herself and begins to remove items from the tray. First, she opens a paper towel and places it on the table in front of her. Next, a small porcelain bathroom soap dish containing a small sponge is then laid next to the hand towel. One at a time, the child removes two small pitchers (like those seen for oil and vinegar at a restaurant salad bar), using the handles of each to place them facing each other on the towel. One pitcher is empty and the second is filled with water colored with blue food dye. The child now "water plays" by pouring the blue water from one container to the other and back again without spilling. If some water is spilled, the child wipes it up with the small sponge. Once the child has finished with the activity, the items are placed back on the tray, the tray is returned to the shelf, and the wet paper towel is thrown in the trash.

Obviously, these are two dramatically different forms of water play with regard to openness for free expression of the child's behavior and demands for control. *Degrees of freedom* is a concept that describes the degree to which children may take play materials and use them in any creative manner they wish. The large outdoor water tub has maximum degrees of freedom, permitting children the widest range of use for expression of their ideas and wishes. The Montessori water pouring has minimum degrees of freedom, and the child must perform the motor meanings or motor actions dictated by how the materials were engineered and how the teacher has instructed that they should be used. Therefore, the Montessori water play would be called structured.

With an understanding of the degrees of freedom concept regarding materials, we may now view all the play materials that are normally placed in a play-based classroom. These materials traverse a continuum that arranges materials from maximum to minimum degrees of freedom, beginning with water play, dry sand, and finger painting and advancing to easel painting, clay, drawing (with any items), blocks, Legos, Montessori equipment, puzzles, Lotto-type games, and, finally, the computer.

The maximum to minimum degrees of freedom construct regarding materials (see Figure 9–2) enables us to design a well-balanced classroom and a balanced play environment that has all these materials available to children daily. Both natural and arranged play unit space or zones would contain a wide variety of play materials ranging from maximum to minimum degrees of freedom. These

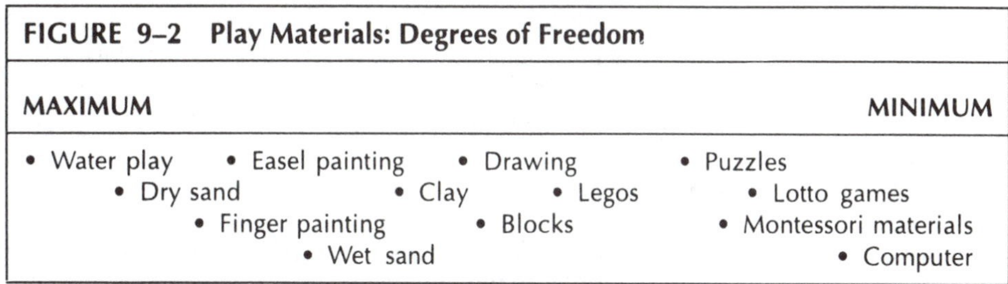

FIGURE 9–2 Play Materials: Degrees of Freedom

materials can be used for construction-structured and construction-fluid types of child play, as well as make-believe symbolic-micro play (miniature life-like) and macro play (dress-up/housekeeping). This design also enables us to assess the effect on the behavior of the highly active aggressive (or introverted passive) child were we to place him with construction-fluid materials that offer maximum degrees of freedom (such as the large outdoor water tank) or with construction-structured materials that offer minimum degrees of freedom (puzzles). Chapter 7 addresses this in detail by showing the teacher how to deliberately use various materials, with their innate degrees of freedom, for purposes of intervening and facilitating the play of these difficult children.

Control of Error

We will return to the example of the disruption caused by the rolling marker (from the beginning of the chapter) to begin to understand the concept of *control of error*. Let's change the scene to a different classroom, where the teacher has taken the markers and cemented (plaster of paris) the marker caps upside-down in an empty, cleaned tuna can. The markers can then be placed back into the cemented caps and placed on the table for the children to use, providing a number of benefits. The children may take out, use, and replace the markers, always knowing where they belong. In addition, storing the markers in fixed caps prevents them from rolling off the table, and since the markers are now always stored facing down, gravity will keep the tips wet for quick use by the child. There is now less likelihood that the markers would be laying about on a table or in a box, accidentally marking the table or drying out in the open air. We have deliberately engineered *control of error* into the activity and materials. Thus, the children are less likely to make a mistake or have a problem using the material, and we have prevented discipline situations such as having children scrambling on their hands and knees under the table and across the floor chasing a runaway marker.

Using these two concepts of degrees of freedom and control of error, one can see that the big outdoor tank for water play offered great freedom but it was engineered with much thought regarding control of error. Since (1) it was placed outdoors, (2) it was placed in a boxed-in surface with gravel to control water runoff, and (3) the children wore bathing suits, there is only a minimal possibility that the teacher would need to intervene to stop or control some action or error made by the children during water play.

We are required to evaluate every space and all materials to determine if we can creatively engineer these items, using the concept of control of error, so that children may be free to actively use materials with little concern for breakage or for the kinds of accidents that may disrupt daily classroom activities. Puzzles that have many pieces that tend to get lost can be stored and used on small cafeteria trays. Legos, with their greater expense and number of pieces to control, may be used on a larger cafeteria tray (2 × 3 feet) or a Lego table can be purchased to help confine the pieces and make them easier to control. Smocks for painting, plastic eye shields for hammering at the carpentry table, mouth guards for the water fountain to prevent children from sucking on the outlet—all these provide control of error.

Symbolic and Color Cueing

Let's return to Happy Harry's Crab House, which we visited in Chapter 8. After imbibing large quantities of the local grog, we find that we must go to the "necessary" room. As we approach the two doors, we must choose between two doors: Gulls and Buoys—no small task under the circumstances. How do we know which door to choose, other than deciphering the "cute" verbal signs? The answer is symbolic cueing, through the symbol of a man or woman placed at eye level on the outside of the bathroom door. In our modern world there are hundreds of symbolic cues that control our behavior. A symbol of a cigarette inside a red circle with a crossing red slash tells us that smoking is not permitted in that area; a blue sign with a white wheelchair emblem tells us that the parking space is reserved for handicapped drivers. We may use similar symbolic cueing, in the form of color coding, to positively control young children's behavior in the classroom.

Our hypothetical classroom has 100 to 125 dozen wooden blocks stored on shelves for the children to use for building (construction-structured play). On this day, it seems that every block the school possesses is scattered across the floor of the block room and needs to be picked up. Young children are only just beginning to learn how to be organizers and classifiers, so if we simply ask them to "put the blocks away," the various shapes will be mixed together and randomly stacked. This produces an unattractive view that detracts from the classroom environment. Also, the next time a child seeks a particular size or shape block, he will be forced to rummage through the entire collection, knocking many blocks to the floor and causing the block room to become even more disorganized.

Instead, we can use symbolic and color cueing to help make sure each block finds its proper home. First, we take all the blocks and place them in an orderly way on the shelves, arranging them so that like blocks are clustered together. To increase the control of error and create an understandable classification system, we place the smallest block on the top left shelf; as the sizes of the blocks grow, we place them in different slots, moving from left to right. When the first row is filled, we drop to the next row and repeat the process, beginning with the smallest on the left and moving toward the right.

Next, we take all the blocks of a single type out of their one cubicle and trace a silhouette of one of the blocks on a piece of colored paper. The silhouette is cut out and glued or taped to the bottom left corner of the cubicle; the process is then repeated for the remaining block storage cubicles. Now when the children have finished playing with all the blocks and it is time to put them back, the symbolic cue—the silhouette of the shape of the block—is there for them to use. They place the first wooden block against the paper silhouette, and the rest of the blocks of that size and shape will follow. With symbolic cueing, the space "speaks" to the children and the teacher does not have to tell them how to put the blocks away.

We can do the same with all play zones and equipment. For example, we may color code puzzles by using pieces of plastic tape in primary colors, coding and stacking them from easiest to hardest. We may sew a ribbon in the inside of a piece of dress-up clothing and tape another piece of the same ribbon under the hook on which we wish to have that item stored. By using the techniques of control of error with color cueing, we can organize all items and space in a similar manner. Every child (or adult) working and playing in this classroom should now be able to pick up almost any item in the room and put it back exactly where it belongs. All objects have a home—our job is to give children the tools to find the proper home for each item.

MOTOR RULES AND "MARS DAYS"

Four-year-old Anthony gets up from snack time; he stands and uses the back of his legs to push out the chair. He then takes three steps to the trash basket, throws out his trash, and begins to walk to the playground door. Suddenly he stops; it is apparent that a thought has entered his mind. He returns to his chair and pushes it in under the table, so that no other child will trip over it.

This act of pushing in the chair is a learned "motor rule."[4] Adults as well as young children go through much of their day as if on automatic pilot, moving from one motor action to the next. Collect your snack waste paper, Stand and move to the trash basket, Push in your chair—these are all motor rules that Anthony has internalized. Once the child learns these motor rules after entering a new school, he understands the structure of the school and gains a sense of security that he can master such a world. This world is predictable. However, if something out of the routine takes place—for example, a photographer appears unexpectedly to take group photographs—the schedule of activities is dramatically altered. The child becomes demanding and whining; he wants to know, "Why aren't we going to color now, Mrs. James? When are we going to have snack?" This shows tension and confusion. What is important, then, is to have the children learn quickly the motor rules for all of the materials and rooms, so that they can return to the order of their school world as smoothly as possible.

Spatial location in our adult world communicates motor rules and behavior, and because we are well-socialized, we respond appropriately. In a movie theater, we act with certain defined motor rules; at a football game, we act in an entirely different way.

The previous chapter suggested that great numbers of today's children are not being taught a sensitivity to spatial rules in their home settings. The teachers may remark about many of today's children, "Where do these kids come from—they don't know how to act! Are they from Mars?" Well, compared to the way the teachers were raised and learned value systems, these children may just as well have come from Mars, because of the dramatic gap between the values of the teachers and those of the children. The mission of the quality early childhood center is now clear: We must make the children socially sensitive to expected and "proper" social behavior based on where they are and the social context of the moment. Developing this awareness is a skill, and once learned by young children, it will enable them to be ready for later formal schooling—typically in a highly rule-based environment. This can be done by declaring "Mars Days."

If a child had come from a foreign land, or another planet, we would not expect him to know our habits, routines, and cultural dos and don'ts. Similarly, we cannot expect many of today's children to know "how to behave" in the classroom, so we hypothetically consider them as just stepping off a spaceship from Mars. In dealing with these "Martians," we cannot expect them to know anything about how our classroom works, so we directly teach it to them. "Mars Days" may be declared when we have a large number of new children entering the school or classroom who will not know our routines, or when general behavior in the classroom begins to deteriorate and we find ourselves dealing with too many discipline incidents, or when too many accidents, especially on the playground, occur.

In small groups of 8 to 10 children, or with an entire class if manageable, the teacher takes the children around the classroom and "teaches walls and objects." With her group, the teacher starts at the front door. Moving to the right, she comes to the block shelves (or housekeeping, puzzle shelf, etc.). Now the teacher conducts a directive lesson.

> ***Teacher:*** "Children, these are our blocks. We like to take the blocks down from the shelves and build lots of neat things here on the floor. When blocks are off the shelf, we keep them here on the big rug" (Step 1: Say). (The teacher removes the blocks from the shelf while the children watch; she then speaks and builds a small house-like structure (Step 2: Show).)
>
> ***Teacher:*** "Now, when we are all done with using blocks, we put them back in their 'home' on the shelf. Here is the small block, and you see that there is a blue paper block shape on the back corner (points to the blue silhouette shape). Watch what I do: When I put the block back, I place the small block against the paper block so they match. Then I put on this shelf all the blocks that are the same size." (The teacher puts all small blocks on this shelf section.)
>
> ***Teacher:*** "Now watch me closely and see if I make a mistake!" (The teacher takes a circular block and deliberately misplaces it on a shelf designated for rectangular pieces.)
>
> ***Teacher:*** "Children, is this correct?" (Step 3: Check).
>
> The children in unison say,
>
> ***Children:*** "No-o-o!"
>
> ***Teacher:*** (The teacher removes the circular block from the improper shelf and places it on the floor.) "Bill, come up and show me how to do it correctly." (Bill jumps up and places the block on the correct shelf.) "Class, did Bill do it correctly?"
>
> ***Children:*** "Yes-s-s-s!"

We have just seen the teacher teaching motor rules, or spatial rules, through the use of a direct instruction *Three-Step Lesson* (Step 1: Say; Step 2: Show; and Step 3: Check) (see Figure 9–3). The teacher *says* by using words, or verbally encoding, the concept or motor rules that she is attempting to teach. She then *shows* visually by having a child model the correct motor behavior or performing it herself. In order to know that the children have understood the say-show, the teacher *checks* their understanding by exhibiting the incorrect action she does *not* want, or what is "not the rule," by doing it incorrectly while asking the children to watch for a mistake. She now asks them to evaluate the action, and they respond with "no" in unison. Finally—and this is an important step that must never be left out—the teacher again models the correct motor behavior, having a child do it correctly, and then asks the children to respond as to the correctness of this final behavior. They, of course, respond in unison, "Yes-s-s!"

Some children build very high block structures and, once completed, deliberately knock them over. This creates a huge crashing noise that stops everyone's action in the classroom, and at times the falling blocks may hurt other children. If we want children to disassemble their block structures rather than knock over the blocks, this must be demonstrated to the children as a motor rule—as a part of "teaching the walls and objects" through the Three-Step Lesson (say, show, and check). Once the children know the motor rules for the entire classroom environment, they have gained a sense of security because they now know how everything works. If they are not taught motor rules (in such a manner through Mars

FIGURE 9–3 The Three-Step Lesson		
Step 1	Say	The teacher verbally labels or encodes the object or process being taught.
Step 2	Show	The teacher models by displaying the object or by having another child or herself motorically enact the process.
Step 3	Check	The teacher now requires each child, by some physical action, to demonstrate that he or she can discriminate the correct object or process. The teacher always ends the lesson by demonstrating the correct example.

Days), they can only learn a rule by accidentally doing a misbehavior and then being reprimanded by the teacher for doing so.

If children are not taught motor rules, they are placed in an unfair and frustrating environment. Let's take an elementary or secondary school example.

> *It is the first minutes of the first day of class. John's pencil tip breaks and he needs to sharpen it to do the work his new teacher has just assigned. He looks at the pencil sharpener across the room, glances at his teacher, and then stares at his pencil. What is he to do? He bravely stands and begins to walk toward the pencil sharpener. "Just a minute, young man, where do you think you are going? Sit down! You need permission before you are to leave your seat. Get back to work."*

In this classroom, since rules were not taught, John must discover each rule by accidentally performing a misbehavior. It is as if this classroom has been seeded with land mines. The child takes one misstep and a bomb explodes! It will take weeks, or even months, before the children have stepped on enough bombs in the classroom to know all the teacher's rules. But by the time that occurs, the children are "shell shocked"—tense, unhappy, and feeling frightened by the environment and the teacher. For the teacher's part, possibly because of not knowing a better method, she feels that "you have to 'sit on these kids' or they will take advantage of you."

In an open-plan play environment where children are able to actively move about and enjoy the activities, the classroom should not be "land mined." Therefore, by declaring "Mars Days" and teaching motor rules immediately and repeatedly throughout the year when they are needed, the teacher enables the children to truly know their environment and have maximum degrees of freedom. The classroom is child centered, not teacher centered.

The following is a review of the process of making classroom materials and space well-organized so that the possibility of misbehavior occurring is minimized:

1. Understand large categories of play—sensorimotor, symbolic play (micro and macro), and construction (fluids and structured)—and provide an abundance of materials to support all forms of this play.
2. Instill a concept of space that involves organizing the materials and space with regard to natural units and arranged units, and eliminate "dead space."
3. Organize each play unit or zone with regard to concepts of complexity (simple, complex, and super-complex) and determine the number of potential play points (ppps) needed based on the number of children in the classroom.

4. Balance the classroom with the three variables of complexity, number of children, and teacher involvement.
5. Organize a wide variety of play materials (fluids to structured); see Figure 9–2.
6. Engineer each play zone and materials with the concept of control of error, permitting the children to have maximum degrees of freedom in the use of the materials.
7. Create symbolic and color cueing systems so that every object has a "home" and every child and teacher knows where that home is.
8. Teach "the walls and objects" by declaring "Mars Days" and using the Three-Step Lesson of say, show, and check.

Through these methods, the environment is designed with scientific precision; it is arranged and organized so that it should require very little direct teacher involvement—it works on its own. Good space and object arrangement frees the teacher from the need to constantly intervene to keep children playing and on task; the environment does this for her. The teacher is freed from needing to "put out fires"; she is empowered to use her professional judgment in deciding how and when to insert herself into the children's ongoing activities and how and when *not* to. She is free to intervene with Jimmy "El Zorro" using the Teacher Behavior Continuum; to intervene with a more difficult child by using the Relationship-Listening, Confronting-Contracting, and Rules and Consequences faces; to do one-to-one intervention with passive or aggressive children; or to teach a lesson to an individual child or a small group.

TEACHER BALLET

Normally, most early classrooms have two or more adults who become involved with children.[5] Having a number of adults present requires a conscious awareness and an agreement as to how these adults will work together in the classroom. In a well-balanced classroom, the teacher can spend time "looking on" or closely observing the actions of the children to skillfully decide to intervene or not intervene. However, as much as we may find young children interesting, they have a limited range of conversation. Adults who work in the classroom for long periods of time every day may literally become lonely and begin to invest emotionally in each other and their adult interests. In effect, within the classroom they can create a sphere of adult-to-adult relationships where they are discussing last night's TV show, a recent friendship, or some personal problems, and they have unknowingly emotionally deserted the 15 or more children in the classroom. If the space traveled by the teacher during the day is closely monitored, one may find that it is less than 40 percent of the classroom. Or one may find that the adults do well indoors but desert the children on the outdoor playground; they cling to each other standing at the top of the playground or at the sidewalk, with the bulk of the playground space lacking their presence.

The concept of the "teacher ballet" places teachers on opposite sides of the classroom or playground looking into and across the space. By their looking, they can radiate a zone of safety and control by just visually "looking on" in that space. If one teacher needs to become involved in a teachable moment in a one-to-one relationship with a child such as Jimmy "El Zorro," the second teacher is immediately aware of this; she knows that she must move deeper into this space, radiating a zone of safety and control over a wider area, picking up the space or zone that had been supervised by the teacher now working with Jimmy. This may be seen as a form of zone supervision (see Figure 9–4).

If children's stress has built to the point that they might be physically aggressive for a split second and they are about to have a conflict with each other, they first tend to scan the nearby area. If they meet a teacher's eyes, they will feel the controlling force of the teacher's simple modality cues because she is physically nearby, and they will inhibit their aggression. If, instead, the children see that the two teachers are "lost in themselves," talking about adult interests and no modality cueing is forthcoming, the aggression occurs. Who is at fault here? The answer is the teachers, because they have emotionally deserted the children. Thus, teachers must work out zones of looking on and engage in a ballet of teacher movement as they work together in the classroom.

SUMMARY

Many constructs and concepts exist to help the teacher design a classroom balanced with appropriate materials and methods for their proper use. But the steam that makes this classroom engine run remains the teacher. Making use of the balanced classroom, she now has the freedom with her co-workers to create a ballet of teacher movement, supervising this space by her presence and her ability to look on. The teacher plans for ways that every young child may get a share of her emotional investment and skilled help. The blend of space, objects, and teacher presence and emotional investment "speaks" clearly to children, telling them that they are safe, secure, and wanted in this classroom environment.

FIGURE 9–4 Teacher Zone of Safety and Control

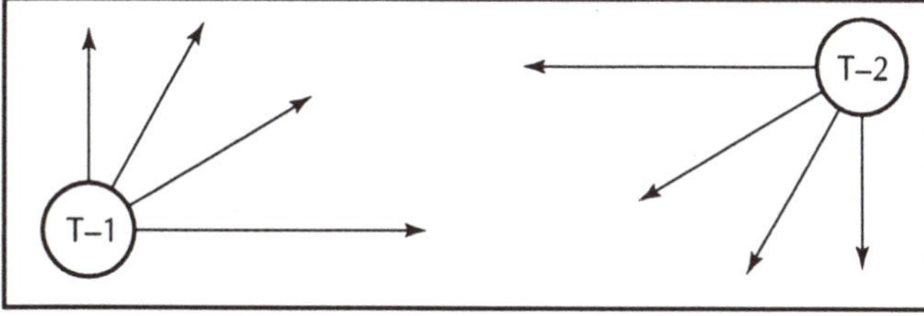

Teacher 2 moves to help the child, and Teacher 1 moves to supervise a wider zone.

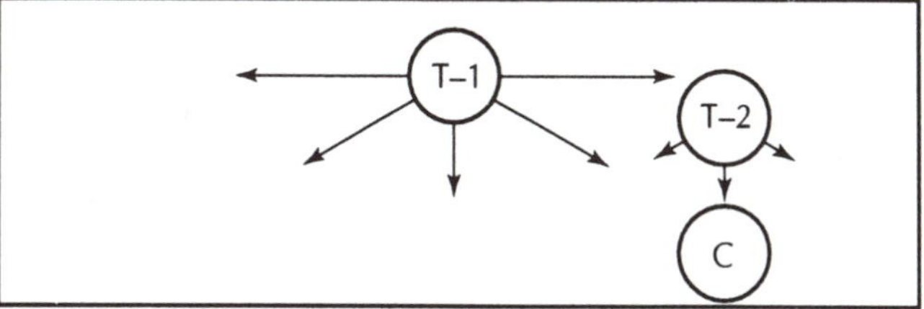

(T) Teacher

(C) Child

Arrow indicates the direction the teacher is facing

Test Yourself

The following questions will test your knowledge of concepts of objects, materials, and spatial arrangements. Answers may be found at the end of this chapter, following the Endnotes.

A. ___ 11 children B. ___ 13 children C. ___ 17 children D. ___ 21 children	1. The classroom has 2 super-complex units, 3 complex units, and 16 simple units. How many children could this classroom properly absorb?
A. ___ color cueing B. ___ complexity C. ___ construction-fluids D. ___ control of error	2. A poster shows pictures of children going through the correct steps of washing and drying their hands. What organizational concept has the teacher used?
	For each material shown on the right, place an x before the proper type of play or classification on the left.
A. ___ construction-fluids B. ___ construction-structured C. ___ symbolic-micro D. ___ symbolic-macro E. ___ sensorimotor	3. Drawing
A. ___ construction-fluids B. ___ construction-structured C. ___ symbolic-micro D. ___ symbolic-macro E. ___ sensorimotor	4. Block building
A. ___ construction-fluids B. ___ construction-structured C. ___ symbolic-micro D. ___ symbolic-macro E. ___ sensorimotor	5. Clay
A. ___ construction-fluids B. ___ construction-structured C. ___ symbolic-micro D. ___ symbolic-macro E. ___ sensorimotor	6. Small rubber animals
A. ___ construction-fluids B. ___ construction-structured C. ___ symbolic-micro D. ___ symbolic-macro E. ___ sensorimotor	7. A play kitchen
A. ___ construction-fluids B. ___ construction-structured C. ___ symbolic-micro D. ___ symbolic-macro E. ___ sensorimotor	8. A balance beam

Glossary

Arranged Unit The clustering of materials with no perceivable boundary, to attract children to the area for social play.

Color Cueing A systematic method of marking toys and other play materials with colored marks so that the child can readily identify the object and its proper shelf or storage location.

Complex Unit Placing together two to four materials so they may productively absorb approximately four children in a zone or unit (receives a ppp score of 4).

Complexity Arranging materials in the classroom with a balance of simple, complex, and super-complex play units so there will be at least 2.5 ppps per child using that space.

Concept of Classroom Organizing classroom materials and equipment with regard to complexity, number of children, and teacher involvement, and to include the use of degrees of freedom and control of error within the zones or play units.

Construction-Fluids Materials such as water play, sand, painting, clay, and drawing, which tend to have maximum degrees of freedom.

Construction-Structured Materials that maintain their shape and form, such as blocks, Legos, Montessori materials, puzzles, and Lotto games, which have predetermined and narrowly defined uses or minimum degrees of freedom.

Control of Error Arranging and putting together materials in a manner that minimizes the chances that children will break, spill, or have accidents while using them.

Degrees of Freedom An indication of the extent to which materials may be used in an open or creative manner by children, as compared to a very narrowly defined use.

Floor Mapping Drawing a schematic map of the classroom with regard to ppps and fluid, structured materials, and symbolic materials in order to provide the best design for the classroom space.

"Mars Days" An agreement to teach all the motor rules for all objects and materials in the classroom, as if the children have just arrived from Mars and have no concept of their use.

Natural Unit A walled space that tends to cluster children into the zone, either indoors or outdoors.

Number of Children One of the variables (along with complexity and teacher involvement) used to determine if a classroom has a proper balance.

Potential Play Points (ppps) The numbered scoring system of simple play units (score of 1 point), complex play units (score of 4 points), and super-complex (score of 8 points) as a system to determine the complexity of an organized classroom space and how many students it can properly accommodate.

Sensorimotor Play Play involving the body and sensory practice.

Simple Unit One item, such as a puzzle, that can be used by only one child (receives a score of 1 ppp); a simple unit lacks the ability to absorb a child's attention for a long period of time.

Spatial Rules Automatic motor actions suggested by the room or zone in which the child is located (e.g., throwing paper in the trash when done with it, closing the door behind you, or putting things away when done).

Super-Complex Unit The arrangement of four or more materials into a zone that will absorb at least eight children (receives a ppp score of 8).

Symbolic Cueing A symbol such as a silhouette or international road sign to signal what is permitted or not permitted or to control and direct behavior (e.g., a frowning face sign on a bottle of poison indicates it should not be consumed).

Symbolic Play-Macro Make-believe play where the child plays a role and uses child-size props.

Symbolic Play-Micro Make-believe play where the child uses miniature life representations.

"Teacher Ballet" A technique through which two or more teachers supervise an assigned zone and maintain an awareness of each other's actions to deliberately move (ballet) themselves about the space in relation to each other so the space is always being supervised by at least one teacher.

Teacher Involvement Direct teacher intrusion into the children's activities to maintain their interest in productive activity.

Related Readings

Frost, J. L., & Klein, B. L. (1979). *Children's Play and Playgrounds*. Boston: Allyn and Bacon.

Gerhardt, L. A. (1973). *Moving and Knowing: The Young Child Orients Himself in Space*. Englewood Cliffs, NJ: Prentice-Hall.

Kritchevsky, S., et al. (1969). *Planning Environments for Young Children: Physical Space*. Washington, DC: NAEYC.

Wolfgang, C. H., & Wolfgang, M. E. (1992). *School for Young Children: Developmentally Appropriate Practices*. Boston: Allyn and Bacon.

Endnotes

1. It is highly recommended that before you begin to arrange or reevaluate current play materials and classroom space, you should obtain and read Kritchevsky's *Planning Environments for Young Children: Physical Space*. In addition, you should obtain a free planning guide from either Childcraft Education Corp., Kaplan School Supplies, or Creative Playthings, which will also provide free slides or videotapes on organizing and selecting materials for your classroom. Kritchevsky's pamphlet-like book, the Wolfgang and Wolfgang (1992) book, and the supply company planning guides recommend a checklist of materials and suggest methods of "mapping" your room before you actually move heavy equipment and furniture. The guides provide a measured grid system with silhouetted cut-out pieces simulating furniture and equipment; these can be laid proportionally on the grid to make a classroom map to assist your organizing.
2. *Note*: A natural potential unit—space barriered off on at least two sides or more but containing no props or play materials—draws children in with nothing to do; this makes them feel trapped with no path out. When one child is in the space, it can serve as a "getting away" space where the child feels safe from others and is able to relax, but when two or more children are drawn into the space without materials, it becomes a "desert" with nothing to do. Therefore, the children look to each other to create activity, and they may begin wrestling and general roughhouse play that leads to injury or conflicts that require discipline action. These areas are called "dead space" (see Kritchevsky, previously referenced) and need to be eliminated from the classroom or playground by boarding them closed, putting a table or other furniture into this space, or creating a pathway to permit the child to move out of the space.
3. It is highly recommended as a routine monthly procedure that the classroom maps be brought to staff meetings to analyze intersections of conflict in the classroom space. The staff should next make a list of all rules that unknowingly have crept into classroom procedures with the children. Efforts should be made to eliminate each of these rules by physically changing the environment and alternating the three variables of space: complexity of the material, number of children, and teacher involvement.
4. Piaget, J. (1965). *The Moral Development of the Child* (M. Gabain, Trans.). New York: Free Press.
5. If there is only one teacher, that teacher must, again, consider complexity, number of children, and the balancing of the environment in order to make this classroom work by herself.

Answers to Test Yourself

1C, 2D, 3A, 4B, 5A, 6C, 7D, 8E

10

Misbehavior and Daily Activities

Why does a young child present no difficulties on the playground, where active physical play is encouraged, but the very same child is disruptive at "circle time," which demands sitting quietly and listening to adults and classmates? Other children are well-behaved nearly all day, with the exception of when they come to the table for snack or meal time—then they transform from Dr. Jekyll into Mr. Hyde. How should one handle these "misbehaviors" and "acting out" during these critical daily time periods?

Nearly every early childhood classroom divides its day through a change of activities, with time being broken into arrival rituals, free-play period, circle or group times, toileting, snack-eating periods, rest-nap periods, and outdoor and indoor times. Within each of these clearly defined time periods and in the transitions between the time periods, acting-out behavior or misbehavior increases, changes in form, or decreases, depending on the demands of that activity. To assist the teacher in dealing with difficult behavior and highly demanding children, each of the common time periods used in most classroom days will be presented here, as well as descriptions of the typical "misbehaviors" seen and the concrete actions a teacher might take in handling such misbehavior.

ARRIVALS

To adults, the movement from home to school or from parent to teacher and classroom seems a simple matter. But for young children, especially 3-year-olds,[1] these changes may have the impact of "culture shock."[2] If you, as an adult, were transported suddenly to a foreign country with a different language, different foods and ways to eat it, different clothing, and the like, you would be under great stress, or culture shock. The school—which is a new place to live and work with others—places similar stress on the young child, who must be wondering to himself: Where do I go to the potty if I need to? Who will keep me safe here when my mother is gone? Will others take my toys from me? Where do I sleep and eat? This fear of the school as an unknown will produce a variety of behaviors on the child's part. Described here is an example of a successful preschool adaptation, with the child progressing through various stages of adjustment.

Lap Stage

Three-year-old Kate enters the classroom door, tightly holding her mother's hand. After Kate and her mother are warmly greeted by the teacher and silently observed by the other children, the full meaning of "going to school" and "mother leaving" begins to come to Kate. She climbs on her mother's lap, buries her face in her mother's chest, and begins to cry softly. For a few minutes she refuses to look at this new world. (This is the lap stage of adjustment.*) The teacher encourages the mother to take the rocking chair to a large upright mirror mounted on the wall and sit with her back to the mirror. The teacher instructs the mother that when Kate feels more relaxed, the mother might demonstrate some of the toys to her. Then the teacher leaves, explaining reassuringly that she will be back shortly to help.*

Customs Inspection Stage

Kate soon stops her crying and begins peeking over her mother's shoulder to watch the classroom activities through the mirror. Kate begins to point things out to her mother, and the two chat about what is occurring. (This is the customs inspection stage.*)*

Practicing Stage

After looking about the room for a while, Kate suddenly slips from her mother's lap, runs out into the classroom to grab a toy, and brings it quickly back to her mother. Then, standing at her mother's knee, she watches to see if anyone will intervene. Kate makes eye contact with the teacher, who smiles an OK at her.

"Oh, this is a toy dog," Mother says. "It goes 'ruff-ruff' and walks like this." Three or four times Kate runs out, grabs an object, darts back, and puts it in her mother's hands; her mother responds by telling her the name of the object and demonstrating its uses. (This is the practicing stage*—practicing being separated from mother for short periods.[3])*

Teacher-Approach Stage

Notice that the teacher did not throw herself at the child but permitted the child and parent time to relax and gradually separate physically. During the gradual separation, the teacher observed the parent-child interaction, noting the sensory modalities employed by the mother.

- *Hearing*: Is the mother trying to reassure the child by using language to explain, "This is what we are doing, this is what will happen next..."? (If so, this may be a verbal mother.)
- *Touch*: Is the mother cuddling and caressing the child, as well as exploring objects with her own hands and encouraging the child to do likewise? (This may be a tactile mother.)
- *Visual*: Is the mother signaling the child with her eyes, telling her to "go ahead and pick up the object" simply by using her eyes and facial expressions? (This may be a visual mother.)

The teacher has just learned something about the sensory modality or combination of modalities that she may now use to make this child begin to feel comfortable in her new preschool world.

- *Hearing-verbal child*: The teacher tells what is happening or going to happen ("We are going to read a book about...; you will sit near me so that you may hear the story," etc.).
- *Tactile-physical child*: The teacher brings a furry puppet or takes the child to the classroom's pet rabbit, encouraging her to touch.
- *Visual child*: The teacher signals with her eyes that there is a free chair, toy, or materials available, and encourages the child to use them.

If the child and mother communicate well verbally but engage in little or no touching, an attempt on the teacher's part to cuddle with or physically cue that child may be seen by the child as frightening or intrusive.

Why, when there are two or three teachers in a classroom, does each child seem to gain a solid emotional relationship with one or two teachers and yet shy away from or reject a relationship with another teacher? It may sometimes be that the child and a certain teacher share a form of sensory communication, whereas the rejected teacher may unknowingly be attempting to communicate in the child's weak or underdeveloped modality. We as teachers might attempt to determine our own strong and weak modalities, and begin to practice ways of "shifting gears" deliberately, moving into different modalities in order to try to communicate with different children. Later in the child's school years, his favored modality may become his best learning style.

Parent Departure Stage

Once communication is established between child and teacher, the parent may depart with minimal stress for the new child. The example just used demonstrated the child's initial fearfulness and a demand for mother to remain. These stress indicators are viewed as positive, because they indicate that there is a healthy attachment between child and parent. The crying and demanding are simply an indication of love.[4] If the child is given time to regress to more infantile behaviors, such as becoming a lap baby, she will gradually emerge from the arms of mother and be able to join the other children.

Surprisingly, the children who act like "little men" or "little women" and show no emotional stress when mother departs often have greater difficulty in making good long-term adjustments in the classroom. These "I don't need mother" children often refuse later to be cuddled or comforted by the teacher, need excessive teacher attention, behave in "run-and-chase" fashion that puts themselves in dangerous situations, and engage in stereotypic play—failing to progress developmentally.

The point is that signs of stress, such as crying and demanding, are normal. Our role is to find ways of bridging the child gradually from home to school. One way this can be done is by giving the parent time to stay with the child in the first hours or days of school. Another way is to provide the child with an ever-present, comforting reminder of the parent, such as pinning Mother's handkerchief with her perfume on it to the front of the child's clothing so the child may finger it and smell "Mother" all day long, or allowing the child to call her mother by telephone during the day (hearing Mother's voice provides reassurance that she will return). Perhaps the parent could bring a family photo for the child to keep and show around, or the teacher could let the child bring a "transitional object" (e.g., a blanket or a cuddle toy) to carry about for the first few days. These "transition objects" give sensory reminders of home, permanence, and Mother, helping the child make the adjustments from home to school.

Another help in this transition is having the teacher and child play "Mommy and Child" with the use of a toy telephone. Remember the previous illustration of the value of make-believe play for helping children digest difficult emotional experiences (the child making her own fantasy ice cream cones in the sandbox)? With the toy telephone, the teacher carries on a conversation with the new child, reassuring him that his mother is thinking about him and will not forget to pick him up at the end of the day.

Similar dramas may be played out with puppets, making one puppet the child and the other the parent. In the puppet modeling by the teacher, the child puppet pleads, "Please don't go, Mommy." The mother puppet explains that she must leave in order to do such and such, and that Mrs. Anderson will keep him safe until she returns. A teacher puppet now appears and helps the child puppet "go potty," eat, sleep, and play. Finally, a knock is heard at the door and mother puppet has returned to reunite warmly with the child puppet.

Here are some further suggestions for helping children make initial adjustments to school:

1. Visit the child's home, watch for parent-child cueing modalities, and learn to communicate with the child on familiar ground.

2. Have the parent and child make a visit to the classroom when no other children are there, possibly after school or on a weekend. Have the mother encourage the child to use the small toilets, be seated with the mother and teacher for a quick snack, and take toys from the shelf and play with them. Have the child take some object home with him that he will bring back the first day, such as an inexpensive toy, a piece of modeling dough, or a crayon with paper. Label the child's storage cubby or cot with his name and, if possible, a photo. (*Note*: Some children, when visiting a store where countless enticements sit on display shelves, have been told not to touch and have even been disciplined harshly for not complying. The classroom, with things stored on shelves, will appear similar to children and they will be fearful of touching or taking things from the shelves. Parents and teachers must communicate that it is safe and permitted for them to take and use the classroom objects.)

3. With a small group of already adjusted children, play a series of imitative games, such as "Thumbkin" or "Simon Says." The object of the play activity is for the new child to be directly introduced to a group of children, so they will at least know each other's names.

4. Cut a large silhouette of the new child, paste a photograph of him on it, and display it in a prominent place so all can see it, including parents arriving in the classroom.

5. Prepare the parents for the routine they should follow when they bring in the child for the first time. Explain to them that the school views the early signs of stress as positive, and that they should expect the stages of separation, lap, customs inspection, and practicing before the teacher-approach stage. Remind the parent, though, that some children might not go through these separation processes the first day of school, but may wait until later in the school year, after a long weekend, or following a holiday period. Some parents say, "He did so well the first two weeks, but now he doesn't want to come to school and makes a fuss!" The child is just now beginning to truly separate; if the parents are aware of this beforehand, they will not be disturbed by these new behaviors. Parents may consider removing the child from the school if they have not been previously warned to expect some stress.

SNACK TIME OR EATING

Midmorning and midafternoon snacks provide not only bodily nourishment for highly active young children but also bring them together to further a sense of group belonging. Business people take clients to lunch; families gather for holiday dinners—sharing food in pleasant settings creates belongingness. It is critical that snack time be a pleasant experience for children. If it is not, the situation may give rise to competition and aggression. Eating periods are *not* times for teachers to have breaks, leaving behind the less-trained and less-experienced teachers or aides to carry on. If negative instances occur at home between parent and child, they will most likely occur at the dinner table or when going to bed at night. Therefore, preschool eating at snack time and lunchtime (as well as nap time) are prime periods for the children to become "difficult," expecting to carry out power struggles with teachers just as they do with parents at home.

Group Snack

In organizing for snack, the concepts of control of error and degrees of freedom are used. We do not want the children to play with food, but we do want them to become accustomed to a routine that is nonrepressive and easy to follow.

What *Not* to Do The teacher instructs a mature child to set out the napkins and cups before each chair at the table. The children come to their seats, which are marked with their names. The teacher, seated at the end of the table, makes an announcement or, where appropriate, says grace. Then, extending a wicker basket of a food such as celery or cookies (not permitting the children to pass the basket), the teacher instructs each child to take one. (If any food remains, the basket is removed from the table so the children will not fight over it.) The children are instructed to set the snack on their napkin and wait until all are ready to eat. Next, the teacher appears with a pitcher of milk or juice and, moving behind the children, fills their 7-ounce paper cups. After the teacher is again seated, the children are told they may begin. They are required to eat and drink everything they have been given, and to wait at the table until everyone else is finished. One child then travels around the table, gathering the used cups and napkins.

This is the classroom "kingdom" where the teacher rules in a regal manner. Such a rigid snacking procedure indicates that the teacher does not believe children can learn responsibility and has an overriding fear that an accident will occur. The teacher shows a limited understanding of control of error as she plays food server to passive children.

What to Do Snack materials should be engineered to allow children to eat with minimal pressures from adults. First, two plastic containers with pouring lids, each holding approximately three cups of juice or milk, are placed on a cafeteria tray, along with two snack-filled wicker baskets lined with napkins and a stack of 3-ounce drinking cups. The pouring-lidded containers will keep spills to a minimum. Also on the tray are napkins in a weighted holder (this will keep the napkins from being blown about when snack time takes place outdoors). Approximately 30 percent more snacks than there are children should be provided. These items are previously prepared by the teacher (or the cook, if the school is fortunate enough to have one).

The responsibility—and opportunity—for bringing the filled cafeteria tray to the table belongs to the children who have finished clean-up from previous activities and have washed their hands. They bring the tray carefully from the kitchen to the center of the snack table. Round tables, each seating eight children, are ideal in that they enable each child to see the face of all the others and have equal access to the cafeteria tray. Rectangular tables always seem to leave the end child out of conversations and access.

After washing up, the children seat themselves as desired, select napkins and cups from the center of the table, pour their own juice or milk, and pass the container to a neighbor. Snack items are then taken from the basket with plastic tongs (for health reasons) and passed from one child to another. Children are permitted to take more than one food item, and the small, 3-ounce cups make it necessary that they refill their cups repeatedly. The teacher is seated at the table or at a nearby table and models behavior by carrying on light conversations and eating and drinking the snack just as she wishes the children to do. Coffee cups and soda cans used by the teacher at the snack table would be inappropriate modeling.

When children have had enough food and conversation, they may get up at will, drop their napkins and cups in plastic-lined waste cans nearby, and move to some quiet activity, such as reading or looking at picture books. This procedure gives the children freedom and control. The teacher is not a food server or "boss," but an equal member of the group.

Open Snack

At some child-centered programs, the children are all "herded together" for snack, regardless of whether they are ready to eat. Why not give the children total autonomy over eating by arranging an open snack?

From 9:00 A.M. until 10:30 A.M. a child-size table with two chairs is placed in the corner of the classroom, arranged with snack materials as described above, with 3-ounce cups, pouring-lidded containers, and snacks in baskets—but this time the basket is covered with a see-through plastic lid with a handle. A child is free during this open snack period to find a friend, wash hands (a container with soapy water and a supply of paper towels are nearby), and eat a snack when desired. The only rule is that the child must bring a friend. If she can't find a friend that morning, the teacher may eat with the child—and then "engineer" socially to help that child make a friend in the next few weeks.

On the wall near the open snack table is a class roster where the teacher keeps a record of the time each child eats snack and with whom. Open snack is especially useful during the beginning of a school year when many children are making an initial adjustment; it may be alternated with group snack for variety and so that the children may benefit from the advantages of both methods.

Eating Difficulties

Some children become "Mr. Hyde" or "The Hulk" when they eat with a group. These carryover behaviors from home are rooted in power struggles and generally are seen in the form of the child who will not eat or the child who becomes verbally aggressive (calling others names), becomes physically aggressive (jabbing others with a finger), harasses others, and hoards snacks. The teacher's attitude toward such children should be to consider this "misbehavior" a sign of basic insecurity and fear of the eating and group situation. They should not be viewed simply as bullies or as "just being mean." The goal is to have these children become comfortable, to eat, and to socialize with others.

Start by permitting the difficult passive or aggressive child to eat in a one-to-one relationship with a friend or adult at a small table. This should not be done in such a manner that the child views it as isolation or punishment, but as a special time with a friend or teacher. Later, a second child can be invited to the small table, with others gradually joining over a period of days or weeks until the child finally is eating with a group. Even after the child has adjusted to the large group setting, there may be "bad days" when she might be permitted to revert to a smaller group for eating. (This may be considered a shaping process; see Chapter 4.)

While she is making these initial adjustments, few eating demands should be made of the child; depend on the other children to be good models of behavior for her. If she refuses to eat, make no demands; simply clean up when snack is over and move on to other activities. Some teachers worry that if the child has not eaten she will become malnourished; however, the failure to eat at school will occur only over a two- to three-week period, and with a well-balanced day of active play, the child will develop a healthy appetite. When the noneating child knows that the pressure is off, she will eat. We as teachers must have faith that this will occur.

It is not surprising to discover that it is the noneating child's parents who demand at the end of the day a full report of the child's eating performance: Did John eat all of his lunch today? This is symptomatic of a power struggle between parent and child at the eating table. The parents' emotional intensity may be strong and possibly intimidating to the teacher, attempting to draw us into the power struggle. We must resist. Our response to the parent would be a statement of encouragement: "He did better today!" or "He is becoming more comfortable at snack and gradually eating more; we are confident that in a few days he will be eating a full serving." We then move on to other positive topics with the parent, telling of the other activities in which the child is doing well. Modeling positive expectations for the child is the best support we can give to parents who appear to be overly concerned.

Dealing with the Aggressive Child

For the hoarding child who takes far too much from the shared snack basket, initially provide items that are very small, such as nuts, dry cereals, or trail mix rather than one large blueberry muffin. State, "Take all that you can eat and leave in the basket all that you cannot eat. You may take seconds, and I will always make sure that everyone gets enough to eat." (Remember: Tell the child what to do, not what *not* to do.) Resist the natural tendency to say, "Don't take so much, Tommy. You are not going to eat all of that." Permit the child, for a period of days or even two to three weeks, to continue to hoard without any comment. The hoarder has a basic "not OK" view of the world, and his life-stance position is that the world is denying him and he must fight to get his needs met.

At the end of snack, during cleaning-up procedures, appear before the hoarding child (who will have a large pile of trail mix in front of him uneaten), make eye contact, touch the remaining food to focus his attention on what is being talked about, and then reassuringly state, "Take all that you can eat and leave in the basket all that you cannot eat. You may take seconds, and I will always make sure that everyone gets enough to eat."

Over the next weeks, begin to "back down" the Teacher Behavior Continuum with the child (see Figure 10–1):

- *Modeling*: Eat with others who exhibit good eating behaviors.
- *Directive Statements*: Before the child takes from the basket of food, state directly, "Take all that you can eat and leave in the basket all that you cannot eat. You may take seconds, and I will always make sure that everyone gets enough to eat."

FIGURE 10–1 Teacher Behavior Continuum: SNACKING/EATING

Modality Cueing	Nondirective Statements	Questions	Directive Statements	Modeling/Physical Intervention
Radiating a zone of safety and control	"We have a rule for taking snacks."	"Jim, what is our rule about 'snacks from baskets'?"	"Take all that you can eat and leave in the basket all that you cannot eat. You may take seconds, and I will always make sure that everyone gets enough to eat."	Teacher and peers model appropriate eating behavior

- *Questions*: Just before the child takes from the shared basket, pose the question, "Tommy, what is our rule about 'snacks from baskets'?"
- *Nondirective Statements*: Say to the group in general, as the basket is passed, "We have a rule for taking snacks." Such nondirective reminders simply bring the desired rule to the child's awareness before he acts.
- *Modality Cueing or Looking On*: Such difficult children need the teacher nearby during snack, radiating a zone of safety and control. If the teacher must supervise a number of tables, she may choose to eat at the table where the target child is seated for a number of weeks. This "looking on" is not done with an attitude of "I have to keep an eye on him every moment or he will get out of hand"; rather, the attitude must be that we want a close positive relationship with the child: supportive, helping, and related.

Acting Out While Eating

Once the child has become relaxed and adjusted to eating with others, there will be times when she, or other members of the class, might begin to disrupt the eating situation in a manner that necessitates direct action by the teacher. This will be done by escalating back up the Teacher Behavior Continuum.

> *Carol has been silly all morning, giggling, challenging the limits imposed by the teacher, and generally refusing to fit into routines. At snack time, she is excessively loud, prevents the child next to her from eating by calling her "bathroom" names, and makes the entire eating atmosphere unpleasant.*

- *Looking On*: The teacher changes her seat location, moving into the direct view of Carol. If need be, she touches Carol or uses other nonverbal actions to make the child aware that she is present. A simple look might get Carol back on track; if not, the teacher escalates up the continuum.
- *Nondirective Statements*: The teacher announces in a nondirective statement, "At snack time we need to remember to use our 'inside' voices."
- *Questions*: The teacher increases the intervention by moving up the continuum to questioning: "Do you need my help to remember rules at snack?" or "Do you

need to move to a smaller, quieter table to be able to eat your snack this morning, Carol?"

- *Directive Statements*: Directive statements tell the child exactly what to do, not what *not* to do. If the child continues to be defiant, follow with a preparatory command or promise to take action in the form of a consequence. "Carol (use name, touch her on shoulder, and make direct eye contact), I want you to turn around, sit up in your chair, put your food in your mouth, and use an 'inside' voice that does not hurt our ears." She remains defiant. "If I see that done again, it is telling me that you do not know the rules for eating snack with others and I will ask you to move to another table, or leave snack time this morning" (logical consequence[5]).
- *Modeling/Physical Intervention*: If the child continues to refuse, the teacher now intervenes physically, if need be, to move the child away from the situation in a nonpunitive manner. (See Chapter 8 for techniques in handling temper tantrums, which are likely to occur when very strong intervention is used.)

REST TIME / NAPPING

It is recommended that for all-day programs, 3- and 4-year-old children might require at least two hours or more of afternoon rest or sleep, whereas 5-year-olds might need a minimum of 45 minutes in quiet, lie-down-on-a-mat rest. Resting is another area where power struggles are fought out between parents or other adults and the child, and these patterns will often be brought into the school during sleeping and resting periods.

Again, children (and we adults) live in three worlds: an inside world of thought and feelings, where our focus of attention is internal; a body world, where we enjoy activities such as swimming, running, or simply relaxing in a bathtub; and an external world in which we play, work, and focus on the world around us. A healthy form of regression[6] for the adult at the end of a very busy day is to crawl into a large comfortable chair, kick off tight shoes, and feel one's tired body relax (the body world), then, take time to daydream or think over the day (the inside world). Adults and children move in and out of these three worlds throughout the day.

In order to sleep, young children must release being attuned to the external world of others and objects, move through the body world by feeling themselves physically relax, and then move into an inner world of thoughts that finally lead to unconscious sleep. Overactive children, children frightened by the new school situation, or children who have patterns of engaging in power conflicts centered on napping will not be able to move back normally through these three worlds. Thus, rest period is not a time to be left to inexperienced staff; teachers need to be present—to rub backs, to talk to children, and to reassure them with their presence that the children are safe and secure.

The difficult child, when asked to lie on a cot, cannot give up an external awareness because his perceptions are outward and defensive. To help counter this, each child should have a cot labeled with his or her name, located at the same spot each day (for health reasons, children should not sleep on each other's cots). This is truly a private space, and other children should not be permitted to invade it by putting their hands or feet on the cots. The teachers should distribute themselves around the sleep area, kneeling near the children who are having difficulty relaxing and helping them with appropriate sensory measures. Soft music without lyrics can be played to mask inside and outside noise. Some children may be permitted to wear headphones to listen to soft music to screen out external sounds (these should be removed after the child is asleep).

The child who is visually stimulated may be placed near a wall, shelving, or small movable screen, so that distractions will be kept from view. For some tactile children, gentle back rubbing will help bring on relaxation. Once the children are relaxed and quieted, teachers may depart the sleeping room, leaving behind one adult, who will always be seated in the same location during rest. This is important because children will awaken, look to the "adult chair," see the teacher, be reassured, and return to sleep. If that chair is deserted, the child will sit up to look for the teacher and will have a very difficult time getting to sleep again.

There are rare children at this age who seem not to need sleep. Their behavior and personality are productive throughout the school day, and being on a cot is, for them, like being in jail. These children should be required to attempt to rest and sleep. But if they cannot fall asleep after 15 to 20 minutes and the teacher has given her best attempts to help them relax, she may decide to give them picture books or miniature toys to use quietly on their cots. If these children still act as if they are in jail, the teacher may permit them to leave the sleeping room quietly and do some tabletop activities (clay modeling or drawing, for example) in another room. Such children should not be harshly reprimanded, which would only cause greater tension and make it even more difficult for them to relax. This would be a real contradiction of action and goals.

CIRCLE/STORY TIME

Bringing together a group of 5-, 4-, and especially 3-year-old children and getting them to focus their full attention on one adult takes great care and technical understanding. It might be helpful to reread the concept of three spheres of communication described in Chapter 2.

One to All

Group time provides third-sphere communication (one to all), whereby the teacher requires all attention to focus on her while her emotions and responses are diffused to all members of a group—generally not to one child. Thus, each child is required to inhibit his own egocentric desires and become a part of the collective activity. This is socially very demanding for the young child, who is still quite self-centered. Care must be given in regulating the amount of time children will be required to maintain themselves in nonpersonal, directly controlled situations. Circle/story time is one such situation. If well-managed, this activity can lead the child toward a greater ability to handle direct instruction.

The transition into and out of group time is critical. If all 15 or 20 young children run into the rug room and try to grab a favorite spot, pushing and shoving will occur with some danger of minor injury. Let's look at a better way of making a transition from, for example, snack time to circle time. The teacher in charge of circle time collects three to six children who have finished with their previous activity and have cleaned up. She directs them to follow her to the rug. Once at the rug, the teacher must take a power position, much like a judge in a courtroom, placing herself higher than the children, such as on a piano stool or rocking chair.

Circle time must be engineered with an understanding of control of error. All children should know the rules about what they should and should not do,

MAKING GOOD TRANSITIONS

1. Generally, never have young children stand in line to wait.
2. Move children in groups of three to six, with the first group accompanied by the teacher, who has these children get the new area ready for those who follow.
3. The last teacher to leave the space, such as the rug room where story time was occurring, uses the remaining three to six children to clean up before moving them to the new location.
4. When children are making transitions to a new space, before they leave their present space they should know where they are going and what they will do when they get there.

and there must be some definition of individual seating space. Two large half-circles, taped or painted, or a circle design in the rug can indicate where each child is to be seated with legs tucked under. The first children will take the inner circle, closest to the teacher; the later children will take the back circle, refraining from trampling over children already seated. The motor rules and circle on the floor are structured to control error; if there is no structure, the children will be randomly scattered over the rug, rolling over, lying down, and getting up and down—all in all, a recipe for potential chaos.

The teacher should not wait until everyone is present and ready (this would cause the waiting children to find negative ways of amusing themselves) but should simply begin a finger game, a song with physical actions, or something similar. Once everyone has come in, the story can be started.

While circle time is in progress, other teachers or aides need to be present at the back of the circle. If certain children cannot relax, and begin to disrupt the story, the helping teachers would move closer to them, touching them on their backs or drawing them into their own laps, generally helping them to relax. Or these teachers may, in the case of very physically active children, move them to child-sized chairs at the edge of the circle. These children literally hold themselves onto the chairs until they gain control of their bodies. If repetitive disruptions by one or more children do occur, the in-charge teacher who is reading or carrying on the activity must take some action, and that action will be based on the Teacher Behavior Continuum.

- *Looking On*: The teacher may simply signal with her eyes to the off-task child that she wants his or her attention. This is also a signal to the helping teacher on the sidelines to move in and help with this child.
- *Nondirective Statements*: At this point it is important for the teacher to understand the concept of high-profile and low-profile correction in a directive teaching situation. If the teacher stops the activities and reprimands one child directly, she is disrupting the shared fantasy of the story for all others, as well as possibly making the other children feel empathetically tense and uncomfortable. "John, you are not listening and you are disrupting the story for everyone." The eyes of all other children now turn to John. This is a guilt-inducing statement. The reprimand has probably disrupted the story more than John's original actions did.

In using low-profile correction, the teacher simply looks at John, says his name, and points out some aspect of the book or object she is sharing. "John, you will notice (pointing to the picture) that the troll is hiding under the bridge." In low-profile corrections, the teacher can use the child's name, her hand, and visual focus, and continue with the rhythms of the story.

- *Questions/Directive Statements*: If disruption by the child continues, move up the Teacher Behavior Continuum to questions and to even more directive actions that will require a high profile. But keep in mind that when two or more adults are teaching in the classroom, the in-charge teacher can depend on the sideline teacher to help with children who need "looking on." The teacher then questions all children, "What are our rules of behavior at circle time?" She then directs, "Show me that you know the rules!" Finally comes a preparatory command to the off-task child: "John, you are showing me this morning that you have not learned the rules for story time, and if __ occurs again, I will ask you to go to the next room and choose something else to do."
- *Modeling/Physical Intervention*: If the misbehavior continues, the in-charge teacher will have the sideline teacher remove John from circle time. Since a very high-profile correction is needed, the teacher may choose to stop the story and play a finger or hand game, and then reintroduce the story.

  Later, in a nonpunitive manner, the in-charge teacher will approach John, moving through the TBC again, with child and teacher seated in chairs facing each other, knee-to-knee. "You had a really difficult time in circle time this morning (nondirective statement). What are the rules for circle time? (questions). In circle time I want you to sit on your spot on the line, look at me, and listen to the story." If the teacher feels that the child truly does not understand the rules, the two of them could go to the rug room and the teacher could reteach the rules (modeling). This knee-to-knee follow-through lets the child know, in a nonpunitive manner, exactly what is wanted.

Departing from circle time can be done quickly and in an orderly manner. Generally, children should be dismissed in groups of six to eight. The in-charge teacher may continue with a simple hand game while the sideline teacher signals a small group of children and leads them to a definite location. The in-charge teacher dismisses another group of six to eight who will "go to Mrs. Anderson" at snack or her location. Finally, the in-charge teacher has the remaining children clean up the room and then follow her to the new location. Notice that no one has had to stand in line. Waiting in lines should never occur in early childhood practice. Children at this age do not move well in herds!

ACTIVE/PASSIVE TIMES

Consider the amount of physical activity a child is doing and try to balance this with a passive activity. Many children tend to get "stuck" in outside or physical worlds and cannot slow down and relax. Some young children, if permitted, would continue to be consumed with running and movement until they were so exhausted they would actually "drop in their tracks." Once the teacher senses that children have had enough activity, they should be moved to story time, puzzles, or similar sedentary activities.

HAVE YOU TRIED THIS?

Putting on many children's coats at one time as the children wait and stand to be attended to is a fertile area for conflict to occur between children. You may teach young children to put on their own coats or jackets independently and quickly by the following:

1. Have each child place her coat on a table with the button (or zipper) up and the coat on its back, with the collar facing the child.
2. The child places her hands into the sleeves (right hand to right sleeve, left hand into left sleeve) while the coat is still on the table. She then raises the coat and hands over her head, keeping her arms straight.
3. Her arms slide down into the sleeves as her arms are dropped.

OUTSIDE CLIMATE AND WEATHER

To balance outside and inside activities, the teacher must be aware of the general climate outside and be prepared to make daily adjustments. In tropical climates during the summer months, the teacher may wish to have the outside time in the early mornings when it is relatively cool, and stay indoors in the afternoon. The opposite is true for cold climates or winter months, when it is probably best to stay inside in the mornings and go outside in the afternoon in the warmer sun.

DEPARTURE

There are some children who do well all day long, until the first parent appears at the end of the day to pick up his or her child. Then the Dr. Jekyll and Mr. Hyde syndrome appears among some of the remaining children, with crying, temper tantrums, and defiance toward the teachers. Perhaps after the first parent of the day comes for his or her child, the "Mr. Hyde" child worries about whether he will be picked up by his own parent. For him, the questions is: Will my mom forget me? This is not an extraordinary worry, but will be a concern for most preschool children.

The goal is to occupy the children's minds (perhaps with a story) and possibly their hands (using structured-construction materials such as puzzles) in some activity that keeps their minds off their worry and separation fears. This can be done by having a small, intimate circle time with the six to eight children who are picked up late. Find a comfortable corner on a rug where children can be on the teacher's lap or otherwise physically close to the teacher. Read stories, play hand games, and carry on lively conversation, permitting individual children to depart from the circle at natural break points when the teacher is aware that the parent has arrived. This should be done whenever the parent is truly late. If the last child to be picked up is simply left on her own while the teacher goes about cleaning up, she will have a real feeling of loss. If possible, she should be engaged in helping to clean up, or the teacher should take time for some one-to-one communication with her until the parent arrives.

SUMMARY

Techniques can be used to ensure smoother handling of arrivals, snack eating, meal patterns, rest/sleeping, circle/story time, transactions, departures, schedules, and teaching motor rules. These techniques are founded on the underlying premise that children can be trusted and that their inappropriate actions stem from their lack of ability to behave as we desire. The objective is to give them a secure environment where they can learn these skills and move forward in their development.

To accomplish this task, the teacher needs to understand how to arrange a well-balanced classroom, allowing for freedom and control of error. Once a well-designed play environment is created, and the child understands the motor rules and time schedules, the classroom runs smoothly without the need for excessive teacher control. The teacher is then free to facilitate the children's ongoing play, usually through the Teacher Behavior Continuum, to further their journey toward effectiveness, autonomy, and increased maturity.

Test Yourself

The following questions will permit you to test your understanding of the techniques, methods, and philosophy as they relate to classroom time periods and schedule. Answers may be found at the end of this chapter, following the Endnotes.

A. ____ true B. ____ false	1. All children must come to circle time, and if they disrupt that time they should be punished.
A. ____ true B. ____ false	2. Parents should be instructed to deliver the child to the classroom, say good-bye, and immediately depart to save the child the stress and crying caused by separation.
A. ____ true B. ____ false	3. Children who "misbehave" during snack time should be viewed as children who lack this ability, and they should gradually be introduced to eating in groups with others.
A. ____ true B. ____ false	4. Being able to rest on a cot is a task that the child must learn quickly, and one teacher should be assigned to the whole group to discipline those children who are disruptive.
A. ____ true B. ____ false	5. Children who make noises at rest time may need earphones or background music to mask outside sounds.
A. ____ true B. ____ false	6. When children do not eat all their snack, they need to stay in their seats until they finish.
A. ____ true B. ____ false	7. When the teacher is seated at the snack table eating and talking with the children, she is demonstrating the one-to-all relationship sphere.
A. ____ true B. ____ false	8. When children refuse to eat at meal times, the teacher should cut their portions and give them less.
A. ____ true B. ____ false	9. Hoarding at snack time is an indication of a child who still has not developed a basic sense of acceptance and is therefore working from a power motivation.
A. ____ true B. ____ false	10. An item such as a cuddle blanket with which the child sleeps is a home toy and should not be brought to school.

Glossary

Customs Inspection When the child regresses appropriately back into a parent's protective arms to be comforted during a strange, new, and potentially frighting experience, the child gradually begins to look out to the wider world beyond the parent's lap. This outward awareness period is called "customs inspection stage."

Guilt Induction (GI) When children misbehave and we "GI" them, we make statements and criticisms that make them feel guilty for their behavior. This is a psychologically harmful form of discipline and is not recommended.

Lap Time Young children live in three worlds: an inner world of thought and feeling; a physical world where they actively disperse their energies through large motor actions; and an external world of working and playing with others. When a child is "flooded," he will regress appropriately into the inner world and seek comfort there. The child should be permitted to "cuddle" in the teacher's lap to emotionally "refuel" during those stressful periods.

Practicing Stage The process whereby the young child tentatively leaves the protective lap of mother and goes off into the new world of snack, toys, or playing with others; the practice of being separated physically and emotional from mother (or other adult "parent" figure).

Related Reading

Wolfgang, C. H., & Wolfgang, M. E. (1992). *School for Young Children: Developmentally Appropriate Practices.* Boston: Allyn and Bacon.

Endnotes

1. Freud, A. (1968). *Normality and Pathology in Childhood: Assessments of Development.* New York: International Universities Press. Freud, A. (1971). *The Ego and the Mechanisms of Defense.* New York: International Universities Press. Mahler, M. S., et al. (1975). *The Psychological Birth of the Human Infant.* New York: Basic Books. Mahler, M. S. (1970). *On Human Symbiosis and the Vicissitudes of Individuation.* New York: International Universities Press. Speers, R. W., et al. (1970). Recapitulation of Separation-Individuation Process When the Normal Three-Year-Old Enters Nursery School. In J. McDevitt (Ed.), *Separation-Individuation, Essays in Honor of Margaret Mahler.* New York: International Universities Press. Speers, R. W., et al. (1970). *Variations in Separation-Individuation and Implications for Play Ability and Learning as Studied in the Three-Year-Old in Nursery School.* Pittsburgh: University of Pittsburgh Press.
2. Toffler, A. (1971). *Future Shock.* New York: Bantam Books.
3. Speers, R. W., et al. (1970). Recapitulation of Separation-Individuation Process When the Normal Three-Year-Old Enters Nursery School. In J. McDevitt (Ed.), *Separation-Individuation, Essays in Honor of Margaret Mahler.* New York: International Universities Press. Speers, R. W., et al. (1970). *Variations in Separation-Individuation and Implications for Play Ability and Learning as Studied in the Three-Year-Old in Nursery School.* Pittsburgh: University of Pittsburgh Press.
4. Speers, R. W., et al. (1970). Recapitulation of Separation-Individuation Process When the Normal Three-Year-Old Enters Nursery School. In J. McDevitt (Ed.), *Separation-Individuation, Essays in Honor of Margaret Mahler.* New York: International Universities Press. Speers, R. W., et al. (1970). *Variations in Separation-Individuation and Implications for Play Ability and Learning as Studied in the Three-Year-Old in Nursery School.* Pittsburgh: University of Pittsburgh Press.
5. Dreikurs, R. (1964). *Children: The Challenge.* New York: Hawthorne Books.
6. Freud, A. (1968). *Normality and Pathology in Childhood: Assessments of Development.* New York: International Universities Press.

Answers to Test Yourself

1B, 2B, 3A, 4B, 5A, 6B, 7B, 8A, 9A, 10B

SECTION IV

Parents, Staffing, Play, and the Difficult Child

In searching for reasons why a child's behavior becomes increasingly difficult, one will at times find that dramatic changes have been occurring in the child's home life involving his or her parents—divorce, moving to a new home, sometimes even destructive incidents of abuse. These actions, and a host of others, can have a profound impact on a child's behavior. Often, the teacher of the very young child is the only one to witness these family changes and the negative fallout for the child. Most teachers feel a strong need to take some action, but this desire is tempered by a concern that their actions might make the situation worse. Teachers could then become the objects of the parent's anger or possibly even the targets of legal action. To successfully intervene regarding parents and the difficulties associated with them takes considerable skill. In addition, teachers can benefit from carefully designed constructs to offer guidance in knowing just which actions to take. Chapter 11 provides a way of viewing these problems and suggests a set of definite guidelines for teacher action.

In Chapter 12, the teacher is given clear steps to follow in establishing a staffing approach for dealing with the child who is a discipline problem. A key to this process is to have clearly focused meetings among the teaching staff; an unfocused meeting can drag on, consuming a great deal of time without resulting in a clear picture of what has been decided. This chapter details a step-by-step procedure with clear responsibilities, so that a staffing meeting will be goal directed, use time well, and produce a clearly understood agreement on future intervention approaches toward the difficult child.

Finally, Chapter 13 is provided to give the teacher a better understanding of the importance of play. A characteristic of the misbehaving child who acts out daily is that he lacks social skills and shows signs of internal stress and emotions. Play is the key to enabling the problem child to develop necessary social skills and to ventilate stored-up tensions, and it is play that fills the young child's behavior void. The chapter offers a clear definition of play, explains its value, and suggests how the teacher may evaluate and facilitate the child's play.

11

Parents: Difficulties and Problems

The day-to-day life of the teacher is almost never free of questions or problems stemming from relationships with the parents of some students. The overwhelming majority of parents love their children deeply and want nothing but the best for them. Even some of these devoted parents, however, can conduct themselves—and their relationships with their children—in ways that adversely affect the children's behavior in school. Parents' statements, questions, and behaviors—sometimes even destructive behaviors—are signals that alert teachers to parents' needs and those of their children. How can a teacher make sense of this continuous parental input, prioritizing needs and making reasonable responses? On what basis would you make a decision to take action as a teacher in the following situations?

> *Situation 1: "The Hole in the Doughnut"*
>
> *Holly's parents are what would be called* yuppies. *They want to do all the best for their daughter. Holly's father is personable, greets you warmly, and is always ready to question you about the latest "how-to" parent book, public television program on children, or article on "how to raise your child smarter" that he found in an in-flight magazine. His attitude is described by one teacher, with some frustration, as "He always sees the hole in the doughnut!"—in other words, he focuses on what is missing rather than appreciates what is there.*
>
> *He wants the school to provide him with a parallel home curriculum through which he and his daughter would have specific hours set aside for instruction at home. Holly's mother is a volunteer for a host of social activities in the city, and is first to respond when parent help is called for. She is well-liked by teachers, but periodically brings questions from her husband ("Tom wants to know..."). There is always an urgency and intensity to their demands, though they are grateful and positive toward teacher observations and suggestions. After a school pageant, they were very displeased that their daughter did not have a more central part in the play.*

Situation 2: New Role Demands and Family Separation

Jason, a new 3-year-old student, has an 8-year-old brother who attends another school. His father has opened a new business located near Jason's school, and his mother has just returned to a full-time job on the opposite side of town. The father's new responsibilities include getting the boys up, getting breakfast, making lunch, and dropping the boys off at their schools. He is at the gate to Jason's school 15 to 30 minutes before the school is to open. When teachers arrive early to make preparations, he requests that Jason be allowed to enter early, so he can drop off his other son and get to his business. Usually, Jason enters the school carrying a bag containing an egg and muffin sandwich and orange juice.

During the first three weeks of school, Dad forgot Jason's lunch on four occasions. On the first and second occasions, he returned at 11:45 A.M. with a small pizza and a cola for Jason, to the envy of all the other children. On the third occasion, he appeared with a fast-food hamburger and soda when the lunch period was almost over and some children had begun napping. The fourth time, he forgot completely. Because of the father's morning haste, there is no time to talk to him, and when the mother is informed when she picks Jason up at the end of the day, her response is, "That's Jim's responsibility. Tell him about it, not me." Jason is a personable child who greets you with a warm smile, much like that of his salesman father—a smile that makes you feel special. However, at times—especially when he is asked to do a task—Jason's expression becomes flat and emotionless. He usually responds to a new activity, no matter how simple, with, "No, I can't do it." During these times, when he seems to pull inside of himself, he also pulls at his hair on one side of his head, and now he has a number of bald spots.

Situation 3: Aggressive Behavior

Brandon is the only son of a rugged, athletic, chain-smoking father and an attractive primary teacher mother. Because of recent moves, he has been in and out of a number of day-care centers. He is a thin-featured, pale-complected (to the point of looking anemic), tense child who appears as tightly coiled as a spring. He cannot look a teacher directly in the eyes, and usually turns away when invited to join activities. At lunch or snack, he seats himself with the more excitable boys, and uses "bathroom talk" in a whispered, covert manner, whipping the boys into a giggling frenzy that usually ends with their throwing food at each other. When the teacher approaches to stop this behavior, Brandon puts his head down, smiles slightly, and acts as if he is totally innocent.

His most productive behavior is during story time, when for the first time his eyes are focused on the teacher and the book. It is rare that the teacher finds a book to read to the group that Brandon's parents have not already read to him. His answers to questions after story reading are insightful and animated, and show understanding as well as enjoyment of books (recall that his mother is a primary teacher).

During play-activity curriculum, he is like a caged tiger, normally crouched in a protective corner in the block room, wanting to use the materials but not feeling free to do so. His attitude stems from his fear that if he starts a block structure, someone will destroy it. This almost totally fearful and untrusting view of his peers causes him to lash out with sharp fingernails, sometimes directly at the other children's eyes, and to repeatedly bite peers for the most minor contact. After an aggressive act, he tells the teacher that the other child was hostile to him, but upon investigation, it usually turns out that the other child merely bumped him accidentally or inadvertently stepped on one of his toys. During conferences his mother refuses to discuss this behavior, changing the topic to his performance in the more academic curriculum.

On the rare occasions when the father picks Brandon up, he seems impatient to get in and get out. Brandon complicates this by refusing to come when called and running to the opposite side of the playground, causing his father to move after him. The frustrated father, when he feels no teacher is looking, strikes Brandon sharply on the backside and departs with the boy crying as he is dragged by one arm. Brandon also refuses to depart with his mother. She reacts by whispering in his ear bribes of candy or gifts that she has for him in the car.

Last week the mother and father separated, and when school closed on Friday, there was no parent to pick him up. The home and emergency numbers provided by parents at registration time were called with no results. Brandon was taken home by the head teacher, who made repeated telephone calls during the weekend without success, and Brandon spent the entire weekend at the teacher's house. It was not until the end of the school day on the following Monday, when the mother appeared to pick Brandon up, that either parent was aware the child had to be cared for by the teacher, in her home, for the entire weekend. When told of this, both mother and father blamed the opposite parent, claiming that it was the other's responsibility.

Situation 4: Sexual Actions and Apparent Injuries

Carol's mother's new boyfriend brings Carol to school, normally an hour or two late each morning. The child appears wearing black leotards, a tank top, and, on one occasion, a red lacy garter belt. The mother's boyfriend does not come into the school, but leaves Carol at the school gate with a kiss that appears passionate and adult-like. Carol is a beautiful 4-year-old child with long black hair and large round eyes, but a nervous smile. She often drops her eyes when spoken to by the teacher and turns away looking over her shoulder in a coy manner. She is not defiant but simply passive and noncompliant toward teachers. For the last two weeks, she has been preoccupied with masturbation, and repeatedly attempts to enlist others to join her in parallel fashion or to touch her in her genital area.

Female teachers first talked to her in a supportive manner, asking her not to "do that." This counseling escalated to outright demands that she stop inviting others to join her. She repeatedly gets the children who are more easily controlled to go behind the storage shed, where they are found with their dresses up and fingers in their panties. The behavior is so repetitive and excessive that a teacher is assigned to watch her at all times, but she is an expert at concealing her lower body behind the toys, or the sand table, or the block shelves, while she signals a nearby child to watch what she is doing. She was seen having the boys place their fingers in her, as she and they giggled. One of the boys reported this to his mother, and she came to school and announced, "My child is being sexually abused by this 4-year-old girl and I want something done immediately or I will call the child abuse number." The following day, Carol came to school walking as if in pain, and was found to be bruised and bleeding in her anal area.

In considering the cases of Carol and the other children, most teachers will realize that some of these parent situations are clearly not serious, whereas others might call for consulting or legal action. However, each of these situations does demand some degree of teacher intervention; each situation requires the teacher to make a reasoned decision.

To respond effectively to these situations, we as teachers must determine what degree of power would be appropriately used in our intervention. Various incidents might call for simply a Relationship-Listening response, whereas others might warrant a Confronting-Contracting response, possibly a Rules and Consequences response, or even a legalistic-coercive approach that goes beyond the teacher's and school's authority. The following construct may be useful in determining appropriate teacher responses to particular parent situations.

NEEDS OF STUDENTS

The preceding four examples concerned Holly's parents (with their competitiveness and "hole-in-the-doughnut" questions), Jason's father (new role demands and family separation), Brandon (aggressive behavior and parent difficulty in handling him), and Carol (excessive sexual actions and apparent injuries). Obviously, each of the situations is related to a need of the parent or child. An analysis of this need can be made by using a construct such as Maslow's[1] hierarchy of needs (see Figure 11–1) to give order to what might appear to be unrelated behaviors of parents and children.

From a Maslowian position, before parents or children can gain self-fulfillment, their lower needs must be met. One must first meet the *physiological* needs of food, water, and basic physical health care (see Situation 4, where Carol was physically injured). Once these physiological needs are attained, *security* can become a focus for a parent's or student's energies. The teacher can attempt to help establish these feelings of security. (Brandon, in Situation 3, exemplified a child with fears of others' aggression.) The next hierarchical need is *belonging* (a situation that is absent in Jason's withdrawal into himself in Situation 2). Last is *esteem*, the need to attain a degree of respect from one's peers and those to whom one is related (Situation 1, Holly's parents' competitiveness).

Within the context of Maslow's theory, it is suggested that a teacher can analyze the behavior of the parents and identify which of the child's needs are being blocked and where this would fall in the Maslowian hierarchy. The teacher is then ready to evaluate the degree of severity of these problems.

FIGURE 11–1 Maslow's Needs Hierarchy

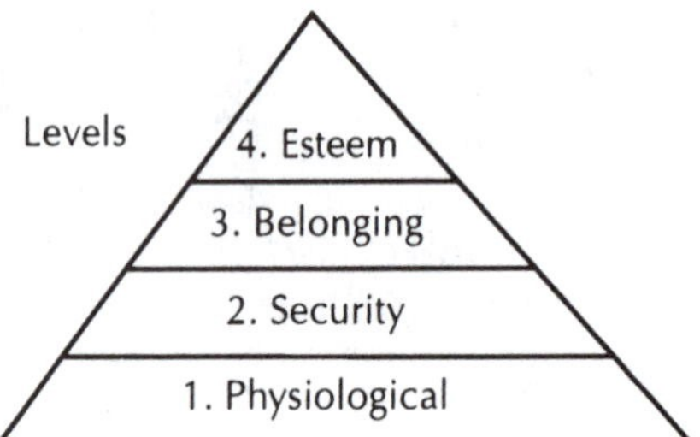

DEGREES OF CRISIS

When looking at the human needs underlying some of the problems portrayed in the four preceding situations, it is apparent that the degree of seriousness of the situation may vary from life threatening or psychologically threatening (sexual abuse, physical injury) to limited seriousness (social competitiveness of Holly's parents). As one moves through Maslow's needs hierarchy, a classification of crises may be seen: (1) imminent crisis, (2) developing crisis, and (3) potential crisis.[2]

Imminent Crisis

An *imminent crisis* would be a situation in which the Level 1 physiological needs are involved, and there is a life-threatening situation. If Carol's injuries are not immediately treated with medical care, irreversible damage will occur and she may already have suffered psychological damage. Time is of the utmost importance with this incident.

Developing Crisis

The *developing crisis* is generally related to the blocked needs of Level 2 security. The consequences are serious but there appears to be more time to head off the event. Brandon's loss of his home stability constitutes a developing crisis. If changes do not occur, his behavior may continue to regress, with the potential of becoming an imminent crisis. In the situation of Jason and his busy parents, another blocked need is belonging, which also suggests a developing level of crisis.

Potential Crisis

With the desire of Holly's parents for their child to always be special, the need level is esteem, and there is a *potential crisis*. The situation might be strongly felt by the parent, but the seriousness is related to a blow to self-esteem.

THE TEACHER'S HELPING BEHAVIOR

With the understanding of the two correlated constructs of Maslow's levels of need and the levels of crisis, the question arises as to what responding actions the teacher should take. The answer is found in the continuum of human relationship faces: Relationship-Listening, Confronting-Contracting, and Rules and Consequences. Though not one of these "faces," another point along this continuum is Coercive-Legalistic, a process through which the teacher follows prescribed procedures to implement actions required by law. The degree of power used for the teacher's intervention would escalate or deescalate relative to the level of needs and the severity of the crisis (see Figure 11–2).

In the case of Holly's parents, with their social competitiveness, the need level is esteem, and there is a potential level of crisis. The helping techniques for the teacher are found in Relationship-Listening. The Relationship-Listening face, described in Chapter 2, discusses such techniques that may be used with Holly's parents as door openers, verbal encoding as active listening, I-messages, the Six Steps to Problem Solving, acknowledgments, conferencing, and problem ownership. Just as the Teacher Behavior Continuum may be used with children, these

FIGURE 11–2 Needs, Crises, and Relationship Faces

Needs Level	Crisis	Face (method of responding)
Level 4: Esteem	IMMINENT DEVELOPING POTENTIAL	Relationship-Listening
Level 3: Belonging		Confronting-Contracting
Level 2: Security		Rules and Consequences
Level 1: Physiological		Coercive-Legalistic

similar techniques can now be used with the parent at needs Level 4 esteem. Such Relationship-Listening techniques permit the teacher to be active in dealing with Holly's parents, but in an accepting relationship to help the parents gain some emotional control and do some problem solving to meet their needs and the teacher's needs in a cooperative, shared manner (see Figure 11–3).

Holly's Parents

Need: Level 4—Esteem

Crisis: Potential

Face: Relationship-Listening

Scene: Parent-teacher conference

Participants: Holly's parents and the head teacher

Teacher: "You were not pleased that Holly did not have the lead part in the school pageant (active listening). Would you like to talk about it?" (door opener).

Father: "Yeah, she never gets picked for 'good' things!"

Teacher: (Nods head [acknowledgment])

Father: "She did have a part in the last two pageants and she is a better speaker than all the other children in that class."

Teacher: "You're not quite satisfied with the experiences that Holly is receiving at this school" (active listening).

Father: "Well, maybe you should learn to pick the best child for your pageants!"

Mother: "Holly had three paintings on display at the art show."

Teacher: "Seeing Holly's products pleases you very much" (active listing).

Father: "How do we know that Holly is going to be ready for kindergarten? We taught her all her colors and letters of the alphabet, and she can count to 100!"

FIGURE 11–3 TBC: Relationship-Listening Face

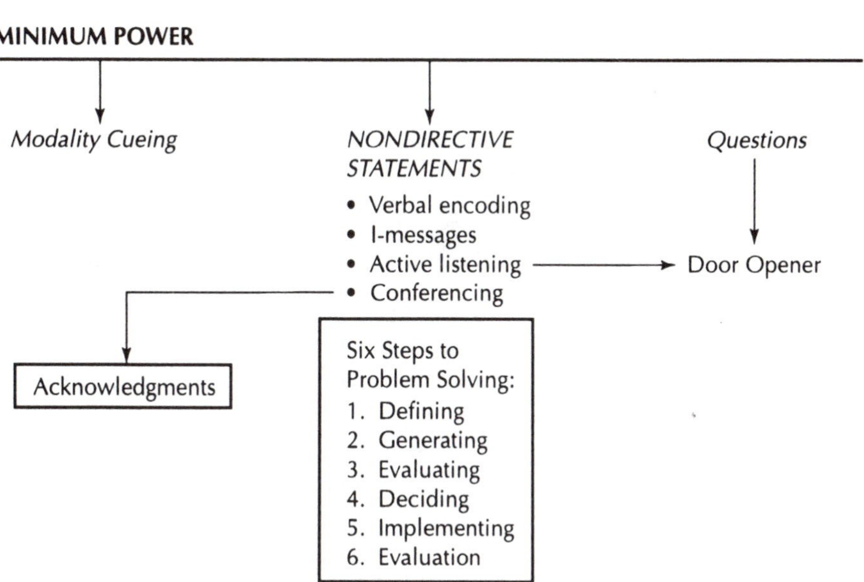

Teacher: "Helping Holly with academics is very important to you" (active listening).

Father: "Yes, we are concerned as to whether she will get into medical school. It's very competitive. Can you guarantee that Holly will be reading before she leaves your classroom this year? We would be glad to help with any homework at home. And is Holly doing A, B, or C work—what grades should she be getting?"

Teacher: "If we were to give grades (behavior) and create competition, this would violate our concepts of how your children need to be educated at this age (effect) and would make us feel guilty (feeling) for contradicting our views (I-message). Let's see if we can identify your needs or problems and then see if we can work on these needs together (Six Steps to Problem Solving—Step 1: Define the problem). Which problem is most important to you?"

Mother: "I think my husband would like to have some help on doing activities with Holly at home that would help her learn."

Father: "Yes."

Teacher: "Okay, helping Dad with activities that he can do with Holly (define the problem). Let's try to do this together—we are studying the farm and farm animals. What ideas can we think up to supplement our unit of study?" (Step 2: Generating possible solutions).

Father: "You're studying farm animals. Well, I saw in the children's section of the newspaper that there is a petting zoo at the Highland Mall."

Teacher: "What other ideas?" (door opener).

Mother: "We could buy some books on farm animals for Holly."

Teacher: "Book reading sounds good. Are there other sources of books?"

Father: "I might take Holly to the public library and get some animal books."

Teacher: "Here is a school activity book for parents on good parent activities with children's literature. You may wish to borrow it for two weeks. Okay, let's see some of the solutions we have designed: (1) Check the newspaper children's section for activities, (2) Go to the petting zoo, and (3) Borrow the school's activity book. Which of these will you choose to do?" (Step 3: Evaluating solutions).

Parents: (in unison) "We could do all of them!"

Teacher: "Who will do what?"

Father: "My wife can take Holly to the petting zoo, I will take her to the library on Saturday morning, and we can get the book from you."

Teacher: "Let's check back at the end of the month and see if this has all worked out" (Step 6: Reevaluation).

The teacher has used Relationship-Listening techniques with parents who are motivated by esteem needs. We have seen that the teacher did not "own" the problem but first encouraged the parents to talk out any negative feelings or problems. She then defined a manageable problem and guided the parents through the Six Steps to Problem Solving process, permitting the parents to come up with their own solutions. This, of course, may possibly empower them to do that for themselves the next time. If the parents' request was not acceptable to the teacher—such as the suggestion of giving grades—the teacher responded with an I-message. Thus, the teacher and school were not defensive about the parents' criticism but actually encouraged more criticism to get it all "out on the table." Once the problem was understood, the problem-solving process could begin.

In the case of Jason's parents with their busy schedules, the blocked need is belonging and suggests a developing crisis. The techniques of Confronting-Contracting described in detail in Chapter 3 would be most useful for the teacher in dealing with such a situation. This "face" places a high value on getting needs met in a social context and gives clear suggestions as to how to accomplish a positive sense of belonging (see Figure 11–4).

FIGURE 11–4 TBC: Confronting-Contracting Dimension Face

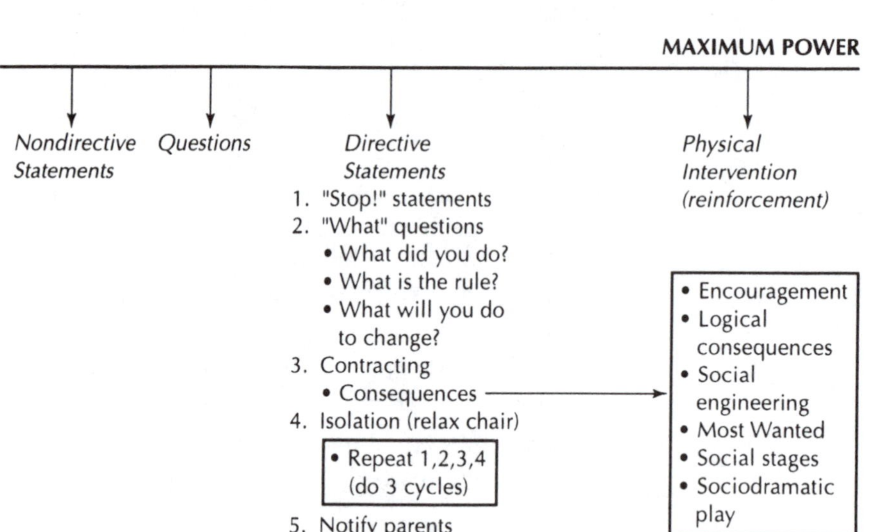

Jason's Parents

Need: Level 3—Belonging

Crisis: Developing

Face: Confronting-Contracting

Scene: Parent-teacher conference

Participants: Jason's parents (both mother and father) and the head teacher

Jason has been showing behaviors that indicate he is feeling more and more stress these days, and it is obvious since last month that roles at home have changed. Things are not working, and this needs to stop for Jason's benefit (Confronting Step 1: Stop it). The teacher seeks to determine what is happening here (Step 2: "What" questions).

Mother: "I pack Jason's lunch in the morning and it is his father's responsibility to get it here in the morning."

Father: "Sometimes Jason is too difficult in the morning. He refuses to let me dress him, and then in all the confusion I have periodically forgotten his lunch."

Teacher: "Things are not working for you at home, things are not working for Jason, and, because Jason comes to us like a bull in a china shop, things are not working with us here at school. Things must change for all of us. We will be glad to help; we must work this out! How can we make things change?" (Step 2: What will you do to change?).

Mother: "This is not my problem. I leave for work at 6:30 A.M. and I can't do anything!"

Father: (Drops eyes and gives no response; neither parent appears willing to speak.)

Teacher: "I see that there is no willingness to work together here. We need to work this out. We can take many actions to help Jason do well when he gets here. But if he goes through home interaction that causes him to 'flood' and he comes to us out of control, we must have one teacher deal with him all morning, and our program is disrupted. We need to work this out. What are your suggestions for change?"

Parents: (Both drop eyes, with mother appearing angry and father looking helpless.)

Teacher: "Well, since there appears to be no willingness to negotiate and contract for change here, I need to tell you the logical consequences of not working together (Step 3: Consequences). Jason will not be permitted to return to our center until we—you as mother and father and I as teacher—have an agreement" (preparatory command and a promise of isolation or logical consequence).

Mother: "Are you throwing us out of your school?"

Teacher: "No. I am saying that we need to work this out. The school is a stable environment for Jason and he needs to be with us and we love him dearly. Things are not going well at home, and this is having a negative impact on Jason and then a negative impact on us and our school. We are willing to work with you—but we need a contract for change to occur. How will you change?" (broken record).

Parents: (No response; four minutes pass.)

Teacher: "Well, we can work this out now, or meet in the morning before school starts, giving you some time to talk this over tonight, or you can call me later in the week when you're ready to work this out and wish Jason to return" (follow through to isolation and logical consequence).

Father: "Well, what do you want us to do?"

Teacher: "We, together, need to come up with ideas so that things can get worked out. I have heard one problem suggested regarding forgetting lunches, so let me make this suggestion. We need you to remember to bring Jason's lunch, but on the rare occasions when you forget, let us take the pressure off you to need to find a lunch later that morning. We will take care of Jason's lunches on those rare mornings. We have snack food, such as fruit, cheese, bread, and milk, and we will make Jason a healthy lunch on the day that you forget. Please don't feel guilty for this. It really will be no big problem for us and it will relieve pressure from you on this one problem. Now, I think bringing lunch is just one minor problem, and there are a host of others. What are they, and how will you work this out?"

Father: "Well, I have just opened an auto-body painting business. I have a great deal of pressure on me to make this business work or we could go bankrupt. It opens at 6:00 A.M., when most customers drop off their cars, but your school doesn't open until 7:30, and I am not able to be there to see how things are working out at my business."

Mother: "Well, I have started a new job as a high school teacher on the opposite side of town, and I am not going to drop Jason off. It's much too far and dangerous for me to travel each morning through all the traffic. This is Jim's responsibility—after all, his business is just two blocks away!"

Teacher: "Well, it seems that dropping Jason off is inconvenient for both of you. How will you solve this?"

Mother: (after much thought) "I know that Amy Gibson's mother and father live in our neighborhood and they bring her here each morning. I wonder if they would mind?"

Teacher: "I know that Mrs. Gibson is having some difficulty in getting here to pick Amy up at the end of the day before school closes on Tuesdays and Thursdays."

Mother: "Well, I don't have any trouble getting here in the afternoons. Maybe I should call Mrs. Gibson about swapping. No, that is Jim's job. It is his responsibility to handle the boys in the morning. Jim, you call."

Father: "I really don't know the lady, and I hesitate to call. Could you arrange that, Mrs. Walker (the head teacher)?"

Teacher: "No. My job is to teach the children and to serve as a leader in this meeting."

Father: "Oh, all right. I'll call."

Teacher: "Are there any other problems we should discuss?"

Parents: "This has really helped. If we can take care of the drop-off problem, that will take a lot of stress out of our life!"

Teacher: "Good, then we have a contract. Jim will call Mrs. Gibson to take care of the morning drop-off problem and Jim will make an effort to have

Jason off to school with his lunch. But on the rare occasion that the lunch is forgotten, I will make him lunch here and relieve you of that concern. Do we have an agreement and a contract?" (The teacher reaches out and shakes both parents' hands.)

Parents: "Yes." (They shake hands with the teacher and smile.)

Notice that in use of Confronting-Contracting techniques, the teacher and school express a willingness to bend their own procedures (making lunch on rare occasions for Jason—social engineering), but they did not assume the parent's responsibilities. The locus of control for solving problems is always with the child when dealing with disciplining a child, or with the parents when in a confronting conference. The teacher and school must be clear as to what logical consequences they have within their power, and is it wise to use this power if the parents fail to contract. This kind of meeting is confrontational and requires the use of some degree of power.

The Teacher Behavior Continuum, with its escalation and deescalation of power, has been a central construct to provide an advanced organizer of teacher behavior and actions. When dealing with parents, the teacher and school must be clear as to the power given to them by law and governing authorities (including licensing authorities, departments of education, or school boards). In the example of Jason and his parents, the school had the power to refuse service (a form of isolation and logical consequences) and was willing to use it. In public schools, where this option might not be available, other consequences must be clearly identified. If the school has not identified its power and the available logical consequences, or it is not willing to use that power for the betterment of the child under its care, the Confronting-Contracting Face will be toothless when used with parents and will be ineffective if the parents refuse to contract. If a developing crisis is not dealt with constructively, it will escalate into an imminent crisis, which could ultimately require the school to call on child abuse or neglect authorities or juvenile legal authorities if the actions are extremely serious. But the "face" of the teacher and school is to socially engineer and encourage the parents to work actively with the school to find solutions to their problems, with the teacher and school being a partner in the contracting.

The example involving Jason's parents was resolved ideally, but more likely a great deal more time will be spent and fewer positive results will be attained in real-life situations with parents involved in a Level 3 developing crisis. This example could have resulted in the parents getting family counseling or other social services to help them over this difficult period. Other options might include their church or relatives, depending on the type of problems faced by the parents in a Level 3 developing crisis. Some other parent difficulties that could result in a developing crisis are divorce, the father's loss of his job, or the destruction of the home by fire or other disaster.

In the case of Brandon, with his aggressive behavior and the family's marital difficulties, the need is Level 2 security and the level of crisis can be considered as developing to imminent. The teacher in this instance may choose techniques from the Rules and Consequences Face and the Coercive-Legalistic approach. This means that in dealing with Brandon's parents, the teacher would first specify actions to be carried out by the parents. If they carry out these actions, every effort will be made by the teacher to be positively reinforcing; if they do not, then negative actions—including moving to the Coercive-Legalistic—might be necessary. The Coercive-Legalistic option for the teacher and school might include using a social services agency to provide family counseling or turning the case over to child abuse or neglect authorities (see Figure 11–5).

FIGURE 11–5 TBC: Rules and Consequences Face

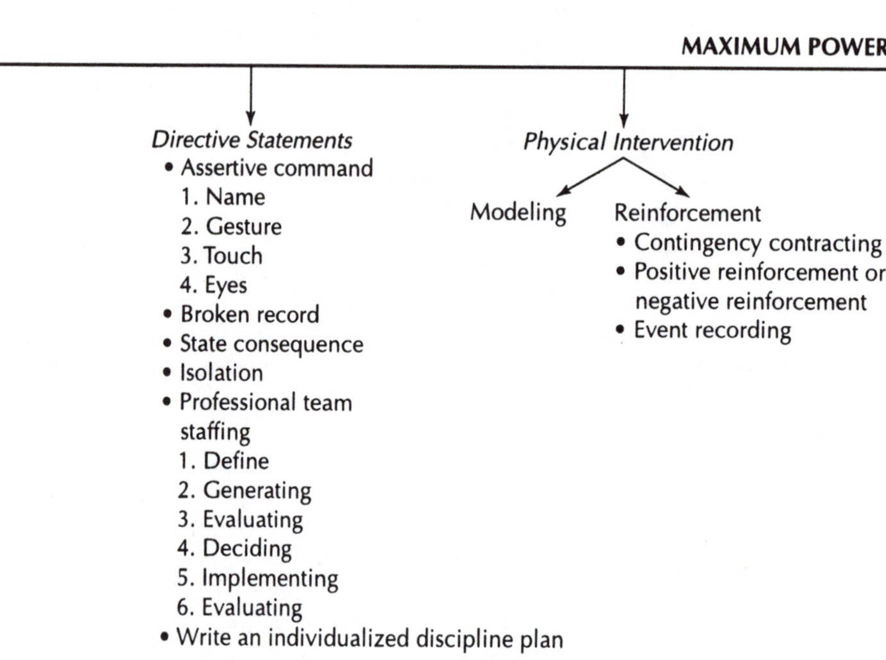

Brandon's Parents

Need: Level 2—Security

Crisis: Developing to Imminent

Face: Rules and Consequences

Scene: Parent-teacher conference

Participants: Brandon's parents and the teacher

Teacher: (Makes eye contact with parents, gestures, touches, and uses names) "Gail and Michael, I want you to obtain the services of a child and family counselor, for Brandon's sake, to help you as a family and Brandon individually to handle the problems related to your home difficulties" (assertive command)

Father: "We are sorry about failing to pick up Brandon last Friday. It won't happen again."

Teacher: "We care for Brandon for 10 hours a day (this is day care) all year-round, and we are an intimate and central part of his life. Brandon is suffering emotionally and socially at this time, and he and you need professional help. I want you to obtain the services of a child and family counselor, for Brandon's sake, to help you as a family and Brandon individually to handle the problems related to your home difficulties" (broken record).

Father: "I can't afford that. We won't forget to pick him up again. I don't want any counselor."

Teacher: "We have a commitment to Brandon and you, and we wish to work with both of you during this difficult time for you and especially for

Brandon. I want you to obtain the services of a child and family counselor, for Brandon's sake, to help you as a family and Brandon individually to handle the difficulties related to your marital situation (broken record). We have a list of private counselors or publicly available ones if you cannot afford the cost. We would like to meet, as a team, with you, a counselor of your choice, and our staff and do some solid problem solving to set up guidelines for us here at the school and you at home so that we may best help Brandon."

Father: "No way. This is none of your business."

Teacher: "We have a commitment to Brandon and you, and we wish to work with both of you during this difficult time for you and especially for Brandon. I want you to obtain the services of a child and family counselor, for Brandon's sake, to help you as a family and Brandon individually to handle the difficulties related to your marital situation" (broken record).

Father: "No way! I am going to remove him from this center."

Mother: "Where will he go, Michael?"

Teacher: "If you remove him from our school or will not work with us to change things for Brandon, then your past actions would suggest the possibility of child neglect, and I will be ethically obligated to report this to the child abuse and neglect authorities."

Father: "What child abuse and neglect?"

Teacher: (opens a folder containing a written anecdotal record and event recordings on Brandon and his parents collected over the past two months) "Our data collected over the last two months would suggest neglect for the following reasons: (1) There were 6 occasions that Brandon wore the same soiled clothing for a period of over five days; (2) On 15 occasions Brandon's lunch contained a coke and two slices of bread—his ferocious appetite suggests he is not being properly fed; (3) There were 12 times you were late by as much as 1½ hours in picking him up at the end of the day, and there was the complete failure to pick him up at all last Friday; (4) Brandon has reported 9 occasions when no one was at home with him for long periods of time; (5) Our records show that Brandon has been physically aggressive 30 to 35 times per day over the last three weeks; and (6) Our data show that Brandon cannot nap at rest time, and is so constipated that his stomach is bloated and swelling and he simply cannot have a bowel movement. Please, be assured that I find it difficult to say these things to you. We have a commitment to Brandon and you, and we wish to work with both of you during this difficult time for you and especially for Brandon. I want you to obtain the services of a child and family counselor, for Brandon's sake, to help you as a family and Brandon individually to handle the difficulties related to your marital situation" (broken record).

Mother: "Michael, this school has been so good to Brandon. He likes it here."

Father: "It's Gail's job to give him a bath and make his lunch. (silence) You mean that Brandon is doing all those things?"

Teacher: "Yes, Brandon is having a very difficult time right now."

Father: "You mean we would have to pay for a counselor? What would he do?"

Teacher: "I can give you a list of publicly supported social service counselors, and you would call and meet with him or her. We would have a team meeting with you, Gail, and our staff to set up a program (IESP) for you working at home and us here at school. (The teacher defines a behavioral objective for the parents.) Michael (identify the person), you will use my phone to call now and set an appointment to meet with a counselor (identify the target behavior) within the next 24 hours (identify the conditions). I will call the counselor two days from now to see if you have made your appointment (identify the conditions). If you have made your appointment with the counselor, I will take no actions to call in outside authorities (negative reinforcement). If you fail to make and attend the appointment, I will call the authorities (punishment)." (This may also be considered contingency contracting.)

In viewing the interaction of the teacher using the Rules and Consequences Face, one might consider her insensitive, cold, and unforgiving in dealing with these parents. But it is important to realize that past actions by the parents have placed Brandon in a psychologically damaging situation; the teacher is one of the few people who sees this occurring, and she has a moral obligation to take actions to safeguard this child's rights and well-being.

HOW TO REPORT SUSPECTED ABUSE OR NEGLECT

Most states require anyone who knows of or has reasonable cause to suspect child abuse or neglect to report that abuse or neglect. Any person who fails to report, knowingly prevents another from doing so, or makes a false report generally is guilty of a criminal offense and may be prosecuted. Normally, state laws specifically mention the requirement of the school teacher or other school officials to make reports. Many state laws protect those teachers reporting child abuse in two ways: immunity from liability and confidentiality. Anyone making a report "in good faith" is specifically immune from any civil or criminal charges that might result. The name of the person making the report will not be released to anyone other than the protective investigating agency or prosecutors without written consent of the person reporting. The reporting individual is not required to give his or her name, although all persons are encouraged to do so to facilitate the investigation.

Though child protection service systems vary from state to state, typically there is a toll-free abuse registry line operated 24 hours per day. Reports should include the following:

- Names and addresses of child, parent(s), guardian(s), or other persons responsible for the child's welfare
- Child's age, race, sex, and siblings' names
- Nature and extent of alleged abuse or neglect
- Identity of abuser, if known
- Reporting person's name, address, and telephone number if desired (normally this is not required)
- Direction to the child's location at the time of the report

While wearing the Rules and Consequences Face, the teacher is not listening to the parents nor is she contracting. Instead, based on the serious nature of the previous actions, the teacher takes a position concerned with the immediate actions she wants the parents to take to help Brandon, and then goes about assertively taking actions toward the parents to obtain compliance. If cooperation does not come in the form of behavioral change by the parents, the teacher would not hesitate to escalate to the next level of Coercive-Legalistic and call social service abuse and neglect authorities. A developing to imminent crisis situation calls for immediate action.

In the case of Carol, the injured student, the need level is physiological and the crisis is imminent. This life- and psychologically-threatening situation calls for very powerful intervention: Coercive-Legalistic. When time is of utmost importance, the teacher's goal is to get immediate help and legal protection for the child. It is no longer necessary—and perhaps not even advisable—to discuss the situation further with Carol's mother. In most serious cases where sexual abuse is suspected, the steps required of the teacher are clearly set by law. The teacher would be ethically bound, and possibly legally bound, to take coercive action for the student's welfare. To clarify, Coercive-Legalistic is not a "face" but a process through which the teacher uses assertive techniques to carry out actions required by law. In its simplest form, the teacher calls child abuse authorities and turns over all records of data gathered to support the charge.

Carol's Parent and "Boyfriend"

Need: Level 2—Physiological

Crisis: Imminent

Face: Coercive-Legalistic

A report must be made to the state child protection service. See Figure 11–6 for physical and behavioral indicators of child abuse and neglect (children are typically defined as persons under 18 years of age).

SUMMARY

The teacher, as a problem solver dealing with parent-child situations, can reexamine his or her own "personal wisdom response" in the broader perspective of the constructs described in this chapter. For discussion purposes, direct parallels were made between situations, needs, and faces; *in reality, such division might be less clear-cut, and actions would have to be adjusted accordingly with the teacher making a professional judgment as to the seriousness of the situation.*

FIGURE 11–6 Physical and Behavioral Indicators of Child Abuse and Neglect

	Physical Indicators	**Behavioral Indicators**
Physical Abuse	Unexplained bruises and welts: • on face, lips, mouth • on torso, back, buttocks, thighs • in various stages of healing • reflecting shape of articles used to inflict injury (extension cord, belt buckle, etc.) • on several different surfaces areas • regularly appear after absence, weekend, or vacation Unexplained burns: • cigar or cigarette burns, especially on soles, palms, back, or buttocks • immersion burns (sock-like, glove-like, or doughnut-shaped on buttocks or genitalia) • patterned like electric burner, iron, etc. • rope burns on arms, legs, neck or torso Unexplained lacerations or abrasions to mouth, lips, gums, eyes, external genitalia	Wary of adult contacts Apprehensive when other children cry Behavioral extremes: • aggressiveness • withdrawal Frightened of parents Afraid to go home Reports injury by parents
Physical Neglect	Consistent hunger, poor hygiene, inappropriate dress Consistent lack of supervision, especially in dangerous activities Unattended physical problems or medical problems Abandonment	Begging, stealing food Extended stays at school (early arrival and late departure) Constant fatigue, listlessness, or falling asleep in class Alcohol or drug abuse Delinquency (e.g., thefts) States there is no caretaker
Sexual Abuse	Difficulty in walking/sitting Consistent touching of genitals Torn, shredded, or bloody underclothing Bruises or bleeding in external genitalia, vaginal or anal areas Venereal diseases, especially in preteens Genital warts Pregnancy	Unwilling to change for gym or participate in physical education classes Withdrawal, fantasy, or infantile behavior Bizarre, sophisticated, or unusual sexual behavior or knowledge Poor peer relationships Delinquency or runaway Reports sexual assault by caretaker
Emotional Maltreatment	Speech disorders Lags in physical development Failure to thrive	Habit disorders (sucking, biting, rocking, etc.) Conduct disorders (antisocial, destructive, etc.) Neurotic traits (sleep disorders, inhibition of play) Psychoneurotic reactions (hysteria, obsession, compulsion, phobias) Behavior extremes: compliant, passive; aggressive, demanding Overly adaptive behavior: inappropriate adult or infant Developmental lags (mental, emotional) Attempted suicide

Test Yourself

Check the correct answer for each of the items presented. Answers may be found at the end of this chapter, following the Endnotes.

A. ____ valuing B. ____ security C. ____ physiological D. ____ praise E. ____ esteem F. ____ belonging G. ____ happiness	1. Rank the needs (Maslow) from most serious to least serious by placing the numbers 1 to 5 on the appropriate needs. (Note: some of those listed are not needs.)
A. ____ valuing B. ____ security C. ____ physiological D. ____ praise E. ____ esteem F. ____ belonging G. ____ happiness	2. Having inadequate food to eat would represent which blocked need?
A. ____ valuing B. ____ security C. ____ physiological D. ____ praise E. ____ esteem F. ____ belonging G. ____ happiness	3. Parents living separately, with the child moving from one house to another each week, has the potential for creating stress for the child around which of the blocked needs?
A. ____ valuing B. ____ security C. ____ physiological D. ____ praise E. ____ esteem F. ____ belonging G. ____ happiness	4. Parents want letter grades to be given by the school for young children. Which need are these parents experiencing?
A. ____ valuing B. ____ security C. ____ physiological D. ____ praise E. ____ esteem F. ____ belonging G. ____ happiness	5. The teacher calls the child abuse number and gives the name of a child and family. What blocked need is most likely to be involved here?

Practice Analyzing Parent/Child Needs, Crises, and Teacher Response ("Face")

Based on the data below, place a check mark for the appropriate need, crisis level, and "face." Answers may be found at the end of this chapter, following the Endnotes.

A. TOO MANY CUTS, BRUISES, AND INJURIES

Brian and Michael live with their grandparents, who were given custody of the boys immediately after Brian's birth. Their biological mother, Jean, was and still is an abuser of drugs and alcohol. The extent to which she used drugs and alcohol during the pregnancy is unknown. Jean is allowed only supervised visits with the two boys. Brian, age 2, and Michael, age 3, are extremely aggressive toward each other and other children. Both children have come into the center with a variety of bruises and cuts the last two weeks. The bruises have been found on their abdomens, buttocks, and backs. Cuts have appeared on their arms, legs, and faces. The teachers have kept a log of each new incident, carefully noting the date and location of new bruises and cuts. During routine diapering and bathroom times, the teachers have asked the boys about the origin of the bruises and cuts. Their response is usually, "I fell down." In addition, the teachers have spoken with the grandparents about each noticeable bruise or cut. There is always an explanation suggesting it was nothing more than a normal childhood accident. Granddad would jokingly say, "You know how rough these boys are. I don't know what we are going to do with them!" Several days in a row the children's uncle came in to pick the boys up while the grandmother waited in the car. The director went out to talk with the grandmother about some paperwork that needed to be completed. As she approached the car, she noticed that the grandmother had a black eye and bruises on her wrists. The grandmother quickly put on a pair of sunglasses. No mention was made of the black eye or bruises. The following week, both boys came to school with what appeared to be cigarette burns on their abdomens.

A. Need	B. Crisis Level	C. Face
___ 1. physiological	___ 1. developing	___ 1. Relationship-Listening
___ 2. security	___ 2. potential	___ 2. Confronting-Contracting
___ 3. belonging	___ 3. imminent	___ 3. Rules and Consequences
___ 4. esteem		

B. FAILING "SANDBOX"

Susan, whose fifth birthday is in July, is a bright but socially immature child. She is the older of two girls. Her parents are both college educated and professionally employed. Dad is 10 years older than Mom and is very involved in his daughters' lives. At the prekindergarten conference held in April, Susan's teacher recommended that she remain in the early childhood center for kindergarten and then go into public school for an additional year of kindergarten. The extra year was suggested to allow Susan the opportunity to develop an adequate repertoire of socially acceptable behaviors and to become more emotional mature. Both parents reacted in a shocked manner. "Why didn't anyone tell us Susan was failing preschool (failing "sandbox")?" was Dad's response. While the teacher attempted to explain that failure was not an issue here, it was apparent that neither parent was hearing her. They wanted to know what remedial steps they could take over the summer so Susan would be ready for "real" kindergarten in the fall. Dad suggested that the preschool had not adequately stimulated his child and it would be the last place he would have her go to kindergarten. Dad left the conference in a huff without his wife. Mom tried to explain that they both had such high hopes for Susan and they were just "crushed" that she was not ready for advancement to the next "grade." The teacher tried to explain the possible positive outcomes of an extra year in kindergarten for Susan. Mom agreed to try to convince her husband.

A. Need	B. Crisis Level	C. Face
___ 1. physiological	___ 1. developing	___ 1. Relationship-Listening
___ 2. security	___ 2. potential	___ 2. Confronting-Contracting
___ 3. belonging	___ 3. imminent	___ 3. Rules and Consequences
___ 4. esteem		

C. FATHER-SON ESTRANGEMENT

Adam, age 4, and Jessica, age 2, are the children of a busy couple, Scott and Janet. The parents have distinctly different approaches to child rearing. Janet is extremely laid back, whereas Scott prefers to maintain a level of control that appears extreme to Janet. Jessica is a typically developing child who is not overly demanding of either parent and appears to be developing positive peer relationships. Adam, on the other hand, is an extremely aggressive child to all the people in his world. He was an aggressive toddler and Janet often comments with a smile that he is just like she was as a toddler and she is just getting paid back. Scott's job requires him to be out of town three to four days a week. When he is in town, he likes to bring the children to school and pick them up so he can have some extra time with them. Adam does not like this break in routine and usually protests loudly and strongly. It is not uncommon for Adam to kick and scream at his Dad as they come into the building. Adam tells the teacher that he only wants his Mom to bring him to school. At the end of the day, if Dad comes for him, Adam runs away to the far corner of the yard or building. A teacher must assist Dad in getting Adam to the car. Yesterday, Mom and Dad came to the school together to get the children. Janet picked up Jessica from the toddler program while Scott picked up Adam from the preschool. Adam saw his Mom across the street. He ran past Dad, out the gate, across the busy parking lot, and across a street to get to his mother. Janet picked him up and with a big smile said, "Oh, Adam, it isn't safe to run across the street. But I am *so* happy to see you." Scott, visibly angered by the situation and Janet's response, asked one of the preschool teachers if someone could take his family home because he was leaving without them.

A. Need	B. Crisis Level	C. Face
___ 1. physiological	___ 1. developing	___ 1. Relationship-Listening
___ 2. security	___ 2. potential	___ 2. Confronting-Contracting
___ 3. belonging	___ 3. imminent	___ 3. Rules and Consequences
___ 4. esteem		

D. BECOMING A SINGLE FATHER

Billy started preschool three weeks ago. His sister, who is age 6, attended this school and Billy visited often with Mom and Dad. His parents wanted both children in the school at the same time, but Dad kept losing his job, so they were unable to afford having two children in the school at the same time. Billy stayed home with Mom and was 3 years old when he started preschool. This was his first separation from Mom. He was scheduled to begin in August, so he and Mom visited extensively in July. This allowed him to become acquainted with the environment and to begin to separate from Mom for short periods of time. A week ago, Mom and Dad separated, and Dad was granted temporary custody of both children. Dad now physically carries Billy into the building every day, although the child is not crying in protest. Dad talked to the teachers about the tremendous sense of guilt he feels over the breakup of his marriage and the effect it may have on the children. During the visits to the school and the initial two weeks of school, Billy had become independent and playful, but now he is helpless and withdrawn. The slightest conflict with another child will reduce Billy to tears. Billy's teacher talked with Dad about her concerns regarding the change in Billy's behavior. She suggested a conference to discuss strategies for reducing the stress in Billy's life. Dad was appreciative of the concern and agreed to come in the next day at 2:00 P.M. Billy did not come to school the next day. When the teacher called to find out what was wrong, Dad told her he decided to keep Billy home for a few days, thinking that some special time with Dad might help Billy perk up a little. When the teacher suggested that Billy needed stability in his life and that school was a possibility for that stability right now, Dad started to cry and hung up the phone.

A. Need	B. Crisis Level	C. Face
___ 1. physiological	___ 1. developing	___ 1. Relationship-Listening
___ 2. security	___ 2. potential	___ 2. Confronting-Contracting
___ 3. belonging	___ 3. imminent	___ 3. Rules and Consequences
___ 4. esteem		

Glossary

Belonging The second highest level of Maslow's taxonomy of needs, in which the person (child) feels the presence of love from individuals on whom he or she can depend.

Crisis Parents and children regularly face problems related to blocked needs that vary in degrees of seriousness. The crisis construct suggests that these difficulties may be classified from the minimal potential crisis, to the more serious developing crisis, and then to the most serious imminent crisis. This classification system enables the teacher to consider an appropriate response and determine how much power, help, or intrusion is needed.

Esteem The highest level of Maslow's taxonomy of needs, where actions are driven by the need to be respected by others and the parallel feelings that this respect brings.

Faces A method of responding to parents or children in which the teacher assumes an attitude regarding the power to be used and the demands to be made on others.

Needs Maslow suggests that how people act or are motivated to act can be based on basic needs, which he has placed on a taxonomy ranging from basic physiological needs to the needs of security, belonging, and esteem.

Physiological The fourth and most basic of needs in Maslow's taxonomy of needs, whereby the person (child) feels that he can depend on having adequate food and basic care for his own existence.

Security The third highest level of Maslow's taxonomy of needs, whereby the person (child) feels that he has dependable shelter or home in which he is protected.

Related Readings

Maslow, A. H. (1968). *Toward a Psychology of Being* (2nd ed.). New York: D. Van Nostrand.

McMurrian, T. (1975). *Intervention in Human Crisis.* Atlanta: Humanics Press.

Endnotes

1. Maslow, A. H. (1968). *Toward a Psychology of Being* (2nd. ed.). New York: D. Van Nostrand.
2. McMurrian, T. (1975). *Intervention in Human Crisis.* Atlanta: Humanics Press.

Answers to Test Yourself

1: A—none, B2, C1, D—none, E4, F3, G—none; 2C, 3B, 4E, 5C
Too Many Cuts, Bruises, and Injuries: A1, B3, C3
Failing "Sandbox": A4, B1, C1
Father-Son Estrangement: A3, B2, C2
Becoming a Single Father: A2, B1, C2

12

Staffing: A Team Approach

Simply put, many minds working together are better than one. Historically, teaching has been a rather solitary profession: one teacher closed in by four walls and a closed door. The teacher is responsible for a collection of children from whom, for discipline's sake, she must maintain an emotional and relationship distance that enables her to set limits for these children at any time she feels it necessary. It is through this limit setting that the teacher expresses her power and adult position and carries out her responsibility of caring for and educating the children toward gradually more mature behavior, or growth. When the teacher's judgment, as projected through limit setting, fails to be effective with the elementary school-aged child, she fails. The misbehaving child may then display frightening actions that endanger himself, other children, and the educational climate of the classroom itself—the shared space within these four walls. The teacher is now ineffective; her actions do not work.

Such misbehaving children can be like small grenades; beyond the teacher's ability to know about it, something or someone may pull their "pins" and they explode as small aggressive power forces that destroy—destroy our climate for learning and destroy our ability to live and work together as a healthy classroom of sharing people. We are teachers, and others—children and parents—depend on us. We are like a conductor who must orchestrate shared space; if our arrangement does not work, we are ineffective and will experience the accompanying feelings of utter helplessness. We feel we are not in control and we have no outlet for getting help. In fact, we might be frightened to admit—especially to those in authority over us—that we are having this disciplinary difficulty, for fear that we may be judged as ineffectual and later evaluated negatively at the end of the school year.

The way to get the help we need is by creating a collegial team association. Rarely do other professions (e.g., law, medicine, etc.) expect the professional to live and work on a four-walled island cut off from colleagues. Doing it alone should not be a virtue that defines our worthiness as teachers. Children have changed in the modern world, and the knowledge base of psychology and education has exploded far beyond the ability of a day-in, day-out practicing teacher to keep pace. It is extremely difficult, if not impossible, for the classroom teacher to maintain immediate updated knowledge on the many problems faced by children and new methods of educational practice. The collegial meeting of professional minds takes the form of a staffing, or brainstorming, session that focuses on one child—his strengths and positive traits and his problems—as well as how the professional classroom teacher might become effective in meeting this problem child's needs with the help of others. Such staffing sessions must be a basic (at least bimonthly) practice. This concept of a staffing team as a collection of problem-solving professionals is a structure to guide the collective minds, so that thinking is orderly and creative and includes everyone on the team.

For the experienced classroom teacher, the mere mention of being a part of a team process brings forth cries of, "Oh, no, not another meeting!" Such verbal aggression from the teachers seems to be justified, as every teacher can remember meeting after meeting that has dragged on with few results. The frustration produced by these futile attempts to work with others drives many teachers to retreat to their classroom "islands" to "do their own thing." It can be hypothesized that the primary reason for nonproductive meetings is the absence of an understanding regarding the possible solutions that may come out of them. Teachers have endured hours of meetings feeling unclear as to the nature of the problem being discussed; finally, they are driven to a state of "helpless passivity" by unfocused conversation that veers off into many directions and appears to have limited connection to solving the immediate problem.

In order to overcome these obstacles to good collective problem solving, a clear orderly process will be proposed based on the Six Steps for Problem Solving[1] of (1) defining the problem, (2) generating a possible solution, (3) evaluating, (4) deciding on a solution, (5) implementing, and (6) evaluating the solutions. In order to maximize the use of time, a clear staff agenda procedure is proposed for the purpose of collectively working as a team to use the host of techniques drawn from the Three Faces of Discipline, the concept of Levels of Crisis (found in Chapter 11), and the development of an Individualized Discipline Plan (IDP) for intervening with and helping the difficult child. The team approach utilizes a creative application of techniques and procedures to fit the needs of a particular school and a particular teacher working with one very difficult child.

STAFFING AGENDA: STEPS AND PROCEDURES

Team members might include any or all of the following people: head teacher, assistant teacher, teacher aides, special education teacher, center director or school principal, school counselor and/or psychologist, social worker or home and family visitor, or any other person having direct contact with the child on a daily basis (including cafeteria or playground supervisors, bus driver, and office staff). On some occasions, it would be helpful to have the child's parents as members of this team. The head teacher, in consultation with the school administrator, will make the decision on just who is invited.

One thing to avoid in team staffing is the notion of rank, as defined as administrative rank (director/principal) or expertise rank (psychologist). If rank is formally or informally asserted in the team staffing, it will inhibit creative problem solving because those members who feel less "in authority" will hesitate to speak up or challenge a position of some member in a position of "higher rank." The attitude, or face, of the staffing meeting is that roles are clearly defined but not necessarily according to rank. The meeting is for the benefit of the teacher, who has daily responsibility for the difficult child, and all members are there to serve as her consultants and advisors with a direct focus on what she and they can do to help this particular child. It is preferable for meetings to be held at a round table where all members can see each other face to face, suggesting an equal power relationship among team members, rather than at a rectangular table with a power figure seated at one end. A wall chart or chalkboard should be nearby and in clear view of all team members.

It is helpful at the beginning of a staffing meeting for the teacher who is being advised to appoint a timekeeper and a secretary. The timekeeper serves as a type of moderator, announcing before each step begins the purpose of that step, who may speak, the amount of time to be spent on that step, and the actions and results needed to be accomplished. A copy of Figure 12–1, Six Steps to Team

FIGURE 12–1 Six Steps to Team Staffing Agenda

Purpose	Speaker	Time	Actions
Step 1: Statement of the Problem			
a. Background Information (Teacher)	Teacher	10 mins.	State general description of the child's behavior problems and desired changes. Present background information using collected data (see Figure 12–2).
b. Background Information (Team)	Team Members	10 mins.	Present information from other team members who may have observed the child under various situations and time periods.
c. Clarifying Information	Team Members	6 mins.	Team members question other team members on data presented and the final changes in desired child behavior.
Step 2: Generating Solutions			
a. Written	Team Members	3 mins.	Each team member writes a list of solutions independently of all other members.
b. Oral	Team Members	10 mins.	Each member quickly reads her or his solution list without comment; secretary writes each solution on a wall chart or chalkboard.
Step 3: Evaluating Solutions	Team Members	10 mins.	Members state their objections (in the form of an I-message) to a suggestion; if there is general agreement to these objections, the suggestion is removed. Secretary strikes out rejected suggestions.
Step 4: Deciding on Solutions	Team Members	5 mins.	Decide on a group plan with roles and each member's responsibility defined. Using the Individualized Discipline Plan (IDP) (see Figure 12–3), the secretary writes solution agreements and completes the IDP form.
Step 5: Implementing (commitment)	Team Members	1 min.	All members sign the plan as a commitment to the strategies.
Step 6: Reevaluation Scheduled	Teacher	2 mins.	A time is established for a follow-up meeting, normally two to three weeks later, to evaluate the success of the plan.

Staffing Agenda, should be mounted on the meeting room wall or included in a handout in front of each member for easy reference. The secretary handles writing activities such as keeping notes, writing suggestions on wall charts, and writing the final plan. These duties should be rotated among the team members for each new meeting. The timekeeper will channel the discussion to conform to the stated goals and will signal when time periods are up. If the team is well disciplined, the entire team staffing activity can be accomplished in 60 minutes.

Step 1: Statement of the Problem (Overview of the Child's Behavior)

a. Background Information (Teacher)

Purpose: The teacher clearly states to the team members a general description of the child's behavior and states clearly those behavioral changes she would like to see in the child.

Time: 10 minutes

Actions: The teacher who has direct responsibility for the difficult child begins the reporting by providing the team with a general description of the child's past behavioral problems. She also summarizes the data on her Child Background Information form (Figure 12–2) and gives a few vignettes to place

FIGURE 12–2 Child Background Information Form

Child's Name ______________________ Date ______________

Team Members ______________________________________

____

Child's Misbehavior(s) ______________________________

____

____

1. Describe misbehavior(s)	2. What activities was the child engaged in at the time?	3. In what physical surroundings?	4. How frequent is each type of misbehavior?	5. What time of day?	6. What peers/adults were involved?
a.					
b.					
c.					

this behavior in context. The teacher also summarizes the Social Competence Graph (see Figures D and E in Chapter 3). Each team member should have a copy of Figure 12–2 before him or her during the reporting.

Finally, the teacher states clearly the behavior changes she would like to see in the child's daily behavior. For example, "Brian will, at snack time, stop throwing food and biting other children, and he will follow my directions and requests when I give them to him."

b. Background Information (Team Members)

Purpose: Each team member adds any information not previously mentioned by the child's teacher.

Time: 10 minutes

Actions: The team members report their data by summarizing their copy of the Child Background Information form (Figure 12–2), moving clockwise around the table in a business-like manner. It is important to get all data out and "on the table," and it is recommended that members refrain from asking questions of clarification until this is accomplished. This process may include a review of any medication the child is taking or any allergic reactions potentially affecting his behavior. (See the Appendix for a general description of medications commonly prescribed for such children.)

c. Clarifying Background Information

Purpose: All members may now ask clarifying questions concerning background information previously presented.

Time: 6 minutes

Actions: All members of the team have the right to question the teacher or any team member who presented information in order to discuss the child in greater detail. This is also time to identify and explore what techniques have previously been tried. Team members should also question the behavior change goals that the teacher stated in Step 1, and a discussion should occur to get a team agreement on the stated behavior changes desired. Once the goals are agreed on, the secretary will write these goals on the IDP form (Figure 12–3).

Step 2: Generating Solutions

a. Solutions (Written)

Purpose: All members write down their proposed solutions or suggestions as to what actions may be taken to help this difficult child.

Time: 3 minutes

Actions: All staff members write down their proposed solutions, listing the actions they and anyone else could take to help the child. During this process, each member should mentally review the teacher-child interaction models of the Three Faces of Discipline. This mental review will help the members decide what teacher methods and techniques would be the most helpful and how these actions can be organized systematically. Writing these possible solutions creates active involvement by each member and establishes their active commitment to the problem-solving process.

FIGURE 12–3 Individualized Discipline Plan (IDP)

Child's Name	Summary of Present Behavior
School	
Date of Staffing	
Long-Term Behavioral Changes Desired	(1)
(2)	(3)
(4)	(5)

Short-Term Behavioral Change	Specific Teacher Techniques	Person Responsible	% of Time	Approx. Date of Completion	Reevaluation Date

Short-Term Behavioral Change	Specific Teacher Techniques	Person Responsible	% of Time	Approx. Date of Completion	Reevaluation Date

Short-Term Behavioral Change	Specific Teacher Techniques	Person Responsible	% of Time	Approx. Date of Completion	Reevaluation Date

Short-Term Behavioral Change	Specific Teacher Techniques	Person Responsible	% of Time	Approx. Date of Completion	Reevaluation Date

Evaluation Criteria for Changes in Behavior	Staff Members
	Date of Meeting
	Reevaluation Date

b. Solutions (Oral)

Purpose: Each team member verbally presents his or her written ideas to the other members without evaluation or feedback.

Time: 10 minutes

Actions: Each member presents his or her ideas orally to the group. The discussion of these ideas is reserved for a later step, in order not to inhibit the free flow of each member's ideas. The attitude in this discussion is that there is no "crazy" idea—no matter how "off the wall" it might initially sound, it is nonetheless put on the table for consideration. Even the seemingly farfetched idea might later trigger an idea from a team member as to how this idea can be turned into a practical and very real creative solution. Criticism in any manner during this step will stifle creative ideas and keep them from surfacing. While the members are reading their ideas out loud, the secretary writes them on a wall chart (or chalkboard) as a visual display of these ideas.

Step 3: Evaluating Solutions

Purpose: All members verbally explore, in a "brainstorming" format, how each of the ideas presented in Step 2 can be interrelated and developed into a comprehensive, collectively agreed upon plan of action, to achieve both the short-term and long-term behavioral changes or other results desired.

Time: 10 minutes

Actions: This step begins with the team taking a quick vote to score the suggestions on the wall chart. One simple but effective method employs a "thumbs up-thumbs down" approach. The timekeeper reads out the number of the solution or suggestion while the secretary points to the numbered solution on the wall chart. The members indicate their feelings by pointing a thumb up if they like the idea or a thumb down if they dislike it; they hold their hand flat if they are unsure but do not immediately disapprove. The secretary writes a plus sign (+) before the number of a proposed solution if *all* team members vote "thumbs up." A question mark (?) is placed before the solution if the members' response is mixed negative and positive. Finally, a minus sign (-) is added and a line drawn through the suggested solution if *all* members vote "thumbs down." This quick vote provides an immediate, overt display of the group's feelings about each suggestion, and members are now ready for meaningful discussion. However, even when a solution has been scratched out, any member may bring it back for further discussion.

Interaction among the members, which has been controlled and limited in previous steps, now becomes of primary importance as the members fully discuss how their ideas are interrelated or have some commonalties. The team might ask itself: Do our solutions cluster into one "face" of discipline? Do these suggestions indicate the amount of power at which we wish to begin our intervention? Do we need to make educational changes beyond the disciplinary actions?

It is important that the teacher and team members recognize in this step that they have progressed beyond the "personal wisdom" kind of speculative thinking, in which the teacher attempts to solve problems in a haphazard manner. The constructs, methods, and procedures provided for the teachers and school staffs here have brought the professional out of the darkness in which she functions as a limited technician, and provide a framework for the scientific problem solving that is characteristic of a true professional.

Step 4: Deciding on Solutions (A Final Written Plan)

Purpose: Decide on an orderly plan of action and put that plan into writing.

Time: 5 minutes

Actions: The members agree on a plan of action, including their own responsibility for carrying out the various segments of this plan. The secretary writes out this Individualized Discipline Plan (IDP) with a designation of each person's responsibilities. (All members should receive a copy.)

Step 5: Implementing (Commitment)

Purpose: The members commit themselves to implementing the plan's procedures.

Time: 1 minute

Actions: Each staff member is asked to sign or initial the IDP, and by doing so agrees to actively carry out the procedures and return for a follow-up reevaluation. The follow-up reevaluation future meeting should be established at a time convenient for all members.

Step 6: Reevaluation Meeting

Purpose: The members return for a meeting to evaluate the plan's effectiveness and call for any changes that might be necessary.

Time: 2 minutes

Actions: All members meet again to assess the progress of the IDP and to determine the effectiveness of the techniques proposed and changes needed. The reevaluation meeting might simply require a short discussion, but if the teacher is still unsuccessful, the group may have to repeat Steps 1 through 6.

SUMMARY

The structured agenda with established procedures is a systematic process loosely based on a six-step problem-solving process, but it can be modified to accommodate team members' own unique working styles. However, it is important to have an agreed-upon structure for such staff meetings. The solutions generated by the staffing procedures can be built out of an understanding of the techniques found in the chapters of this book and augmented by the individual and collective ideas of the team members.

Test Yourself

Test your understanding of the concepts related to staffing by writing the correct number in the right column for the corresponding step listed in the left column. Answers may be found at the end of this chapter, following the Endnote.

1. Step 1: Statement of the Problem 2. Step 2: Generating Solutions 3. Step 3: Evaluating Solutions 4. Step 4: Deciding on Solutions 5. Step 5: Implementing the Plan 6. Step 6: Reevaluating	_____ A. As an indication of commitment, each team member signs the plan. _____ B. A quick vote is taken. _____ C. A time for a second meeting is agreed upon. _____ D. The teacher describes the child's misbehavior. _____ E. The teacher states the behavioral change she wants from the child. _____ F. The team establishes the behavioral changes wanted from the child. _____ G. Data from the teacher's background form are presented. _____ H. Data from all team members' background forms are presented. _____ I. Members write down their proposed solutions. _____ J. The secretary writes out the IDP. _____ K. Members question other members on background data. _____ L. An open and free discussion of all possible solutions and techniques takes place.

Glossary

Individualized Discipline Plan (IDP) A written plan created at the end of a staffing process detailing the specific techniques to be utilized in dealing with a difficult child and those who will be responsible for carrying them out.

Quick Vote A nonbinding process to quickly gauge support for the list of proposed solutions in Step 3: Evaluating Solutions. The solutions are ranked according to those the group likes (+), dislikes (-), or is not sure of (?).

Secretary One team member appointed by the teacher of the difficult child, assigned responsibility for carrying out the writing duties during the staffing process.

Staffing Agenda The established six-step process (statement of the problem, generating solutions, evaluating solutions, deciding on solutions, implementing, and reevaluating) that defines team members' roles, the purposes of each step, the amount of time to be used, and the actions needed to be accomplished.

Team Staffing A meeting held to help a teacher who is experiencing considerable difficulty handling a child who is disrupting her classroom or endangering himself or others.

Timekeeper A team member appointed by the teacher of the difficult child, assigned responsibility for carrying out the time keeping and keeping the staffing process on task.

Related Readings

Gordon, T. (1974). *T.E.T.: Teacher Effectiveness Training.* New York: David McKay.

Wolfgang, C. H., & Glickman, C. D. (1980). *Solving Discipline Problems: Strategies for Classroom Teachers.* Boston: Allyn and Bacon.

Endnote

1. Gordon, T. (1974). *T.E.T.: Teacher Effectiveness Training.* New York: David McKay.

Answers to Test Yourself

A5, B3, C5, D1, E1, F1, G1, H2, I2, J4, K1, L3

13

Play: Key to the Child's Full Development

In today's work-oriented society, play often has a negative meaning.

> "Quit playing around!"
>
> "You're wasting your time playing."
>
> "You're such a playboy!"

All of these expressions show our lack of respect for play. By looking closely, however, one will find that play is the central activity of young children. It is play that enables children to grow socially, emotionally, intellectually, and physically to their maximum potential. This chapter on play is included because a common characteristic of the misbehaving child during the ages from 2 to 7 is that they generally are not players! If we as teachers change young children's behavior, such as with the use of any of the Three Faces of Discipline, we may leave the child in a behavioral vacuum;[1] play will fill this vacuum. We cannot discuss discipline without talking about the positive behaviors that we do want to see in the child's repertoire—play behaviors.

THE VALUE OF PLAY

Social Development

The young child is not born with the ability to get along with others or to cooperate in activities of give and take. This skill of learning to live and work with others begins in the first year of life, and obtaining the ability to be truly cooperative is normally accomplished by age 7. It is in the early years that children move through prestages to cooperation. These prestages are (1) unoccupied behavior, then developing to (2) solitary independent play, followed by (3) onlooker, (4) parallel play, and (5) associative play, which then results in true (6) cooperative play. This level of maturity of cooperative play occurs when the young child has developed the ability to do sociodramatic play.

In the prestages, *unoccupied behavior* is introverted and nonactive, but in *solitary independent play*, the child starts to manipulate objects and begins to make believe, although by herself. In *onlooker play*, the child becomes interested in others and watches them play. This is followed by *parallel play*, which can be seen when older toddlers play side by side, each doing a similar imitative activity (e.g., washing dolls) but without true communication or cooperation.

The true social stage of play, near age 3, is *associative play*, in which the children work on one task, sharing materials with peers. Two children might build a garage with blocks or work together to create a sand city. Later, after much experience with other children, we begin to see the development of highly valued sociodramatic play as true *cooperative play*. This is the dress-up and make-believe role-play that adults find so appealing during the preschool to kindergarten years (ages 3–7). Young children learn to understand social roles through role-playing mommy, daddy, doctor, grocer, firefighter, and a host of other roles.

Finally, near the beginning of middle childhood (ages 7 to 11) and the beginning of formal schooling, the child acquires the ability to play games with rules. These include competitive games (sports and board games) and mental games (word games and those often played in the car while traveling) (see Figure 13–1).

Emotional Development

Young children, whose language is limited, are better able to express their feelings and understand their world through play rather than complicated words. The child who has had a highly emotional negative experience (e.g., a trip to the dentist) or positive experience (e.g., a birthday party) can retreat to his or her play world and play out "dentist" or "birthday." This replaying in the safe world of play allows the child to digest both pleasurable and unpleasant experiences, to better understand them, and to begin to gain some control over his or her feelings related to the emotional experiences.

Intellectual Development

Learning is not a simple process of putting information into the child and then having the child regurgitate it. The child must play with the new information in order to understand it. Children use toys and gestures symbolically in play as attempts to understand objects and experiences in their real world.

The symbols seen in children's play and artworks indicate the development of the ability to use representation (one thing stands for another). Just as a block can symbolize or represent a truck to the 4- or 5-year-old child, the letters *c-a-t* will represent the animal that says "meow" to the older, school-age child. The

FIGURE 13–1 Social Stages

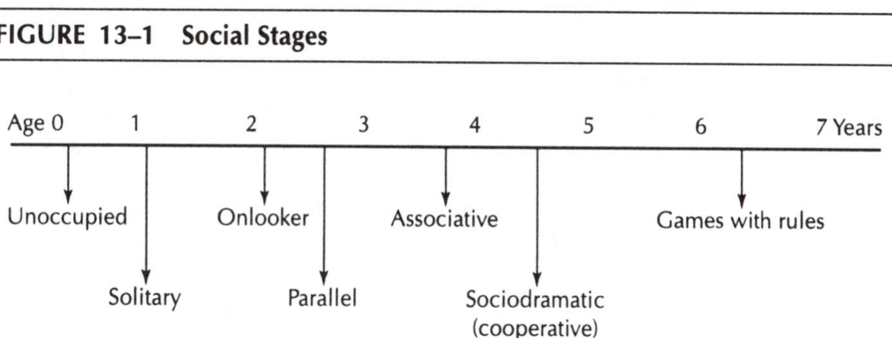

young child needs many experiences of playing with symbols (e.g., pretending the block is a CB radio) before he or she is ready to unlock the world of words (e.g., the letters *c-a-t* stand for the animal: cat), and this is required for success in beginning reading.

It is during the preschool years that the child is moving from the make-believe symbols in play to the world of words in reading and writing. The activities in this book will help the child to bridge the process.

Physical Development

It is through *sensorimotor play* (play with the senses and muscles) that the infant or toddler discovers his or her own body and its abilities. The preschool child is still developing this awareness through both small muscle activity (getting hands and eyes to work together) and large muscle activity (crawling, walking, running, balancing, and climbing). It is also through play with the body senses of taste, smell, touch, sight, and hearing that body feelings become coordinated and useful for testing and gathering information about the world. The sensorimotor play of preschool children helps them master an understanding of their bodies and the ability to control the use of their bodies more effectively.

WHAT IS PLAY?

Play, broadly defined, is an activity engaged in for the purpose of enjoyment. The play of children helps them to understand and master their feelings and to practice and master new intellectual, social, and physical skills. In order to discuss and effectively use play activities, it becomes important to understand the terms used to describe the various forms of play.

Sensorimotor play (SM) is the free movement of small and large muscles and the exploring of body senses to give the body practice with its sensorimotor functions. Some examples of sensorimotor play would include a young child making countless mud pies or riding endless hours on a tricycle. In the development of sensorimotor play, the young 3-year-old still needs a great deal of time and space for sensorimotor practice. As the other forms of play develop (sociodramatic and construction), the preschooler seems to need to devote less time to body practice. This need continues to lessen as the child grows older. Finally, at around the age of 7, these motor activities begin to be tied with rules and become the middle childhood (ages 7–11) "games-with-rules" type of play.

Symbolic play (SP)[2] is the make-believe play in which children express their ideas through gestures and the movement of toys or objects. Symbolic play is *sociodramatic (SD)* when the child (1) undertakes a make-believe role (or uses a toy) and expresses it in imitative actions and/or language; (2) uses toys, unstructured materials, movements, or verbal declaration as substitutions for real objects; (3) engages in make-believe with actions and situations—verbal descriptions are substituted for actions and situations (e.g., "I'll save you"; "Come"; "I'll pick you up"; or "So that's what's wrong with the engine—the round part goes 'chug, chug'!"); (4) persists in role play—the child stays with a single role or related roles for most of a five-minute time period; (5) interacts with at least one other player within the framework of the sociodramatic play episode; and (6) verbally communicates—there is some verbal interaction related to a sociodramatic play episode.

The development of symbolic play begins around the age of 2, when the toddler pretends to "drink from a cup" or "speak on the telephone," and it makes up a large part of a 3-year-old's play. The child begins to express his or her ideas in symbolic make-believe play with toys and objects. For the 3-year-old, symbolic play is generally seen in the form of parallel play and sometimes in simple dramatic play. A 4-year-old can usually do sociodramatic play, which is more complex and shows a wider scope of roles as the child moves through ages 4, 5, and 6. Finally, at school age, the child begins to give up make-believe play and incorporates make-believe into what he or she reads and writes. The ability to play symbolically changes as the child grows intellectually during the first seven years of life.

- Stage 1 (2 years): First, the young toddler needs a real object with which to play. The child must have a real cup, although he is simply pretending and not really drinking from a cup.
- Stage 2 (2–2½ years): The older toddler can use an object that is similar in shape to the real object being symbolized. A circular block can be used as a substitute for a cup.
- Stage 3 (2½–3 years): Now the child can use any object, regardless of the shape or purpose, to substitute for the real object. For example, a child can pick up wooden letters and pretend, "This is the mommy and this is the daddy."
- Stage 4 (3-3½ years): At the beginning of nursery school, the child often does not need an object for pretending. He can hold up his hands as if he is drinking from a cup and can feed his doll or himself. This is an intellectual challenge for the child and shows developmental growth.
- Stage 5 (3½–4 years): Gradually, the preschooler begins to add other children to his play and is able with experience and parallel intellectual growth to engage in sociodramatic play. That is, the child can (1) take on a make-believe role, (2) pretend with objects, (3) pretend with actions (4) persist in role-play, (5) interact with at least one other child, and (6) verbally communicate (see Figure 13–2).

Understanding these developmental stages of symbolic growth permits teachers to evaluate the symbolic level at which children are using toys in their play. By using the chart shown in Figure 13–3, a record can be kept of the child's symbolic play development. Keeping a record of the child's use of symbols in his or her play will enable the teacher to evaluate the child's progress through those stages. When introducing real objects into the environment, introduce them for Stage 1—even with older children who may need to recapitulate the process or

FIGURE 13–2 Symbolic Development

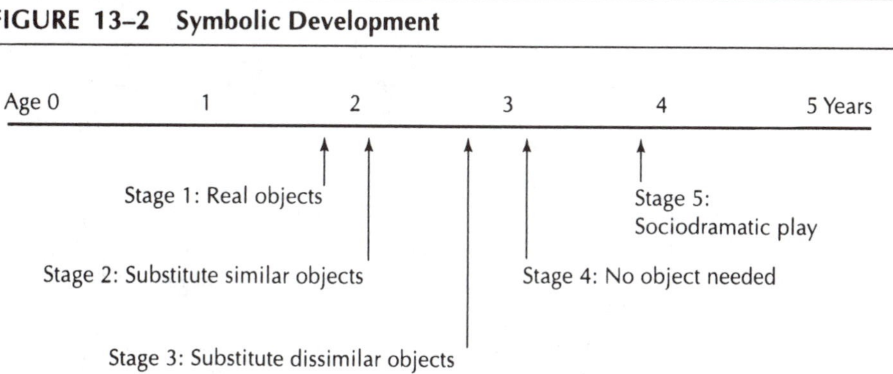

FIGURE 13–3 Symbolic Play Record

	Stage 1	Stage 2	Stage 3	Stage 4	Stage 5
Child's Name	Real Object	Similar Object	Dissimilar Object	No Object	Sociodramatic Play
Alice	*				
Ben					
Martha					
Andy					

Record dates when each stage is acquired.

who may have gone through Stage 1 at an earlier age. Then encourage their movement to higher levels of symbolic play. A new riding toy might be introduced to a group of preschoolers as a "truck." Younger children may continue to play with it as just a truck, whereas older preschoolers may soon be using it as a school bus, a dune buggy, or a UFO. The teacher's role, then, is to give a wide variety of props and support with a variety of teaching behaviors (see Figure 13–8 later in the chapter) to help the child develop these symbolic abilities.

Construction (CN) is the making of symbolic products by using materials, such as paints, paper, clay, and a wide array of similar art materials. The symbols within the product grow, develop, and become more detailed and elaborate as the child grows intellectually and gains more skills with the materials. Because of the symbols used, construction is considered a form of representational play.

The child's symbolic growth can also be evaluated through art activities, a form of construction play. By looking closely at the product the child produces in such construction as fingerpainting, easel painting, clay, and so on, the teacher will find symbol development. As an example, look at the key symbols that develop in drawing or painting shown in Figure 13–4. (The ages given in Figure 13–4 are a guide; they are approximate, not rigid.)

The human figure, which evolves into the face-like house, is given as an example in Figure 13–3 and does appear as such in many children's symbolic development. However, each child will express the symbolic objects that are most meaningful for him or her, and some might not draw the human figure or house. What is important to understand is that no matter what symbols children draw, they will progress with experience and intellectual growth through very similar development and changes. Therefore, when keeping a record on symbolic development in construction (artwork), the teacher should sketch in the symbol of interest to the particular child (see Figure 13–5). It will be helpful to save samples of the child's products over a period of many weeks. Mark them with the date and place them in sequence so that there is a concrete record of the child's symbolic development.

Three-dimensional materials, such as clay, follow a similar line of development. In working with clay, expect to see (1) random pounding, (2) controlled pounding, (3) rolling clay into snake-like rolls and later into circles, (4) adding of pieces to the rolls and circles (facial features and body parts), and (5) combining products, such as people in cars or a boy on a horse. Development in three-dimensional art could also be sketched in the child's chart to keep a record of his progress in the use of that particular medium.

Figure 13–4 Stages of Symbolic Development in Construction

1-2 years – Random Scribbling: The child uses random scribble marks simply as a sensorimotor activity.

2-2$^1/_2$ years – Controlled Scribbling: The child begins to develop some control of his fine motor abilities, and scribbles gain some direction and control. After some experience with controlled scribbling, you may hear a child name his picture a "motorcycle" or a "big wheel," although there appears to be no resemblance. This is an intellectual accomplishment for the child and an indication that he is beginning his first step toward representational thinking.

2$^1/_2$-3 years – The Face: The next major development is for the circle, which then becomes a face.

3$^1/_2$-4 years – Arms and Legs: The circle "person" develops stick arms and legs, which at first lacks a body, as the "appendages" stick out of the face.

4 years – The Body Appears: The human figure begins to acquire a body. Gradually, more and more body parts are added (hands, feet, hair, ears, etc.).

5 years – Floating House: First "house" drawings usually resemble a face, with windows placed like eyes and the door like a mouth. These first houses are usually somewhere in the middle of the picture and seem to be floating in space.

5$^1/_2$-6 years – House on Bottom Line: Next, the bottom of the paper is used as a baseline and the house rests on it.

5$^1/_2$-6 years – Baseline Supports House in Drawing: A baseline appears within the drawing and the house rests on it.

6-7 years – Two-Dimensional Drawing: The baseline begins to take on the quality of a horizon, which indicates the child's awareness of two-dimensional space.

FIGURE 13—5 Symbolic Record in Construction

Name	Date	Date	Date	Date	Date	Date

Game with rules (GWR) requires socially agreed upon rules to hold together the cooperative play. Since most preschoolers do not yet have the intellectual ability to understand the point of view of others, they usually are unable to engage productively in games with rules that involve other participants. Only the most simple games with rules, such as Lotto, are included in this collection.

PLAY AND ITS DEVELOPMENT

The play of children during the preschool years will change in its complexity and duration as each child matures socially, emotionally, intellectually, and physically. The young 3-year-old will have some success with construction using media such as crayons or paints, but will find working with three-dimensional media such as clay difficult. This will change as the child matures and gains experience and mastery over materials. Figure 13–6 should be viewed as a hypothetical representation of 100% of the child's play capacities between ages 3 to 7. The central goal of the play activities in this book is to help the young child develop his or her symbolic abilities both in symbolic play and construction. This will lay the foundation for the ability to understand and use school skills successfully.

FIGURE 13–6 The Developmental Play Capacities of Young Children

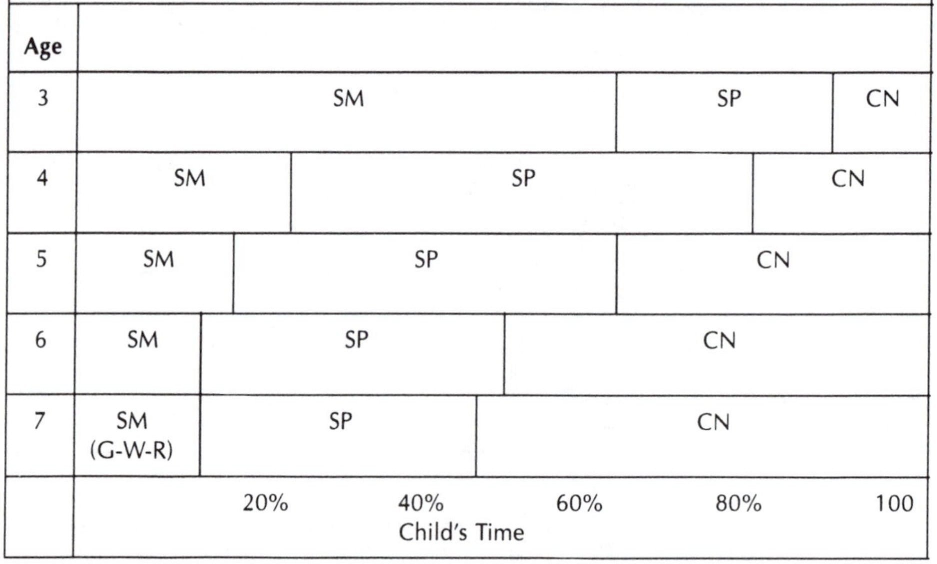

Age			
3	SM	SP	CN
4	SM	SP	CN
5	SM	SP	CN
6	SM	SP	CN
7	SM (G-W-R)	SP	CN
	20% 40% 60% 80% 100 Child's Time		

SM = sensorimotor play; SP = symbolic play; CN = construction; G-W-R = games with rules

Materials for Construction Play

Materials used by young children to create products that show their symbolic development are often very challenging for the children to master and control. It is therefore suggested that the materials be placed on a continuum from maximum freedom (fluid) to minimum freedom (structured materials), as in Figure 13–7. Materials on the maximum-fluid end of the continuum are more difficult to control. The materials on the minimum-structured end are usually easier to control. Providing a wide array of materials along this continuum enables the child to gain mastery over many challenging experiences and to develop symbolic thought.

Fluids Materials such as water, fingerpaints, dry sand, easel paints, wet sand, clay or flour and water dough, and crayons or pens can be thought of as fluid materials. They seem by their natural form to encourage the child to explore them through sensorimotor play. But to produce symbolic construction and products, the child must control or master the materials. The child must deliberately structure the materials to his or her liking. After starting with the use of brush and paints on the paper (sensorimotor), the child next moves through the stages of symbolic development: Stage 1 (Random Scribbling), Stage 2 (Controlled Scribbling), Stage 3 (The Face)—to the stages of two- and, later, three-dimensional drawings (see Figure 13–4). This type of progress occurs with most of the fluids, with the exception of water and dry sand.

As the materials appear on the continuum, from left to right (from fluid to structured), they become easier to control and master. For example, dry sand is quite fluid but if water is added, it becomes less fluid—easier to form into a shape such as a castle. Drawing is the most structured of the fluid materials, as crayons on paper are easier for the child to control. The goal of this book is for the child to play with and master all these materials and to develop symbolic abilities within each.

Structured Materials The materials placed on the right of the continuum are the structured materials. They basically maintain their shape and, at the most structured end, have a particular use (minimum degrees of freedom). Often, the

FIGURE 13–7 Play Materials versus Degrees of Freedom (Fluid to Structured)

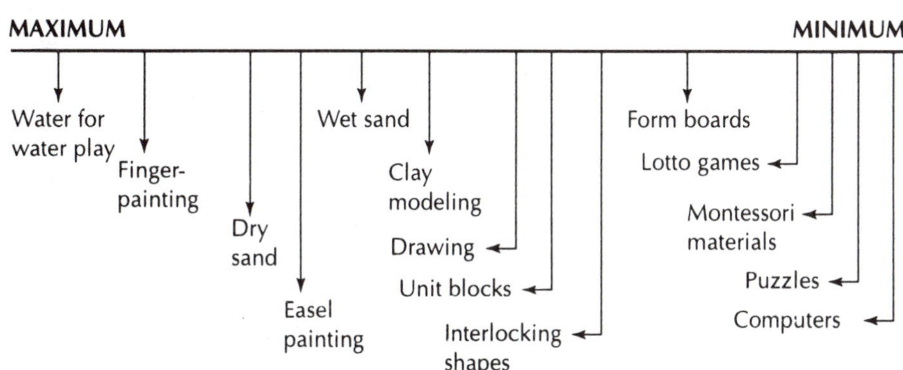

symbols are built in. For example, puzzles have a set form and can be used in only one way. As one moves to the more open end of structured materials on the continuum, the materials begin to have a less clearly defined use. The child begins to structure and change the materials to fit his or her own symbolic ideas. For example, blocks, the least structured of the structured materials, maintain their shape, form, and size, but the child can work with these "givens" and arrange the material to make any symbolic product he or she may wish to create. Similar symbolic growth will be seen in the use of less structured material as was seen in the fluids. Block play will first be random, then controlled, and eventually more elaborate. The most structured materials will limit symbolic development, so it will be necessary to lead the child into more advanced or elaborate Lotto games, Montessori materials, form boards, or puzzles.

Symbolic Materials Another group of materials to support children's play is called symbolic material, including both micro (small) and macro (large) materials. These are the materials and toys that encourage make-believe play. The micro (small) symbol toys include such items as small people figures, zoo and farm animals, small playhouses and furniture, miniature vehicles, puppets, and other toys that are generally used in "hand play." In the microworld of toys, the child can create elaborate make-believe dramatic episodes.

The macro (or large) symbol toys and equipment would include such items as housekeeping equipment of all kinds (stove, iron, ironing board, sink, refrigerator); costume boxes for dress-up clothing; toy luggage; toy telephones; and larger dolls. The large equipment permits the child to develop symbolic play into sociodramatic play with other children in the larger classroom space.

It pays to have on hand a well-balanced supply of materials for construction that would range from fluid to structured, as well as abundant symbolic materials, both micro and macro. Finally, the amount of each will depend on the age level of the children. Keep in mind that the materials should parallel the amount of sensorimotor play, symbolic play, and construction play seen in Figure 13–6.

TEACHER BEHAVIOR CONTINUUM (TBC)

Adults usually do not belong in the child's play world, and often the teacher can be most helpful by maintaining a supportive stance by looking on. However, if the child does not play or if the play is stereotypic (abnormally repetitive), the teacher may gradually move along the Teacher Behavior Continuum, taking care to use the least controlling behavior necessary to facilitate the play activity (see Figure 13–8).

The Teacher Behavior Continuum is a way of viewing the teacher's actions of getting into and out of the child's play. The teacher may move back and forth on the continuum, beginning at the open end (giving the child maximum degrees of freedom) and moving to the structured end (minimum degrees of freedom), especially when the child is competent. If the teacher anticipates that the child will have great difficulty with a task, she will start with the structured intervention of modeling and physically help the child before gradually moving back along the continuum to less control. It is her responsibility to evaluate and choose the amount of control needed to best support the child's attempts.

The TBC provides a framework for deciding on the types of interventions appropriate to the child's play ability. When the child is in control and playing well, less teacher structure is required and the more "open" behaviors of visually

FLUID, STRUCTURED, AND SYMBOLIC MATERIALS

The following list is provided to give examples; many other materials could easily be added.

Fluids

Water play toys; bubble set; fingerpainting materials; clay on wooden clay board; sand and sand toys; sand or water table with aluminum or plastic measuring cups, hand water pump, siphon, hose, funnels, sand tools, and can and sifter set; unbreakable, small family figures and animals; balance scales; boats; scoops; double easels with nonspill paint pots and smocks; felt-tip markers, colored chalk, and wax crayons

Structured

Inlay puzzles; matching games; hammer, nails, and soft wood with work bench; unit blocks, giant blocks, and play planks; scissors, variety of paper, paste, paper punch, felt pieces, bits of cloth, bits of wood, yarn, and pipe cleaners; typewriter; manipulative (string and beads, sewing basket, chunky nuts, pegboard, lacing boards); interlocking blocks; sorting boards and box for shape, color, and size; simple card games; dominoes and number boards or games; stand-up mirrors

Symbolic

Micro

Washable, unbreakable doll for dressing and undressing; assorted floor blocks with small family figures; farm and zoo animal sets; puppets; animal families; wooden vehicles; table blocks; open-top doll house, including furniture and people

Macro

Housekeeping equipment of all kinds; costume box for "dress-up" clothes; toy luggage; steering wheel; ride-a-stick horse; sheet or blanket for play tent; large cartons for making stores, houses, gas stations, and for climbing into; rocking chair; large cuddly toy animals; dolls of all types; doctor equipment; plastic food; balance scales; cash register and play money; variety of hats; toy telephones

looking and nondirective statements are most appropriate. However, when a child is having great difficulty controlling his or her play, the more structured behaviors of directive statements and physical intervention may be needed. Examples of using the TBC with teacher type of play activity are given in Figures 13-9 through 13–11.

FIGURE 13–8 TBC: Degrees of Freedom

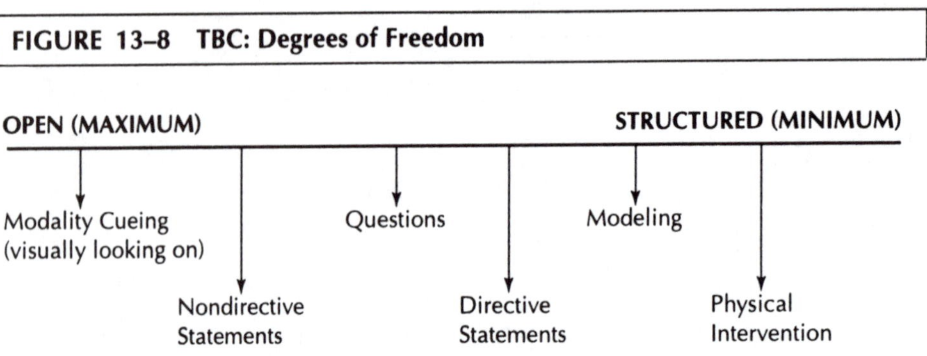

FIGURE 13–9 The Teacher Behavior Continuum with Sensorimotor Play

Visually Looking On	Nondirective Statements	Questions	Directive Statements	Physical Intervention
The adult supportively looks on to encourage the child in the use of equipment and is ready to provide help if needed.	The adult verbally mirrors the child's actions. (Examples: "You're walking with your hands out for balance." "You like to walk all the way to the end and then come back.") The adult helps develop concepts by using such descriptive words as *fast, slow, long, short, over, under,* and *between.*	The adult uses questions to challenge the child to explore new ideas and skills. (Examples: "How many different ways could you go across the beam?" "What could you carry across the beam?")	The adult helps the child who is having some difficulty with a task by direct instruction. (Examples: "Place your foot here and your hand here." "You need to wait for Billy to finish before you begin.")	The adult physically moves the child's body while modeling the proper action. (Example: Physically help the child who cannot walk backwards on the balance beam as another child demonstrates how to do it.)

FIGURE 13–10 The Teacher Behavior Continuum with Symbolic Play

Visually Looking On	Nondirective Statements	Questions	Directive Statements	Physical Intervention
The adult supportively looks on to encourage children to play out a variety of fantasies that might potentially be frightening. The adult stands by to assist those children who get overexcited or lost in a fantasy.	The adult verbally mirrors the beginning play actions of the child. (Example: "I see you have the dishes and are ready to set the table.")	The adult uses questions to encourage the child to play out and further develop fantasy themes. (Example: "Now that the table is set, what's going to happen next?")	The adult helps the child select, start, or further develop his play theme by directly assigning roles ("You're the mommy." "You're the doctor.") or by directly describing a new development in his play theme. (Example: "Now that you've finished setting the table, the doorbell rings and the mail carrier has a special delivery letter.")	The adult introduces a new prop to encourage further play or assumes a part and inserts herself into the play. (Example: Pick up the telephone and call the doctor.)

FIGURE 13–11 The Teacher Behavior Continuum with Construction

Visually Looking On	Nondirective Statements	Questions	Directive Statements	Physical Intervention
The adult provides the materials and supportively looks on to encourage the child to freely and creatively use the materials.	The adult supports the child's efforts in using art media through such statements as, "You're working hard." The adult verbally mirrors the concepts found in the child's construction. (Examples: "You're using blue." "You've made a circle." "You've added ears to your person.")	The adult uses questions to have the child verbally describe the concepts in his product. (Examples: "Can you tell me about your drawing?" "Is there a story in your drawing?" "What have you made with your clay?")	The adult helps the child to control materials or equipment with which he is having difficulty by using directive statements such as, "Keep the paint on the paper." "Brushes are used this way."	The adult helps the child develop his construction abilities by providing direct physical experiences, such as feeling a tree before drawing one, providing a model for the child's clay animal construction, or having a pet visit the classroom.

SUMMARY

If very young children are performing behaviors that cause teachers to take disciplinary actions, these children are characteristically found to lack social skills. These critical and valuable social skills develop through the young child's growing play abilities. Classrooms designed for young children must provide a play curriculum and materials for young children to develop to their highest play abilities.

Play is often misunderstood by teachers. This chapter has defined play and its value, and has discussed how to organize and facilitate that play. Finally, a method was given for evaluating or assessing play development. It is basic to the development of all children during these early years that they have a wide variety of play experiences with a teacher who understands the value of play and who can facilitate or teach the misbehaving child how to play.

Test Yourself

Test your understanding of concepts related to play. You will find the answers at the end of this chapter, following the Endnotes.

A. ___ crayons B. ___ clay C. ___ blocks D. ___ puzzles E. ___ water F. ___ Legos G. ___ fingerpaints	1. In the space before each play material number from 1 to 7, from the most fluid materials (being #1) to the most structured (being #7).
Place an (x) before the concept on the left that is defined on the right.	
A. ___ sensorimotor play B. ___ microsymbolic play C. ___ sociodramatic play D. ___ games with rules E. ___ fluid-construction F. ___ structured-construction	2. Baseball, ping pong, checkers
A. ___ sensorimotor play B. ___ microsymbolic play C. ___ sociodramatic play D. ___ games with rules E. ___ fluid-construction F. ___ structured-construction	3. Johnny is wearing a firefighter's hat and Jane is wearing a police officer's badge and hat; they are racing their "cars" to the fire.
A ___ sensorimotor play B. ___ microsymbolic play C. ___ sociodramatic play D. ___ games with rules E. ___ fluid-construction F. ___ structured-construction	4. A painting of a house
A. ___ sensorimotor play B. ___ microsymbolic play C. ___ sociodramatic play D. ___ games with rules E. ___ fluid-construction F. ___ structured-construction	5. Mark builds a castle out of blocks.
A. ___ age 3 B. ___ age 4 C. ___ age 5	6. How old normatatively is Andy? He spends 60% of his time doing sensorimotor play, 35% doing symbolic play, and 5% doing construction.

Glossary

Associative One of the developmental social stages whereby the child plays with other children. The children borrow and lend materials with conversation related to their activity. All members engage in similar activities, but there is no division of labor and no organization of activities around a clearly defined theme or product.

Construction The use of materials to create an identifiable product.

Cooperative One of the developmental social stages whereby the child plays as a member of a group that is organized to make a product or carry out a theme. There is a leader, with clearly identified roles and responsibilities for each member.

Degrees of Freedom The openness of materials or equipment to create a product determined by the children, as opposed to being required to produce something predetermined and engineered by the adult.

Fluid-Construction Creating a product with materials that have a fluid quality, such as paints, clay, or crayons.

Games With Rules Highly social games beginning at age 7 or later, involving either sensorimotor skills (baseball, softball, etc.) or board games (checkers, Monopoly, Candyland, etc.) held together by arbitrary socially agreed-upon rules.

Macrosymbolic Materials Make-believe play with the use of child-size props and toys.

Microsymbolic Materials Make-believe play with miniature life-like props and toys.

Onlooker One of the developmental social stages whereby the child becomes socially interested in others by watching peers play; the child may speak to the group but does not overtly join the group's activity.

Parallel One of the developmental social stages whereby the child plays with toys similar to those used by others and in physical proximity to them; the child plays beside others rather than with them.

Sensorimotor Play Play with materials that have a high modality (touch, taste, smell, etc.), or motor activity for the pure pleasure of the movement, not to produce or for make believe.

Sociodramatic The highest level of social play reached by the child age 2 to 7, requiring the child to imitate a role, sustain a make-believe theme, use gestures and objects, interact with others, and engage in verbal exchanges.

Solitary Independent Play One of the developmental social stages whereby the child plays alone without interacting with others.

Structured-Construction Creating products with materials that maintain their form and shape, such as blocks, Legos, and puzzles.

Symbolic Play Make-believe play whereby the child uses objects and gestures to represent adult world or nonexistent objects and actions.

Teacher Behavior Continuum (TBC) An inductive teaching process whereby the teacher gradually uses more intrusive behaviors to facilitate the child's play. The steps moving from minimum to maximum use of power are visually looking on, nondirective statements, questions, directive statements, and modeling/physical intervention.

Unoccupied Behavior The first nonsocial activity on the developmental social stages whereby the child is not playing but simply looks off to whatever catches his eye or manipulates his own clothing or body.

Related Readings

Parten, M. B. (1971). Social Play Among Preschool Children. In R. E. Herron & B. Sutton-Smith (Eds.), *Child's Play*. New York: Wiley and Sons.

Smilansky, S. (1968). *The Effects of Sociodramatic Play on Disadvantaged Preschool Children*. New York: Wiley & Sons.

Smilansky, S., & Shefatya, L. (1990). *Facilitating Play: A Medium for Promoting Cognitive, Socio-Emotional and Academic Development in Young Children*. Gaithersburg, MD: Psychosocial & Educational Publications.

Wolfgang, C. H., & Wolfgang, M. E. (1992). *School for Young Children: Developmentally Appropriate Practices*. Boston: Allyn and Bacon.

Wolfgang, C. H., Mackender, B., & Wolfgang, M. E. (1981). *Growing & Learning Through Play*. Paoli, PA: Judy/Instructo.

Endnotes

1. Alberto, P. A., & Troutman, A. C. (1990). *Applied Behavior Analysis for Teachers*. New York: Merrill.
2. Smilansky, S. (1968). *The Effects of Sociodramatic Play on Disadvantaged Preschool Children*. New York: Wiley & Sons. Smilansky, S., & Shefatya, L. (1990). *Facilitating Play: A Medium for Promoting Cognitive, Socio-Emotional and Academic Development in Young Children*. Gaithersburg, MD: Psychosocial & Educational Publications.

Answers to Test Yourself

1: E, G, B, A, C, F, D; 2D; 3C; 4E; 5F; 6A

Appendix
Medication and the Difficult Child

The following is a list of typical types of drugs or medication given to children with behavioral problems. The purpose, names, warnings, and side effects are provided here to inform the teacher who may have a student taking these drugs. It is not intended as a comprehensive listing of all possible medications or their effects; instead, it provides an overview of some of the more common ones.

Drugs Commonly Used with Behavioral Problem Children			
Types of Drug	**Purpose**	**Trade Name**	**Generic Name**
Stimulants	Used as a part of a treatment program (psychological, educational, social) for a stabilizing effect on children with a behavioral syndrome and including a history of: moderate-to-severe distractibility, short attention span, ADD with hyperactivity, emotional irritability, and impulsivity. Given in gradually increased doses.	Ritalin Cylert Dexedrine Prozac	Methylphenidate HCL Magnesium Penoline Dextroamphetimine Fuoxetine Hydrochloride
Tranquilizers (Major)	Used to control aggressive, self-abusive, stereotyped, acting-out behavior or psychotic states. Normally used only in severe psychoses. Most children using these would be hospitalized or under very close observation.	Mellaril Thorazine Haldol Stelazine	Thioridazine Chlorpromzine Haloperidol Trifluoperazine HCL
Tranquilizers (Minor)	May be used to calm mild agitation, anxiety, or tension. Also used as a muscle relaxant for individuals with cerebral palsy. Will sometimes be used to control seizures in epileptic children and to induce sleep.	Valium Atarax Librium Vistaril	Diazepam Hydroxyzine HCL Chlordiazepoxide HCL Hydroxyzine Pamoate
Anticonvulsants	Used primarily to control grand mal seizures and psychomotor difficulties.	Dilantin Eskabarb Mebaral Mysoline	Phentoin Phenobarbital Mephobarbital Primidone
	Used primarily to control petit mal seizures (absence epilepsy).	Zarontin (Enteric Depakene) Depakene	Etaosuximide Valproic Acid
	Used to control psychomotor seizures and grand mal.	Tegretol	Carbamazepine
	Sometimes used to try to control myoclonic seizures but relapse rate is high.	ACTH Corticosteroids	Corticotropin

Sources: Westling, D. L. (1986). *Introduction to Mental Retardation*. Englewood Cliffs, NJ: Prentice Hall; and Barnhart, E. R. (1991). *Physicians' Desk Reference, 45th edition.* Oradell, NJ: Medical Economics Data.

Drugs Commonly Used with Behavioral Problem Children	
Warnings	**Side Effects**
Should not be used with children under 6 years. Should not be used with children under 3 years (may be used for weight reduction for children older than 12). Given for depression; mostly for adolescents and adults.	Loss of appetite, insomnia, mood changes, headaches, stomachaches, nausea. Possible suppression of growth may occur with long term use. With psychotic children, these drugs may make their condition worse.
Should not be used with children under the age of 2 years. Should not be used with children under 6 months of age. Not recommended for use with children under 3 years. Recommended for use with children 6 years or older under close supervision.	May cause dry mouth, increase in appetite, shaking of hands, shuffling walk, difficulty in speech, restlessness. Drowsiness.
Not for use with children under 6 months. Not usually given on a long-term basis. May be given before dental procedures. Use for allergic conditions; may cause skin itching. Often used short term. Not recommended for use with children under the age of 6 years. Given for itching, allergies.	Drowsiness, dry mouth, constipation, headaches.
Contact doctor if skin rash appears. Habit forming; barbiturates. Habit forming; barbiturates. Habit forming; barbiturates.	Nausea, vomiting, constipation. Somnolence. Somnolence. Somnolence.
May impair physical abilities.	Frequent g.i. symptoms; drowsiness.
Not recommended for children younger than 6 years.	Abrupt discontinuation can cause seizures—do not skip doses! Possible fever, bruising, sore throat.

WORKSHOPS ON DISCIPLINE

Workshops on *The Three Faces of Discipline* will be regularly offered during the summer months both for teachers (three-day workshops) and trainers of teachers (plus two more days for trainers) throughout locations in the United States and Canada. Training can also be arranged at your school site, county, or district office.

Write for workshop information:

Three Faces of Discipline Workshops
Wolfgang and Associates
713 Middlebrooks Circle
Tallahassee, FL 32312

Phone: 904-385-1640
Fax: 904-386-1640

Index